Contesting the Wo

Over the past thirty years, norms research has evolved into a significant sub-field within International Relations and beyond. *Contesting the World* delves into the development of norms, exploring their emergence, change, and legitimacy on both domestic and international levels. This in-depth volume presents the interpretation–contestation framework, positioning it as the primary theoretical mechanism for understanding norms.

Leading scholars spanning diverse sub-fields and epistemological perspectives investigate the crucial aspects of norm development, including norm strength, collision, and conflict; interaction and linkages; and the illumination of historical norm development through contestation.

Contesting the World offers a fresh perspective on norms research, focusing on ideas, social facts, norm adaptation, and the shift towards viewing norms as processes. It is an invaluable resource for anyone interested in understanding the complexities of norms and their impact on international relations – a fascinating exploration of norms, contestation, and the ever-changing world of global politics.

Phil Orchard is Professor of International Relations at the University of Wollongong and Co-director of the University of Wollongong Future of Rights Centre. His books include *Protecting the Internally Displaced: Rhetoric and Reality* (Routledge, 2018) and *A Right to Flee: Refugees, States, and the Construction of International Cooperation* (Cambridge University Press, 2014), which won the 2016 International Studies Association Ethnicity, Nationalism, and Migration Studies Section Distinguished Book Award. He is co-editor, with Alexander Betts, of *Implementation in World Politics: How Norms Change Practice* (Oxford University Press, 2014), and, with Charles Hunt, of *Constructing the Responsibility to Protect: Contestation and Consolidation* (Routledge, 2020).

Antje Wiener holds the Chair of Political Science, especially Global Governance at the University of Hamburg. Before coming to Hamburg, she held chairs in international studies at Queen's University Belfast and the University of Bath. With James Tully she is Co-founding Editor of *Global Constitutionalism*, published with Cambridge University Press since 2012, and she edits the Norm Research in International Relations Series with Springer. Her book *Contestation and Constitution of Norms in Global International Relations* (Cambridge University Press, 2018) was awarded the International Law Section's Book Prize in 2020. Her other books include *A Theory of Contestation* (Springer, 2014) and *The Invisible Constitution of Politics: Contested Norms and International Encounters* (Cambridge University Press, 2008). She has been an elected by-fellow of Hughes Hall, University of Cambridge, since 2017, a fellow of the Academy of Social Sciences since 2011, and a member of Academia Europaea since 2020.

Contesting the World

Norm Research in Theory and Practice

Edited by

Phil Orchard

University of Wollongong

Antje Wiener

University of Hamburg and University of Cambridge

Shaftesbury Road, Cambridge CB2 8EA, United Kingdom

One Liberty Plaza, 20th Floor, New York, NY 10006, USA

477 Williamstown Road, Port Melbourne, VIC 3207, Australia

314–321, 3rd Floor, Plot 3, Splendor Forum, Jasola District Centre, New Delhi – 110025, India

103 Penang Road, #05–06/07, Visioncrest Commercial, Singapore 238467

Cambridge University Press is part of Cambridge University Press & Assessment, a department of the University of Cambridge.

We share the University's mission to contribute to society through the pursuit of education, learning and research at the highest international levels of excellence.

www.cambridge.org
Information on this title: www.cambridge.org/9781009479172

DOI: 10.1017/9781009479141

When citing this work, please include a reference to the
DOI 10.1017/9781009479141

First published 2024

A catalogue record for this publication is available from the British Library

Library of Congress Cataloging-in-Publication Data
Names: Orchard, Phil, 1976– editor. | Wiener, Antje, editor.
Title: Contesting the world : norm research in theory and practice / edited by Phil Orchard, University of Wollongong, New South Wales, Antje Wiener, University of Hamburg and University of Cambridge.
Description: Cambridge, United Kingdom ; New York, NY : Cambridge University Press, 2024. | Includes bibliographical references and index.
Identifiers: LCCN 2023053233 | ISBN 9781009479165 (hardback) | ISBN 9781009479141 (ebook)
Subjects: LCSH: International relations. | Norm (Philosophy) – Political aspects. | Political science – Philosophy. | Political culture.
Classification: LCC JZ1251 .C664 2024 | DDC 320.01–dc23/eng/20240222
LC record available at https://lccn.loc.gov/2023053233

ISBN 978-1-009-47916-5 Hardback
ISBN 978-1-009-47917-2 Paperback

Contents

Figures

Tables

Contributors

HALIMA AKHRIF works at the German Federal Employment Agency. Her research investigates emotional responses to norm violations in public debates. She has worked as a research assistant to the Chair of International Relations and European Integration at the University of Stuttgart and held a teaching position at the University of Konstanz. She received her MA in political science and public law from the University of Trier.

MICHAL BEN-JOSEF HIRSCH is an associate professor in the Political Science and Legal Studies Department at Suffolk University and an International Security Program Fellow at the Belfer Center for Science and International Affairs, Kennedy School for Government, Harvard University. She holds a PhD from the Massachusetts Institute of Technology. Her research and teaching interests include International Relations theory, with a focus on the role of international norms and ideas, transitional and historical justice, and the contested narrative of the conflict in Israel/Palestine.

JENNIFER M. DIXON is Associate Professor of Political Science at Villanova University. She is the author of *Dark Pasts: Changing the State's Story in Turkey and Japan* (Cornell University Press, 2018), which was awarded the 2019 Dr Sona Aronian Book Prize for Excellence in Armenian Studies. Her research focuses on the development of international norms, the politics of memory, genocide, and mass atrocity, and transitional justice.

SASSAN GHOLIAGHA is a postdoctoral researcher at the European New School of Digital Studies. His research focuses on norms, the responsibility to protect, international criminal law, drones, and the role of artificial intelligence in analysing arguments. He has published in edited volumes and in journals such as the *International Journal of Political Theory*, *Global Constitutionalism*, and *Global Society*. He is the author of *The Humanisation of Global Politics: International Criminal Law, the Responsibility to Protect, and Drones* (Cambridge University Press, 2022).

JAKOB V. H. HOLTERMANN is an associate professor in legal philosophy at iCourts – Centre of Excellence for International Courts, Faculty of Law, University of Copenhagen. He teaches and researches in the fields of the philosophy of punishment and the philosophy of legal science. He has published extensively on Scandinavian legal realism and on the empirical turn in (international) legal scholarship.

CECILIA JACOB is Associate Professor of International Relations in the Department of International Relations at the Australian National University. Her work focuses on civilian protection, mass atrocity prevention, and international human protection norms. Cecilia is Co-editor of the journal *Global Responsibility to Protect* and Co-chair of the Asia-Pacific Working Group of Global Action Against Mass Atrocities.

AUDIE KLOTZ is Professor of Political Science in the Maxwell School of Citizenship and Public Affairs at Syracuse University. Her award-winning work spans theories of international relations, qualitative methods, transnational activism, global migration, and identity politics, with an overarching emphasis on race. She builds upon a specialisation in the Southern African region and, more broadly, the former British Empire.

SIMON KOSCHUT holds the Chair for International Security Policy at the Department of Political and Social Science at Zeppelin University in Friedrichshafen. His research lies at the intersection of security governance, norms, and emotions in world politics. In 2018, his book *Normative Change and Security Community Disintegration* (Palgrave Macmillan, 2016) received the Ernst Otto Czempiel Prize from the Peace and Conflict Research Frankfurt for the best postdoctoral monograph in peace and conflict research.

ANDREA LIESE is Professor of International Relations in the Faculty of Economics and Social Sciences at the University of Potsdam and a member of the Centre for Advanced Studies in the Humanities and Social Sciences research group 'The International Rule of Law – Rise or Decline?' Her current research focuses on the authority, expertise, and neutrality of international organisations, on norm collisions in international relations, and on the rise and decline of norms in international law.

MIKAEL RASK MADSEN is Professor of European Law and Integration at the Faculty of Law, University of Copenhagen. He is the Founder and Director of iCourts, the Danish National Research Foundation on International Courts, also at the University of Copenhagen. His research focuses on international law and institutions, the evolution of the legal profession, human rights, and the transformation of the state since World War II.

PHIL ORCHARD is Professor of International Relations at the University of Wollongong and Co-director of the University of Wollongong Future of Rights Centre. His books include *Protecting the Internally Displaced: Rhetoric and Reality* (Routledge, 2018) and *A Right to Flee: Refugees, States, and the Construction of International Cooperation* (Cambridge University Press, 2014), which won the 2016 International Studies Association Ethnicity, Nationalism, and Migration Studies Section Distinguished Book Award. He is co-editor, with Alexander Betts, of *Implementation in World Politics: How Norms Change Practice* (Oxford University Press, 2014), and, with Charles Hunt, of *Constructing the Responsibility to Protect: Contestation and Consolidation* (Routledge, 2020).

SUSAN PARK is Professor of Global Governance in Government and International Relations at the University of Sydney. She focuses on how international organisations and global governance can become greener and more accountable, particularly in the transition to renewable energy. Her most recent books are *The Good Hegemon* (Oxford University Press, 2022) and *Environmental Recourse at the Multilateral Development Banks* (Cambridge University Press, 2020). She is Co-lead Editor of the journal *Global Environmental Politics* and a research lead of the Earth Systems Governance project.

JASON RALPH is Professor of International Relations, University of Leeds. He was Head of the School of Politics and International Studies, University of Leeds, from 2016 to 2019 and Co-editor of the *European Journal of International Security* from 2020 to 2023. He is the author of four books, and his articles have been published in journals such as the *European Journal of International Relations*, *International Organization*, and *Review of International Studies*.

ANCHALEE RÜLAND works as a policy advisor for foreign affairs at the German parliament. She holds a PhD in International Relations from the European University Institute and is the author of *Norms in Conflict: Southeast Asia's Response to Human Rights Violations in Myanmar* (Oxford University Press, 2022).

MITJA SIENKNECHT is a postdoctoral researcher at the European New School of Digital Studies/European University Viadrina Frankfurt

(Oder). Previously, she held positions at Bielefeld University, Berlin Social Science Center, and the University of Münster. Her research focuses on the transformation of war through technological developments, questions of responsibility in world politics, inter- and intra-organisational relations in security studies, and the role of artificial intelligence in analysing arguments.

NORA STAPPERT is Associate Professor at the Center of Excellence for Global Mobility Law, Faculty of Law, University of Copenhagen. Her research is situated at the intersection of international law and International Relations, with a focus on international practice theory, legal authority and legitimacy in world politics, and legal change dynamics. Her work has appeared in *International Theory*, *Global Constitutionalism*, the *Leiden Journal of International Law*, and the *Journal of International Relations and Development*, among other journals.

ANETTE STIMMER is a lecturer in International Relations at the University of St Andrews. She studies norm contestation and change, the interplay of norms and moral convictions in foreign policy decisionmaking, and international law. Her research has been published in *International Studies Quarterly*, *European Journal of International Relations*, *Journal of Global Security Studies*, and *International Affairs*. Her book on norm contestation in international politics is under contract with Cambridge University Press.

JACQUI TRUE is Professor of International Relations at Monash University and Director of the Australian Research Council Centre of Excellence for the Elimination of Violence against Women. She is a leading scholar on the gender dynamics of international politics, women, peace and security, and feminist foreign policy, and she is the author of sixteen books and over 150 articles, including *The Oxford Handbook on Women, Peace and Security* (Oxford University Press, 2019) and *Hidden Wars: Gendered Violence in Asia's Civil Conflicts* (Oxford University Press, 2024) with Sara E. Davies.

JENNIFER WELSH is Professor and Canada 150 Research Chair in Global Governance and Security at McGill University, where she directs the Centre for International Peace and Security Studies. Her research and policy engagement focus on civilian protection, humanitarian assistance, and the ethics, law, and politics of military intervention. She is a fellow of the Royal Society of Canada and an international member of the American Academy of Arts and Sciences.

ANTJE WIENER holds the Chair of Political Science, especially Global Governance at the University of Hamburg. Before coming to Hamburg, she held chairs in international studies at Queen's University Belfast and the University of Bath. With James Tully she is Co-founding Editor of *Global Constitutionalism*, published with Cambridge University Press since 2012, and she edits the Norm Research in International Relations Series with Springer. Her book *Contestation and Constitution of Norms in Global International Relations* (Cambridge University Press, 2018) was awarded the International Law Section's Book Prize in 2020. Her other books include *A Theory of Contestation* (Springer, 2014) and *The Invisible Constitution of Politics: Contested Norms and International Encounters* (Cambridge University Press, 2008). She has been an elected by-fellow of Hughes Hall, University of Cambridge, since 2017, a fellow of the Academy of Social Sciences since 2011, and a member of Academia Europaea since 2020.

CARLA WINSTON is a senior lecturer in International Relations at the University of Melbourne. She received her PhD from the University of British Columbia and previously taught at the University of Victoria (Canada). She is interested in norms and norm diffusion, complexity theory, human rights and transitional justice, peace and conflict, and the uses of popular culture in politics and international affairs.

Acknowledgements

For financial support we would like to thank the International Studies Association's Research Workshop Grant program, and Antje Wiener acknowledges funding by *Deutsche Forschungsgemeinschaft* (DFG), German Government's Excellence Strategy. EXC 2037: Climate, climatic change, and society (CLICCS), award number 390683824.

Abbreviations

AB	Appellate Body
ANSA	Armed non-state actor(s)
APL	Anti-personnel mines
ASEAN	Association of Southeast Asian Nations
BIC	Bank Information Center
CAO	Compliance Advisor/Ombudsman
CEDAW	*Convention on the Elimination of All Forms of Discrimination against Women*
CEO	Chief executive officer
CIA	Central Intelligence Agency
CSO	Chief sales officer
DAWN	Development Alternatives with Women for a New Era
DSM	Dispute Settlement Mechanism
ECtHR	European Court of Human Rights
EDF	Environment Defense Fund (now Environment Defense)
EPI	Environment Policy Institute (now Friends of the Earth)
GHP	Global Health Partnerships
GNI	Gross national income
GNWP	Global Network of Women Peacebuilders
HRC	Human Rights Council
HPTLO	Human Protection Transnational Legal Order
IAW	International Alliance of Women
IBRD	International Bank for Reconstruction and Development
ICAO	International Civil Aviation Organization
ICC	International Criminal Court
ICERD	International Convention on the Elimination of All Forms of Racial Discrimination
ICJ	International Court of Justice
ICSID	International Centre for the Settlement of Investment Disputes
IDA	International Development Association

ICW	International Council of Women
IFC	International Finance Cooperation
IHL	International humanitarian law
IHRL	International human rights law
IIM	Independent Investigation Mechanism
IL	International law
ILO	International Labour Organization
IO	International organisation
IOM	International Organization for Migration
IPAM	Independent Project Accountability Mechanism
IR	International Relations
IRN	International Rivers Network
IRM	Independent Recourse Mechanism
IRM	Independent Review Mechanism
KGB	Committee for State Security (Soviet Union)
LIO	Liberal international order
MBT	Mine Ban Treaty
MDB	Multilateral development banks
MICI	Consultation and Investigation Mechanism
MIGA	Multilateral Investment Guarantee Agency
NATO	North Atlantic Treaty Organization
NGO	Non-governmental organisation
NGOWg	NGO Working Group on the Women, Peace and Security Agenda
NRDC	Natural Resources Defense Council
NWF	National Wildlife Federation
OECD	Organisation for Economic Cooperation and Development
OHCHR	Office of the High Commissioner for Human Rights
OP	Operational policies
OSCE	Organization for Security and Cooperation in Europe
PCM	Project Complaint Mechanism
RO	Regional organisation
R2P	Responsibility to Protect
TFN	Transnational Feminist Network
TLO	Transnational legal orders
TRIPS	Trade-Related Aspects of Intellectual Property Rights
UNCLOS	United Nations Convention on the Law of the Sea
UNDRIP	United Nations Declaration on the Rights of Indigenous Peoples
UNHCR	United Nations High Commissioner for Refugees
UNSC	United Nations Security Council

UNSCR	United Nations Security Council Resolution
VAW	Violence against women
WILPF	Women's International League for Peace and Freedom
WEDO	Women's Environmental and Development Organization
WHO	World Health Organization
WIDE	Women in Development Europe
WPS	Women, Peace and Security (agenda)
WTO	World Trade Organization
WWI	World War I
WWII	World War II

1 Introduction
Norm Research in Theory and Practice

Phil Orchard and Antje Wiener

It has been three decades since constructivism emerged as an approach to the study of international relations. Its emergence at that time is not surprising, as it took place in the wake of one of the largest international events of the twentieth century – the peaceful end of the Cold War and the break-up of the Soviet Union. Those events had fundamentally challenged the then dominant theoretical perspective in International Relations (IR), that of neo-realism (Kratochwil 1986). They had shown the importance of ideas as part of the explanation (Lebow and Risse-Kappen 1995), whether it was the Helsinki process opening up the Soviet Union to human rights challenges (Thomas 2001), the role of wider transnational forces, or Soviet 'New Thinking' within its own foreign policy (Evangelista 1999). Today, faced with the Russian aggression towards Ukraine, questions about the role and function of fundamental norms and their contestation have reached a new urgency. Do fundamental norms endure as a quasi-constitutional 'glue' (Polanyi 1957) of the future global order and the many suborders it entails? The rising number of contestations of foundational constitutional elements across the globe (Lake et al. 2021; Börzel and Zürn 2021), including in some of the world's leading democracies, such as the USA and the UK, indicate a shift in the target of contestatory practices from contesting norms to contesting order. Does the kind of fundamental breach of the liberal international order (LIO) as witnessed by the Russian aggression against Ukraine and the "deep contestation" (Lake and Wiener 2023) it triggers undermine or strengthen global order? Answers to these questions depend on detailed and updated knowledge about norms research.

As we are observing contestations of the world in a context of polycrisis (Tooze 2023) including a range of policy sectors such as security, climate, health, economics, migration, and politics, *Contesting the World* comprises a representative selection of advanced studies of norm contestation conducted by a group of world-leading scholars. The intention is to present the potential of a field that has been growing over more than three decades and to identify challenges that are generated by these crises and what to make of them as students of IR (Wiener and Puetter 2009: 1). To that end, the contributors have been asked to explain and illustrate how to best use the toolkit of norms studies by distinguishing norm-types and practices of contestation and interpretation that bring norms to light and reveal their role and function.

Key academic work in the 1980s initiated the constructivist turn – not least Alexander Wendt's (1987; see also Dessler 1989) – and began to situate the agent–structure problem as a critique of neo-realism's structural focus, as did Kratochwil and Ruggie's (1986: 764) criticism that regime theory faced the debilitating problem that its "epistemology fundamentally contradicts ontology!" But the 1990s became a watershed for the development of constructivism following Nicholas Onuf's (1989: 1) coining of the term in 1989 – as he had argued, "people always construct, or constitute, social reality, even as their being, which can only be social, is constructed for them."

Within the next five years, constructivism directly addressed some of the key questions – and problems – for both neo-realism and wider rationalist approaches, including the role played by national interests (Finnemore 1996; Weldes 1996) and how ideas and norms could be critical factors even in the sphere of national security (Katzenstein 1996). As Jeffrey Checkel (1998: 326) would note, the constructivist approach opened up "the black box of interest and identity formation; state interests emerge from and are endogenous to interaction with structures." It did this by bringing in, as Adler put it, a "conception of social science that is – *social*" (Adler 1997: 320). Such a conception intersubjectively focused on the behaviours of both state and other actors in conjunction with the constitution of normative structures of meaning as an understudied and undertheorised dimension in IR (Kratochwil and Ruggie 1986).

Thirty years on, constructivism has become entrenched as one of the main perspectives in IR, with a quarter of IR academics identifying it as their approach to the study of the field (Maliniak et al. 2017).[1] As an approach, constructivism remains unified around the concept that ideas – along with material factors – matter at the international and

[1] The question posed was "Which of the following best describes your approach to the study of IR?" Realism was the second most cited approach, with 18 per cent of respondents selecting it, while almost 27 per cent stated that they did not use paradigmatic analysis. There do remain questions about how entrenched constructivism is in critical gatekeeping institutions, such as key US-based universities, with Jelena Subotic (2017) finding that only 6 per cent of academics in the fifty top-ranked political science departments identify as such.

transnational levels, and that norms, in particular, play a key role in constituting and guiding the behaviour of states and a plethora of other actors at these levels. It is seen as a pluralist theoretical 'mosaic' (Diez and Wiener 2018); but it continues to have its own divides, frequently identified as falling between 'conventional' and 'critical' constructivists. These divisions were initially cast around their theoretical positioning – in particular the use of social theory – and epistemological positioning, with conventional constructivists generally using positivist/post-positivist approaches or a scientific realist epistemology, while critical constructivists tended to use an interpretivist epistemology (Hopf 1998).[2]

This divide in framing constructivism has also given emergence to new interpretations. It may reflect how practices of contestation are understood as either solely problematic, as reflections of the material interests of the existing geopolitical order (Lake et al. 2021), or as an integral part of norm creation (Havercroft and Duvall 2017: 206).[3] It may, alternatively, indicate a generational divide reflecting the evolution of constructivism as a research approach.[4] Or, as Simon Pratt (2020: 62–3) has recently suggested, it may merely reflect different waves of constructivism, with the first bringing forward the concept of norms and the second focusing on their dynamic nature. Irrespective of how we understand these divides, however, the critical question becomes: how have our understandings of norms developed over this period?

We use this Introduction to the book to make three main arguments. The first is that the process of norm contestation not only significantly aids our understanding of norms but has the potential to be the primary theoretical framework through which norms are understood. We show this by considering the history of norm research as a series of three distinct and theoretical moves: first creating an interest in ideas and social facts in IR, then focusing on norm adaptation, and finally shifting to a view of norms as processes. While each move has generally occupied a particular time, and each follows approximately in sequence from the previous one, each

[2] This labelling is certainly not uncontested in itself, as Roxanne Doty (2004: 379) has noted, because much of 'critical' constructivism has "been subjected to so much intentional misrepresentation on the part of those who self-identify as 'critical constructivists'." Other language used to frame this divide includes 'modern' and 'postmodern' by Richard Price and Chris Reus-Smit (1998: 267–8), who note that the principal difference "tends to be analytical"; or "conventional" and "radical" (Fierke and Jørgensen 2001: 5).

[3] In fact, Jonathan Havercroft and Raymond Duvall see these distinctions as so critical that they propose a third term, 'agonistic constructivists', to incorporate scholars who examine norms "as principles and standards constantly open to generation, critique, and renewal through practices of contestation at all scales of human life from the local to the global" (Havercroft and Duvall 2017: 206).

[4] For a critical assessment of this divide, see Lantis and Wunderlich (2022).

move has also had significant overlaps and interconnections. The second argument is that norm contestation illuminates how norms emerge, change, and are replaced, but, as a process, it is inherently *neutral*. While arguments have been made that norm contestation undermines norms and is therefore a negative process, we argue that contestation is actor-driven, and it is actors' choices that determine whether a particular contestation affects a norm in a positive or a negative way. Thus, we propose the interpretation–contestation framework to demonstrate that contestation possesses three main forms: *reactive*, whereby actors seek to object to norms, and which can, at the extreme, lead to norm violation; *proactive*, whereby actors seek to engage with norms in order to improve them; and *interpretive*, whereby actors possess different understandings of norms from those that are held by the wider international community. Finally, the third argument is that while the process of contestation may be neutral towards the norm, contestations are norm-generative practices themselves – whether strategically intended or not – and as such they have an effect on the normativity of the norm. Public proactive contestations in particular allow for a greater number of would-be stakeholders at the macro-, meso-, and micro-levels to become involved in the process and, through their deliberations, enhance a norm's legitimacy and validity.

To assess these three arguments and illustrate how they have contributed to shape the sub-field of norm-contestation research and what they hold for future research, *Contesting the World* brings together a range of junior, mid-career, and senior scholars, working at the leading edge of norm research, across a diversity of issues and sub-fields, and using different epistemological perspectives. This introductory chapter recalls the past trajectory of the field to set the framework from which the following chapters demonstrate why and detail how norm research continues to hold significant potential and promise both about theorising within IR and for studying current issues and problems in world politics. As the world and its constitutive parts have become increasingly contested, this book seeks both to dismantle the looming perception of contestation as a threat and to firmly establish the potential of the concept not only as a virtue but also, in fact, as a *sine qua non* for establishing sustainable and legitimate order in the world.

Three Theoretical Moves towards an Established Sub-field

This book is not interested in divisions – whether between 'conventional' and 'critical' perspectives or between 'first' and 'second generation' constructivists – but, instead, takes a more pragmatic approach. In this section, we argue that three moves have coined today's status of the field of norms research, spanning programmatic, applicatory, and conceptual advances, respectively: the focus on the 'social' in global politics, the adaptation of norms in processes in policymaking, and a renewed focus on the role politics plays in processes of norm contestation. Each of these moves, we argue, has been integral to the development of norm research as an established sub-field. At the same time, each move has introduced its own set of issues and limitations, while a range of enduring questions continue to affect the sub-field.

The First Move: A Focus on the Social

The *first move* was framed by the constructivist focus on the 'social' in global politics (Adler 1997) and included two important developments. The first was to forge an interest in analysing the role of 'social facts' in addition to material facts that had previously set the standard conditions for political decisions in international relations (Ruggie 1993; Searle 1995). These social facts included norms, standards, regulations, rules, and ideas. The second development was to move away from an agent-centred perspective to instead examine agents and structures existing in a mutually constitutive manner (Wendt 1999; Dessler 1989). Together, these two developments represented a conceptual shift that helped to broaden the research programme in IR considerably (Finnemore 1996; Klotz 1995a; Adler 1997; Finnemore and Sikkink 1998; March and Olsen 1998).

Attached to this first move were models designed to portray the cyclic representation of the process of norm emergence, diffusion, and internalisation. This was initially developed by Kathryn Sikkink (1993) and was then adopted to frame a comparative multi-country case study on human rights norms edited by Risse, Ropp, and Sikkink (1999). It is most concisely summarised by Finnemore and Sikkink's now seminal article in *International Organization* (1998). The norm life cycle is a three-stage model, with norm entrepreneurs playing a critical role in the initial stage of norm emergence in placing issues on to the international agenda. Following the emergence of a new norm, early adopting states become 'norm leaders' and socialise other states to follow them through a variety of mechanisms, including legitimation effects, self-esteem effects, and pressure for conformity (Coleman 2013: 166; Finnemore and Sikkink 1998: 901–2). Once a critical mass of states adopts a new norm, it passes a threshold, or tipping point (Finnemore and Sikkink 1998: 896–906). After this point, they argue new norms may become so widely accepted that they are "internalized by actors and achieve a 'taken-for-granted' quality that make conformance with the norm almost automatic" (Finnemore and Sikkink 1998: 904; see also Risse and Sikkink 1999: 15–17).

But the first move also created a limited understanding of how norms emerged and, more importantly, changed. In this work, there was an underlying assumption of *stability* once a norm emerged (Wiener 2004: 23). A norm was seen as having an endpoint once it became "the prevailing standard of appropriateness against which new norms emerge and compete for support" (Finnemore and Sikkink 1998: 895) and hence became relatively 'fixed' (McKeown 2009: 9), or settled, following which arguments would require "special justification" to deny it (Frost 1996: 105–6).[5] Yet, as others have pointed out, "[w]hile norms may appear as stable over a prolonged, albeit limited, period of time, drawing the analytical conclusion of norms as stable social facts implies ontologising norms" (Wiener 2004: 54). Given that "as observable units, norms not only cause or structure behaviour, they also evolve in relation with social interaction" (Wiener 2007: 55). That is, norms are not ontological 'billiard balls' but complex ontological units that represent a range of 'meanings-in-use', which are enacted by agents in different places and at different times (Wiener 2007: 54, 2009; see also more recently Wilkens and Datchoua-Tirveaudey 2022). The first move also privileged the international level, presuming that international institutionalisation created this fixed norm, which would then diffuse downwards in a unidirectional manner.[6]

The Second Move: Norm Adaptation and Diffusion in Policymaking

The *second move* acknowledged these limitations by focusing on how norms were adapted in processes of policymaking. Rather than presuming a norm was fixed or stable, this move introduced new questions

[5] Others have raised similar critiques: Pratt, for instance, suggests that this period approached "norms as reified social objects" (Pratt 2020: 64). In our view, however, this may be too far a step (and it does depend on the definition of 'reification' used) as it goes beyond an assumption of stability or fixed properties, which reduces the agency to a great degree.

[6] As a two-dimensional process this stable norm transfer may be illustrated with reference to the metaphor of up- and down-loading material. Thus:

> [f]rom a global governance perspective, the transfer of norms from national constitutional contexts into the global context of international organisations could be dubbed as 'uploading'. Conversely, following international negotiations, agreements, and treaties, the implementation of these norms by norm-followers around the world could be dubbed 'downloading'. Most of the compliance literature has sought to enforce the latter through shaming, sanctioning, or coercion of states that were unwilling to comply. The point of this illustration is the reification of a norm's formal validity whilst neglecting its substantive content, and, therefore, its potential for change. (Wiener 2022: 313)

around how norms were diffused and localised, why actors complied with them, and how norms could be generated at the domestic as well as international levels (Acharya 2004; Betts and Orchard 2014; Niemann and Schillinger 2017; Orchard 2018; Risse and Sikkink 1999; Risse et al. 2013; Simmons 2009; Zimmermann 2017; Ben-Josef Hirsch and Dixon 2021). Distinctions that mattered specifically to this move included aspects of norm salience, degree of fit, stability, robustness, and power – all of which were considered to lead to more resilient norm implementation (Risse et al. 2001; Checkel 2001, Schimmelfennig 2001; Deitelhoff and Zimmermann 2019; Stimmer and Wisken 2019). But alongside this focus on resilience, this work also began to critically analyse norm decline, either from cases of "contested compliance" (Wiener 2004) or full-scale "norm violation," when a norm degenerates if it loses its prescriptive status due to widespread non-compliance, leading to it either fading away or being replaced (Panke and Petersohn 2012).

Finally, this move problematised norm transmission. Rather than assuming a single international norm would diffuse downwards, this literature instead saw such norms as being subject to significant changes. At the regional level, they could be subject to 'framing', 'fit', and 'grafting' on to regional cultural contexts (Börzel and Risse 2001, 2019; Acharya 2004, 2013) or to significant reinterpretation including through regional organisations (Checkel 1999, 2005). At the domestic level, a range of distinct issues can affect implementation (Betts and Orchard 2014). Materially, state capacity has been shown to be central to implementation (Urpelainen 2010; VanDeveer and Dabelko 2001). Institutions can also play a significant role. National legal and constitutional frameworks have been shown to matter for how norms are implemented in different states (Simmons 2009; Risse-Kappen 1995: 16; Cortell and Davis 2000: 66; Legro 1997). Domestic institutions can play the role of policy gatekeepers or veto players if they have "sufficient power to block or at least delay policy change" (Busby 2007: 254; see also Tsebelis 2002: 442).

While this move produced considerable knowledge about handling specific norms under given conditions, it inadvertently led to the 'ontologisation' of norms that reflected the predominant interest in the *structuring* as opposed to the socially constructed quality of norms (Wiener 2007; Wendt 1987; Melucci 1989). The unintended consequence of this shared norm ontology largely led to emphasising the role of agents such as norm entrepreneurs or antipreneurs and norm followers vis-à-vis a norm while bracketing questions of normative legitimacy (Orchard 2014; Bloomfield 2016). This meant that hybrid sources of norms – as both social fact *and* as rooted in moral values: the normativity of norms, in other words (Erskine 2012; Havercroft 2018; Wiener 2020) – tended to be overlooked. This omission meant that diversity too was less examined. Norms as solely social facts worked well with an underlying liberal community assumption, but such accounts were less effective in the context of a globally pluralist and diverse world (Krook and True 2012; Krieger and Liese 2019), one which is less united and one in which norms sources are multiple and varied. Effectively, this

> community ontology relies on a fixed community. It implies that any contestation about the normative structure of meaning-in-use, which guides actors in international relations as they enact that normative meaning, remains bracketed. This bracketing of the norm-generative dimension of practice forfeits the central interactive potential of contestation as a social practice that is not limited to notions of opposition, questioning or protest, but which also represents the basis of legitimate global governance. (Wiener 2014: viii)

The third move begins from taking a critical stance on this ontology and the stability assumption about norms that it carried. The following section details this move and its implications for the growing interest in the contestation of norms as a research theme for IR scholarship more generally.

The Third Move: Norm Contestation

This book embraces and argues that we are now in the midst of a *third move*. This move arguably begins with Krook and True's (2012: 105) reintroduction of the idea of "norms as 'processes', as works-in-progress, rather than as finished products" or 'things', echoing Onuf's call of two decades earlier that norms are both a "a thing and a process" (Onuf 1994: 1). Norm contestation is critical to this move in order to understand norms as processes. Contestation, following Wiener, is a societal practice in which rules, regulations, or procedures are critically questioned (Wiener 2014: 1–15). Contestation lets us highlight new-found understandings of the role of politics at both global and local levels as well as new plural understandings of agency in norm generation and resistance (Wiener 2018; True and Wiener 2019; Pratt 2020).

Most importantly, contestation focuses on the multiplicity who can have 'access' to shaping norms and their meaning-in-use through participation in politics. By asking whose norms and whose practices count, this research introduces a more specific attention to societal agency in the field while also acknowledging North–South and regional power biases that have existed in norms research (Acharya 2004, 2013; Draude 2019; Wiener 2017a, 2022). But, beyond agency, this also acknowledges the dual quality of norms, that "they are both structuring and socially

Time Stage of Norm Implementation / **Place** Scale of Global Order	**Stage 1:** Constituting	**Stage 2:** Negotiating	**Stage 3:** Implementing
Macro	*Site 1*	*Site 2* ***Formal Validation***	*Site 3*
Meso	*Site 4* ***Social Validation***	*Site 5*	*Site 6*
Micro	*Site 7*	*Site 8* ***Cultural Validation***	*Site 9*

Figure 1.1 Cycle-grid model
Source: Wiener (2018: 44)
Reprinted with permission

constructed through interaction in a context. While stable over particular periods, they always remain flexible by definition" (Wiener 2007: 49).

To identify, locate, and evaluate instances of norm contestation and their role in norm(ative) change in the global order, Wiener has introduced the cycle-grid model (Figure 1.1). Rather than focusing on the international (or domestic) levels, or a particular phase of a norm life cycle, the model demonstrates that contestations which can reformulate normative meaning can occur *in principle* at any time.

The model reflects two processes. The first is descriptive and consists of a three-by-three grid including nine ideal-typical sites of contestation with reference to the scale of a given order on the vertical axis and the stages of the norm-implementation process on the horizontal access. On each site the normative opportunity structure sets distinct rules of engagement that determine affected stakeholder's access to contestation. The second process is evaluative. It consists of the cycle, which entails three distinct practices of validation to indicate the potential range of access for a stakeholder – pending their positionality in the normative opportunity structure – allowing for an evaluation of a stakeholder's potential to influence norm(ative) change based on constitutive, habitual, and/or cultural validation of normative meanings-in-use. That is, contestations take place within specific normative opportunity structures that frame the context in which actors operate. Nine ideal typical sites can be identified, revealing a "normative grid" (Walker 2008, 2014;

Hofius 2016). These sites identify where contestations may occur across the macro-, meso-, and micro-scales of a given order, representing levels of governance and layers of society (Wiener 2018: 52), and as norms move through a process of implementation, focusing on the constitution stage, then negotiations, and finally on implementation.

It is through this process of contestation that norms become validated. Initially, formal validation occurs through negotiations involving committee members of international organisations, negotiating groups, ad hoc committees, or similar bodies involving high-level representatives of states and/or governments. Formal validation therefore makes specific claims with regard to formal documents, treaties, conventions, or agreements. Habitual validation is practised habitually through interactions within a social environment and therefore depends on the context of social groups. The higher the level of integration among the group, the more likely a norm becomes uncontested. This reflects a different process from formal validation, where validity claims are explicitly negotiated, with habitual validation reflecting mediated access to validity claims qua prior social interaction within a group. Finally, cultural validation is an expression of an individual expectation mediated by individually held background experience. Importantly, the qualifier 'cultural' is used to distinguish individual from group practices. It refers to background experience derived through everyday practice and as such carries a thin rather than a thick meaning of culture (Wiener 2014: 9).[7] Norm clashes, then, indicate the sites for empirical research to study the sources of conflict by mapping meanings on to the normative grids as part of the cycle of contestation.

Mapping contestations about universal validity claims of a norm – for example, the rule of law – in one of the nine sites takes account of the shared normative substance with regard to a selected fundamental or *type 1* norm (Wiener 2018: 58–9). The approach enables norms researchers to determine which practices of norm validation are available to legitimate stakeholders at these sites. It therefore offers a novel perspective that allows for the exploration of the opportunities and constraints of agency in global governance. It also opens up important empirical questions including: what is the highest set of *type 2* norms (i.e., organising principles) that is aggregated through cultural validation of *type 3* norms (i.e., standardised procedures and regulations)? The arrow on the spinning cycle (Figure 1.1) indicates the normative condition for the

[7] Also compare Wenger (1998) and more recent world democratic survey analyses that stress the crucial impact of cultural diversity expressed by attitudes towards 'moral values' (Kistler et al. 2017).

best-case scenario, namely that each of the three practices of norm validation becomes available for the stakeholders affected by a norm.

Against the backdrop of these conceptual advances, the three moves can be summarised with reference to the concept of norm as a *three-layered theoretical advancement* in IR, which included *the identification of norms*, then *working with and applying norms*, and finally bringing in critical questions of *order, legitimacy, and normativity* which address the 'goodness' of norms. This book argues that these three conceptual layers (i.e., norms as social facts, norm implementation, and norm-/ative legitimacy) represent the breadth and depth of the current conceptual background against which to put the value-added of norms research to the test, for example, with reference to the two globally shared crises of climate change and the COVID-19 pandemic. At present, the theoretical claims of norms research span theories of interaction, discourse, order, identity, normativity, and justice. They are more than matched by outstanding methodological advances that have attracted attention beyond IR, especially from international lawyers. This is an excellent point in time to turn to the proof of the pudding, as it were. Against this background, this book seeks both to reassess how norm studies around these three moves have advanced over this period and to identify and seeks to theorise some of the most critical outstanding questions and divides that exist within the contemporary study of norms. To that end, *Contesting the World* takes a practice-based approach to norms that centres on practices of contestation and/or interpretation. And with it, the conceptual balance between approaches that address the normalcy (i.e., taken-for-grantedness) of norms as social structures, on the one hand, and engaging with the normativity of norms that is inherent to assumptions about norms' 'moral reach' and 'ethical value' (Wiener 2008, 2014; Erskine 2012; Havercroft 2018), on the other, have been highlighted.

In sum, contestation can be either a negative or a positive process, which can help to improve the legitimacy of norms. This has raised the ongoing lively debate among norms scholars about the question of when contestation ends. One position sees any evidence of contestation as an indication that a norm is not a true norm. For example, Michelle Jurkovich has recently suggested that norms need both a sense of oughtness and to "link a specific actor to a specific expected action" in order to create a clear social rule (Jurkovich 2020: 696); this implies, however, that all justificatory and applicatory contestations over the norm have by necessity been concluded in order to have this specific pattern of behaviour created. The other sees norms as "stable over particular periods" but that "they always remain flexible by definition," with the degree of contestedness of individual norms being variable (Wiener 2018: 58). This then opens up a question of when norms are more likely to be stable. Here norm robustness – which is defined as encompassing both a norm's validity and facticity – becomes important, with norm robustness "said to be 'high' when its claims are widely accepted by norm addressees (validity) and generally guide the actions of these addressees (facticity)" (Deitelhoff and Zimmermann 2019: 3). Robustness, as we argue later, can also be increased not just when a norm's claims are widely accepted but also when potential access to processes of norm validation are high. As an alternative, Ben-Josef Hirsch and Dixon (Chapter 2) suggest a twofold approach focused on how norms change, reflecting both norm strength – the extent of collective expectations relating to a principled idea at a moment in time – and norm content – focusing on the changes in behaviour, applicability, and distinctiveness – of a given norm. Finally, Anette Stimmer (Chapter 10) suggests we instead focus on individual states' sense of obligation towards a norm, reflected in both their words and actions as well as wider engagement with the international community.

Enduring Questions

In addition, there are two enduring questions that have not been answered by any of the three moves so far. The first – perhaps surprisingly – is *what are norms?* The first move began with identifying and putting selected fundamental norms on the map of IR. Early IR constructivist scholarship understood norms to be shared understandings of appropriate behaviour for actors with a given identity (Jepperson et al. 1996: 52; Finnemore and Sikkink 1998: 891). Yet norms research "soon noticed that the cocoon of that community was fragile" (Wiener 2018: 59), with the notion of shared understandings being extended from a specific set of primarily liberal states to the global community as a whole. Further, early definitions such as Finnemore and Sikkink's were careful to include language specifying that the norm definition "isolates single standards of behaviour" (Finnemore and Sikkink 1998: 891), whereas today 'norms' are used in an increasingly flexible way (Jurkovich 2020: 694). Finally, this early perspective neglected a value-based ethical dimension that raised questions about the legitimacy of norms (Erskine 2012; Havercroft 2018).

Against this background, this book argues that while norms represent shared understandings, they also need to be understood as constituting a form of *soft institution*. Following Peter Hall and Rosemary Taylor (Hall and Taylor 1996: 938), institutions are defined as "formal and informal procedures, routines, norms and conventions embedded in the organisational structure of the polity or political economy." Alongside hard institutions such as international organisations, soft institutions include principles, values, rules, and common standards. Importantly, norms need to be understood as being *both* value-based and fact-based. As a category of analysis, norms have advanced the analysis of international relations insofar as they offer both an explanation for behavioural change and a yardstick for ethics and moral values. Treating norms as a form of soft institution allows them to be viewed as both a thing and a process (Onuf 1994: 1). And given that norms lie in the practice, and all practices are normative (Wiener 2018: 27–49), *Contesting the World* draws in the main on relational approaches to norms that centre on practices of interpretation and contestation.

The second enduring question concerns a tendency to focus on individual norms at the expense of a wider set of structures. Norms rarely exist in isolation. Other structures including institutions are needed in order to "*emphasize* the way in which behavioural rules are structured together and interrelate" (Finnemore and Sikkink 1998: 891, authors' emphasis; Donnelly 2012: 625). Therefore, beyond individual norms, we also need some form of structure which can "provide processes to interpret those rules; and … demark who should have a role in interpreting the rules" (Orchard 2014: 20). These other structures have been marked by a variety of different concepts. These include 'norm complexes' (Finnemore and Sikkink 1998: 891; Bernstein 2000), and as an alternative, Lantis and Wunderlich have made the case recently for examining 'norm clusters', which are "collections of aligned, but distinct, norms or principles that relate to a common, overarching issue area; they address different aspects and contain specific normative obligations" (Lantis and Wunderlich 2018: 571). Winston uses the same term to refer to the fact that clusters within a family group may exist as bounded collections "of interrelated specific problems, values, and behaviours," which can be combined in an number of distinct combinations (Winston 2018: 647). Orchard has argued, following Goertz (2003: 15), that regimes can be understood as similarly bringing together a range of what might otherwise be disparate norms in order to provide a clear sense of the scope of international behaviour required. The regime, rather than individual norms, can "frame the nature and scope of a given problem and provide potential response scripts" (Orchard 2014: 241). In turn, True and Wiener have demonstrated how the concept of a 'norm bundle' works to analyse the connectivity between different types of norms in a given policy sector such as the Women, Peace and Security agenda (WPS) in peace and conflict studies (True and Wiener 2019).

In sum, linkages between individual norms can increase cluster resilience alongside higher levels of institutionalisation and legalisation (Lantis and Wunderlich 2018: 572). Here, too, however, a question remains open: is it that norms work better when they are clustered or embedded together in a cohesive manner, with inconsistences between individual norms, logical gaps in their overall structure, and procedural incoherence reducing their effectiveness (Donnelly 1986: 605)? And does this require these norms to be fixed within a formally legalised or institutionalised regime, or can these norms still assume the property of oughtness in less formal regimes, based around soft law or reflecting policy norms?

The Interpretation–Contestation Framework

The practice of norm contestation reflects the third move of norm research. It is important to clarify that while practices of contestation alter norms, contestation itself should be considered as a neutral process because of a range of positive, negative, or neutral effects on how a norm is understood. This also differentiates our view of contestation from an alternative perspective that focuses on norm robustness and has seen contestations as primarily negative: that they can undermine norm strength (Panke and Petersohn 2016) or challenge the authority of international institutions or even the liberal international order as a whole (Börzel and Zürn 2021: 7). Thus, Deitelhoff and Zimmermann (2020: 52) note, "for scholars of potential norm decay, contestation is per se a sign of norm weakening." But this reflects a notion of a norm as a thing, rather than as a process in which contestation is a *sine qua non* for normative legitimacy, one in which "contestation all the way" (Tully 2002) is conceptualised as a normative asset to strive for, and "contestation all the way down" becomes an imperative for international politics (Niemann and Schillinger 2017).

The practice of norm contestation generates norm conflict, which is distinguishable according to two distinct takes of how agents interact among each other and vis-à-vis specific norms. The first take considers the challenge–change relationship to occur between a given agent (A) and a given norm (N1), which produces a specific understand of that norm for that agent – this is the A–N1 relationship. While this interaction may be repeated, it is always between one or more agents (A+1) and a given norm and may reflect two types of contestation: one that is deliberate or one that is interpretive. By contrast, the second take considers the challenge–change relation to occur between a variety of agents (A1, A2, and so on) who are part of a conflictive encounter. During that encounter, norms are challenged and changed. And it is expected that as a norm-generative practice, contestation generates mutually recognised norms or normative meaning, as it were, in addition to normality.

These two takes indicate that the practice of contestation can be either a deliberate or inadvertent process: Stimmer and Wisken (2019: 516–19) have argued that contestation should be understood as including "any differences in the understanding of norms, no matter what the source." Deliberate contestations reflect societal agents knowingly contesting different understandings of a norm's validity, which leads to a norm conflict. But agents can also have *unknowingly* adopted different interpretations of what a given norm means. Societal agents reflect a notion of a corporate actor: they are composed of many individuals, whether in a state, organisation, or other agglomeration. Particularly as a given norm moves downwards through the meso- and micro-levels, it will primarily be subject to contestations by societal agents within the state (or within large organisations). Specific implementation processes, during which formal legal and policy mechanisms are introduced in order to routinise compliance (see Betts and Orchard 2014: 22) will be particularly prone to these forms of contestation. Betts and Orchard note: "the implementation process itself can open up a new arena for interpretation and contestation of the norm by relevant actors, with the result that the adopted norm is understood differently across states and other international actors" (Betts and Orchard 2014: 3).

The key issue here is that this domestic implementation process (as it occurs across the micro-level sites) may incorporate both visible factors – such as formal constitutional functions – and invisible factors – including "expectations of norms and the interpretation of their respective meanings derived from the historical and cultural contingency." These constitutional functions are "crucial for the interpretation of norms" (Wiener 2008: 7, 23) and yet may remain hidden or opaque to actors beyond the state.

Therefore, we can see three distinct types of norm contestation. *Interpretive contestation* reflects that any given agent may have interpretive variance on how they understand a given norm. Such variances may not be readily apparent without direct application of the norm and, in theory, can exist between any agent and any norm. Thus, interpretive contestations have a distinctly different character from other types; they may be inadvertent rather than deliberate and more likely to appear in the form of applicatory contestations[8] rather than validity contestations

[8] For example, see Matthew Adler's legal essay on the correctness of legal interpretations of the US constitution (2012).

as the agent believes their understanding of the norm is the same as others. This contrasts with two deliberate and distinct practices: *reactive* and *proactive contestation* (Wiener 2017b). As a reactive practice, contestation is indicated primarily as an objection to norms. By contrast, when conceptualised as a proactive practice, contestation is undertaken in order to engage with norms. Through these three practices of contestation, agents create both normality and normative effects.

Constitutive (behaviourally induced) generative practices focus primarily on norm content. Proactive contestations generally seek to improve the norm, while reactive contestations are generally about challenging the standards of behaviour indicated by a norm leading (at the extreme) to norm violation. Reactive contestations, however, can also have constructive effects by leading to norm improvements; hence, they too can be norm generative (Wiener 2020). Interpretive contestations may shade into both forms but will most likely take on the appearance of contested compliance by actors who feel that they are already following the norm's content. Constructive (normatively induced) generative practices focus instead on the legitimacy of a norm and its moral purposes. Proactive contestations more frequently focus on emergent norms, seeking to improve the norm's legitimacy. Reactive contestations will more frequently focus on challenging the legitimacy or moral principles of extant norms. Interpretive contestations focus on hidden understandings that an agent may have of the norm and implicit efforts to bring the wider understanding of the norm's precepts in line.

These three types of contestation can lead to five possible outcomes on how a societal agent interprets a given norm (Figure 1.2). Returning to the A–N1 relationship, these outcomes see N1 potentially split between its domestic understanding (N_d) and the international understanding of the norm (N_i). The *first* outcome is that the societal agent fully endorses the existing international understanding of the norm: N_d and N_i are the same and no contestation occurs. The *second* outcome is that the societal agent does not implement the norm – it may engage in rhetorical support with no follow-through (either as a fair-weather process or due to reputational concerns or pressure): N_d does not exist, and the agent does not support N_i leading to the potential for reactive contestations or even norm violation. The *third* outcome is that the societal agent deliberately endorses a different understanding of the norm: N_d is different from N_i but the societal agent does not engage in a contestation of N_i. This may reflect a localisation process, for example, and the agent may either understand the norm as different at either the discursive or behavioural/facticity levels. With this outcome, the societal agent knows it has a different interpretation of the norm,

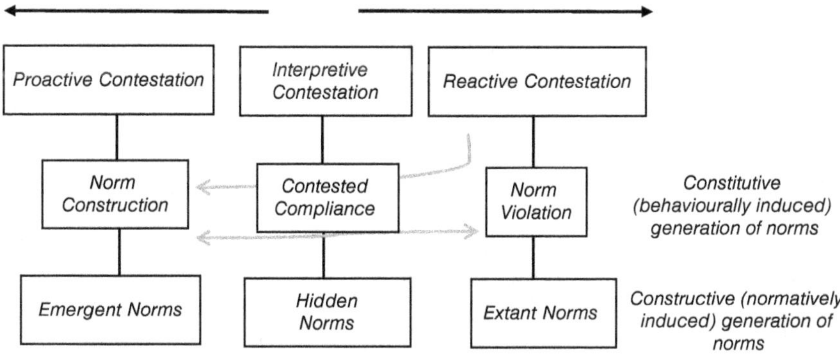

Figure 1.2 Types of contestation

and in effect follows it in parallel to the international norm. Over the longer term, this may not be sustainable and can then lead to reactive or proactive contestations. The *fourth* outcome is that the societal agent deliberately endorses a different understanding of the norm: N_d is different from N_i, and, further, the agent will seek to deliberately either reactively or proactively contest N_i. Finally, there is the *fifth* outcome. In this case, the implementation process has seen understandings of the norm that vary from what exists at the international level. The agent endorses a different understanding of the norm: N_d is different from N_i but the agent does not realise this is the case. This may lead to interpretive contestations. Stimmer (Chapter 10) adds further nuance to these five outcomes in her discussion of how much commitment to a norm different kind of implementation efforts reflect.

The issue with the fifth outcome is that it creates interpretative variation between how this societal agent and others understand the norm. But, as opposed to other types of contestation, the agent 'thinks' that it understands the norm in the same way as other agents within a given community; it 'thinks' a shared understanding exists. And – unless the norm is challenged or violated – these differences in interpretation may be very difficult to detect. In addition, this type of outcome can occur across a series of agents, with the result that the A–N1 challenge–change relationship creates a web of different meanings for a given norm.

As opposed to interpretive contestations, reactive and proactive contestations are also more likely to take on the second form of challenge–change relation, between a specific norm and a variety of agents (A1, A2, and so on). During such encounters, norms are challenged and changed. And it is expected that as a norm-generative practice, contestation generates mutually recognised norms or normative meaning, as it were, in addition to normality. While a conflict is likely to be ignited through contested universal validity claims of a fundamental norm – such as human rights, the rule of law, or the ban on landmines – it is expected to settle the ground rules or the organising principles according to which these universal validity claims are sensibly implemented. These ground rules, or organising principles, reflect a compromise considering constraints and opportunities of sustainable normativity in a given context. The central research question is the effect on the meaning of the involved norm/s: does the contestation only take effect at the implementing stage (reactive contestation), or does it imply a more substantive impact at the constitutive stage of norm implementation (proactive contestation)?

It is therefore through the practice of contestation that we can see a legitimate and accepted understanding of the norm develop. The practice of contestation itself varies in two ways. The first is that different types of contestations can occur, including interpretive, reactive, and proactive contestations. The second is that different forms of contestation can occur, focusing either on a norm's validity or on the norm's application, or what actions the norm requires in a specific situation (Deitelhoff and Zimmermann 2020: 56–7).

The Normativity of Norms

The practice of contestation itself is a neutral process, able to alter interpretations of norms in a variety of ways. That is, contestation works both as an indicator of objection to norm compliance as a 'reactive' practice potentially leading to violation and as a means to critically engage in constructing international politics as a 'proactive' practice. As we have shown earlier, the three moves of norm research can be summarised as a *three-layered theoretical advancement* in IR, which included *the identification of norms*, then *working with and applying norms*, and finally bringing in critical questions *of order*, *legitimacy*, and *normativity* in order to address the 'goodness' of norms. In this final section, we wish to discuss this last point, how the practice of contestation also increases the legitimacy and normativity of individual norms. We have already sought to demonstrate how a norm's validity is created, reflecting the hybrid qualities of a norm: both its *normalcy* and its *normativity*. Because of this hybrid quality, validity can be shown on the one hand by 'fitting in' with reference to the number or magnitude of norm-followers in a given contest; but on the other hand, validity is enhanced through public contestation, for only through contestation can a norm gain legitmacy (Havercroft 2018; Brunnée and Toope 2010; Wiener 2020; Staunton and Ralph 2020). Hence, the axiom "only a contested norm can ever be a good norm" (Wiener 2019; Kurowska 2019).[9]

By focusing solely on validity, we would appear to be going against Deitelhoff and Zimmermann's (2020) work, which argues that either validity or applicatory contestations can occur. This is an important argument. They see validity contestation as attacks against "the very core of a norm, that is, the basis of its normative obligation" while applicatory contestations deal with questions of whether a given norm is appropriate for a given situation, which actions a norm requires in a specific situation, or which norm must be prioritised in a specific situation if several norms apply (Deitelhoff and Zimmermann 2020: 56–7). These are useful distinctions between the forms that norm conflicts can take. However, we do not view these as distinct and unique 'types' of contestation for two reasons. The first is that by treating these as distinct, they are presuming a fixed and stable understanding of a norm, a specific behavioural rule, that will not be affected by an applicatory contestation. This distinction is untenable however, given the normative structure of meaning-in-use. This is the discourse "within which norms are re-enacted as carriers of meaning. As such, norms reflect validity claims of involved stakeholders, and, at the same time, their meanings change through direct engagement" (Wiener 2018: 13). Applicatory contestations affect meaning; they create new understandings of a norm even if only at the margin. Hence, applicatory contestations are a specific form of validity contestations.

The second reason is that Deitelhoff and Zimmermann's applicatory contestation as a distinct and separate type primarily occurs at the level of implementation and does not provide pathways to norm generation, including access to proactive and reactive contestations. For instance, contestations over the torture taboo could be viewed as applicatory in nature (Price and Sikkink 2017) but also reflected reactive contestations (see Akhrif and Koschut, Chapter 6). In this case, agents did object to the implementation of the norm. The key interaction at the offset for empirical research is therefore the reaction of agent A *to* norm N1, which is most likely to be substantiated by further reactions of agent B (+1) to norm N1; the reactive contestation quickly becomes linked to a validity contestation.

We can see a similar pattern even in contestation conflicts involving multiple agents in international encounters. For example, while a norm such as the right to fish is defined by the statutes of the United Nations Convention on the Law of the Sea (UNCLOS), it is interpreted

[9] For a more general international law perspective, see also Brunnee and Toope (2012).

differently by the involved agents who do not share the same national roots. Upon these agents' encounter in international contexts, the contested implementation of the norm comes to the fore. The key interaction, that is, the offset for empirical research, is an inter-national conflict between agents A and B (or more) about which norm (N1 or N2) to refer to, in order to warrant proper implementation, or what is the norms' hierarchical orderings. Here, the key question is whether the contesting agents agree on the authority of one norm N1 (the right to fish according to the rule of law under UNCLOS) or another norm N2 (sustainable fisheries according to regional experience in the Northwest Atlantic Ocean). While this can also be seen as an applicatory contestation (over norm hierarchical ordering), agreement on which norm to follow requires engagement and a struggle over the recognition of a shared ground rule to guide further common action, thus also wrestling with questions of norm validity.

Which types of contestation are used do depend on the normative structure of the environment which can most easily be observed from instances of norm conflict. It is through these conflictive encounters that we can shed light on stakeholder access to distinct practices of norm validation. These encounters therefore help localise empirically where and when *reactive* and *interpretive* contestation is expected to stand in the process of norm implementation. Relatedly, they also point to the sites where facilitative conditions for *proactive* contestation ought to be established. Sociological research on norms has generated manifold data to map distinct patterns of access to contestation on behalf of the variety of stakeholders. They can be distinguished with reference to type of actor (i.e., state vs. non-state), role in the process of norm implementation (i.e., designated norm-setter or designated norm-follower), and socio-cultural background experience (i.e., individual background experience). While the former two have been thoroughly studied by social constructivists over the past two decades, the latter have been predominantly addressed by more recent pragmatist and Bourdieusian research (Adler-Nissen and Pouliot 2014; Kornprobst and Senn 2016; McCourt 2016; Sending 2016). And it is through enhanced access to contestation that we can then see normative robustness emerge as it is based on a given norm's legitimacy in global society. The more access to practices of norm validation, the higher the robustness of a given norm global society.

Contestations, therefore, are critical for understanding the forms norms take, how they gain validity, and whether they achieve widespread legitimacy. As we have shown, when contestations over normative meaning are empirically mapped, the distinct practices of norm validation generate normative grids. But the expectation is that, in most cases, these grids will reveal an uneven distribution of stakeholder access to the three practices of norm validation and hence also unequal access to the practice of contestation. There will be a power imbalance, tipped in favour of agents who enjoy access to multiple practices of norm validation. This inbuilt condition of injustice, with some agents not having a say in the norms that govern them, will generate a gap between a desirable modicum of norm robustness and the actual observed normative structure. And this condition of injustice increases the likelihood that when these norms are engaged with, it will be either through reactive contestation as agents challenge and undermine the norm, or through interpretive contestations as agents become disconnected from the norm. The empirical challenge therefore consists in both identifying *and* facilitating the institutional means for access to proactive contestation.

Thus exploring the legitimacy of norms in such empirical ways, mapping these practices, matters greatly for real-world politics. Reactive contestation can spiral out of control; they can lead to the undermining and violation of norms and even open political conflict. Interpretive contestation can also undermine the norm if not specifically targeted by political or policy means. Another pattern is possible. By enhancing access to practices of norm validation, by seeking to combat this inbuilt condition of injustice, norm ownership by all affected agents can increase and with this, an increase in proactive contestation becomes possible.

Contents and Organisation of the Book

In light of *Contesting the World's* aim of assessing the trajectory and impact of norms research as a sub-field in IR, we seek to offer a concise presentation of the field's trajectory, core concepts, and approaches. In addition, we flag future paths of norms research in practice and in theory as the field is benefitting from a rich repertoire of methods, fieldwork, and cutting-edge theorising that has received increasing interdisciplinary appreciation. The contributions are grouped in four parts that focus on the themes of (1) norm strength, collisions, and conflicts, (2) the historical development of norms, (3) meta-theorising about norms, norm theory, linkages, and international law, and (4) different dimensions of norm contestation. In the four parts, thirteen substantive chapters address the changes that advanced the field in programmatic, applicatory, as well as conceptual moves over the past four decades. Each batch of chapters details one of the leading themes of norms research including, first, the importance of the social in global politics, second, the adaptation of norms in policymaking processes, and third, the renewed focus on politics which is addressed by norm contestation. Notably, the logic of this sequencing is substantial rather than spatiotemporal.

Accordingly, Part I focuses on norm strength, collisions, and conflicts to address core contributions to the field's first move towards the social in world politics. In Chapter 2, Michal Ben-Josef Hirsch and Jennifer M. Dixon begin by arguing that norm content and norm strength need to be understood as distinct and constitutive elements in processes of norm development. Similar to Gholiagha and Sienknecht, this chapter conceives norm content as reflecting the behaviours that are prescribed or proscribed, for whom, and under what conditions, while norm strength is defined as the extent of collective expectations related to a principled idea. Both proactive and reactive contestations most directly affect a norm's strength by affecting its legitimacy, but can also trigger norm content changes including from one norm to another related, yet distinct, norm. In Chapter 3, Anchalee Rüland and Jennifer Welsh examine the nature of norm conflict as affecting both how to immediately respond to the conflict and how to address wider identity problems created by it. They therefore propose a typology of five possible response strategies actors can use to manage the expectations and costs they face associated with either norm compliance or norm violation. They use two sets of cases of norm conflict to examine these response strategies. The first is how Southeast Asian states managed conflicts between the norms of non-interference and protection of human rights in response to ongoing violence in Myanmar. The second is how the United Nations (UN) has addresses conflicts between norm associated with the prevention and response to atrocity crimes and those associated with respect for sovereignty and state consent. In Chapter 4, Andrea Liese concludes the section by focusing on the specific issue of norm collisions during crisis periods. Like Rüland and Welsh, Liese sees collisions as occurring when the behavioural prescriptions of two or more norms are incompatible with each other. But whereas Rüland and Welsh focus on how such conflicts can be responded to, Liese focuses on crises as desterilising an extent balance or hierarchy between norms. She analyses two such cases: the European refugee crisis and the COVID-19 health crisis.

Part II sheds a critical light of the historical development of norm research, thereby laying the ground for the second move. The chapters take account of the historical development of norms and research about norms. In Chapter 5, Audie Klotz leads this discussion by genealogically examining disruptive episodes of interpretative contestations over racial equality and apartheid norms. She argues that IR as a field – alongside international politics – have treated such norm contestations silently, that there is a norm against noticing, when opposition to apartheid actually played a crucial role in challenging domestic jurisdiction and supporting the development of international human rights norms. In Chapter 6, Halima Akhrif and Simon Koschut examine the relationship between emotions (as moral value judgements) and norms, arguing that emotional resonance – the ability of social norms to evoke and suggest emotional images, memories, and collective feelings – is crucial to the impact and enforcement of norms over time in response to reactive contestations and norm violation. They use the Bush administration's reaction to torture allegations to demonstrate that when there is a lack of emotional resonance, enforcement measures including naming and shaming campaigns are less likely to work. In Chapter 7, Susan Park examines how proactive contestations associated with the World Bank's development of the international accountability norm has shaped not only how the bank understands its responsibilities – with a focus on internal standards rather than legal obligations – but also the efforts of activists to hold the World Bank and other multilateral development banks to account. In Chapter 8, Sassan Gholiagha and Mitja Sienknecht conclude the discussion of this theme by exploring the relation between norms and responsibility. Studying norm-related behaviour, they develop a typology of four ideal types: appropriate, responsible, inappropriate, and irresponsible behaviour. They focus specifically on responsible behaviour and identify three configurations of responsible behaviour, which are then illustrated through instances of responsible behaviour from diverse actors and different norms, including gender equality, anti-personnel landmines and armed non-state actors, and the NATO intervention in Kosovo.

Part III refines the conceptual tools of norms research with a focus on meta-theorising, norm theory, and interdisciplinary linkages with international law. In Chapter 9, Carla Winston sets out the discussion by arguing that norms can be understood through the lens of complex systems theory, which provides a different framework and sets of insights for understanding the process of norm diffusion. Because actors in a system are connected to each other by multiple pathways, different actions can have non-linear effects. Contestations both provide information to actors and can trigger negative feedback loops – which die out – or positive feedback loops – which can undermine a norm. She illustrates these effects through contestations with respect to the rule of law, including the USA's attempts to redefine the use of torture. In Chapter 10, Anette Stimmer argues for a new approach to judge the interaction of international law and politics by exploring the grey zone between empty words and purposive action. She argues that by examining actions and justifications, the degree of commitment to international law can be identified as can the level of obligation that states feel. This allows for norm implementation to be used to expose the weakness or strength of law and attempts at exceptionalism or norm change. And in Chapter 11, Jakob v. H. Holtermann, Mikael Rask Madsen, and Nora Stappert conclude the section by arguing that IR and international law's approach to norms research can be bridged by empirically examining interpretive contestations of legal validity among groups of legal professionals, drawing on Bourdieusian approaches and the concept of communities of practice. They outline this approach by exploring the construction of, and interpretive contestations in, climate change law.

Finally, Part IV addresses different dimensions of norm contestation as the signature card of the third move with its growing emphasis on politics. Here, chapters focus on the role of distinct practices of norm contestation. In Chapter 12, Jacqui True begins with a contribution that argues that networks play an integral role in processes of norm contestation. Networks are part of the political opportunity structure that gives rise to new norms, and also shape their evolution by creating novel spaces and enabling greater access to contestation and thereby enhancing the validity and legitimacy of norms. In her chapter, she highlights the critical role that network structures can play in affecting the dynamism and diffusion of norms by examining the Women, Peace, and Security norm bundle including with respect to the response to COVID-19. In Chapter 13, Cecilia Jacob addresses the concept of regulatory contestation, which focuses on the decisionmaking process in the design of regulatory mechanisms as opposed to the underlying norm itself. Using a case study of the accountability turn in the implementation of human protection norms, she argues that regulatory contestation illuminates the power dynamics that shape international order at a micro level. And in Chapter 14, Jason Ralph concludes with an exploration of how norm research has generally eschewed a clear commitment to normative theory to its detriment from the perspective of European pragmatism. Such a commitment, he argues, would need a defence of certain norms against contestation. The point is explored based on critical scrutiny of contestation theory making special reference to the concepts of normativity, practice, and pragmatism in order to advance the third move of norms research.

In the concluding Chapter 15, Antje Wiener and Phil Orchard revisit the core themes of the book with an examination of how the three moves mark the progress of norms research over the past three decades from a focus on norm stability to contestedness. The chapter uses as vignettes the Bush administration's efforts to contest the norm against torture and the contested international politics around the forced landing of Ryanair Flight 4978 by the government of Belarus in May 2021. The chapter then turns to three core themes developed across the book: around norm interpretation and conflict, the process of contestation, and the role of other structures. The chapter concludes the book by reaffirming the centrality of contestation to understand how norms develop and a call to understand even such large questions of contestations of the international liberal order from the bottom-up. It is by establishing and enhancing pathways that enable affected stakeholders to access proactive contestation and interpretation, not through a top-down project, that orders gain legitimacy and can be restored.

Part I

Norm Strength, Collisions, and Conflicts

2 Rethinking Norm Change
Content and Strength in Norm Development

Michal Ben-Josef Hirsch and Jennifer M. Dixon

When does a norm become a norm, and how does it change and develop over time and across space? For example, the origin of the concept of the Responsibility to Protect (R2P) can be clearly dated to 2001, when the principle was introduced in a Canadian government-sponsored report issued by the International Commission on Intervention and State Sovereignty (Capie 2012: 76–7). However, in the years since this report's issuance, scholars, policymakers, and advocates have disagreed over the normative status of this idea. One scholar refers to R2P as a "nascent norm" (Capie 2012: 75), whereas others characterise it as a "principle" (Bellamy and Drummond 2011; United Nations 2014: 2). Scholars further disagree over whether R2P constitutes a single norm (Evans and Thakur 2013: 207; International Coalition for the Responsibility to Protect 2020) or "a collection of shared expectations" (Bellamy 2010: 160). Or, in a somewhat different example that speaks to the same problem, there is broad agreement about the normative status of international expectations related to dealing with the past following gross human rights violations. At the same time, there is a *lack* of consensus over whether transitional justice constitutes a single norm (Gready 2011; Sikkink 2011) or multiple related norms (Ben-Josef Hirsch 2014; Kim and Sharman 2014; Wiebelhaus-Brahm 2016), and about its origins. Some trace the origins of transitional justice ideas to the post-World War II Nuremberg Tribunal (Teitel 2000), others pinpoint the emergence of a justice norm in Latin America in the late 1980s to early 1990s (Roht-Arriaza 2006; Sikkink 2011), and yet others argue that a distinct truth-seeking norm emerged after the 1996 South African Truth and Reconciliation Commission (Ben-Josef Hirsch 2014).[1]

As these examples illustrate, there are real discrepancies about when a principled idea is a norm, defined as "collective expectations for the

[1] In related work (Ben-Josef Hirsch and Dixon 2021), we argue that there is a transitional justice normative regime, within which there are at least two norms with distinct origins and differing strengths.

proper behaviour of actors with a given identity" (Katzenstein 1996: 5)[2] and not a "partial" (Axelrod 1986: 1110), "proto-" (Bailey 2008: 291), "emerging" (Coleman 2013), "nascent" (Capie 2012: 75), or "pre-"norm (Ben-Josef Hirsch 2009). As this proliferation of labels suggests, and as the editors highlight in their discussion of enduring questions (Orchard and Wiener, Chapter 1: 12–14), the literature is plagued by lack of clarity about when an idea can be called a 'norm' and how this threshold should be defined and identified. Among early work on international norms, several scholars attempted to explicitly define when an idea can be called a norm, but these definitions fell short of providing a clear guide or measure. For example, Florini wrote that, "no matter how a norm arises, it must take on an aura of legitimacy before it can be considered a norm" (Florini 1996: 365). Price offered a more observable, but still fuzzy, rule for judging when a norm is a norm, arguing that "one can say that a norm exists when the dominant discourse shifts in such a way that puts opponents on the defensive or even relegates direct contestation of its central validity claims to the margins" (Price 1998: 631). Such definitional variation – and imprecision – has persisted, signalling the need for a way to distinguish between fully fledged norms and principled ideas. This is particularly complicated in the context of norms within a normative regime or a so-called norm cluster, such as transitional justice and the R2P norm or norms. As noted by Orchard and Wiener (Chapter 1), "norms rarely exist in isolation" (p. 13) and are often studied within structures (Orchard 2014), clusters (Winston 2018; Lantis and Wunderlich 2018), or systems of norms. Indeed, much of what has been written about international norms are in fact about collections or systems of norms that establish collective expectations for appropriate behaviour (Sandholtz 2017). This chapter's contribution can thus be used to parse individual norms within clusters as well as individual 'stand-alone' norms.

Having identified the status of the study of international norms as an "established sub-field," the editors of this book (Orchard and Wiener, Chapter 1) outline two "enduring"' questions: what are norms and how do they relate to broader structures? Indeed, the lack of clarity about when a norm becomes a norm and how norms relate to other norms reflects two key shortcomings in existing understandings of norm development. First, norm development has focused primarily on norm

[2] A principled idea is an idea about "the proper behaviour of actors with a given identity" (Katzenstein 1996: 5) that might – or might not – become a norm. A principled idea consists of a fundamental underlying normative belief, but the idea is not necessarily collectively held, nor does it necessarily connote a clear behavioural expectation (Goldstein and Keohane 1993).

content, often implying or assuming that changes in norm *content* constitute the main or only form of norm change. For example, "second move" scholarship (Orchard and Wiener, Chapter 1) has identified several mechanisms of norm change, including localisation (Acharya 2004) and translation (Zimmermann 2017), contestation and interpretation (Wiener 2004, 2014; Sandholtz 2008), implementation (Betts and Orchard 2014), institutionalisation, and violation (McKeown 2009; Panke and Petersohn 2012). With the exception of the latter two processes, most conceptual and theoretical work has been centred on mechanisms and processes of *content* change. Second, there has been little consideration of norm strength.[3] Exemplifying this relative neglect, scholars frequently refer to strengthening and weakening, and strong and weak norms, without offering clear definitions or measures of norm strength. Even work that explicitly focuses on norm strength has neglected to define the concept or offer clear ways to measure it (e.g., Percy 2007; Liu and Kinsey 2018).

Together, these shortcomings have contributed to idiosyncrasies in the study of norms in general and norm development in particular. Notably, the field lacks a generally accepted framework for the study of norms and features a burgeoning of highly idiosyncratic concepts. As the editors suggest (Orchard and Wiener, Chapter 1, citing Diez and Wiener 2018), norm research is currently in a pluralist "mosaic" stage. This pluralism is welcome for raising and exploring questions about the legitimacy of norms and the politics that shape norm dynamics. At the same time, however, it contributes to the deepening of existing conceptual gaps and inconsistences. In particular, the lack of a clear and shared conceptual framework for norm development has made it difficult to test competing hypotheses about the consequences of norm violation, contestation, and localisation, and has hindered the development of general theories about normative causes and effects. Furthermore, it has hindered the potential for dialogue and exchange between constructivists and International Relations (IR) scholars who do not study norms but might consider including norms in their models or theory-testing.

This chapter thus proposes a typology that identifies four forms of norm change, along with an updated conceptual framework for understanding norm development. The chapter proceeds as follows. We first revisit the norm life cycle model and its impact on thinking about norm development. This section of the chapter corresponds with what

[3] Exceptions are Legro (1997), Deitelhoff and Zimmermann (2019), and Ben-Josef Hirsch and Dixon (2021).

the editors have identified as the *second move* in norms scholarship, which challenged the model's assumptions, specifically the stability assumption. These challenges have led to a more dynamic understanding of *norm content*, which we define as that which is prescribed or proscribed, for whom, and under what conditions. Next, we discuss recent scholarship on *norm strength*, which we have elsewhere defined as "the extent of collective expectations related to a principled idea" (Ben-Josef Hirsch and Dixon 2021). Building on this conceptualisation, this chapter introduces an original typology of norm change and a new framework for thinking about norm development. We argue that norm development has two constitutive elements – norm content and norm strength – which are analytically distinct, individually necessary, and together sufficient to capture changes over time and space. The framework introduced in this chapter corresponds with what the editors have identified as the *third move* in constructivist literature, which focuses on norms as processes. Norm strength helps identify norms and their applicability, while norm content helps answer questions about the legitimacy and normativity of norms. Paraphrasing the editors, norm strength relates to the normalcy of norms as social structures/institutions, while norm content captures the normativity of norms (Orchard and Wiener, Chapter 1: 18). Together these elements capture a more complete notion of norm development. We conclude by highlighting how our proposed rethinking of norm development overcomes existing conceptual gaps and inconsistences and offers a way to move beyond the tendency to study single norms and the sometimes-conflicting findings these studies yield. In so doing, it offers an important tool that opens new directions of enquiry and promises to advance existing debates.

The Norm Life Cycle Model and Its Limitations

Existing approaches to norm development have both shaped and limited thinking about norms.[4] The most influential conceptualisation of the processes by which a norm emerges and diffuses is Finnemore and Sikkink's norm life cycle model. With more than 12,000 citations since its publication,[5] it introduced important propositions concerning the development and impact of international norms and fundamentally shaped how scholars describe and analyse international norms. Notwithstanding its contributions, three key limitations of the model

[4] The discussion in this section borrows in part from Ben-Josef Hirsch and Dixon (2021).
[5] According to Google Scholar, as of January 2024.

and its legacy are the linear conception of norm development, the static treatment of norm content, and the neglect of norm strength.

Like other early scholarship that suggested that norm development had an "evolutionary" character (Axelrod 1986; Florini 1996), the norm life cycle model argued that norms emerge and evolve in a general "patterned" (Finnemore and Sikkink 1998: 888) way. It thus offered a relatively narrow and unidirectional conceptualisation of norm development. In response, for example, Payne critiqued the norm life cycle model's "depict[ion of] a linear and reactive communicative process," in contrast to which he emphasised the fundamentally contested and discursive nature of "norm-building" (Payne 2001: 42). Krook and True similarly highlighted the discursive nature of what they term "norms as processes" (Krook and True 2012: 106), while Zwingel (2012) critiqued the model's unidirectional conceptualisation of norm diffusion. As we discuss later, these and other scholars have demonstrated that norm development is complicated, iterated, and contingent.

Since the linearity and categories of the norm life cycle model often did not coincide with researchers' own knowledge of specific norms, many scholars – typically motivated by specific research questions and informed by specific areas of geographic, temporal, and substantive expertise – have highlighted different elements of norm development. While such an informed, inductive approach makes sense and has clear merits, a distinct downside has been the introduction of many new and often idiosyncratic terms that are rarely applied to other norms. For example, recent conceptual innovations have unpacked some of the ways in which states attempt to resist pressures arising from international normative expectations. This work has introduced several different terms – including "rhetorical adaptation" (Dixon 2017), "norm immunization" (Nuñez-Mietz and García Iommi 2017), and "norm evasion" (Búzás 2021a) – for behaviour that generally falls within this ambit. Similarly, other scholars have conceptualised forms of norm 'backlash,' including "transgression" (Evers 2017) and "deviance" (Terman 2020). While such conceptual contributions are often well defined and empirically substantiated, the extent to which such terms overlap – or do not – and whether and how they relate to scholarship on norm contestation and violation are often not fully clear. Moreover, there is a tendency for subsequent scholarship that treads similar terrain to introduce new concepts rather than adopt existing ones, which is understandable given professional incentives but prevents the accumulation of knowledge about norm development. Consequently, scholarship on international norms includes many innovative and sophisticated conceptual developments, but they rarely yield replicable empirical applications. Overall, this hinders the development and advancement of a coherent body of research.

Another consequence of the emphasis on linearity in norm development has been the use of behavioural measures to assess the progress of given norms along the 'stages' of norm development. This tendency has arisen in particular from the fact that the 'norm emergence' stage of the norm life cycle model captures processes related to the development and promotion of a norm's *content*, whereas the 'cascading' and 'internalisation' stages focus on the effects of or behavioural responses to a norm. However, using behaviour as a measure of stages in norm development is problematic for several reasons. First, norms are best understood as social and collective *expectations* about appropriate behaviour, not as mere descriptions of behaviour or as aggregations of practices. As other work has shown, practices and observable behaviours often fall far short of the expectations embodied in a norm. Full compliance is extremely rare. Even strong norms are violated on occasion, and other norms are regularly violated to some extent. Second, the behaviour of an individual state or the aggregation of many states' behaviours do not necessarily reflect *collective* expectations. States might adopt a norm when they have no interest in complying or no opportunity to reject it (Cardenas 2007; Hyde 2011; Risse et al. 2013). Consequently, adoption may or may not reflect a norm's strength or stage of development. Also, a state might violate or reject a norm because the state is particularly strong, or for identity-related reasons (Evers 2017: 786). In such cases, compliance reflects states' capabilities and identities, not a norm's strength or stage of development. Finally, as others have noted (Legro 1997: 33; Cortell and Davis 2000: 69–70), using behaviour as an indicator of norm strength and development would obviate the possibility of assessing the relationship between norm development and other outcomes.

In addition, early work on international norms implicitly assumed that a norm's meaning remains unchanged once it has successfully 'emerged'. In response, subsequent work sought to address the model's relatively static understanding of norm content. Thus, rather than looking at an existing norm and tracing the processes through which the norm came into existence, scholars problematised the notion that the content of a principled idea remains unchanged through processes of emergence, contestation, institutionalisation, and violation. As the editors (Orchard and Wiener, Chapter 1) discuss, critiques by Sandholtz (2008), Wiener (2004, 2009, 2014), and others (Krook and True 2012; Ben-Josef Hirsch 2014; Hadden and Seybert 2016) have established that norms are dynamic and are produced and reshaped via processes of interpretation, implementation, and contestation.

However, whereas processes of norm content change have been explored in some depth, norm strength has been largely overlooked and underspecified in thinking about norm development, leaving us with a limited understanding of whether and how a norm's *strength* changes over time or space, how it interacts with norm content and changes therein, and how changes and interactions in both shape norm development. Of course, norm content and norm strength are not fully distinct. For example, work on norm emergence and localisation has demonstrated that the more an idea resonates or 'fits' with prevailing norms, the more likely it is to emerge and spread (Florini 1996: 376; Price 1998; Checkel 1999; Cortell and Davis 2000: 73–6; Acharya 2004). Precisely for this reason, we contend that a complete understanding of norm development should include distinct conceptualisations of both content and strength.

Rethinking Norm Development

As noted earlier, the norm life cycle model and its critiques have left a mixed legacy for understanding norm development: sophisticated yet idiosyncratic conceptualisations of norm change as content change, a conceptual lacuna with regard to norm strength, and an overreliance on behavioural measures as indicators of norm stages or trends. In this section, we propose a way forward. Based on extensive review of the literature on norm change, we identify three types of change in norm content, which we argue is a necessary element of norm development. We then draw on our own recent work on norm strength to identify a fourth type of change: change in a norm's strength. We define both content and strength in relation to Katzenstein's definition of international norms as "collective expectations for the proper behaviour of actors with a given identity" (Katzenstein 1996: 5). Building on the components of this definition, norm strength is defined as *the extent of collective expectations related to a principled idea,*[6] while norm content is defined as the *behaviours that are prescribed or proscribed, for whom, and under what conditions*. Together, the explicit articulation of norm content and strength as distinct from each other and from complying and/or violating behaviours helps clarify when an idea can be called a norm. Instead of debating tipping points, scholars can describe and assess changes over time in the content and strength of norms to reach a more complete understanding of norm development. The chapter closes with a discussion of how the proposed approach to norm development draws together these two elements.

[6] See fn2 for our definition of principled idea.

Existing Approaches to Norm Change

What is norm change? There is a significant body of work on norm change, which is organised along three main lines of enquiry. The first includes work that theorises the *determinants* and *mechanisms* of norm change, typically via 'dynamic' and iterated processes of contestation and interpretation (Van Kersbergen and Verbeek 2007; Sandholtz 2007, 2008; Sandholtz and Stiles 2009; Badescu and Weiss 2010; Krook and True 2012; Wunderlich 2013; Stimmer 2019a; Deitelhoff and Zimmermann 2020). Such processes arise in the context of practice (including violations) (Sandholtz 2008), implementation (Van Kersbergen and Verbeek 2007; Betts and Orchard 2014), and localisation and translation (Acharya 2004; Zwingel 2012; Zimmermann 2017); in response to exogenous shocks; and from 'tensions' in and between competing rules and norms (Sandholtz 2007, 2008; Sandholtz and Stiles 2009; Krook and True 2012; O'Mahoney 2014). A second line of enquiry theorises *agents* of norm change (Wunderlich 2013; Lantis 2016; Jose 2017). A final line of enquiry *conceptualises* the nature and process(es) of norm change (Sandholtz 2007, 2008; Sandholtz and Stiles 2009; Wunderlich 2013; Stimmer 2019a). Sandholtz (2017), for example, notes the inherent dynamism of international norms or systems of norms and defines norm change as a phase in this dynamic, one that follows the cycles of disputes and argumentation over emerging normative structures.

Across all three lines of enquiry, norm change is primarily understood as change in a norm's content, that is, in *the behaviours that are prescribed or proscribed, for whom, and under what conditions*. The first type of norm change refers to the behaviours that are understood to fall within and outside the purview of a norm (e.g., Sandholtz 2008; Krook and True 2012; Stimmer 2019a). This type captures changes in the goals, values, and virtues – or the logics of appropriateness – that are associated with a norm (March and Olsen 1998). An example of this type of change is the shift in perceptions of the appropriateness of truth commissions as a mechanism of justice-seeking (Ben-Josef Hirsch 2014), and the emergence of the convention that financial deregulation (e.g., of global monetary flows) is an essential part of economic growth (Abdelal 2007). This type of norm change is also a key focus of "applicatory" norm contestation (Deitelhoff and Zimmermann 2020). For example, the Bush administration sought to situate 'waterboarding' outside the boundaries of the norm against torture (Sanders 2011), and the Turkish government has sought to reinterpret the norm against genocide by claiming that "genocide only involves 'totally innocent' victims who are killed 'simply because of their membership in a specific group'" (Dixon 2017: 90).[7] While both examples illustrate the same type of content change, according to the editors' proposed framework, the former would be an example of reactive contestation and the latter an example of proactive contestation (Orchard and Wiener, Chapter 1: 16–18).

The second type of content change is in the applicability of a norm, which can include the actors for whom and the conditions under which a norm applies. This type of change roughly aligns with what Sandholtz refers to as the "scope of application" of a norm (Sandholtz 2008: 104), what Badescu and Weiss refer to as refinements in a norm's "scope and boundaries" (Badescu and Weiss 2010: 368), or what others refer to as "applicatory contestation" (Deitelhoff and Zimmermann 2020). Examples of this type of change include the broadening of the applicability of the norm of truth and reconciliation commissions (also referred as the norm of truth-seeking) from countries transitioning to democracy to include countries emerging from civil conflict (Ben-Josef Hirsch 2014); the broadening of the boundaries of the norm of reparations from its initial application to cases of genocide to its application to an expanded range of historical wrongs (Engerman 2009); and the broadening of the types of states for which the norm of election monitoring is applicable from democratizing states ("true-democrats") to include "pseudo-democratic" states (Hyde 2011).

The third and most fundamental type of change is from one norm to another related, yet distinct norm. It is in the context of this type of change that scholars often conceptualise and empirically investigate a norm's substance (what the norm is about) and its form (how well it is elaborated).[8] Examples of this type of change include the shift from the norm of colonisation to the norm of decolonisation (Crawford 1993); the shift from the "the anti-commercial whaling norm" to the "proto-norm" that "whales are not just another commodity" (Bailey 2008: 291, 314); and the "change in the rules of war in the early 20th century … from the rule 'to the victor go the spoils' to … the rule that states should not profit from aggression" (O'Mahoney 2014: 834).

[7] While targeting based on group identity is a necessary element of the definition of genocide, whether or not members of the targeted group are 'innocent' is not part of the definition of genocide.

[8] On the distinction between a norm's substance and its form, see Bailey (2008). Winston (2018) bypasses this type of change by conceptualising a broader and more flexible structure – the norm cluster – that encompasses a wider combination of value-behaviours.

Bringing Norm Strength In

In addition to these three types of changes in a norm's content, a fourth type of change is in a norm's strength, which is defined as *the extent of collective expectations related to a principled idea.*[9] The main axis along which change in a norm's strength occurs is by becoming stronger or weaker, either over time or space. Thus, a norm's strength can strengthen (or weaken) via changes in concordance *or* institutionalisation.[10] As the editors discuss, proactive and reactive contestation focus on and can affect the legitimacy of a norm (Orchard and Wiener, Chapter 1: 20), which in turn has the potential to affect its strength. The most obvious way in which a norm's strength changes is from not being a norm – or from being a 'principled idea' without wide agreement about its appropriateness – to being a norm. This change is often labelled 'norm emergence' and is typically discussed in terms of the content of an 'emerging' norm and the agents who shape and promote it. Instead of the typical focus on content and agents (or 'norm entrepreneurs'), and in line with the definition of international norms, a focus on norm strength is attuned to the degree to which international actors and institutions agree that a principled idea is 'appropriate' and should be considered a 'standard of conduct'. Changes in the norms of legal accountability and truth-seeking, which together with the norm of reparations comprise the transitional justice normative regime, are examples of this form of change in a norm's strength. In particular, the norm of "legal accountability became a norm in the early 1990s and is today a strong norm, [while the norm of] truth-seeking emerged later and remains a weak norm" (Ben-Josef Hirsch and Dixon 2021: 521). The emergence and subsequent strengthening of the anti-personnel land mine ban (Price 1998), the "nuclear taboo" (Tannenwald 1999, 2005), and the norm of election monitoring (Kelley 2008) are other well-documented examples of change from principled idea to widely accepted norm. Similarly, change in the opposite direction, that is, from being a norm to no longer being considered a norm, is also possible. This has been referred to by others

[9] In recent work (Ben-Josef Hirsch and Dixon 2021), we conceptualise norm strength and propose two indicators to assess it: concordance, which is the degree to which international actors refer to and accept a principled idea as appropriate; and institutionalisation, which is the degree to which a principled idea is codified and ensconced in international law. As we note in our earlier work (Ben-Josef Hirsch and Dixon 2021: 528), a norm's strength should be understood and assessed in relative terms, either over time, over space, or in conjunction with closely related norms.

[10] As we note elsewhere (Ben-Josef Hirsch and Dixon 2021: 527), concordance and institutionalisation are discrete and do not necessarily change in tandem. Thus, a principled idea may have a high level of concordance and a low level of institutionalisation and vice versa.

Table 2.1 *A typology of norm change*

	Type of Change	Example(s)
Norm Content	Change in the behaviours that are understood to fall within and outside the purview of a norm	• Shift in perceptions of the appropriateness of truth commissions as a mechanism of justice-seeking
	Change in the applicability of a norm, which can include the actors for whom and the conditions under which a norm applies	• Broadening of the applicability of the norm of truth-seeking (also referred as the norm of truth and reconciliation commissions) from countries transitioning to democracy to include countries emerging from civil conflict • Broadening of the boundaries of the norm of reparations from its initial, relatively limited application to cases of genocide to its application to an expanded range of historical wrongs and dark pasts • Broadening of the types of states for which the norm of election monitoring is applicable from democratising states ("true-democrats") to include "pseudo-democratic" states (Hyde 2011)
	Change from one norm to another related, yet distinct norm	• Shift from the norm of colonisation to the norm of decolonisation • Shift from the "the anti-commercial whaling norm" to the "proto-norm" that "whales are not just another commodity" (Bailey 2008: 291, 314) • "Change in the rules of war in the early 20th century … from the rule 'to the victor go the spoils' to … the rule that states should not profit from aggression" (O'Mahoney 2014: 834)
Norm Strength	Change from a 'principled idea' without wide agreement about its appropriateness to a norm, as well as change along the axis from a weak to a strong norm and vice versa	• Emergence and subsequent strengthening of the anti-personnel land mine ban, the "nuclear taboo" (Tannenwald 1999), and the norm of election monitoring • Weakening of the norm of state sovereignty • Obsolescence of the norm of colonisation

as "backsliding" (Hadden and Seybert 2016), "regress" (McKeown 2009), "obsolescence" (Wunderlich 2013), and "death" (Panke and Petersohn 2016). As Sandholtz (2008) observes and the earlier discussion illustrates, this typically occurs in the context of a shift from one norm to another related, yet distinct norm. Examples of norms that have weakened over time include the norm of state sovereignty (Ramos 2013) and the now-obsolete norm of colonisation (Crawford 1993).

Table 2.1 summarises the typology discussed in this section, which provides a basis for a generalisable approach to norm development.

Towards an Integrated Model of Norm Development

Two questions remain: what might be gained by disaggregating the content of a norm from its strength, and how to do this? In the first place, disaggregating norm content from norm strength makes possible the analysis of the effects of changes in norm content on a norm's strength and vice versa.[11] This would allow scholars to explore questions such as how the shift away from an 'absolute' conception of sovereignty to one that is 'contingent' on human rights practices has affected its strength (Ramos 2013). Disaggregating the two elements would also help resolve debates that are currently confused by the conflation of content and strength. For example, scholars disagree about whether ambiguity in a norm's content facilitates its diffusion: Bailey (2008) argues that the ambiguity of the anti-commercial whaling norm facilitated its emergence and then obstructed its institutionalisation,[12] whereas Sandholtz (2008) and Ben-Josef Hirsch (2014) both suggest that more clearly specified and elaborated norms are stronger.[13] Along related, but slightly different lines, Stimmer argues that "narrowing the scope of a norm weakens it" (Stimmer 2019a: 273).

Disaggregating content and strength in processes of norm development would also facilitate the analysis of relationships between different norms, particularly those situated within broader norm clusters.

[11] Hadden and Seybert (2016: 251) point in this direction and note that norms can be institutionalised (which is an indicator of strength) before gaining coherence (which is an aspect of content), which supports the idea of viewing these as distinct. Similarly, Wunderlich's (2013) discussion of norm dynamics/development includes possible changes in norm content and strength. Where her approach differs from ours is that she focuses on the determinants and agents of norm change, whereas we conceptualise the elements of norm development.

[12] Similarly, Widmaier and Glanville (2015) highlight that institutional ambiguity can help facilitate consensus and hence norm development.

[13] As we argue elsewhere (Ben-Josef Hirsch and Dixon 2021), both formal and informal forms of institutionalisation can strengthen a norm. In most cases, depending on the identity and scope of the relevant organisation that issues the formal treaty, the former is likely to be a more significant form of norm strengthening.

For example, the norms of truth-seeking and legal accountability are part of the transitional justice normative regime. Analyses of the content of these two norms reveal changing ideas about states' obligations to "deal with the past" of human rights violations (Ben-Josef Hirsch 2014; Dixon 2017). This insight can be paired with assessments of the changing strengths of these norms to better understand how and to what extent shifts in the content of these ideas have affected their strength (Ben-Josef Hirsch and Dixon 2021). In so doing, this approach has the potential to help address the "enduring" questions about norm structures and resiliency that are raised by the editors (Orchard and Wiener, Chapter 1: 12–14).

For the study of norm development, the disaggregation of content and strength should help answer existing and new research questions. For example, scholars studying norm localisation could use this framework to better understand how international norms interact with the content and strength of relevant domestic norms and the factors that shape domestic actors' scope for agency in localising or translating a given international norm. This typology is also a step towards a theory of norm change and development (Sandholtz 2017: 10), one that accounts for the conditions under which norms are more (or less) likely to gain or lose strength. This conceptualisation should also allow scholars to better understand and assess how and when a norm's content and strength shape states' perceptions of the costs and benefits attached to a given norm, along with their assessments of the likelihood of having to pay certain costs or of reaping particular benefits. Refocusing on states' agency fits with the research agenda outlined by Stimmer (2022), who proposes studying states' actions and justifications to explain compliance and violation decisions, along with broader patterns of norm adoption. This also fits with the research agenda charted by the editors, inasmuch as the framework introduced here provides a path to systematically study the role of different agents (as independent variables) in shaping changes in the content and/or strength of international norms.

Finally, a distinct contribution of our approach is that it resolves the question of when a principled idea becomes a norm. To borrow Finnemore and Sikkink's (1998) language, the 'tipping point' from a principled idea to a norm cannot be reduced to the number of states that have adopted a prescribed behaviour. Instead, we contend that an idea can be called a norm when it contains behaviours – either prescriptive or prohibitive – that are understood to fall either within or outside its purview, along with actors for whom and conditions under which it applies; when it is distinct from other related norms; *and* when these content components are accompanied by at least a moderate level of concordance.[14] Beyond this answer to the question of when a norm is a norm, which is raised both in this chapter's introduction as well as in the editors' introduction (Chapter 1), our typology allows us to generalise about patterns of norm development and at the same time capture the idiosyncrasies of different norms, including within a norm cluster. As noted earlier, we have elsewhere introduced indicators of norm strength. Future work should focus on specifying indicators that could be used to identify and assess the three types of content change identified here. Potentially, for example, the different types of contestation outlined in the book's introduction (Orchard and Wiener, Chapter 1: 15–16) could be integrated into a theory that systematically identifies the causal mechanisms that shape changes in the content and strength of norms (i.e., norm development.)

Overall, this conceptualisation adds analytical precision to the study of norms and their development by disaggregating norm content and strength and differentiating them from both complying and/or violating behaviour. Gaining analytical precision is an important factor in the advancement of research programmes as it opens new directions of enquiry and allows for rigorous empirical applications. This framework thus promises to advance a broader research agenda on international norms, including better dialogue among constructivists as well as with non-constructivist scholars.

[14] To identify these content components and assess concordance, hindsight is assumed. Therefore, it should be noted that the approach proposed here will not be able to identify which ideas will emerge as norms, but it will be useful to understand norms once they emerge.

3 Understanding and Resolving Norm Conflict

Anchalee Rüland and Jennifer Welsh

International Relations (IR) theory has dealt extensively with norms and agency through the three 'moves' of norms research surveyed in the Introduction to this volume. Yet to date, the issue of norm conflict has remained theoretically and empirically understudied in our discipline.[1] We still have little understanding of the judgements that governments or institutions make regarding compliance when the directives inherent in the norms to which they have committed appear to be mutually exclusive. The objective of this chapter is to conceptualise norm conflict as a challenge to decisionmaking in international normative environments and to outline a theoretical framework for studying norm conflict, including the ways in which states and international institutions seek to resolve it. We suggest five possible 'response strategies' for addressing norm conflict and theorise these as efforts by states and international institutions to meet the expectations of key audiences and minimise the social costs entailed by norm violation or compliance. In developing our approach, we speak to the norm contestation framework set out in the Introduction, but also draw from international law and sociology – two disciplines that have extensively dealt with norm conflict.

Defining Norm Conflict

Understood as "shared understandings of appropriate behaviour for actors with a given identity" (Jepperson et al. 1996: 52; Finnemore and Sikkink 1998: 891), norms follow a deontic logic. In other words, they reflect patterned behaviour of a particular kind that both reflects and contributes to normative expectations about what *ought* to be done. At the same time, norms are *collectively* held by groups of actors, which

[1] Two exceptions are Saltnes (2019) and Peltner (2017), though neither attempt to develop a theoretical framework for analysing norm conflict. One recent article, which builds on our earlier work on strategies for addressing norm conflict (Welsh 2019; Rüland 2018), develops an approach for analysing the management of norm conflict by the United Nations (UN). See Buitelaar and Hirschmann (2021).

distinguishes them from ideas, which are often held by individuals (Wiener 2008: 41). While there will be a degree of consensus about the validity of a norm within a group, the claim that norms are 'shared' should not be understood in absolute terms: norm contestation and normative change are core features of international politics. We therefore conceive of norms as 'works-in-progress' that must be analysed as both "static and changing" (Wiener 2004: 191; Sandholtz 2009: 1).

Norm conflicts arise from the relatively stable quality of norms, which make them recognisable and, in some cases, enforceable prescriptions for behaviour. According to Pauwelyn, "two norms are ... in a relationship of conflict if one constitutes, has led to, or may lead to, a breach of the other" (Pauwelyn 2003: 176). As we define it, a norm conflict occurs whenever actors find themselves in a situation in which different normative directives are incompatible or not uniquely action-guiding (Beirlaen 2011: 1; Elhad et al. 2000: 209; Milanovic 2010: 8). The clearest example can be found where one norm prohibits a certain behaviour, whereas another norm obligates the same behaviour. Neither norm is applicable without seeming to conflict or 'collide' with the other (Liese, Chapter 4).

The distinction between regulative and constitutive norms is also relevant to understanding norm conflict and how it creates uncertainty about behaviour in systems governed by norms (Kammerhofer 2005: 1). By creating expectations for compliance, regulative norms can serve as important problem-solving devices for dealing with recurrent issues of social life (Hurrell 2002: 11; Kratochwil 1991: 69). In situations of norm conflict, however, this action-guiding function of regulative norms is seriously impaired. By contrast, constitutive norms shape identities: how agents perceive of themselves and want to be seen by others. But given that both states and institutions may have different identities that relate to their normative commitments, constitutive norms – like regulative ones – can give rise to norm conflicts, some of which are particularly difficult to resolve. A situation of norm conflict thus raises important questions not only about the right immediate response or decision, but also about the resolution of *identity problems* for both states and international institutions (Wendt 1999: 230).

The Management of Choice and Expectations in Norm Conflicts

Our framework for understanding how actors address norm conflict builds upon the three 'logics' that IR theorists have used to explain behaviour in situations of choice: the logics of consequences, appropriateness, and arguing. Our own approach is in part consequentialist, but also "socially embedded" (Rüland 2018). It allows for the possibility that actors – whether they be officials of states or international institutions – may engage in 'rational' approaches to norm following, while at the same time incorporating into their action consideration of the *social costs* that follow from their pre-established commitment to norms and the expectations they have raised with different audiences. Responses to norm conflict can thus be explained as attempts by actors to manage potential costs to legitimacy and reputation that can arise from norm violation. To put it most simply, we expect that states and international institutions will adopt the form of resolution to a norm conflict that minimises these costs.

This emphasis on expectations and social costs points to the role of *perceptions* in the context of efforts to manage norm conflict. Even if an actor's intention may be to proactively contest a norm, or its meaning, as a way of resolving norm conflict, it may be viewed by others as seeking to undermine it. This also implies that some response strategies may work better than others in lowering the costs of choosing to follow or violate a norm – a theme we return to later.

It is important to note that our socially embedded but consequentialist approach to understanding responses to norm conflict does not negate the possibility that actors believe in the norms in question. Nor does it suggest that they never pursue policy-choices based on their inherent sense of appropriateness. We simply argue that in situations in which notions of appropriateness are not uniquely action-guiding, actors must resort to a conscious process of decisionmaking that relies on an additional mechanism for norm following. This strategy has several advantages. First, it leaves the processes of decisionmaking open to relations of power and influence, thereby recognising that actors do not treat all expectations equally. Second, by conceptualising norm conflicts as 'moments' of decisionmaking, our framework allows for the fact that international events often require quick responses and thus little time for deliberation about a norm's superior validity claim (Wiener and Puetter 2009). Third, a consequentialist but socially embedded approach can capture patterns of relative stability as well as change in patterns of norm following by incorporating both the internal transformations that may be occurring within states or institutions and broader normative changes in their surrounding international environment.

A Typology of Responses to Norm Conflict

If we rely solely on the logic of appropriateness, decisionmaking appears virtually impossible in situations of norm conflict. Neither norm can be followed without violating the other, leaving a respective actor seemingly paralysed and unable to act. But in a world in which agents do not operate in complete isolation, and in which normative commitments create expectations of others regarding compliance, paralysis is not a satisfying or viable outcome for most actors in world politics. It therefore seems reasonable to assume that actors will work hard to avoid such an outcome or at least prevent its recurrence.

In what follows, we propose a typology of response strategies to situations of norm conflict. Response strategies are conceived here as the visible representation of the policies that actors adopt, over time, to manage the expectations and costs associated with norm compliance or norm violation. Theoretically, at least five strategies are possible for actors confronting norm conflicts.

Consistent Norm Prioritisation

The first strategy entails the prioritisation of one norm over another, thereby creating a "hierarchical ordering" of the two prescriptions (Orchard and Wiener, Chapter 1; Kreuder-Sonnen and Zürn 2020). By adopting our consequentialist but socially embedded perspective, we might expect consistent norm prioritisation as a response to norm conflict in those cases in which an actor faces compatible and relatively constant expectations that favour compliance with one of the two conflicting norms. In this situation, there is a reasonably 'settled' interpretation of what constitutes legitimate action. For an institution, this is most likely under two conditions: first, when a norm conflict is relatively weak, as measured by degree of obligation generated by the institutionalisation of the two norms (Buitelaar and Hirschmann 2021) and the relative strength of the norms' respective proponents and opponents (Panke and Petersohn 2016); and second, when an institution's mandate and mission have evolved to strongly favour one of the two norms, thereby giving it greater salience (Foot and Walter 2013: 331). For a state, the strategy of prioritisation is most likely when both domestic and international expectations converge in favour of compliance with one norm. This will be even more likely if there is relatively uncontested and strong normative leadership within the state's shared normative system and a firm domestic engagement with the norm in question. The compatible domestic and international expectations thus reinforce each other and raise the stakes of non-compliance with the favoured norm (Boekle et al. 1999: 11). By addressing those expectations and complying with the norm prioritised by its most relevant audiences, an actor will avoid both legitimacy and reputation costs and experience very little fall-out from its encounter with norm conflict.

Some cases in which an actor consistently chooses norm A over norm B will be relatively benign, and thus represent what Orchard and Wiener refer to as "proactive contestation" of the second norm (Orchard and Wiener, Chapter 1). Over time, however, consistent norm prioritisation could also affect the validity of the violated norm, leading to "norm replacement" (Sandholtz 2016: 7). For example, a prohibition can be replaced by a permissive rule and a permissive norm can be replaced by a prohibition or a requirement. As a result of the consistent prioritisation of one of the two norms, the perceived validity of the violated norm would diminish, and relevant audiences might start to question its relevance – and thus its status as a shared standard of behaviour in a particular domain. As the norm degenerates, non-compliance becomes the rule rather than the exception. The consistently prioritised norm would then assume an exclusive action-guiding function and stipulate what constitutes appropriate state behaviour in future situations of choice (Krook and True 2012; Panke and Petersohn 2012).

Norm Replacement

As a conscious strategy for responding to norm conflict, norm replacement actively pursues normative change. Like consistent norm prioritisation, over time it manifests as a uniform response pattern, as an actor consistently complies with the same norm. But unlike the former, norm replacement would be a viable as a strategy only when an actor faces conflicting expectations for norm compliance from relevant audiences *and* when that actor is relatively certain that the audience supporting its course of action will continue to do so in the foreseeable future. Otherwise, removing one of the two norms from the normative environment would create more social costs than it would prevent. Norm replacement is also more likely when an actor is relatively confident in its abilities to convince others of the benefits of compliance with the prioritised norm. To manage the social costs that can arise from leaving one set of expectations for norm compliance unaddressed, an actor would likely try to undermine the validity of the violated norm within a shared normative system and to replace it with the rival – thereby resolving the norm conflict. By challenging the validity of the conflicting norm and seeking to replace it, a strategy of general norm replacement also tries to prevent conflicting expectations for norm compliance from arising in the future.

While *general* norm replacement is on the face of it an attractive approach to resolving norm conflict, it is a demanding strategy. At a minimum, an actor would need to generate acceptance of the prioritisation of the norm among audiences with dissenting views on legitimate conduct. However, the strategy's ultimate goal is to shape the behaviour of others in accordance with the favoured norm so that compliance becomes 'normal' and does not require constant legitimation. Very few actors have the sufficient power or capacity to influence others within a shared normative system in this way (Sandholtz 2009: 12; Ikenberry and Kupchan 1990: 288), especially given the way in which norms can interact with the core identity of other actors.

As a result of these demanding conditions, we expect that actors will rarely pursue general norm replacement as an approach to norm conflict. Instead, they are likely to engage in more context-specific or *strategic* norm replacement. This is most likely where the prioritised expectations in a particular context diverge from those which exist more generally – perhaps as a function of unique circumstances or a 'special relationship' between two actors. In such a scenario, an actor does not intend to undermine the violated norm's general validity and thereby potentially weaken the compliance of others with that norm. Instead, it tries to affect the expectations of a dissenting audience regarding its own behaviour within a specific context, through processes of legitimation that argue for exceptional circumstances (Hurd 1999: 386; Kratochwil 1991: 9). While these arguments can take many forms, scholars have observed that in cases of "horizontal reasoning", arguments that stress similarities with past situations can be particularly powerful (Crawford 2002: 17; Sandholtz 2009: 13–14). As part of a strategy of strategic norm replacement, we therefore expect actors to try to legitimise their norm following by referring to precedents in that particular context.

Norm Reconciliation

A third response strategy to norm conflict, norm reconciliation, aims at removing overlap between the two norms' obligations by altering their meaning in a way that an actor believes to be most acceptable to its various audiences. The actor then tries to establish the modified interpretation of the norms as new shared standards of behaviour. In other words, norm reconciliation targets *both* the expectations of relevant audiences *and* the behaviour of others in future in situations of norm conflict.

This strategy is frequently used in law as a technique for resolving norm conflicts. By employing the legal maxim of *lex specialis*, jurists can resolve the conflict in a way that enables both norms to continue to co-exist, but in a modified way. *Lex specialis* suggests that if both a general standard and a more specific rule regulate a matter, then the latter should take precedence over the former, since it has greater clarity and relevance (Cholvy and Cuppens 1995: 201). In a norm conflict, priority would thus fall to the provision with a more precisely delimited scope of application to a particular a priori defined context (Lindroos 2005: 44), while the general norm remains in the background and re-emerges to regulate behaviour that falls outside the scope of the more specific norm.

Analogous to this legal maxim of *lex specialis*, states or institutions may try to assign a 'general' and a 'specific' norm in response to situations of norm conflict. Two moves are necessary. First, in order to remove the overlap between two norms' obligations, a gap has to be identified within the general norm (Kammerhofer 2005: 5). And second, the specific norm needs to be 'derogated' so that it henceforth only regulates the specific subject matter of the gap within the general norm. The more specific norm therefore becomes an exception to the general norm, while at the same time a hierarchy of order between the norms is created (Ratti 2015: 147). An additional way in which reconciliation can be achieved, particularly for international organisations, is through institutional adaptation: the design of particular policies or mechanisms to address the tensions that arise between two norms in particular contexts to ensure that the institution remains in compliance with both sets of normative commitments.

For norm reconciliation to be a successful approach to norm conflict, the altered meaning of the two norms – and their inter-relationship – has to be accepted by relevant audiences. The likelihood of acceptance, and therefore the success of this strategy, will increase with the legitimacy of the actor that is promoting reconciliation, which in turn is grounded in that actor's own adherence to the new spheres of the norms' application. Since norm reconciliation represents a kind of compromise between the two norms, both of which continue to 'live on' in the shared normative system, we expect this strategy to be more viable for a larger number of actors than the demanding strategy of general norm replacement.

Conflict Denial

Another possible strategy for managing norm conflict is conflict denial. This response strategy focuses upon the interpretation of a particular situation and challenges the conclusions about legitimate action that others have drawn from the perceived facts. In other words, it rejects a particular interpretation or framing of a situation that pitches two conflicting norms (both of which an actor has previously committed to) against each other.

Conflict denial differs from what the editors refer to as "reactive contestation" (Orchard and Wiener, Chapter 1) in that it does not question the validity of a norm per se or a shared understanding of its general sphere of application (Wiener 2004; Krook and True 2012). Rather, it rejects the perceived facts of a situation, which appear to invoke the two norms as standards of behaviour, and hence assumes that norm conflict in this context can be interpreted away. In so doing, an actor must argue that the 'wrong' conclusions have been drawn from the interpretation of the situation and, in fact, only one of the two norms presents a legitimate standard for response to the crisis (Crawford 2002: 17). The strategy of conflict denial – which can also be understood as a form of "interpretive contestation" (Orchard and Wiener, Chapter 1: 15) – is most likely when an actor can provide a powerful counter-narrative of a situation which combats expectations towards compliance with a competing norm. Its chances of success will depend on a number of factors, including the power and status of the actor engaging in denial, the credibility of the information presented by that actor, and how widely the competing interpretation and framing of the situation is shared.

Since conflict denial does not target the general validity of either norm, and thus does not affect future expectations for norm compliance, it is likely to be less attractive as a long-term response strategy to norm conflict. Instead, we expect it to serve as a short-term strategy for actors that face conflicting expectations, but that are uncertain about how these expectations will develop going forward. By targeting the interpretation of a particular situation, as opposed to a norm's general validity, the actor retains the flexibility to align its stance with expectations in favour of compliance with either norm in the future.

Ad Hoc Responses

A final strategy of resolution within our typology acknowledges the possibility that there may be no systematic approach to addressing norm conflicts. Where none of the other approaches are seen as possible, there are at least two options for response: sequencing (whereby one norm is pursued first and then the other); or principled inconsistency, through a case-by-case assessment of which norm to privilege in any given situation (Rüland 2018). While it would be tempting to see these behaviours as merely forms of "organized [*sic*] hypocrisy" (Krasner 1999), we argue that they can still be underpinned by an actor's genuine commitment to both norms and a reluctance to abandon either as part of its identity. We therefore conceive of sequencing and mixed response strategies as conscious attempts to manage norm conflict.

In concluding this discussion of our typology, we note that it is theoretically possible for different actors, who face the same norm conflict, to use alternative strategies (depending on their identities and assessments of social costs associated with compliance and/or violation). It is also possible for an actor that faces multiple instances of a norm conflict to use different strategies, given that concerns for domestic legitimacy or international reputation may evolve over time.

Responding to Norm Conflicts in Practice

Given limitations of space, our application of the preceding theoretical framework focuses on three of the five response strategies: reconciliation, replacement, and denial. (We leave aside the first strategy outlined in the preceding section, given that it is the most familiar form of managing norm conflict, as well as the final strategy, given that it is likely to tell us less about actors' efforts to minimise the social costs of norm violation.) We use two cases of norm conflict to illustrate these response strategies: first, how states within Southeast Asia managed the conflict between the norms of non-interference and protection of human rights in response to violence and crisis in Myanmar; and second, how the United Nations (UN) addressed the conflict between norms associated with the prevention and response to atrocity crimes and those associated with respect for state sovereignty and consent. In the former, we illustrate how Indonesia pursued a strategy of norm reconciliation, Thailand a strategy of norm replacement, and Malaysia a strategy of conflict denial. In the latter case, we illustrate how the UN pursued norm reconciliation through its Human Rights Due Diligence Policy in UN Peacekeeping and the strategy of conflict denial through the development of the Human Rights Up Front initiative.

State Responses to Norm Conflict

Myanmar experienced three major human rights crises during the country's period of democratisation from 2003 to 2012: the 2007 Saffron Revolution, during which thousands of citizens peacefully protesting for economic and political reform were beaten and detained by state enforcement agencies; the aftermath of Cyclone Nargis in 2008, which saw high-profile NGOs describe the government's blockage of life-saving humanitarian assistance as a violation of human rights (Human Rights Watch 2008; Amnesty International 2008); and the 2012 state response to riots in the Rakhine state, in which the Myanmar government failed to stop the discrimination, persecution, and eventual displacement of the Rohingya. These events saw the junta in Myanmar categorically characterised as violator of human right obligations, and yet three powerful Southeast Asian member states – Indonesia, Thailand, and Malaysia – responded to these episodes in different ways. Their reactions were shaped by the need to address conflicting domestic and international expectations regarding two conflicting norms: the promotion and protection of human rights, and non-interference in the internal affairs of states.[2]

Indonesia

Indonesia's policy in these three instances of human rights violations illustrates the strategy of *reconciliation* as a response to norm conflict. Recall that as a strategy for managing norm conflict, norm reconciliation assumes that both norms remain within a state's normative framework, but in a slightly modified way. One of the two conflicting norms is assigned to be the 'general' and the other one the 'specific' norm. In Indonesia's case, this strategy was shaped by two factors: conflicting expectations for norm compliance from domestic and international audiences; and Indonesia's limited persuasive and soft power to convince other states in its region to engage in a process of norm replacement.

At first Indonesia complied with the human rights protection norm during the Saffron Revolution, by individually condemning the Myanmar junta's use of force against protesters – going as far to suggest that the case be taken to the UN Human Rights Council – and mobilizing colleagues with the Association of Southeast Asian Nations (ASEAN) to call for restraint. Domestic and international expectations initially worked together in favour of this position. Presiding over a comparatively weak coalition government, Indonesian decisionmakers were extremely responsive to domestic expectations that flowed from the country's experience of democratic transition, in which respect for human rights had thus become a central element of political legitimacy. This domestic pressure was coupled with the government's sensitivity to the expectations of Western states – who following Indonesia's democratisation had become the country's primary international audience – and its desire to improve Indonesia's international reputation by joining the 'democratic club' (Acharya 2015; Katsumata 2009). Several world leaders, speaking at a meeting of the UN General Assembly in September 2007, vocally condemned the junta's violent crackdown and framed the Saffron Revolution as a case of extraterritorial human rights protection.

[2] The discussion in this section draws from Rüland (2022).

As a non-permanent member of the UN Security Council, Indonesia thus confronted strong pressures to meet expectations for appropriate behaviour as a democratic and rights-respecting country.

While Indonesia's early position therefore enabled it to minimise legitimacy and reputation costs at the domestic and international levels, its stance shifted over time as the crisis in Myanmar evolved. As the junta renewed its fight with various ethnic minorities, Indonesia perceived an increasing risk that Myanmar could be 'balkanised', thereby prompting the Indonesian government to reassess the costs and benefits of complying with either of the two norms. The new territorial dimension to the conflict – which evoked Indonesia's own struggle with territorial integrity – activated a strong domestic expectation for the continued validity of non-interference in cases involving risks of secessionism or state disintegration and for the avoidance of precedents that one day might be mobilised in relation to Indonesia's own internal affairs. Ultimately, the government considered the potential for domestic legitimacy costs to be stronger than the international expectations for compliance with human rights protection. Though Indonesia believed that it was legitimate to discuss governance and human rights with fellow ASEAN members states, it deemed it unacceptable for those members to interfere directly in the affairs of another by assisting rebels or supporting secessionist movements.

The Indonesian government again prioritised human rights protection in the aftermath of Cyclone Nargis in 2008. Not only did it donate US$1million in the early days after the disaster, but it also dispatched Hercules aircraft with emergency relief supplies, along with an Indonesian delegation to accompany the aid – despite the junta's refusal to issue visas for foreign observers and to allow relief teams to enter the country. Contrasting this approach with Indonesia's cooperation with the international community following the tsunami in Aceh in 2005, Indonesia's foreign minister denounced the junta's path of isolation – which had left large segments of the population destitute – and openly questioned Myanmar's membership in ASEAN. While Indonesia's stance in this case was again shaped by the government's reading of domestic expectations, it was primarily Indonesia's international audience – in the form of UN officials and Western foreign ministers – that articulated expectations for interference in Myanmar on the basis of human rights protection.[3]

[3] At the same time, while Indonesia was willing to adopt a leadership role, including by 'naming and shaming' Myanmar, its government was openly critical of Western threats to use force to intervene in the reclusive country based on the international community's 'responsibility to protect' (see Rüland 2022: 79).

By contrast, in the final case of the Rakhine riots in 2012, Indonesia firmly adhered to the norm of non-interference. Despite the intensifying crisis, it delayed any public comment on the violence and denied that religious conflict or ethnic cleansing was taking place. It was only when Myanmar officially invited Indonesia's assistance that the latter offered to provide advice in addressing issues related to citizenship for the Rohingya (Hari 2013), but in so doing continued to stress that the conflict between the Rakhine and Rohingya was an internal problem of Myanmar.

Indonesia's prioritisation of the non-interference norm may on first sight seem surprising, given the strong domestic outcry from civil society, the media, academia, and parliamentarians, who highlighted not only human rights concerns, but also the need to express solidarity with fellow Muslims (Rüland 2022). However, Indonesian decisionmakers were motivated by a countervailing concern that, given perceived human rights violations in relation to Indonesian minorities, any action in support of the Rohingya could create a precedent for interference in Indonesia's internal conflicts with religious and ethnic minorities. Furthermore, the government's position did not incur reputational costs with regional or global audiences, given ASEAN's collective stance in favour of non-interference and the relative lack of Western pressure for human rights protection during the crisis. The government therefore tried to appease strong domestic expectations regarding human rights protection by working with partners to address the crisis through the Organization of Islamic Conference, and supporting the Indonesian Red Cross mission in Rakhine state.

In sum, although Indonesia did not consistently prioritise one norm over the other, or pursue a strategy aiming at norm replacement, its response pattern nevertheless followed a clear logic: the government mainly complied with the 'general' norm of human rights protection, unless the case in question involved a secessionist dimension or risk of territorial disintegration (as seen in the later stages of the Saffron Revolution and the Rakhine riots), in which case the more 'specific' norm of non-interference would apply. This behaviour can best be described as an attempt to reconcile the two norms by shaping expectations of state behaviour within Indonesia's immediate region to be more in line with its normative preferences.

From a consequentialist perspective, the general emphasis on human rights protection avoided domestic legitimacy and international reputation costs: top officials wanted Indonesia to be seen at home and abroad as a 'good democracy' and a promoter of human rights within the region. Yet, the derogation of non-interference and its prioritisation in particular circumstances responded to strong domestic expectations for the maintenance of the territorial integrity of the Indonesian state, given the country's long experience of disintegrative forces and recent 'loss' of East Timor. Hence, while expectations about extraterritorial human rights protection flowed directly from Indonesian self-identification as a democracy, the latter expectation, which made compliance with non-interference necessary in some cases, was a more existential concern linked to domestic legitimacy. Moreover, since it was presiding over a relatively weak coalition, the government lacked the means to remove the underlying causes of the domestic concern for state survival, which would have been necessary for any strategy of general norm replacement to succeed.

Thailand

Thailand's response to the three episodes of human rights violation in Myanmar saw the consistent prioritisation of non-interference over human rights protection. In light of strong but conflicting expectations on the part of domestic and international audiences, the Thai government justified its response by framing non-interference as the only appropriate norm to regulate inter-state relations between Thailand and Malaysia, given the special geopolitical context created by the long and porous border between the two states.

Thailand's muted response to the Saffron Revolution clearly prioritised non-interference over human rights protection. The interim government of General Surayud Chulanont, which had come to power after a military coup in 2006, only condemned the violence following a collective ASEAN statement and then swiftly returned to a strict policy of non-interference. Only as international pressure mounted did the prime minister agree to communicate concerns to the junta in Yangon, but his subsequent letter was largely aimed at expressing solidarity and stressed that he was "speaking as one soldier to another" (Chongkittavorn 2007).

In the aftermath of Cyclone Nargis, the Thai government again prioritised non-interference, even though it was in a strong position to exercise influence over Myanmar's generals. Although Thailand did assume the role of a logistic hub for the international relief effort, its government ensured that it did not directly pressure or criticise Myanmar for its handling of the humanitarian fallout from the disaster. This stance was emblemised by the fact that several Thai medical teams were left on standby in Bangkok waiting for an invitation to be dispatched, as the junta insisted on distributing the aid on its own. Even after the Thai prime minister visited the devastated areas of Mynamar in May 2008, he forcefully defended the country's generals and reiterated that they did not want or need interference from the international community (Cartan 2008).

Compliance with the norm of non-intervention continued through the riots in Rakhine state and subsequent violence against the Muslim Rohingya. Indeed, during the entire period of the crisis not a single official government statement was issued by Thailand, which instead invested efforts in strengthening bilateral relations through an official state visit to Myanmar. Furthermore, while human rights groups and liberal forces within Thai civil society expressed concern, and critical voices in the press called for stronger action, the broader Thai population appeared less sympathetic. The government had used the fear of the arrival of thousands of stateless Muslims, with the potential to further destabilise the situation in Thailand's southern region, to diffuse any domestic expectations for action on behalf of the Rohingya (Parnini 2013).

Thailand's prioritisation of non-interference over human rights protection across these three episodes was therefore relatively uniform, despite various changes in the country's government. Nevertheless, the country's strategy is best characterised as a case of *strategic* rather than general norm replacement, since the Thai government did not intend to undermine the general validity of human rights protection in its region. In pursuing strategic norm replacement, Thailand aimed to minimise its own social costs within a specific context without impacting the behaviour of other actors.

Thailand's reluctance to comply with the norm of human rights protection was internally driven. In particular, it spoke to the strong domestic expectation – particularly within the rural population[4] and country's powerful business class – that the Thai government would maintain friendly relations with the neighbouring regime in order to preserve Thailand's border trade with Myanmar and access to the country's natural resources. Violation of the non-interference norm not only would have risked reputation costs in relation to ASEAN member states within the region that embraced non-interference, but more importantly, would also have risked legitimacy costs at home if economic activity was affected by a deterioration in relations with Myanmar. In the case of Cyclone Nargis, the government's compliance with the norm of non-interference

[4] Thailand's rural population, which had been hard hit by the Asian financial crisis, perceived the Democrat Party's liberal foreign policy as a threat to flourishing border trade with Myanmar, upon which many of them depended to earn a living. Given that this population outnumbered the urban middle class at the polls, its electoral support had become critical for the government (Rüland 2002: 100–2).

was facilitated by the fact that the urban middle class viewed the situation as a humanitarian disaster, and therefore articulated few expectations for an alternative approach. Against that backdrop, Thailand was believed to have 'done its bit' in delivering humanitarian aid to Myanmar.

Internationally, however, Thailand's non-interference policy following the Saffron Revolution and Cyclone Nargis proved more problematic. Not only did it threaten to incur reputation costs given the international community's emphasis on human rights, but it also seemed to contradict Western expectations of a country that, unlike most other ASEAN members, had long-standing ties with the West. In addressing the strong international expectations for action, the Thai government rhetorically acknowledged the need for it to perform as a 'good democracy' and ally but proved reluctant to substantively change its position. Instead, to minimise the reputational fall-out from its prioritisation of non-interference, Thai officials asked their Western counterparts to consider the country's 2,000-plus kilometers of shared border with Myanmar. For the Thai government, these "unique circumstances" (a phrase used by British foreign minister David Miliband in 2007) justified a measured rather than confrontational approach with the junta, aimed at working through ASEAN and the UN special envoy to Myanmar (Khundee 2007).

In the end, it was dominant domestic expectations, and related concerns over legitimacy costs, that were decisive in shaping Thailand's response strategy to these cases of norm conflict. But it is crucial to add that these pressures encouraged Thai policymakers to choose non-interference over human rights protection *in relation to Myanmar*. The government argued that because of its geostrategic position as a direct neighbour of Myanmar with an extremely long and porous shared border, Thailand could not engage in a policy of confrontation. The prioritisation of the norm of non-interference was therefore context-specific, rather than general. The government did not desire a general weakening of the human rights protection and promotion norm within the region, or to actively seek to alter the behaviour of other actors.

Malaysia

When the Malaysian government was faced with the set of protection crises in Myanmar, its compliance with the two conflicting norms alternated. In the case of the Saffron Revolution, it prioritised human rights protection through forceful condemnation of Myanmar's military regime, called for the junta to both engage in dialogue and release Aung San Suu Kyi, pushed for a more interventionist stance by ASEAN, and managed potential legitimacy and reputational costs through a strategy of norm reconciliation. On the other hand, when faced with the aftermath of Cyclone Nargis and escalating violence in Rakhine state, the Malaysian government adhered firmly to the norm of non-interference, primarily through a strategy of norm conflict denial. In part, this uneven pattern can be explained by the fact that Malaysia's democratisation process set in later (beginning with Abdullah Badawi's premiership in 2003), and thus internalisation of the human rights protection norm was more nascent than in the cases of Indonesia and Thailand. In addition, the government in Malaysia changed in 2008, prior to the onset of the riots in Rakhine state, bringing to power a leader who was particularly sensitive to the regional expectations for behaviour set by ASEAN.

In the case of the Saffron Revolution, addressing compliance expectations at the domestic level was particularly important for Prime Minister Badawi, for two main reasons. First, his administration had declared its commitment to greater political participation through consultation and accommodation and had sought to empower minority groups beyond the numerically dominant ethnic Malays (Musa 2012). Given expectations to act in accordance with the government's commitment to human rights protection, Badawi moved quickly to condemn the violence against the protestors and distanced himself from former prime minister Mahathir Mohamad, who been a staunch support of Myanmar's membership in ASEAN. Second, after decades of Mahathir's anti-Western stance internationally (Dosch 2014), Badawi sought to project Malaysia as a cooperative and moderate Islamic state that respected democracy, good governance, and human rights, both at home and abroad (Noor and Qistina 2017).

Nevertheless, the Malaysian government also recognised that the majority of ASEAN member states did not share its forwarding-leaning stance. This prompted the Badawi administration to consciously pursue a strategy of norm reconciliation, with the hope of changing the long-term trajectory of the non-interference norm in ASEAN. Instead of framing Malaysian interference in the case of Myanmar's Saffron Revolution as a singular exception, Badawi's government attempted to establish certain forms of interference as justifiable exceptions to the norm. More specifically, it argued that interference should be considered legitimate when a situation inside a country has a tangible impact, through spillover effects, on other neighbouring member states or the ASEAN region as a whole. By attempting to solve the norm conflict at the regional level through modification of the two norms, ASEAN's normative framework could once again serve as an action-guiding device for the organisation's member states (Rüland 2022: 140).

By the time of the ASEAN summit in November 2007, however, Malaysia had backed away from its pressure on the junta in Myanmar and was prioritising non-interference. This change followed a weakening of domestic expectations in favour human rights protection, especially among the government's dominant constituency, the Malays. Following the prime minister's significant losses in the 2008 general elections, expectations for strong action by Malaysia in the aftermath of Cyclone Nargis were almost exclusively articulated by the parliamentary opposition and human rights activists; for its part, the government chose to tack closely to the norm of non-intererence. While this approach failed to address international expectations that ASEAN would take the lead in protecting the population in Myanmar following the cyclone, Malaysia's policy – which focused exclusively on providing humanitarian relief and only with the explicit consent of the junta – was compatible with the majority of ASEAN members.

Finally, although Malaysia was the first ASEAN country to comment on the 2012 riots between the Muslim and Buddhist communities in Rakhine state, the government at no point criticised the junta for standing by or for the involvement of its security forces in the ensuing violence. Under its new leader, Najib Razak, Malaysia continued to comply with the non-interference norm, despite influential Muslim voices calling on the government to take a more prominent role in defending the Rohingya and similar requests by other Islamic states (such as Iran, Turkey, and Saudi Arabia) who lobbied for an intervention by the Organisation of Islamic Cooperation (OIC).

Two main factors explain why there were fewer voices calling for Malaysian interference based on human rights concerns (as opposed to religious affiliation). The first was the noticeable decline in the protection and enforcement of rights within Malaysia itself, which in turn affected domestic belief in the appropriateness of human rights protection as part of Malaysia's foreign policy. The second was a growing fear of a Muslim Rohingya refugee 'wave' hitting Malaysia, which led members of the Indian and Chinese minorities to openly oppose Malaysian involvement in the Rakhine riots. Added to these factors was the absence of any reputation costs at a regional level, since the majority of ASEAN member states had maintained compliance with the non-interference norm.

In order to minimise legitimacy and reputation costs with the Muslim-Malays at home and Islamic nations abroad, the Malaysian government pursued a strategy of norm conflict denial. More specifically, it sought to undermine domestic pressure for action by framing the Rakhine riots as a humanitarian disaster – which required Myanmar's consent for any international assistance – as opposed to a case of human rights violations. As the crisis in Myanmar progressed and calls for interference intensified, the government eventually made concessions to its domestic and international audiences by supporting the work of the OIC in Rakhine state.

In sum, the mixed response pattern evident in Malaysia's management of norm conflict can be explained as the result of a shift in the government's estimation of the strength of domestic expectations and its perception of the legitimacy costs of complying with human rights protection as opposed to non-interference. In order to address changing domestic as well as conflicting international expectations for norm compliance, the government over time adapted its response strategy from attempted norm reconciliation to conflict denial.

Institutional Responses to Norm Conflict

While individual nation-states frequently face norm conflicts, international organisations (IOs), as key actors in world politics, can also encounter situations where the imperative to give effect to one institutional norm can appear to challenge compliance with another. These contexts pose a particular challenge to IOs, which usually lack coercive power and thus rely on legitimacy in order to function and secure compliance with their decisions (Lenz and Viola 2017; Tallberg and Zürn 2019; Dellmuth and Schlipphak 2020). For example, analysts have shown that legitimacy is the core ingredient that enables the UN to achieve everything from its narrowest operational goals to its broadest international purposes (Zaum 2013; von Billerbeck 2017). While the UN's legitimacy has a range of sources, one central element is a strong conformity between a legitimating audience's socially embedded expectations of what is desirable or appropriate – which is informed by norms and values – and the UN's actual procedures, conduct, and performance (Suchman 1995; Lenz and Viola 2017). Researchers have also found that when a UN peace operation is considered to be legitimate – that is, if its objectives and actions are considered appropriate and effective when measured against a shared set of expectations – societies in host states are more likely to comply with the directives of a UN mission, donors that fund the operation are more likely to continue providing resources, and UN member states responsible for the authorisation of a mission will prove more willing to renew its mandate (Whalan 2017; Von Billerbeck 2017).

Two foundational norms that have long guided UN policy and practice, particularly in the domain of peacekeeping, are impartiality and host-state consent. The former implies that the UN sets aside particular interests and preferences with respect to any given conflict and seeks the equal application of unbiased rules and policies. The latter stipulates that UN peacekeeping operations receive the consent of host governments and seek to partner with them in rebuilding peace (Paddon Rhoads 2016).

From the late 1990s onward, partly as a response to perceived failures to address systematic killing of civilians in Rwanda and Srebrenica, UN peace operations moved beyond their traditional roles to adopt the additional task of protecting civilians. This expansion of peacekeeping mandates coincided with a broader normative imperative for the organisation to strengthen its promotion of human rights and seek to prevent and respond to atrocity crimes (Paddon Rhoads and Welsh 2019). But this new imperative soon bumped up against UN missions' long-standing practice of providing material and technical support to the armed forces of host states, some of whom were implicated in serious violations of human rights and/or violence against civilian populations. As a result, the UN now faced a conflict between two institutional norms: the imperative to work 'hand in hand' with the forces of the host-state and the imperative to protect local populations. Withholding support from host-state security forces risked diminishing a mission's ability to fulfil its broader mandate and objectives, as established by the Security Council, while continuing to cooperate with and assist those forces exposed the UN to charges of complicity in violations of international humanitarian and human rights law (Aust 2015).

The organisation responded to this norm conflict with a strategy of reconciliation: both norms continued their applicability to peacekeeping settings, but the UN's conduct would be regulated by new context-specific institutional procedures, embodied in the Human Rights Due Diligence Policy (HRDDP). The policy stipulates that in the context of its missions, the UN must refrain from providing support to non-UN armed actors "where there are substantial grounds for believing there is a real risk of the receiving entities committing grave violations of humanitarian, human rights or refugee law" (United Nations 2013). It then goes on to define what constitutes support and to identify procedures for ongoing risk assessment and compliance measurement. The HRDDP was thus a form of institutional adaptation designed to safeguard the reputation of the UN with key audiences and its institutional legitimacy, by ensuring the organisation would continue to meet its responsibility to promote and respect key bodies of international law and ensure the protection of civilians.

The UN's Human Rights Up Front initiative, also launched in 2013, was a more comprehensive and ambitious form of institutional adaptation, which can be characterised as a strategy of conflict denial. In this case, the catalyst for change was a damning report by an Internal Review Panel of the UN development and humanitarian officials' failure to protect civilian populations in the final phase of the civil conflict in Sri Lanka in 2008–9 (United Nations 2012). The report claimed that UN agencies had not only under-reported violations of human rights and humanitarian law by state-sponsored actors, but also deferred to government restrictions on their presence and operations in order to avoid confrontation with the authorities in Colombo and maintain access for humanitarian relief operations.

The Review Panel acknowledged that the UN appeared to face a conflict between two norms: the imperative to seek a government's consent and support to deliver humanitarian assistance, and the imperative to respond to serious violations of international humanitarian law in ways that might require criticism of that government. Yet it advocated a response strategy that would alter the organisations's identity and thus render the dilemma a false choice. The subsequent Human Rights Up Front initiative, launched by Ban Ki-Moon, sought to elevate the promotion of human rights into *all* UN departments and agencies, with the aim of resolving the apparent tension between protecting humanitarian access and robustly condemning and responding to systematic violations of human rights (United Nations 2015). Through a system-wide reform programme to make human rights *the* basis for UN action – via changes in information gathering and assessment, staff training, and new decisionmaking frameworks – the UN's leadership sought to prioritise the protection of populations and alter perceptions of appropriate behaviour for all UN staff. By framing situations such as the one in Sri Lanka as cases of human rights violations, as opposed to humanitarian crises, it was legitimising more robust behaviour vis-à-vis UN member states and signalling that protection was now part of the 'core business' of the organisation (Welsh 2018).

Conclusion

This chapter has sought to address a gap in IR's treatment of norms, by conceptualizing norm conflict, developing an account of how actors seek to resolve it, and creating a typology of potential response strategies. Our theorisation of norm conflict also has at least two implications for the interpretation–contestation framework set out in the Introduction. First, as we have illustrated, the way in which actors respond to a conflict between two norms can reveal something about the nature of contestation. While some actors' responses can be seen as straightforward cases of interpretive contestation, an actor's strategy for managing norm conflict could involve into more deliberate contestation, designed to either strengthen one norm (proactive contestation) or undermine another (reactive contestation). Second, as "practices of interpretation" (Orchard and Wiener, Chapter 1), responses to norm conflict may entail a "hierarchical ordering" of norms that reflects applicatory contestation. But such practices could go even further. If one actor's response initiates a broader agreement on which norm to follow, this could galvanize collective engagement – and potentially struggle – over the recognition of a new shared ground rule to guide further common action, thereby also raising questions about norm validity.

4 Norm Research on Conflictive Norm Relations

How Norms Collide in Times of Complexity, Contestation, and Crisis

Andrea Liese

Introduction

Over the past three decades, a substantial body of scholarship has shown how norms evolve and matter in global politics. Questions on norm emergence, diffusion, and impact formed the centre of what this volume specifies as first and second 'move' of constructivist norms research (Orchard and Wiener, Chapter 1: 4–8). This literature has significantly advanced our knowledge of the social structures of international relations. However, each approach or move has both expanded and limited our understanding of norms.

The first two moves have foremost analysed relatively stable individual norms and hardly researched how norms relate to one another (for a similar assessment, see Fehl and Rosert 2020: 1–2; Lantis and Wunderlich 2022: 3, 5). In particular, this research took little notice of ambivalent or conflictive norm relations. Instead, scholars focused on adjacency, consistency, or congruence in norm emergence and diffusion processes or, more recently, on a norm's (congruent) embeddedness in larger norm clusters or norm complexes. In the rare instances where the International Relations (IR) literature on norms identified norm conflicts or collisions, research focused on how such tensions could be overcome by prioritising or reconciling norms (see, for instance, Buitelaar and Hirschmann 2021; Rüland and Welsh, Chapter 3).

The third move of norms research has introduced an alternative view of "norms as 'processes'" (Krook and True 2012: 106) and "flexible by definition" (Wiener 2007: 49). Moreover, the core concept of contestation emphasised the role of agency in (re)shaping and (re)validating norms (Orchard and Wiener, Chapter 1: 8). In this view, norms possess a dual quality as "both structuring and socially constructed through interaction in a context" (Wiener 2007: 49). The third move is thus much more attentive to norm dynamics and actors' engagement with norms and diverging expectations. Nevertheless, the third move still has to tap its full potential to understand potentially conflictive norm relationships, given that much of the respective research has focused on the effects of contestation of *individual* norms – that is, whether and when norm contestation leads to a norm's validation, robustness, change, or even death (Wiener 2014; Lantis and Wunderlich 2018; Deitelhoff and Zimmermann 2019, 2020; Schneiker 2020; Panke and Petersohn 2012).

This chapter reassesses how norm studies around the three moves have both advanced and limited our understanding of ambiguous and conflictive relations between norms and how the second and, notably, the third move could contribute to a better and more nuanced understanding of a specific type of norm relation: a norm collision. A norm collision is characterised by conflicting or incompatible behavioural prescriptions of two or more norms (Gholiagha et al. 2020: 291, 295; Buitelaar and Hirschmann 2021: 551; Holzscheiter et al. 2022: 29; Mende 2022).[1] In other words, actors find more than one social expectation regarding their appropriate behaviour in a given situation, and adherence to one norm may result in the breach of another (Milanović 2009: 465). Norm collisions provide an excellent example of how the view of norms as processes – essential for the third move and the editors' first argument – aids and enriches our theoretical and empirical understanding of norms. In line with the second argument of the book's Introduction (Orchard and Wiener, Chapter 1: 4), norm collisions may not only appear as a threatening and problematic fate of norm proliferation and regime overlap but can – alternatively – be conceptualised as a pluralistic outcome of productive actor-driven norm engagement (Gholiagha et al. 2020: 291).

The chapter sheds light on a phenomenon still underexplored in the norms literature: colliding or conflicting norms (see also Rüland and Welsh, Chapter 3). In research on international institutions and regimes, a burgeoning literature on regime complexity or institutional fragmentation has stressed that competing rules overlap and render international institutions ineffective. Research on international legal rules and fragmentation has also stressed that public international law is not as coherent as national law and discussed techniques to resolve conflicts between legal norms (Michaels and Pauwelyn 2012). Norm research in international relations has hardly reflected on this debate, although the

[1] This chapters builds on discussions and joint research with Anna Holzscheiter and Sassan Gholiagha. Where appropriate, I reference our common publications. The application of this edited volume's analytical framework to the concept of norm collisions as well as the review of the three moves' conception of ambiguous or incongruent norm relations remain my own responsibility.

regime complexity debate's underlying concepts of norms, rules, and institutions resemble the norm concept of the first move scholarship. Until recently, only the 'second move' of norms research acknowledged competing norms when examining the (non-)diffusion of or (non-) compliance with global or transnational norms in domestic settings. These vertical norm collisions, that is, collisions at the intersection of global, regional, national, and local norms (or practices) in multi-level governance were typically seen as a negative phenomenon, hindering compliance, norm diffusion, and norm internalisation (Cloward 2016; Cortell and Davis 2005). A few contributions also examined horizontal norm collisions, with the chief interest in understanding strategies for "reducing the tensions generated by these norm conflicts" (Buitelaar and Hirschmann 2021: 548). However, this literature's focus on norms as "things" (Krook and True 2012: 106) or "stable social facts" (Wiener 2007: 54) has likely hindered the identification of collisions that occur once a norm's meaning-in-use changes or norms are applied to new situations. As a consequence, scholars may underestimate the prevalence of norm collisions. Furthermore, mirroring the dominant assessment of contestation as an inherently harmful process, norm collisions have primarily been understood as a soon-to-end plague.

This chapter proceeds in three steps. First, it engages with the neglect or limited perspective of norm collisions in the three moves of norm research. Second, it shows how choosing a specific norm concept – as connected to one of the three 'moves' in norm research – matters for theorising and identifying a norm collision and how core insights of the third move can shed additional light on the phenomenon. It refers to the Mediterranean refugee crisis as an illustrative example. Third, it discusses how crises, such as the recent COVID-19 pandemic, nurture norm collisions by providing actors with the opportunity to destabilise agreed-upon norm balances, on the one hand, and forcing them to engage with the meaning-in-use of norms, on the other.

From Adjacency and Congruence to Contestation

Norm relationships have only recently caught the interest of norm research. The traditional constructivist approaches in IR viewed norms as relatively stable and focused on adjacency, consistency, or congruence in norm emergence. Concerning the *first move*, Lantis and Wunderlich state that:

> Critically, works that focus on norm development sometimes fail to incorporate a broader context to understand the structure of the normative architecture. Constructivist interpretations of discrete norms often miss larger structural

components of normative meaning and, therefore, impede theoretical advancement. They may also not fully capture the dynamic relationships between norms and how normative meaning evolves through contestation. (Lantis and Wunderlich 2022: 5)

There are several explanations why norm relations, in general, and norm collisions, in particular, have been widely neglected in the *first wave of norm research*. First, the highly influential contribution by Finnemore and Sikkink (1998: 891) defined norms as "single standards of behaviour" and reserved the term 'institution' for the "way in which behavioural rules are structured together and interrelate" (Finnemore and Sikkink 1998: 891). The model launched a new research agenda, which analysed the emergence, diffusion, and impact of various individual norms, such as personal integrity norms (see, for instance, Risse et al. 1999; Price 1998), but hardly considered normative ambivalence and norm plurality within or among institutions (see also the critique by Ben-Josef Hirsch and Dixon, Chapter 2).

Second, scholars representing the first move in norm research typically assumed coherent rule systems and normative environments. Ideas of congruence in international law encouraged this explanation, which inspired much of the early IR constructivist research agenda.

The resonance or "fit" (Finnemore and Sikkink 1998: 908; Keck and Sikkink 1998: 201) with previously established norms or connected normative systems (see also Price and Tannenwald 1996: 376; Price 1998; Grillot 2011) is commonly regarded as crucial for a new norm to emerge. New norms must prove to be "acceptable extensions of the existing normative framework embodied in international law" (Florini 1996: 377). In the relatively rare instances where scholars acknowledged contradictory expectations and prescriptions, they turned to an international legal scholarship to assess how competing normative claims are adjudicated and to explain why some norms are more persuasive than others: "Since normative contestation in law is so explicit and well documented, and since much of contemporary norm politics in the world has a strong legal component, we believe an examination of legal mechanisms for norm selection and dissemination will be instructive for IR scholars" (Finnemore and Sikkink 1998: 915). Indeed, several international law and IR scholars point to conventions of legal argumentation, such as analogical reasoning, that keep (legal) norms robust (Sandholtz 2008: 106; Kleinlein 2023). While some of the early work on the evolution of norms pointed out that norms "are in competition with other norms … that carry incompatible instructions" (Florini 1996: 364), norm collisions have not made it to the fore of the first and second move of norms research. For example, although Florini raises the point of norm competition, she mainly seeks to understand why one norm, and not another, prevails or survives or why different norms may co-exist. This may be the case when competing norms address actors with different identities or each norm is applied in a different situation:

> With regard to norms, which call for specific behaviours, the competition is relatively direct. An actor cannot follow two opposed norms at once. However, when norm variation is present, that is, when neither of the two competing norms has driven the other to extinction, it is quite possible either for the population to be polymorphic (with some actors following one norm and some the other), or for an individual actor to pursue a mixed strategy, following one norm on some occasions and its competitor on others. (Florini 1996: 373)

Third, early norm research treated norms as "relatively stable" structures (Finnemore and Sikkink 1998: 891) and "shared assessments" (Finnemore and Sikkink 1998: 892). A norm's effect as structuring relied on a shared, if not taken for granted and, thus, uncontested, understanding of what a norm means: "We recognize norm-breaking behavior because it generates disapproval or stigma and norm conforming behavior either because it produces praise, or, in the case of a highly internalized norm, because it is so taken for granted that it provokes no reaction whatsoever" (Finnemore and Sikkink 1998: 891–2). Thus, the leading model of a progressive life cycle – emergence, diffusion, and internalisation of a norm (Finnemore and Sikkink 1998) – and the subsequent research agenda hardly considered norm ambivalence and conflictive relations between norms.

Expectations of adjacency and congruence also feature prominently in the *second move of norms research* that turned to implementation. The literature on norm diffusion and adherence stresses the importance of a "cultural match" between global norms and domestic practices or norms (Cortell and Davis 2000: 74; Checkel 1999: 86). While this literature acknowledged "competing norms" (Krampf 2013) or norm collisions, it initially located them only in the vertical sphere of international politics. In instances where norms collide vertically, that is, between the transnational and local context, scholars anticipate and observe resistance to norm acceptance and implementation by local veto players (Checkel 1999; Cortell and Davis 2000), decoupling of norm acceptance and norm adherence (Berkovitch and Gordon 2016; Hafner-Burton and Tsutsui 2005), or adopting transnational norms in processes of localisation (Acharya 2004). Again, research deems it unlikely that actors endure conflicting or incompatible behavioural prescriptions of two or more norms. Instead, they are expected to respond by avoiding one of the colliding norms through outright rejection, decoupling, or reshaping the colliding (transnational) norm to eventually fit the dominant normative (local) context.

For quite a while, horizontal norm collisions, that is, conflicts between sectoral spheres and regime complexes, did not feature prominently in the second move of norms research. Indeed, horizontal collisions first caught the attention of regime theorists who studied the fragmentation of regimes and the proliferation of norms and rules (Alter and Meunier 2009; Gehring and Faude 2013). These challenged the idea of normative coherence and congruence and argued that the web of transnational norms has become denser and more diverse over time. Regime complexes capture functional overlaps between different regimes and non-hierarchical institutions. One result of the rising density is that 'conflicting rules' are institutionalised in overlapping but discrete regimes, at least "during periods of transition to new interests and rules" (Raustiala and Victor 2004: 295). In line with the assumption of adjacency and congruence, the regime complex literature expects that "the architects of new rules will attempt to avoid conflicts by demarcating clear boundaries. They will negotiate devices such as 'savings clauses' and other mechanisms for disentangling one regime from another" (Raustiala and Victor 2004: 297). However, conflicts may be unavoidable, for instance, when the issue at stake is somewhat complex and interactions are manifold. Even when states succeed in avoiding collisions within the elemental regime, they may still fail to prevent inconsistencies "at the 'joints' between the elemental regimes" (Raustiala and Victor 2004: 300). In addition, research has also found "explicit efforts to create conflicts to force change in another regime" in a few instances (Raustiala and Victor 2004: 298).

In line with the view of norms as relatively stable, most norm collisions or norm conflicts were analysed between legally codified rules. The most prominent collisions at the horizontal level are norm conflicts at the intersection of international humanitarian law and international human rights law (Milanović 2009), trade law with environmental law (Pauwelyn 2003), or trade law with human rights law (Helfer 2003).

Recent research on norm implementation has investigated horizontal norm collisions more thoroughly and, in particular, studied responses by norm addresses to such collisions. In their analysis of norm conflicts between the international criminal accountability norm and three traditional peacekeeping norms, Tom Buitelaar and Gisela Hirschmann (2021) show how the United Nations (UN) either prioritised one norm over the other or adopted one or both of the colliding norms to resolve the collision. Janne Mende (2022: 728) argues that norm collisions are inferred in practices of delegitimation in regime complexes, where adversaries are excluded.

Still, little emphasis was put on the intersubjective and, therefore, the malleable character of norms (Stimmer 2019a: 271). Not surprisingly, collisions between norms that do not qualify as legal norms or between norms that are interpreted differently and have changed their intersubjective meaning over time have remained under the radar in second move norm research. Furthermore, research hardly reflected on how a norm balance or norm hierarchy, including one that arose from the prior application of traditional conflict rules (such as *lex posterior*), is contested and changing. As I will argue further in the following sections, even relatively stable norm relationships are changed in times of crisis – a moment that legitimises the destabilisation of an extant balance or a hierarchy between potentially colliding norms.

The more recent *third move in norm research* seems particularly well suited to address changing norm relations. As Orchard and Wiener (Chapter 1: 8–9) delineate, this move is particularly interested in how norms are structured in interaction (see also Wiener 2007: 49).

Norm research now widely recognises that although norms are "stable over particular periods, they always remain flexible by definition" (Wiener 2007: 49). This flexibility concerns their meaning, applicable situation, and the actors whose behaviour they prescribe. The malleable and ambiguous character of norms also affects relations between norms and, thus, their potential to collide. In their debates and discourse, actors shape the meaning of a norm and its application to a given situation. Whereas norm defenders and supporters of the established order may regard a contestation and a norm collision as threatening, historically marginalised groups may regard them as beneficial, as True-Frost (2022) has argued for people with disabilities and Holzscheiter, Gholiagha, and Liese (2022) for indigenous peoples.

By now, the third move of norms research has convincingly shown that contestation does not have to result in norm decay (Percy and Sandholtz 2022). On the contrary, it may strengthen a norm's validity. Scholars studying norm contestation but also robustness or resilience (Deitelhoff and Zimmermann 2019; Sandholtz 2019; Percy and Sandholtz 2022) emphasise how norm clusters or institutions in which a norm is embedded stabilise norms and shield them from change. Still, contestation may change the intersubjectively held meaning of a norm and modify the norm's value, range of applicability, or prescription.[2] The modified norm

[2] Third wave research on the effects of norm contestation offers, by now, various contestation outcomes. Stimmer (2019a: 270) proposes to break norms down to two core elements, that is, "norm frames (justifications) and claims (to action)." Combined, they may lead to four outcomes: norm clarification, norm recognition, norm impasse, and norm neglect.

may now collide with another slightly changed or stable norm previously standing in congruence. Hence, contestation, norm interpretation, and other mechanisms of norm change may provoke norm collisions.

Theorising Norms Collisions: Complexity, Lack of Authority, Contestation and Interaction

The lack of attentiveness regarding norm collisions in the first move of norm research might have to do with the centrality of the assumptions that norms emerge coherently to each other (see previous section). Another caveat in analysing the potentially conflictive relation between norms stems from the challenge of recognising norms empirically. The preceding sketched ontological choices have implications for 'norm research in theory and practice', that is, for explaining when and why collisions emerge and for the methodological strategy of identifying collisions.

Traditionally, constructivist norm research – the *first move* – has defined norms as "collective expectations for the proper behaviour of actors with a given identity" (Katzenstein 1996: 5) or as "a standard of appropriate behaviour for actors with a given identity" (Finnemore and Sikkink 1998: 891). Typically, two types of norms have been distinguished depending on their function (Rüland and Welsh, Chapter 3). Constitutive norms prompt expectations regarding proper behaviour; they shape the interests and identities of actors in international relations and "specify an actor from whom an appropriate behaviour is expected" (Jurkovich 2020: 697). Regulative norms enable and constrain behaviour because they signal the appropriate behaviour in a particular situation and mobilise or legitimise (social) sanctions that impose costs on norm violators (Gelpi 1997). Norms are, thus, conceptualised as standards of behaviour and prescriptions on which actors have agreed at a given time. A formal act of agreeing to a norm or establishing a norm – for instance, following international negotiation – is to codify the norm in international law. Many norms studied in IR have been codified at one point in time. This outcome enables researchers to identify the norm by examining which behavioural prescriptions have been legally codified.

Critical constructivist norm research instead pays attention to cultural context (Gurowitz 1999) and agency in re-enacting "the normative 'structure of meaning in use'" (Wiener 2009: 176), notably in actors' discourse. Such a non-essentialist and non-formal understanding of norms compels the researcher to grasp prescriptions of appropriate behaviour from sources other than explicit agreement, law, or authoritative (legal) interpretation. Instead, it considers the intersubjective interpretation, re-negotiation and re-articulation, and norm-generating practice of actors (Gholiagha et al. 2020). I will return to these conceptual differences once the concept of a norm collision has been introduced.

Why do norms collide? Depending on each move's concept of norm and research interest, norm collisions have been mainly identified as a result of regime complexity, fragmentation, and "overlapping spheres of authority" (Kreuder-Sonnen and Zürn 2020), or as a result of various forms of norm contestation, norm (re)interpretation, and lack of robustness or validity of collision rules, including opposing views on the priority of norms that are relevant to the same situation (Holzscheiter et al. 2022: 31). In addition, this chapter highlights how norms are pitted against each other in times of crisis.

First, norm collisions may stem from rule systems that eventually intersect or overlap, either horizontally or vertically (Kreuder-Sonnen and Zürn 2020). This assumption speaks to the notion of regime complexes understood as "nested, partially overlapping and parallel international regimes that are not hierarchically ordered" (Alter and Meunier 2009: 14) and mirrors the *first move of norms research*'s concept of a norm as a rather stable prescription. Norm collisions may occur once new norms generate unintended expectations in neighbouring fields or for the behaviour of other actors. For example, when the United Nations Security Council mandated the UN to assist the International Criminal Court (ICC) in supporting criminal justice efforts in conflicts or post-conflict zones, the ICC's international criminal accountability norm prescribed a different behaviour from the equality norm that guides the UN's operations (Buitelaar and Hirschmann 2021: 558). These and related norm conflicts arose because norms had been developed in international institutions with only partly overlapping membership, with initially hardly overlapping mandates (inter-organisational overlap), under pressure, or where the same institution developed norms in different bodies and at different periods (intra-organisational overlap).

In contrast, the rationalist literature on regime complexes and institutional fragmentation has argued that states intentionally create separate rule systems with contradictory norms to allow forum shopping and, thus, minimise the constraining effect of one particular norm (Drezner 2009). For example, states disagree on the state-market relationship and its role in food security, that is, the relationship between the colliding norms of trade liberalisation and food security. States support either the World Trade Organization's view on free trade and trade liberalisation as beneficial or the alternative view of the United Nations Food and

Agriculture Organization (FAO) that the current asymmetries in market access hinder the needs of food insecure countries and that certain staples or crops should be exempt from liberalisation (Margulis 2013: 61, 62). In rare instances, strategic efforts to maximise conflicts between regimes are even intended to "force change in another regime" (Raustiala and Victor 2004: 298). In addition, an established norm may be challenged by actors advocating and refering to an emergent norm. Such a normative change may result in conflicting prescriptions, and thus a norm collision, when each norm is still intersubjectively accepted by a group of actors and both expect a third actor to orient its behaviour to the respective norm. An example are competing norms in global health governance, which the World Health Organization could not both live up to (Kreuder-Sonnen 2019).

Contradictory rule systems do not necessarily weaken expectations of appropriate behaviour, as those who hold such expectations may not be satisfied with an actor's choice to apply one norm but not another. Considering the possibility that the violation of a shared norm mobilises norm defenders, a concept of norm collisions reminds us that contradictory prescriptions do not only offer the promise of autonomous decisionmaking, forum-shopping, and forcing changes in another regime, which the rationalist literature on regime complexes and fragmentation has accentuated (see earlier), but also carry the risk of reputation cost and social sanctions for violating one of the colliding norms, at least from the group of those social actors that expect appropriate behaviour (see also Buitelaar and Hirschmann 2021: 551). Finally, divergent rules and norms may impede institutional reform and international cooperation to solve transnational problems, such as hunger (Margulis 2013).

The legal literature has been highly attentive to dissonance at the intersection of various (legal) regimes: in the absence of a central authority such as "a court of last resort" or an "appellate body" that exists in a domestic system, conflicting norms cannot be reconciled in a consistent and binding way (True-Frost 2022). Furthermore, the various decentralised actors tasked with norm intepretation, such as the UN treaty bodies, whose constituencies and mandates vary, have generated "conflicting and varying interpretations of human rights treaties" (True-Frost 2022: 365) on issues such as involuntary detention or the right to live in a family. Given that these bodies' interpretations affect norm development and norm implementation (Reiners 2022), further norm collisions could rise. In the absence of a central cross-sectional authority and a common standard, common tools to resolve norm collisions, such as *lex superior*, *lex specialis*, and *lex posterior* or the principle of the primacy of the most favourable norm, may not only be contested but also even ignored (Michaels and Pauwelyn 2012; Graf-Brugère 2013). Therefore, norm relations may remain uncoordinated and norm conflicts unresolved.

Second, the concept of norm collisions is compatible with the notion that norms are not stable in different political arenas, as actors can contest the quality and meaning of a norm, and various actors can interpret a norm in various ways (Wiener 2018; Deitelhoff and Zimmermann 2020). When one takes the idea of certain flexibility of norms seriously, as the *third move of norm research* does, then discourses and interaction can change the meaning of one norm, consequently affecting or changing the relation to other norms. For example, in the field of human rights, there is an ongoing debate between a generalised and dominant interpretation of human rights norms, on the one hand, and the interpretations, contestations, and demands of marginalised groups regarding the interpretation of these very norms and their relationship, on the other (True-Frost 2022: 368). In the case of colliding norms, the researcher should then enquire whether an actor finds more than one social expectation regarding its appropriate behaviour in a given situation. Consequently, research on colliding norms is less interested in studying the conditions and processes of contesting *one* particular norm than in how a changed meaning-in-use of one norm affects the relation to other norms.

How can norm collisions be identified? Several strategies to identify a norm collision become feasible when the different norm concepts of the three 'moves' are applied. The following section will illustrate how the three perspectives differ in identifying norm collisions.

Where Do We Find Norm Collisions? How Conceptual Choices Matter

Norm collisions have been identified by employing different perspectives. A first and second move perspective puts a norm's fixed meaning into focus. A norm collision could then be identified by studying norm collisions that arise at the intersection of different functional spheres of authority at the international level or between vertical levels (Kreuder-Sonnen and Zürn 2020), or when established and newly emerging norms compete (Kreuder-Sonnen 2019). An external observer may determine the incompatibility of two prescriptions in a particular situation by drawing on each norm's prescription; for instance, as stated in a treaty or declaration. In addition, one may examine the collisions that come to the fore when international courts or quasi-judicial institutions (Birkenkötter 2020; Krisch et al. 2020) or the dispute settlement bodies of international organisations address a norm collision (Flonk et al. 2020). This approach may be labelled an "externalist" perspective to norm collisions (Kreuder-Sonnen and Zürn 2020: 243).

The third move perspective may object that this approach could underestimate the prevalence of norm collisions (Gholiagha et al. 2020) and fail to grasp the social validity necessary to speak of a norm. As recently pointed out by Jurkovich, not all legal rules are standards of appropriate behaviour that members of a society share. Some legal rules are unknown, others are no longer or not yet shared, and others lack a sense of oughtness (Jurkovich 2020).

When one refrains from treating norms as given, then norms must be identified by studying how norms are interpreted, validated, and prioritised by various actors, including norm addressees, whose behaviour and justification change the meaning-in-use of norms. Viewing norms as subject to changing interpretations unsheathes changes that have not (yet) manifested in changed legal meaning. For instance, in examining how political actors have defined the rules of sovereignty, Barkin and Cronin (1994) find that these vary throughout modern history, although the legal content "changes little" (Barkin and Cronin 1994: 107). Yet, even when norms are captured by their meaning-in-use, how can we be sure that actors regard them as colliding? Sassan Gholiagha, Anna Holzscheiter, and Andrea Liese (2020) propose identifying norm collisions in discourse by looking for collisions that actors articulate or stress as problematic. Their research has shed light on the ubiquity of norm collisions in various policy domains. Examples include incompatible normative prescriptions between the prohibition of certain drug use practices and Indigenous People's rights (Gholiagha et al. 2020) or the prohibition of child labour and the children's rights of self-determination (Holzscheiter et al. 2022). This internalist perspective unsheathes collisions that emerge despite supposedly stable, that is, legally codified norms and even where a previously agreed upon norm hierarchy should have settled the collision. However, from a norms perspective, the shared expectations on the appropriate behaviour of a specific actor cannot be fulfilled at once. This more interpretivist identification strategy resonates with the norm concept of the 'third move' of norms research. Such a perspective focuses on norms as processes subject to interpretation and contestation. Hence, it can accommodate the malleable character of norms.

This section illustrates how the different approaches to norms represented in each of the three moves affect the identification of norm collisions. The section complements Chapter 3 by Rüland and Welsh and pays particular attention to how the second and the third move perspectives can 'see' collisions as a much more likely phenomenon than perspectives that treat norms as fixed. I have chosen the European refugee crisis and the COVID-19 crisis as contexts in which collisions may play out.

Transnational crises, such as the European refugee or Mediterranean migration crisis (Panebianco 2016) or the COVID-19 crisis compel states to adopt and change policies in order to manage the crisis. While crisis management occurs ad hoc, it is still shaped by norms and must comply with legal standards. In the Mediterranean, European states not only engaged in border protection, but also launched common policies to protect migrants' lives at sea. Guided by the first move in norm research, one may examine whether behavioural prescriptions were colliding. The normative framework of international law offers legally codified norms to guide such policies, notably the norm to rescue people at sea. The behavioural prescription to assist persons in distress at sea holds regardless of their nationality or status and the circumstances. This norm can be considered one of the oldest humanitarian norms and is part of customary law (Papanicolopulu 2016: 494). Several maritime conventions adopted between the mid-1970s and the beginning of the 1980s and amendments after the turn of the century (United Nations High Commissioner for Refugees (UNHCR) 2002) specified the norm. First move norm research would argue that the norm was fixed over time and became "the prevailing standard of appropriateness against which new norms emerge and compete for support" (Finnemore and Sikkink 1998: 895). Yet, the turn of the century marks the emergence of another norm, expressing the shared expectation that states should prevent smuggling at sea. This norm has been codified in the 2000 Protocol against Smuggling of Migrants by Land, Sea and Air, supplementing the United Nations Convention against Transnational Organized Crime. In line with the expectation of the first move in norms research, the new norm was made to 'fit' or resonate with previously established norms, that is, the norm to rescue people at sea. Under the Protocol, 'the fact that migrants, including asylum-seekers and refugees, were smuggled does not deprive them of any rights as regards access to protection and assistance measures' (United Nations High Commissioner for Refugees (UNHCR) 2002). One of its core obligations that states shall cooperate to prevent and suppress migrant smuggling (Article 7 of the UN Smuggling Protocol) is explicitly bound to "accordance with the international law of the sea." Again in line with the expectations sketched earlier, a conflict between the different regime complexes was avoided by a savings clause

(Raustiala and Victor 2004). The respective savings clause in Article 19 states: "Nothing in this Protocol shall affect the other rights, obligations and responsibilities of States and individuals under international law, including international humanitarian law and international human rights law" (United Nations 2000). Consequently, it has been argued that the UN Smuggling Protocol "does not alter the underlying legal framework provided by the international law of the sea" (Gallagher and David 2014: 431). Hence, from an externalist perspective on norm collisions or a first move perspective of norms as 'things', one might argue that the respective behavioural prescriptions are not colliding. This is also the dominant position in legal interpretation and analysis. Similar assessements could be made for the various human rights obligations that states have to uphold during emergencies, such as during the COVID-19 pandemic. Here, a slightly different collision rule applies: restrictions of human rights, such as freedom of expression or freedom of movement, are permitted, when they are lawful, necessary, and proportionate (Human Rights Watch 2020).

The second move in norm research would shift the focus from congruence to implementation and (non-)compliance and contestation and thus focus on actors' behaviour and their shared assessments of a norm. When more and more people tried to reach Europe by sea, states withdrew from search and rescue in the Mediterranean and criminalised non-governmental organisations (NGOs) and individuals that filled the gap. In addition, representatives of several European states started to engage in reactive contestation, mainly contesting the duty to assist any person irrespective of status and circumstances. For example, in 2014, Joyce Anelay, the minister of State, Foreign and Commonwealth Office of the United Kingdom, announced that her country would not support planned search and rescue operations in the Mediterranean, as they "create an unintended 'pull factor.'" Instead, the government should and would take "steps to fight the people smugglers who wilfully put lives at risk by packing migrants into unseaworthy boats" (Anelay 2014). Frontex and other European governments also framed search and rescue as a pull factor (Cusumano and Villa 2021: 28, 29) and addressed the need to prevent that rescue at sea builds a "bridge to Europe" (de Maizière 2014, my translation). The widely reported position of the Italian government to stigmatise and criminalise sea and rescue humanitarianism marks the strongest reactive contestation of one norm in favour of another. In contrast, humanitarian NGOs and the UN agencies, such as the International Organization for Migration (IOM) and the UNHCR, emphasized the humanitarian imperative of the rescue at sea norm (UNHCR and IOM 2019; United Nations High Commissioner for Refugees (UNHCR) 2002; Ponthieu 2016). In other words, actors with different identities engaged in a vivid debate on the appropriateness of rescue operations and opted to privilege compliance with one norm over the other. Therefore, the second move in norm research can already see a lacking fit, incongruence, or conflict. However, it would likely frame it as a behavioural contestation of the rescue at sea norm by some actors or as a form of reactive contestation questioning the norm's applicability in the context of the Mediterranean migration crisis. A subsequent question could be whether these contestations eventually weaken or alter the rescue at sea norm or whether the manifold interpretations by various authorities affirming its legal validity and superiority secure the norm's robustness.

A more internalist perspective on norm collisions that resonates with the third move in norms research would shift the focus from incompatibilities between codified norms and their legal interpretation to social interactions in which actors reveal shared and intersubjectively held expectations. It studies how actors engage with the meaning of each norm and a potential collision between two or more norms. Do they find two norms to collide, that is, argue that their behavioural prescriptions are incompatible, even when the norms' codified prescriptions are structured as non-colliding? Do they even find the collision problematic, potentially inviting a reconfiguration of each norm's relation to the other such as an established norm hierarchy? Do they argue that adherence to one norm might lead to a breach of another? In other words, "do actors 'construct' norm collisions and frame them as problematic in their social and discursive interactions" (Gholiagha et al. 2020: 293)? This is a process that Gholiagha, Holzscheiter, and Liese (2020: 295) term as 'activation'. In the context of the Mediterranean migration crisis, one may find first indications of such activations, for instance, when, in 2017, the then director of Frontex, Fabrice Leggeri, argued that the norm to rescue at sea is not unaffected by the norm to prevent smuggling but instead colliding: "Everyone at sea has the duty to save people in need. This also is what Frontex stands for. But we must not support the business of criminal networks and traffickers in Libya by having European ships pick up migrants ever closer to the Libyan coast" (Bewarder and Walter 2017, my translation). Similar concerns were voiced by French president Macron and the Italian minister of the interior Matteo Salvini (Harlan 2018). By focusing on how actors shape the meaning of norms in interaction, collisions come to the fore that other perspectives overlook. These invite further enquiry. First, collisions of shared but not necessarily codified norms may generate responses by a variety of actors, including states and international organizations (for the effect of norm collision on conflict management, see Rüland and Welsh, Chapter 3). Second, by invoking an alternative norm, actors cannot only 'forum-shop' but also shift public opinion or (de)legitimise actors and their claims, that is, affect their power. Third, collisions resulting from interpretation and contestation could prompt actors to further engage with one of the norms and related practices and policies (effect of norm collision on further engagement with norms). The cases used for illustration here, COVID-19 and the Mediterranean refugee crisis, show that international organisations, notably those hosting a norm, and states and international organisations implementing one of the colliding norms engaged much more proactively with the respective norms by issuing guidelines for effective policy responses, fostering cooperation and improving norm compliance.

As the brief illustration indicates, regime complexity, the lack of a central authority and processes of contestation provide a fertile soil for actors activation of norm collision. In addition, I argue that that moments of crisis destabilise existing (or presumed) norm hierarchies. They provide actors with an opportunity to strategically contest the superiority of a given norm and strengthen an alternative norm (on norm strength, see also Ben-Josef Hirsch and Dixon, Chapter 2) but also force them to (re-)assess the validity and meaning of norms, which may bring a collision to the fore.

Norms and Crises: Destabilising Hierarchies, Rebalancing Relationships, and Unsettling Settled Norms

The final section of this chapter will introduce an additional setting in which norm collisions become likely. It argues that a crisis affects the relations between single norms and norm clusters and, thus, provokes norm collisions as it intensifies norm contestation, norm re-interpretation, or norm expansion. Following the literature on crisis management, a crisis is defined as "a serious threat to the basic structures or the fundamental values and *norms* of a system, which under time pressure and highly uncertain circumstances necessitates making vital decisions" (Rosenthal et al. 1989: 10, emphasis added).

Whereas in principle, norms can be contested at any time (Orchard and Wiener, Chapter 1: 9), a crisis can intensify processes of contestation. Indeed, crises such as war and depression are typically understood as drivers of norm change (Acharya 2004; Legro 2020; Barkin and Cronin 1994). While the effect of a crisis on policymaking and the fate of single norms is well explored, norm research has just started to pay attention to the effect of a crisis on the relationship between norms. Research has so far theorised and demonstrated how new norms arise and spread to respond to a crisis (Acharya 2004; Berger 1996; Florini 1996) and how established norms change or shift in meaning in response to a crisis (Sandholtz 2007; Wiener 2009). For example, Florini argues that the spread of the transparency norm and the evolution of the Chemical Weapons Convention was spurred by three external shocks, including Iraq's near success in developing weapons of mass destruction (Florini 1996: 387).

Crises affect the process of normative contestation in various ways. First, crises are a sign that previous institutional structures are inadequate and extant beliefs are "wrong-headed" (Legro 2020: 423), tempting actors to question the previous norm set and the hierarchical order of norms (Acharya 2004: 247). In security, economic, or health crises, a range of societal and private actors get access to reactive and proactive contestation, that is, to object to prevailing norms and engage with emergent norms (Orchard and Wiener, Chapter 1: 16). For example, in response to the severe acute respiratory syndrome (SARS) outbreak, the World Health Organization engaged with the not yet (legally) established but emerging norm of global health security and brought it in collision with the established norm of non-interference (Kreuder-Sonnen 2019). Second, a crisis often truncates the regular policymaking process and, thus, empowers executives to interpret a given norm or previous norm relationship, such as a norm hierarchy. For instance, a crisis can legitimise exceptional measures and swift responses, thus, enabling the contestation of in-principle validated norms. Third, and related, a crisis changes or challenges actors' identities. This has consequences for norms, as norms are regarded as prescriptions for actors with an identity. The norm literature has long acknowledged that "individuals have multiple roles and identities and the number and variety of alternative rules assures that only a fraction of the relevant rules are evoked in a particular place at a particular time" (March and Olsen 2004: 6). If the sense of the particular place and time changes, then actors may contest that a formerly prioritised norm is still applicable or should still be prioritised. In the latter case, a previously reconciled norm collision may be reactivated. A frequently discussed example of the second and third mechanisms is the response to the 9/11 terrorist attacks. Several transnational norms were subject to interpretative contestation, notably the prohibition of torture and the long-held interpretation that the right to self-defence does not include the use of force towards non-state actors (Liese 2009; Reinold 2023; Lesch and Zimmermann 2023).

Yet, while a crisis has been found to offer a window of opportunity to contest a norm reactively, proactively, and interpretatively, less attention has been paid to how crises affect relations between previously accepted, shared, or practised norms. Previous research has shown that a crisis empowers actors to activate a latent contradiction between two norms or question a long-practised norm hierarchy. In other words, a crisis might disrupt the fragile compromise of a former response to a norm collision. A severe crisis – such as a war – might also terminate the dominance of one coalition and give rise to a new one (Barkin and Cronin 1994: 108). The new coalition may interpret norms differently or promote different norms. For example, the SARS crisis in 2002 activated a conflict between prescriptions stemming from sovereignty and non-intervention norms, on the one hand, and a norm of global health, on the other (Kreuder-Sonnen 2019). Again, the COVID-19 pandemic, illustrates how various governments reprioritised human rights norms that have come to be seen as "indivisible, interrelated, interdependent and mutually reinforcing" (United Nations Secretary General 2013). In the wake of the COVID-19 pandemic, several human rights norms were restrictively applied, often because governments prioritised public health and shifted resources accordingly (Human Rights Watch 2020). The COVID-19 pandemic has also revealed a lacking consensus on the proportionality of restrictions of rights such as freedom of movement, freedom of expression, or the right to education, leading to renewed engagement with the Siracusa Principles, the General Comments of the United Nations Human Rights Committee, and the rights of vulnerable groups, such as children and refugees.

Conclusion

By reviewing and applying the three moves of norm research, this chapter has shown how norm collisions can be theorised and examined as one type of norm relation. It has argued that norm complexity and lacking authority, on the one hand, and contestation and interaction, on the other, make norm collisions a likely phenomenon with important consequences that warrant further examination. Furthermore, it has proposed that even relatively stable norm relationships are changed in times of crisis – a moment that legitimises the destabilisation of an extant balance or a hierarchy between potentially colliding norms. Norm collisions are therefore critical for understanding the forms individual norms take over time, how, why, and when their relations are (re)shaped, and how practices and policies are legimated or delegitimated.

Part II

Development of the Field

5 A Brief History of Norms about Race

Audie Klotz

Introduction: Contesting Origin Stories

Twitter briefly exploded in February 2020 after former South African president F. W. de Klerk pronounced that apartheid had not been a crime against humanity and that United Nations (UN) resolutions labelling it that way merely reflected Soviet propaganda.[1] Commentators, some more knowledgeable than others, vented outrage, while experts quickly dug up and circulated links to the most relevant primary documents. Nearly three decades after the formal demise of apartheid, why do international rights resolutions – going back to condemnation of apartheid in the International Convention on the Elimination of All Forms of Racial Discrimination (ICERD 1965: Article 3) – feature prominently in domestic South African debates over structural inequalities? And why is apartheid still an international concern, as evident in Article 7 of the Rome Statute, which lists it among the crimes against humanity that are grounds for potential prosecution by the International Criminal Court?

We can glean fundamental insights about international norms, in practice and in theory, from this incident. Even a cursory glance at the diplomatic record, for example, reveals that racial equality has morphed in the human rights agenda over the past century, partially in response to apartheid. Segregation in South Africa received considerable attention within British imperial conferences during the interwar period before appearing on the UN agenda in 1946. By the 1960s, some critics used 'anti-apartheid' to mean universal franchise, whereas others stressed that eliminating segregation required socio-economic restructuring as part of decolonisation. After decades of disagreement, many countries coalesced around sanctions policies in the late 1980s, with substantial effects on

[1] The comment and his subsequent backtracking received plenty of media coverage, domestically and internationally. *Quartz Africa* (26 February 2020) provided a summary, which also put the controversy into context, https://qz.com/africa/1808502/south-africa-fw-de-klerk-tried-to-reframe-apartheids-impact/.

South African reforms in the early 1990s, thus providing evidence of a 'strong' norm that spans discourse, institutionalisation, and policy outcomes (Klotz 1995; Ben-Josef Hirsch and Dixon 2021; Chapter 2).

Consistent with a linear cascade model of norm diffusion and internalisation, this conventional narrative ends in 1994, with universal suffrage elections (Black 1999). Yet persistently fierce contestation over the meaning of 'apartheid' fits better within the alternative cycle-grid model, which resists neat chronologies and acknowledges recursive processes (Wiener 2018; Orchard and Wiener, Chapter 1: Figure 1.1; see also Moses et al. 2020). A malleable concept, 'anti-apartheid' has transformed over decades from an emergent norm into a pervasive rhetorical reference point upon which activists have projected comparisons as a legitimation tactic, from critiques of racism in other countries to global inequalities, such as 'vaccine' apartheid (Klotz and Boehme 2022).

Apartheid plays this unique role, past and present, because mobilisation for racial equality in South Africa successfully challenged claims of domestic jurisdiction as a fundamental norm (Klotz 1995: ch. 3; Burke 2010: ch. 3).[2] For example, Ben-Josef Hirsch (2014) explores the contemporary legacies of apartheid through the South African Truth and Reconciliation Commission for the emergence of transnational justice norms, while Amnesty International (2022) deploys an apartheid frame as a call for global action on Palestine, with roots of this frame going back to controversies over Zionism as racism in the 1960s (Lyons 1989). This persistent salience of an apartheid frame supports core claims by Percy and Sandholtz (2022) that individual norms typically morph rather than 'die' because of their position in broader social structures.

Because these recursive and layered debates do not neatly follow a teleological sequence, my analysis simultaneously traces the multi-dimensionality of contestation noted by Orchard and Wiener (Chapter 1: Figure 1.2). To capture these intertwined processes, I adopt a genealogical approach in two ways: as a methodological tool that stresses disruptive episodes of interpretative contestation and as an epistemological tool that reveals theoretical meta-narratives (Lynch 1999; Vucetic 2011). Thus, I argue that devolution in the practice of apartheid-related norms parallels disciplinary treatment of racism and racial hierarchies (Vitalis 2015; Zvobgo and Loken 2020). For example, political fracturing around apartheid resulted in the theoretical marginalisation of racial equality in the human rights literature

[2] Seidman (2000: 353) drew a similar lesson from the anti-apartheid movement for social movement theorists – that transnational activism bridged national and international articulations of race, within a context of institutionalised hierarchies.

too, evident in its routine omission of ICERD alongside invocations of the two contemporaneous covenants on political-civil rights (ICCPR 1966) and economic-social-cultural rights (ICESCR 1966).

Vitalis (2000: 333) aptly labelled such silences as deriving from a 'norm against noticing' (with attribution to novelist Toni Morrison). Building on the growing reckoning with race in International Relations (IR) as a field, this chapter highlights how a bifurcated mix of racial equality as a contested human right alongside widespread appropriation of apartheid as a general signifier of racial inequality has deeper roots in the overlooked legacies of imperialism for the normative architecture of the international system. The first section delves into macro-level debates about South Africa as a focal point that connects back to the waning years of the inter-imperial system, instead of privileging US hegemony from 1945 onward. Once we revisit the 1920s, other micro-level controversies jump to the forefront, notably domestication of racism within immigration restrictions, covered in the second section. With a quick conceptual stroke, IR eliminates imperialism, in theory and in practice, by presuming that domestic jurisdiction is a static feature of the inter-state system, rather than as a persistently disputed constitutive norm.

Macro-processes of Contestation: Whose Rights?

Selective disciplinary memory provides a window on what IR has gained and lost as 'norms' moved to the mainstream. The multi-dimensional marginalisation of race underscores that our analyses of norms in the world 'out there' are also embedded within a professional normative fabric derived from that world: the liberal imaginary. The field gradually tempered the critical edge of path-breaking claims in the late 1980s and early 1990s, leaving race outside the mainstream theories, even as post-colonial perspectives gained traction in many other venues (Doty 1993; Inayatullah and Blaney 2004; Anievas et al. 2015; Búzás 2021b).

In contrast, my analysis builds on insistence that opposition to apartheid played a crucial role in the development of international human rights norms, especially successful challenges to domestic jurisdiction in the 1960s (Willets 1982; Klotz 1995; Black 1999; Thörn 2006; Burke 2010). Unfortunately, this centrality of apartheid specifically, and racism generally, has been sidelined.[3] Notably, in influential writing about rights

[3] The early 'regimes' literature, gaining momentum by the late 1970s and early 1980s, rarely referenced human rights. Notably, Young (1980: 333–4) used the word 'right' only in the general sense of entitlement, whereas his word 'rule' approximates current

over three decades, Sikkink frequently reiterates this 1970s timeframe, variously as a tipping point in a cascade of ratifications especially related to torture and as a pivotal reorientation by the United States (e.g., Risse and Sikkink 1999: 21; Sikkink 2011). So does Moyn, another well-known human rights scholar, who recently co-edited a book titled *The Breakthrough: Human Rights in the 1970s* (Eckel and Moyn 2014), which includes his own chapter on the 1970s as the turning point.

Furthermore, influential early writings about the human rights regime ignored or glossed over apartheid, even at the height of its global political salience in the mid-1980s. In just one footnote, Ruggie (1983) demoted apartheid and racial discrimination – along with genocide, war crimes, crimes against humanity, slavery, women, children, refugees, and stateless people. Such relegation to the margins continued across decades, even in his later work on corporate responsibility (e.g., Ruggie 2004: 501–2), an agenda closely linked historically to anti-apartheid boycotts (Crawford and Klotz 1999). Similarly symptomatic of the silo effect, Donnelly acknowledged apartheid in passing (Donnelly 1986: 618) but stressed the weakness of ICERD (Donnelly 1986: 630), while labelling both racial discrimination and women's rights as separate issues from other human rights (see Lyons 1989: 85–7, for an explanation of this fragmentation).

Subsequently, this regime framework led to a large literature on human rights in IR, which offered a selective reading of mobilisation against racism, including apartheid. For example, the abolition of the slave trade as a 'prohibition regime' (Nadelmann 1990) reframed the issue away from race. In sharp contrast, Quirk (2011) dissected the relationship between racism and liberal imperialism. A complementary literature documenting transnational advocacy networks followed the pathbreaking publication of Keck and Sikkink's *Activists beyond Borders* (1998). Addressing apartheid only as a precursor case, they did not probe the relationship between racism and the human rights agenda. Also, Risse and Sikkink (1999: 2) relegated to a footnote the distinctiveness of racial equality as a normative focal point. Sporadic references to South Africa in their follow-on book, *The Persistent Power of Human Rights* (Risse and Sikkink 2013) explored questions of regime type, not the after-effects of apartheid.

notions of norms. Concentrating on political economy, Haas (1980) ignored rights but did establish the possibility that 'knowledge' could alter goals and hence national interests, which set the stage for later claims about constitutive effects of norms (Klotz 1995: ch. 2). More recently, Búzás (2021b) coined the term 'racial diversity regimes' to analyse domestic underpinnings in similar ways to export- and import-oriented coalitions in analyses of trade regimes (apartheid receives merely passing reference).

As these influential works illustrate, the anti-apartheid movement features narrowly in the predominant liberal imaginary as a struggle for universal franchise rather than a challenge to structural racism. One partial exception was the substantial resources that the Ford Foundation provided to a wide range of anti-apartheid activities, spanning individual rights and social justice agendas (Wong et al. 2017: 96). Still, Ford fits within the elite establishment. Deeper critiques about structural racism, meanwhile, hived off into fractious divides over colonialism and Zionism, among other controversies (Lyons 1989).

Similarly, international law textbooks often treat ICERD as a postscript, after prioritising ICCPR and ICESCR. For instance, von Glahn and Taulbee (2017: 387) offer passing reference on the general theme of discrimination, with race and women's rights in a short section labelled (presumably with unintentional irony) 'other' conventions. A bit better, Scott (2017: 248–50) does provide an explanation of the anti-racism convention, although again mixed among 'other' rights treaties. For Scott, as well as Donnelly, what is notable in ICERD is the procedural possibility of individual complaints (also detailed by Burke 2010: 60–71). No attention, not to mention analysis, then queries how race appears as one of many factors in so many rights conventions, often lumped together as race–ethnicity–nationality to avoid any rigid or essentialist conceptualisation. Nor do these discussions acknowledge any potential implications of this pervasiveness of race as a dimension of discrimination. In effect, race is simultaneously central yet marginal.

Admittedly, one reason for such analytical omission is that opposition to apartheid did not fit neatly into existing categories. Instead, it intersected with pan-Africanist anti-racism, decolonisation, democracy, torture, and many other rights frames, as well as within a broad coalition of social justice movements (Willets 1982: 23; Thörn 2006: ch. 2). The keystone of its significance – beyond any of these specific themes, and because of their intersection – centred on its *uniqueness*. The egregious nature of South Africa's draconian segregation policies and their transnational implications undermined claims to domestic jurisdiction, thereby setting the stage for a wide range of subsequent rights movements.

The multifaceted role of the UN as a formal setting for validation offers a window on these intersections. Even before the term 'apartheid' framed international attention on discrimination in South Africa, the UN served as a venue for intense disagreements over the definition and scope of domestic jurisdiction, a principle enshrined in its charter, alongside various caveats. At its very first session, India successfully placed the issue of "treatment of people of Indian origin in the

Union of South Africa" on the agenda of the General Assembly, while South Africa and some of its sympathisers objected based on domestic jurisdiction.[4]

But what did 'domestic jurisdiction' even mean since neither India nor South Africa was an independent country in 1946? Although both were UN members, and had been League members, each was still a self-governing colony within the British Empire (Pienaar 1987: ch. 1). This ambiguous status was hidden in plain sight. For instance, the question quickly arose whether prior bilateral agreements reached in 1927 and 1932 should be viewed as treaties. Yet, negotiated within the overarching auspices of empire, of course neither had been registered as a treaty with the League of Nations. Indeed, India had agreed not to take the dispute over discrimination to the League venue. Only when South Africa failed to deliver did India ramp up pressure by shifting to the UN venue.

The status of 'people of Indian origin' also did not fit neatly within a state-centric tenet of domestic jurisdiction. Britain and the Dominions had made strides in aligning their naturalisation policies, but with the notable exception of overt racial exclusion in South Africa (Ollivier 1954: 321; Gorman 2006). For decades, Indians within South Africa had challenged discrimination based on their trans-territorial status as British subjects (see, e.g., Bhana 1997). Various political pressures finally led to the creation of separate citizenships, albeit still within the empire, starting with Canada in 1946. South Africa had no citizens per se until 1949, and then only for people categorized as white; everyone else remained nationals, as well as British subjects (Klaaren 2000). Still, in the UN, advocates of domestic jurisdiction claimed to differentiate between Indians and South African Indians. Thus, a harbinger of the collapse of empire, 'domestic jurisdiction' was fundamentally a generalised defence of a right to be racist.[5]

Furthermore, taking literally the texts of those non-treaties of 1927 and 1932 adds to the confusion. In earlier decades, the 'Government of India' meant the Viceroy in Calcutta, as distinct from the India Office in London; British elites ran both offices. Only through an incremental and oft-violent process did India gain domestic self-government during the interwar years, followed by greater autonomy in 1947, and finally full independence as a republic in 1950. The UN debates only allude to these shifts when resolutions mention support for ongoing negotiations

[4] *Yearbook of the United Nations* (1946–7: 144–8).

[5] Britain finally consolidated its own post-colonial definition in 1981 (Cooper 2005; Gorman 2006).

to recognise Pakistan (which became a republic in 1956). By the 1950s, the practical meaning for 'domestic jurisdiction' was settling into its contemporary state-centric usage.

This lesser-known phase of anti-apartheid mobilisation in the 1950s generated a turning point for human rights, easily overlooked because attention turned to brutal shootings at Sharpeville in 1960 and Soweto in 1976, events extensively documented and discussed elsewhere as critical junctures. If we want to hold onto a linear model, the early 1960s could be characterised as the tipping point on racial equality, with the late 1970s marking its intensification, and the mid-1980s to early 1990s as the endgame. Still, this alternative timeline overlooks factors that underscore racism and colonialism, not just 'human rights' in its mainstream liberal meaning.

Methodological nationalism encourages analyses that portray countries in isolation, at most within diffusion processes. Apartheid, in contrast, led to reconfigured terrain in the region and complex interconnections between the disputed status of Rhodesia and Namibia. For example, Security Council arms embargoes intertwined Rhodesia and South Africa. My view of the 1960s rather than the 1970s as the cascade makes more sense in this broader context of decolonisation. Consequently, we should not be surprised that UN resolutions retain salience long after the transition to universal suffrage in South Africa, as evident in the vociferous response to de Klerk in 2020.

Illustrating how formal validation shapes opportunity structures, the Special Committee on Apartheid, established in 1963, served as the central node for information sharing and political networking. Only later did liberation movements receive recognition within the UN system. Based on interviews with activists, Thörn (2006: 32) argues that the committee's innovative approach created the general foundation for future participation of non-governmental organisations at side conferences during UN meetings, now routinely expected as part of global governance. Much of this anti-apartheid infrastructure, building on the Apartheid Convention (1973), plays a central role in both how and why 'apartheid' continues to frame the Israeli–Palestinian conflict (e.g., Amnesty International 2022). Even Sikkink (2011: 104–5) traces an extraordinary, seemingly serendipitous, connection between Article 5 of the Apartheid Convention and eventual creation of the International Criminal Court.

For the field of IR, the main theoretical lesson of apartheid as a normative focal point is not to privilege domestic jurisdiction as an abstract principle of the international system. Rather, domestic jurisdiction has always been historically constructed and hence inherently mutable.

Although we concentrate on different geographies and histories, Reus-Smit and I agree on this crucial point: sovereignty and rights need to be analysed as intertwined constitutional norms (see, e.g., Reus-Smit 2001: 520, 528; Reus-Smit 2011: 232–5; see also Vincent 1984; Crawford 2002; Cooper 2005: ch. 6; Klotz 2017; Búzás 2021b).

The next section leverages migration history to disrupt further the conventional static view of domestic jurisdiction by emphasising micro-processes of norm internalisation. Greater emphasis after 1919 on territorial control over human mobility, combined with anomalies over family status, set the stage for significant policy shifts, with ripple effects on rights more broadly. By the 1960s, the meaning of racial equality internationally had morphed again, due to this phase of domestication, especially in the context of post-war US hegemony

Micro-processes of Contestation: Why Domesticate?

A genealogy of 'domestic jurisdiction' takes us deeper into the inter-war era. Recall the origins of apartheid on the global agenda, rooted in the trans-nationality of British Indians, who migrated within the empire. Ambiguities in their citizenship status were not unique to South Africa; all the British colonies manifest such complexities. For instance, recent controversies over the status of intra-imperial Caribbean migrants to the British metropole in the 1950s demonstrate a similar misreading; the so-called *Windrush* generation were not immigrants who required paperwork, as now demanded by xenophobes. Echoes of contemporary prejudices that favour displaced Ukrainians manifest in prior British recruitment of white immigrants from Central Europe (Paul 1997).

While such porous borders and complex citizenships characterise many parts of the world, I concentrate in this section on Japanese responses to anti-Asian immigration restrictions, because restrictions over mobility led to its League of Nations proposal for a racial equality clause, with unintended long-term consequences. The reasons for rejecting the Japanese proposal bring to light not only the starkly overt prejudices of luminaries such as Woodrow Wilson; rejection of the racial equality clause marks a crucial turning point in the evolving norm of domestic jurisdiction. Not surprisingly, we also rarely learn about Chinese efforts to revive the racial equality clause in meetings to design the UN. By erasing the centrality of racism in all these ways, the field of IR reaffirms its myths about sovereignty (see Grovogui 2001; Quirk and Vigneswaran 2015).

The relationship between racism and domestic jurisdiction has received passing attention, but without sufficient recognition of how specifically the politics of migration motivated this confluence. The conventional narrative in IR frames Japan as an aggressor, by concentrating on its occupation of Manchuria and the failure of the League to prevent war. I do not seek to rewrite this narrative, only to highlight that any actor viewed as inherently aggressive will likely be presumed, by practitioners or by analysts, to be proactively seeking to overturn rules rather than reactively objecting to prior mistreatment. In contrast, Japan become profoundly frustrated, as an ally within racial hierarchies, which is a perspective readily discussed in migration debates, but typically omitted in IR, because its theories overlook migration.[6]

Conceptual vocabularies, especially the term 'settler societies', also play a key role in how analyses do or do not incorporate specific issues or places. For instance, British imperialism created a two-tier system, with white settler colonies gaining self-government (later known as the Dominions), while the Crown colonies continued to be administered directly from London. (Even then, Ireland and India did not fit in either category.) The meaning of settler colonialism has become equated with white supremacy in Australia, Canada, New Zealand, and South Africa. Rarely do Argentina and Brazil, major destinations for migrants, get comparable attention (notable exceptions include Belich 2009; Fitzgerald and Cook-Martin 2014).

Where does Japanese settler colonialism fit into this framework? Lu (2019: 7–10) poses this question as the entry point to rethinking Japanese imperialism across the Asia-Pacific region, as far as South America. IR explains expansion in terms of access to resources, whereas Lu concentrates on complementary concerns about overpopulation. Suzuki (2009) has already pointed to imperialism as a factor in seeking recognition as a great power. Nuance about these two tiers within British imperialism further explains why Japan mimicked settler colonialism in certain locations and among certain classes, leading Lu (2019: 22–3) to delve into its underlying logic (see also Azuma 2019: 163). For instance, modelling Anglo-expansionism initially generated keen attention to the American West as a desirable destination for Japanese emigrants.

Emigration and expansion entail complex interconnections that have typically been conflated in studies of the Anglophone world, perhaps because of the shear scope of British imperialism. In contrast, Lu distinguishes between emigration inside and outside the boundaries of

[6] The interdisciplinary field of migration studies has developed in recent decades mostly disconnected from IR, which has barely acknowledged the profound impacts of migration on the international system (e.g., McKeown 2011; Mayblin and Turner 2021). For instance, world systems theory underpins many explanations of how inequalities drive mobility, whereas Marxism no longer gets much attention in IR.

Japanese imperial control. Engineered emigration without conquest (across the Pacific Ocean to Hawaii, along the west coast of North America, and within multiple South American countries) manifested similar thinking about settlement: to establish integrated immigrant communities through the acquisition of land and citizenship. The outcome would be co-prosperity, a term only later associated with wartime aggression (Lu 2019: 24). This Japanese view of emigration as diaspora development differed from classic images of European immigrant peasant-farmers on the North American prairies.

Whether Japanese emigration projects succeeded or not depended in part on how well they navigated local politics in territories beyond their direct administrative control. The acceptance or rejection of Asians by predominantly white settler communities varied considerably. Mediated by diplomacy, some projects adapted in response to resistance, but others faced insuperable barriers. For example, a brief foray into rice farming in Texas failed, for economic and social reasons, compounded by political and legal factors (Lu 2019: ch. 4). Still, that new idea of encouraging emigration by settler farmers, instead of labourers, led to successful proactive schemes in Brazil (Lesser 2013: ch. 6; Lu 2019: ch. 5). As anger intensified over humiliating treatment in North America, the Japanese government expanded its role in managed migration by the 1920s.

Studies of immigration in Anglo-settler colonies typically pay little attention to Japanese migration, whereas many studies explore Chinese migration and exclusion. Best known is the so-called Gentlemen's Agreement in 1907 that voluntarily ended Japanese labour migration to the United States, although other classes of migrant, including farmers, could still enter and settle (Azuma 2019). Canada reached a similar agreement. Such diplomatic deals were only possible because the Japanese government could control emigration, a point rarely mentioned yet essential for comprehending the link between their reactions to exclusionary policies and wider foreign policy agendas. Also, IR rarely notices the sense of humiliation that these policies inflicted on Japan, at a time when its aspirations for great power status had been bolstered by victory against Russia in 1905 (Lake and Reynolds 2008: 271–8).

Although not new, anti-Asian sentiments across the Anglosphere intensified in the 1910s. Dissatisfied especially with increased family settlement, California legislators banned Asian land ownership in 1913, with its Alien Land Law written in terms of ineligibility for naturalisation, already limited to 'free white' people by the federal Naturalization Act of 1790. Similar legislation sprouted in other parts of the country. Court rulings affirmed that Japanese, among others, were not considered white (Lake and Reynolds 2008: 263–7). As systematic discrimination gathered strength, despite their wartime alliance, deepening resentment led to Japan's call for a racial equality clause in the Covenant of the League of Nations.

This context of migration as an issue embedded in treaties and diplomacy explains the connection between the racial equality clause and contestation over domestic jurisdiction as an emergent norm. Woodrow Wilson's rhetoric about equality as the foundation for peace led Japan, and many others, to have high expectations. At the same time, imperial powers, including Japan, remained wary of his emphasis on self-determination. British and American leaders expected Japan to claim the colonial territories of defeated Germany in Asia and also worried over its likely claims to removing restrictions on immigration (Lake and Reynolds 2008: 281–2). For Japan, these were inseparable elements of equal status as the only Asian great power, with its potential membership in the League conditional on the outcome of the racial equality debate.

Unpacking the reactive steps in Japan's efforts, especially evolution in wording of its proposal, reveals this underpinning and illustrates the micro-processes of normative contestation. The failure to adopt a proactive racial equality clause proceeded in two phases. Both the venue and who had a vote played a significant but not determinative role: one dominant storyline grants Australia responsibility for the outcome, despite lacking a formal vote, whereas another concentrates on Wilson's procedural maneuvers. Each narrative thus highlights a piece of the contestation puzzle: the interplay between formal rules and stakeholder agency.

The first version of the proposed clause underscores the centrality of migration:

> The equality of nations being a basic principle of the League of Nations, the High Contracting Parties agree that concerning the treatment and rights to be accorded to aliens in their territories, *they will not discriminate, either in law or in fact, against any person or persons on account of his or their race or nationality.* (quoted in Lake and Reynolds 2008: 289, emphasis added)

Initially, Japan sought its inclusion alongside religious freedom in Article 21, but the Commission drafting the Covenant decided instead to remove Article 21 completely (Lake and Reynolds 2008: 290–1). Side negotiations led nowhere. Wilson cared about US domestic politics, where xenophobic Californians carried electoral significance. And Britain cared about preserving its empire, letting Australia object the loudest among the white-settler Dominions, in defence of an intra-imperial principle already affirmed at the 1917 Imperial War Conference.

Rebuffed, in March 1919, Japan omitted direct reference to racism in a revised clause to be included in the Preamble:

> Equality of nations being a basic principle of the League of Nations, the High Contracting Parties agree *to endorse the principle of equal and just treatment to be accorded to all alien nations* of State members of the League. (quoted in Lake and Reynolds 2008: 297, emphasis added)

Britain again deferred to the Dominions but facilitated further attempts at compromise with even weaker reference to migration. Still, Australia continued adamantly to reject it (Lake and Reynolds 2008: 297–9). Japan did try one more time, at the final meeting of the Commission in April. Despite widespread support from other countries, Wilson insisted on unanimity to advance the proposal, unlike prior procedures. No formal vote was taken, once Britain indicated its deference, again, to Australian objections (Lake and Reynolds 2008: 300–1).

Analysts who look only at the final version of the failed proposal miss the substantive meaning of racial discrimination at that historical moment – a reminder that taken-for-granted interpretations may be hidden in plain sight. IR also minimises this controversy because it typically treats migration as low politics. Consequently, self-described 'realists' who portray the League as an 'idealist' failure overlook the puzzling primacy of semi-sovereign Australia over great power Japan. The confluence of these oversights and omissions helps us understand how a norm of domestic jurisdiction crystalised at this juncture, based on the overtly racist Australian argument against any racial equality clause. Its implementation, then, provides an opportunity to track cyclical processes of norm internalisation and renewed internationalisation that, decades later, produced an expansive convention against racial discrimination (ICERD).

Racism submerged domestically in the interwar era, partly obscured by the rise of nationality as a key feature in the regulation of human mobility. The newly legitimated idea of controlling borders translated into a plethora of policies and procedures, including widespread use of passports (Torpey 1998; Salter 2003), with inevitable loopholes and omissions. For instance, the United States first policed its borders for fear that Europeans would evade restrictions by entering through Canada (Ramirez 2001). Procedural uses of family status (Schrover and Moloney 2013; Bhabha 2014) provided a subtler filtering tool. For example, when Britain shifted (based on *jus sanguinis*) from grand-paternal descent to paternal descent in its 1914 Nationality and Status of Aliens Act, the rules needed to delineate the implications (for *jus soli*) of being born on a British or foreign vessel, while in British or foreign waters. Meanwhile, married women received the same status as children – and 'lunatics' (§27). Later, Britain switched back to grand-paternal lineage to reinforce its ties with the Dominions.

Across the Anglosphere, racist restrictions based on nationality and naturalisation provided a means to filter Asian migration. The voluntary limits on emigration that Canada and the United States had negotiated with Japan focused on labourers, but family members could still relocate. Similarly, exceptions within Chinese exclusion laws fostered a robust industry of documenting so-called paper families to circumvent barriers (Lau 2006). And while head taxes reduced numbers by raising the cost of entry into Canada, some people could afford those fees. Thus, Asian migration to North America continued, albeit at a diminished rate, and their locally born children became citizens (based on *jus soli*), regardless of parental nationality.[7] Such exceptions drove xenophobes to demand increasingly stringent restrictions.

Typical for diffusion processes, many countries adopted nationality quotas by the 1930s, due to a mix of policy effectiveness and regional pressures (FitzGerald and Cook-Martin 2014).[8] Varying only at the margins, hierarchies within these quotas, from desirable northern Europeans to less desirable southern and eastern Europeans to undesirable non-Europeans, served as an overt proxy for race. Ending their negotiated approach in 1917, the United States declared an 'Asiatic Barred Zone', followed by quota policies in the 1920s that blocked almost all Asian migrants as aliens ineligible for citizenship based on the 1790 statute. Not until the United States revived migration diplomacy and ended racial barriers to naturalisation in 1952 did Japan receive even a scant quota of 185 within an overall cap of 2,000 for all Asians (Azuma 2019: 162; Oh 2019: 237). Although shockingly low, the quota for Japanese immigrants was slightly higher than the infinitesimal 105 spots allocated for all people of Chinese descent, a blatantly racialised category that disregarded variation in nationality (Lau 2006: 17–18). The strictures of tight quotas turned family status into an intractably ambiguous category.

However, as the status of family gathered policy significance in subsequent decades, its role as a proxy for race diminished, setting the stage for renewed international demands to validate racial equality

[7] While Canadian naturalisation laws ostensibly did not discriminate – in contrast to explicitly racist exclusions in the U.S. – Asians faced significant barriers to qualify in practice (Anderson 2013: 118–20).

[8] Eschewing quotas as too rigid, Canada relied on Cabinet discretion, thereby enabling a compromise to populate its prairies with less desirable Eastern Europeans while maintaining insurmountable barriers against Asians (Klotz 2013: 239–41).

as a constitutive human right. Crucially, Cold War priorities shifted attention to ideologically driven security provisions, which reinforced executive discretion (Friman 2019). Exceptions for Asian-born wives of soldiers created ripple effects, starting with the formal repeal of Chinese exclusion in the Magnuson Act of 1943, albeit replaced with a miniscule quota that served the same purpose. The 1945 War Brides Act, which coincided with the occupation of Japan, enabled a select few returning soldiers to bring home non-white spouses. Pressures built during the Korean War to expand family unification. In 1952, the controversial McCarran–Walter Act went further to prioritise family unification over race, even while reaffirming discriminatory quotas (Oh 2019: 232–7).

Conventional wisdom characterises the Hart–Celler Act of 1965, on the heels of major civil rights legislation, as the end of racist immigration policy. Yet only unintentionally did these reforms lead to more immigrants from Asia and Latin America; many congressional legislators aimed to affirm ties with Europe. Furthermore, the law retained regional quotas and extended, for the first time, numerical limits to the Western Hemisphere (King 2000). In that light, support for family unification looks more like a 'tactical concession' (Risse and Sikkink 1999: 20–8) than a principled disavowal of racism, much like concurrent foreign policy efforts to parry criticism of segregation (see, e.g., Van Eschen 1997; Dudziak 2000). Another result was US support for ICERD, signed in 1966 but not ratified until 1994.

Still, mainstream IR insists that the United States leads, even when it follows. I made this argument in 1995, but people too often inaccurately reference my analysis of US sanctions against South Africa as an example of its hegemony rather than a reaction to pan-African mobilisation. Then and now, US policies on issues of race result from its ontological vulnerability. Should we be surprised, then, that race and racism receive little attention in the US-dominated field of IR? What does surprise me is how so much of constructivism, even the 'third move' emphasis on norm contestation (Orchard and Wiener, Chapter 1), evades self-reflection on such meta-theoretical silences (Klotz 2018). Unlike Vitalis (2000: 334–5), however, I do not see theoretical formulations themselves as an inherent barrier to addressing race and racism. For instance, recent scholarship at the intersection of diplomatic history and security studies delves into white supremacist ideas and US expansionism (see, e.g., Kramer 2006; Immerwahr 2019; Maass 2020).

Clearly, my genealogical stress on the 1920s and 1950s as key historical junctures echoes contemporary questioning of the so-called liberal order, including resurgent white supremacist movements, with implications for theory and practice far beyond the scope of this chapter. Norms of self-determination and domestic jurisdiction remain fundamentally unsettled. In lieu of a conclusion, therefore, I underscore one overarching recommendation from a burgeoning literature on race in IR: contesting the 'norm against noticing' entails attention to episodes of contestation omitted in conventional meta-narratives.

Implications: Contesting Marginalisation

The terminology of 'civilisation' recurs in key international law texts, typically now dismissed as merely archaic rhetoric, despite its alternative inflammatory usage in 'clash' discourses. Scrutinising the word illustrates how racism remains deeply embedded in formal rules and informal assumptions. Diplomatic negotiations over migration in the late 1800s and early 1900s, for example, demonstrate a multifaceted conception of discrimination built on hierarchical degrees of civilisation. While seeking equal status with European great powers, Japan also viewed itself as more civilised than China or India, and Europeans agreed. Thus, exclusionary immigration policies used these same terminologies.

Contestation over racism generated an emergent norm of domestic jurisdiction in 1919, with the definitive rejection of Japan's proposed racial equality clause for the League of Nations. Yet boundaries of the domestic realm remained porous because empires were still the key actors. Invoking civilisational hierarchies, immigration policies created a plethora of new procedures to regulate human movement, with inevitable gaps. For instance, anomalies in the nationality status of married women received remarkable attention in the 1920s, although negotiations to codify one international standard failed (Waltz 1937; Rosenne 1975; Sluga 2013).[9] By the 1950s, however, family unification as a principle had chipped away at some of the staunchest discriminatory immigration policies, based on nationality as a proxy for race. Migration disputes also provide a reminder that both British and American variants of liberalism deserve greater scrutiny, beyond the occasional acknowledgement that Wilson promoted democracy abroad and segregation at home.

Myriad proxy terms for race and, consequently, its persistently covert use underscores the need for context-sensitive analysis. Defining South African 'apartheid' narrowly as the dichotomous ideological interplay between white supremacy (avowedly in defence of

[9] In 1957, the UN affirmed the right of married women to retain their nationality, also subsequently incorporated in the CEDAW in 1979 (Hevener 1983).

civilisation) and universal suffrage (presented as modernity) did not sufficiently capture the complexity of colonial legacies. By recognising such oversights, newer rhetorical uses of apartheid may, inadvertently, capture structural inequality while letting policymakers and academics rely on geography to evade contentious arguments about racism. Use of nationality as a proxy for race in (US) immigration quotas should caution us, as researchers or practitioners, not to accept any stark separation of ethics from empirics if we hope to tackle the multiple manifestations of racism.

6 Emotion and Norms in International Shaming Practices

Halima Akhrif and Simon Koschut

Introduction

On 13 December 2016, US Ambassador to the United Nations Samantha Power (2016) took a firm stance on the Syrian, Russian, and Iranian representatives in the UN Security Council about the siege of Aleppo:

> This is what is being done by Member States of the United Nations who are sitting around this horseshoe table today. This is what is being done to the people of eastern Aleppo, to fathers, and mothers, and sons, and daughters, brothers, and sisters like each of us here. … To the Assad regime, Russia, and Iran, your forces and proxies are carrying out these crimes. … It should shame you. Instead, by all appearances, it is emboldening you. You are plotting your next assault. Are you truly incapable of shame? Is there literally nothing that can shame you? Is there no act of barbarism against civilians, no execution of a child that gets under your skin, that just creeps you out a little bit?

This statement vividly illustrates the link between emotions and norms in international politics. On the one hand, there is a strong emotional attachment to human rights norms, as Samantha Power's speech testifies. The targeted addressing of emotions by means of naming and shaming[1] plays a prominent role in the strategy of predominantly Western actors who are committed to the enforcement of human rights (Keck and Sikkink 1998). On the other hand, norms sometimes appear to lack enforcement power because so many actors do not seem to feel any shame or guilt for their actions. Russia's UN ambassador Vitaly Churkin, for example, did not appear to be very impressed by Power's speech.[2] Thus, the question arises as to why particular norms produce emotional resonance in some cases and with some political elites and not

[1] We are aware that naming and shaming are distinct concepts. Our focus is here specifically on the aspect of naming, as this component is particularly fundamental for evoking emotional responses. Shaming rather presupposes a discursive process (see also Hafner-Burton 2008). Furthermore, it already reflects the emotional response as such.

[2] See the video recording of the UN Security Council session (US State Department 2016). Churkin appears at minute 1:28.

in others. This has significant implications for norm research: if persuasion or arguing – for example, through naming and shaming – is to have an effect by inflicting social suffering, such mechanisms already implicate an emotional dimension. For, if an international actor can be forced to comply with social norms through non-physical forms of coercion, that actor must *feel* the negative implications in order to be persuaded or forced into compliance. Otherwise, these mechanisms of norm compliance would be useless (Koschut 2018).

The aim of this chapter is to address this question by examining the link between emotions and norms in international shaming practices. We argue that emotional resonance supports the maintenance and enforcement of international norms: the capacity of norms to evoke shared emotional images, memories, and collective feelings among different international actors facilitates compliance. We also show how emotional resonance is helpful for explaining failures of norm compliance. The way in which the absence of emotional resonance facilitates non-compliance is illustrated by the example of the Bush administration's reaction to torture allegations in Abu Ghraib and Guantanamo. We deliberately selected torture to illustrate our theoretical argument on a hard case – that is, for a country that has traditionally seen itself as a pioneer or protector of human rights in international relations (see also Ralph, Chapter 1, Stimmer, Chapter 10, and Winston, Chapter 9). Our analysis embraces a new understanding of the psychological characteristics and emotional make-up of agents in shaping norms and their meanings over time through contestation. In doing so, we build on the three forms of contestation indicated in the Introduction to this volume. We are focusing on reactive contestation here, as naming and shaming addresses the gap between a certain – norm-violating – behaviour and the behaviour expectations' indicated by the norm itself. Emotion can also be found in other forms of contestation. For example, the capacity of norms to evoke shared emotional images, memories, and collective feelings implies that the agent not only 'thinks' but also 'feels' that it understands a given norm in a different way as other agents in the community (interpretative contestation) and/or may feel emotionally inclined to improve the norm (proactive contestation).

Theorising the Link between Emotions and Norms

Our conceptualisation of the link between norms and emotions illuminates a hitherto understudied area in norm research. Many constructivists have highlighted that persuading states and non-state actors to comply with international norms is determined by rational deliberation, rhetoric, and argument (Deitelhoff 2009; Krebs and Jackson 2007; Müller 2001; Payne 2001; Risse 2000; Schimmelfennig 2001). The preoccupation with norms as the primary medium of global governance in mainstream constructivist research has arguably led to a neglect of the emotional underpinnings of these norms, which extends beyond the rational or cognitive representation of shared understandings that are thought to lie outside the affective realm of international actors. Addressing this theoretical-conceptual gap in mainstream constructivist research adds significant analytical value to linking emotions more closely to norm-based approaches in International Relations (IR). The conventional constructivist view on the agency of actors in world politics fails to capture other, more emotional ways in which norms exercise influence. Most norm scholars accept emotions as relevant but accord them a taken-for-granted status (Chaiken et al. 1996; Elster 1989; Fearon 1997; Finnemore and Sikkink 1998; Keck and Sikkink 1998; Risse et al. 1999). More specifically, while the importance of emotions is by and large recognised in norms research, its theorisation and empirical operationalisation remains underdeveloped. As a result, we still know little about the psychological micro-foundations of norm-based behaviour. In order to address this gap, we take the constructivist debate on the link between emotions and norms a step further by suggesting ways in which social norms may be relevant not only as to how actors *think* and *behave* but, importantly, also as to how they *feel*. Moving away from conceiving norms as being solely rooted in cognitive categories and drawing on emotional forms of practices that currently fly under the radar of constructivist norm research allows for a better and more comprehensive understanding of how international actors interact in world politics.[3]

The link between emotions and norms can be theorised in at least two ways. First, emotions contribute to the maintenance and enforcement of social norms (Illgit and Prakash 2019; Kowert 2012; Mercer 2005). According to this bottom-up approach, emotions assign meaning to norms and restrain undesirable attitudes and behaviour; for example, through shaming. Paul Kowert (2012) sees in its emotional appraisal precisely that quality that turns cognitive ideas, considerations, and assumptions into explicitly normative convictions: it is their emotional sounding board, an emotional force of norms, which gives them value and, if they are of high value, fundamental commitment. The value of norms therefore does not arise (solely) from social pressure or deontic language but fundamentally depends on emotions that justify normative qualities of mutual obligation: "To function normatively, beliefs require evaluative,

[3] On emotions as practices in IR, see Bially Mattern (2011).

emotional force. Put more simply, normativity depends on creating feelings of obligation. ... Norms are thus inescapably emotive, cognitive, and linguistic phenomena" (Kowert 2012: 37). Some scholars suggest that the legitimacy of a given norm even depends on emotion. As Jon Mercer (1996) notes: "One way to test for the presence of norms is to look for emotion." Indeed, neurological research shows that people who suffer from brain damage, having lost their ability to feel joy or pain, are incapable of adhering to social norms simply because they cannot feel the negative consequences of their inappropriate behaviour (Damasio 1994).

The second way in which the link between norms and emotions can be theorised is by turning the causal link around. According to this top-down approach, social norms and conventions prescribe what is felt, who is entitled to feel, and in what ways. In sociology, this phenomenon is known as emotion norms (Thoits 2004: 359). Emotion norms are collective expectations that govern the emotional experience and expressions of members of a particular group. By emotional experience, we mean the emotions that individuals are supposed to feel in a specific situation (e.g., 'You should feel sad at a funeral', 'You shouldn't be angry with her'). By emotional expressions, we mean social prescriptions about the appropriate forms of emotional display in a given context (e.g., 'Men shouldn't cry', 'You should show gratitude for receiving a gift'). Both emotional experience and expressions may be subject to emotion norms. Emotion norms specify and prescribe the meaning, intensity, and duration of emotional experiences and expressions that are appropriate in a given situation. Individuals undergo emotional socialisation to acquire the emotional knowledge and skills of their particular peer group. Emotional deviants will be subject to social disapproval, labelling, and stigmatisation. Individuals are thus pressured to conform in order to achieve social approval and avoid social sanctions. Such efforts at emotional conformity, in turn, serve important social functions; for example, to help sustain the social order, hierarchies, and social cohesion of the group. Some IR scholars have analysed how emotion norms explain group cohesion at the international level following traumatic events (Hutchison 2016), the appropriate control and expression of emotion among military men and women (Basham 2015), state practices against marginalised groups (Head 2019), the stabilisation of security communities (Koschut 2014), and the practice of suicide terrorism (Fierke 2013). Our chapter offers a fresh perspective on the link between emotion and norms in IR by zooming in on the norm addressees and the targeting of state actors through shaming practices to evoke a particular emotional response. This provides a genuine contribution to the state-of-the-art literature on norm contestation in IR.

Emotional Resonance

While IR scholars have tacitly accepted that emotions contribute to the maintenance and enforcement of social norms as well as studying how emotions themselves can be subject to social norms, we believe the potential of linking emotions to norms in IR can be taken a step further. We suggest that the constitutive role of emotions for social norms can shed new light on an old empirical puzzle: why international norms sometimes resonate and sometimes not. For this purpose, we introduce the concept of *emotional resonance*. We define emotional resonance as the ability of social norms to evoke and suggest emotional images, memories, and collective feelings. These images, memories, and feelings originally stem from prior emotional experiences that gave rise to the social norm in the first place. Here, we borrow from Émile Durkheim (1982), who famously claimed that the moral value of social norms originates from and is sustained by collective emotions. For example, the creation of the Universal Declaration of Human Rights originated from and was reinforced by a collective emotional experience of human atrocities committed by Nazi Germany: "Man's desire for peace lies behind this Declaration. The realisation that the flagrant violation of human rights by Nazi and Fascist countries sowed the seeds of the last world war has supplied the impetus for the work which brings us to the moment of achievement here today" (Roosevelt 1948). Political leaders collectively felt that there must be a better way for the nations and peoples of the world to live together and subsequently drafted the Universal Declaration. The legal framework of the Universal Declaration of Human Rights constitutes the outcome of a kind of "epistemological contract" that established precontractual emotional solidarity and which answers the question of certainty: 'How can I be sure of what I know?' Put differently, the only reliable basis that international human rights could have, if legal obligation was to be guarded from fluctuating self-interest, lay in charging it with emotional value.

We argue that emotional resonance is crucial to the impact and enforcement of norms because it charges abstract legal norms with emotional value: without the ability of norms to evoke shared emotional images, memories, and collective feelings among international actors, we cannot expect compliance. We suggest that this process of 'emotionalising' is important because it underpins the moral value of the norm. Only when there is emotional resonance can we assume that the actor appraises the norm to be important. Here, we follow emotional appraisal theories that view emotions as expressions of a moral evaluations of events that causes specific emotional responses in different people (Arnold 1960;

Nussbaum 2001). Human rights norms, for example, are attached to collective images and memories of human atrocities as well as feelings of what is right and wrong, moral and immoral. People who follow the norm should feel good about themselves whereas people who fail to comply should (ideally) feel bad. Only when such emotional resonance occurs can we assume that the actor considers the norm to be important. As we will show further in the following discussion, this is what makes shaming practices effective in international politics.

The concept of emotional resonance builds on but also differs from existing approaches as part of the 'emotional turn' in IR. Some scholars theorise how emotions create and sustain "circulations of affect" (Ross 2014: 22) by which individuals – diplomats, protesters, or political leaders – tend to take on the emotions displayed by other individuals with whom they interact (Holmes and Wheeler 2020; Ross 2014). While emotional resonance also assumes the synchronisation and alignment of emotions between actors, it links these emotions to specific norms. Rather than to involuntarily align the emotional expressions of others in face-to-face encounters, emotional resonance assumes that actors strategically employ emotions to facilitate norm compliance. Other scholars have focused on the specific mechanism through which individual emotions are socially embedded through language and images (Bleiker and Hutchison 2008; Hutchison 2016; Hansen 2015; Ross 2006). Emotional resonance plays a crucial role in these processes, as socially shared images, words, symbols, or gestures evoke an emotional reaction in some cultural contexts and among some people but not in others. A very good example is Philippe Beauregard's (2019) excellent study of emotional resonance to explain the emergence and maintenance of international leadership. However, these scholars do not link their insights to the study of norms.

We suggest that the degree to which norms emotionally resonate depends on at least two factors. First, it depends on the moral framing of actors. Emotions evoke moral value judgements about specific norms, so we can assume the evocation of emotional images, memories, and feelings puts the targeted actor in the position to also react with an emotional assessment of the norm's value (all else being equal). Conversely, if emotional images, memories, and feelings are absent or weak, we can expect non-compliance. When discussing emotional resonance, we focus on political leaders. Political leaders are defined here as "responsible decision-makers," having a political mandate in one form or another which includes heads of state, heads of governments, cabinet members, and other representatives (Hill 2003). That said, we would also expect this form of resonance to exist among other audiences, such as (trans) national publics, albeit perhaps to a different degree.

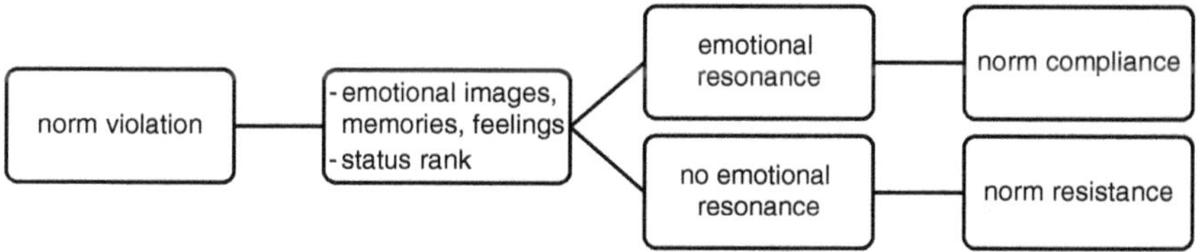

Figure 6.1 Pathways of emotional resonance

Second, we suggest that the impact of emotional resonance depends on the target actor's relative status in the international system. The targeted actor has to perceive itself as a member of the respective community for which the norm in question is regarded as a fundamental principle in the first place in order to produce emotional resonance.[4] Here, we borrow from Arlie Hochschild's (1983) work on emotional labour and suggest that states assuming a particularly powerful position in the international system may be able to withstand the evocation of emotions in some situations. For Hochschild, emotions are tied to social hierarchies and inequalities. Those actors that rank higher within a group are able to define the proper ways of feeling and expressing emotions, which means that actors in the lower ranks will be forced to alter their performance in order to better adapt to the prevailing cultural script. This pertains particularly to situations in which emotions may jeopardise the respective state's relative status position, as is the case with *shaming*. The alternative pathways of emotional resonance are summarised in Figure 6.1. Our model does not preclude the existence and possibility of alternative mechanisms of compliance, such as coercion (Hafner-Burton 2005), domestic institutions (Sandholtz 2017; Simmons 2009), state reputation (Tomz 2007), or norm internalisation and diffusion (Risse et al. 2013). Nor do we exclude additional factors, such as time, power capabilities, or strategic considerations. We simply suggest that greater attention should be paid to the psychological and emotional micro-foundations that underpin these mechanisms of compliance.

Shaming and Emotional Resonance in International Relations

The practice of *naming and shaming* vividly illustrates our argument about emotional resonance for understanding norm compliance in IR. Traditionally, the strategy of calling out states for norm violations has

[4] In some cases, states may strategically violate international norms to assert their identity as insiders or outsiders (Evers 2017).

been a prominent means of governmental and non-governmental organisations to pressure states into a change of behaviour (e.g., stopping human rights violations). Actors thereby exert moral leverage by pointing to and condemning deviations of state's actual practices from their own claims or standards (Keck and Sikkink 1998: 23).

Naming and shaming is a practice that can be considered paradigmatic for explicating how norms – here in their specific expression of human rights norms – work in international politics. IR scholars have been at the forefront of theorising the purposes for which states and non-state actors may be shamed into compliance. Shaming has been employed, for example, to punish deviation from international norms (DeMeritt 2012; Finnemore and Sikkink 1998; Hafner-Burton 2008; Keck and Sikkink 1998; Klotz 2018; Krain 2012; Lebovic and Voeten 2006; Murdie and Davis 2012; Nadelmann 1990; Risse et al. 2013; Sandholtz and Stiles 2009), enforce international taboos (Price 1997; Tannenwald 2005), or to make international status claims (Adler-Nissen 2014; Paul et al. 2014; Subotic and Zarakol 2013; Zarakol 2011).

Some scholars have recently begun to unpack shaming practices by looking more closely at the conditions that shape their effectiveness (Carraro et al. 2019; Friman 2015; Terman and Voeten 2018; Woo and Murdie 2017). Previous research has yielded inconclusive results: Jacqueline DeMeritt's (2012) as well as Matthew Krain's (2012) findings suggest that particularly instances of *shaming* from human rights and international organisations are correlated with a decrease of government violence against civilians. Emile Hafner-Burton (2008), by contrast, finds that governments even tend to step up abusing policies after being put in the spotlight of international criticism. Some results point to a general effectiveness of *shaming*, but suggest its contingency on conditional factors such as the target state's economic interconnectedness with other countries (Franklin 2008), the presence of human rights organisations (Murdie and Davis 2012), or regime type (Hendrix and Wong 2013).

As some authors have noted, the mixed and at some points contradictory results concerning the effectiveness of *shaming* campaigns could be related to a misleading understanding about the outcome of interest. Ilgit and Prakash (2019) note that most empirical assessments of the issue consider tactical concessions by the target government as the prime indicator for successful *shaming* practices, with the evocation of a "genuine emotional reaction" (2019: 1301) typically being deemed irrelevant. DeMeritt's (2012) empirical assessment is a case in point: the author assumes governments not to end abusive policies merely on the grounds of resonance with the emotion of *shame*, but rather out of fear from sanctions by third-party states. However, the literature dealing with the enforcement of human rights norms considers the socialisation of the latter as a crucial component in *naming and shaming* practices.

It is against this backdrop that Asli Ilgit and Deepa Prakash (2019) have advocated for a more thorough investigation of the emotional dimension of *naming and shaming*. Rees et al. (2013) note that actors can only feel shame when a self-relevant value has been seriously violated. Therefore, situational adjustments in behaviour may not be sufficient reactions to reduce the feeling of shame. Rather, it requires a rectification that allows "the one's own or the group's actions to be seen as living up to or consistent with" the violated value (Rees et al. 2013). As an emotion, the public denouncement or *shaming* of a suspected norm-violator carries a value judgement of the norm under question (and its violation, respectively) in the context of a community's broader set of norms. If we think of norm violation as an extreme form of reactive contestation, shaming indicates the presence of an objection to the norm and the value it carries. It thereby markedly departs from only spotlighting human rights abuses, as its potential impact does not lie merely in the indication of the deviation from the individual norm.

This prompts an obvious question: if *shaming* yields the effect of placing norm-violators in a distinctive out-group, why should these actors respond to *shaming* in the desired way nonetheless? A possible explanation for this puzzle lies in the fact that *shaming*, albeit implicitly separating the wrongdoer from compliant states, nonetheless assumes the respective state's membership in the community for which the norm is deemed essential. *Shaming* signals a "temporary decrease in status of the targeted state within the club" (Rousseau 2018: 325). It is against this backdrop that some authors assign specific importance to the socialising role of *shaming* practices given the norm-violating state's aspiration to regain its status in the community (Risse et al. 2013).

Implicit to this argument is the expectation that *shaming* is most likely to be effective when the target state actually aspires to be a part of the community for which the violated norm is deemed essential. States met with *stigmatisation*, by contrast, sometimes even embrace and capitalise on international ostracism for strengthening domestic legitimacy (Adler-Nissen 2014; Rousseau 2018). *Shame* "is an aversive experience" and motivates actors "to think and act in ways that best reduce their levels of shame" (Rees et al. 2013: 390). If successful, *shaming* results in the evocation of *shame* on behalf of the targeted state. This may manifest itself most directly in the form of apologies or in commitments to assume a responsible role as a member of the international community, sometimes combined with the evocation of shared collective memories and images. In some cases, however, states may respond to allegations of norm violations with counter-discourses qualifying the norm deviation (Adler-Nissen 2014). States may either try to justify the norm transgression with other norms that are deemed more important or downplay the violation as individual instances over which the actor had no control (Jetschke and Liese 2013). These observations mirror our earlier assumptions. First, *naming and shaming* evaluates an actor's compliance with a norm – or, more precisely, non-compliance – and calls its relative status or even membership in the community of states into question. From this follows that for *shaming* to be effective, the target country has to perceive itself as a member of the respective community for which the violated norm is regarded as a basic principle. Second, however, the degree to which *naming and shaming* is capable of evoking emotional resonance – even for states that typically consider themselves to be part of the community – is dependent on the state's relative status and its ability to successfully respond with the emotionalisation of counter-norms. Only when international criticism actually succeeds in evoking an emotional resonance on parts of the violating state can *shaming* be deemed effective in the sense that it reflects the discursive persuasion to norm compliance by actors.

Case Vignette: The Bush Administration's Reaction to Torture Allegations in the 'War on Terror'

We illustrate the salience of emotional resonance for explaining non-compliance with norms by referring to the US administrations' reaction to torture allegations during the 'War on Terror'. This instance represents a hard case insofar as the traditional self-perception of the United States as a norm entrepreneur in the international system – specifically with regard to democracy and human rights promotion – would make it particularly amenable for emotional resonance. Nonetheless, the case shows to which extent the distinctive status of the United States in the international system allowed it to withstand attempts to make it *feel* ashamed. Shortly after the attacks on 9/11, the US administration authorised 'enhanced interrogation techniques', which were classified by international organisations and human rights advocates as forms of torture (International Committee of the Red Cross 2007). First reports on abusive practices of prisoners of war surfaced early in the war; for example, with regard to Central Intelligent Agency (CIA) interrogation techniques at Afghanistan's Bagram Air Force base in December 2002 (Priest and Gellman 2002). The public outcry over ostensible US human rights violations abroad arguably found its climax when reports about torture and humiliation of prisoners of war in Guantanamo and Iraq's Abu Ghraib surfaced.

In the course of these scandals, international human rights organisations condemned the US practices, stressing the illegitimacy of interrogation techniques and their incompatibility with basic human rights norms. Since the beginning of the allegations, human rights advocates stressed the gravity of the violations by emphasizing the discrepancy of actual practices to historical commitments, especially with regard to the Geneva Conventions (e.g., Human Rights Watch 2001). For example, Amnesty International in a statement on the Abu Ghraib incidents accused the US administration of "consistent disregard for the Geneva Conventions and basic principles of law, human rights and decency" (Amnesty International 2004). Specifically, since the incidents in Abu Ghraib became known, the criticism on US human rights violations was underpinned by the expression of emotions. The statements made by then-UN general secretary Kofi Annan demonstrate how emotions were accompanied by the attempt to show how the United States through the continued use of torture acquired a lower status within the international system. After noting that "[a]gain and again, we see fundamental laws shamelessly disregarded," he mentions "Iraqi prisoners [being] disgracefully abused" as an example along with human rights violations in Uganda, Sudan, Russia, Israel and the Palestinian territories, closing that "[t]hey put all of us to shame" (Annan 2004). The emotional resonance of the norm violation was enhanced by appealing to collectively shared memories and images and implicitly pointed to a relative status loss by putting US abuses in line with practices by other states, some of which with a known record of human rights abuses. Annan's statement regarding the "shameless disregard" of "fundamental laws" represents an evaluation of the founding principles of the United Nations and individual states. He says that "[many] nations represented in this chamber can proudly point to founding documents of their own that embody that simple concept [rule of law]" (Annan 2004).

In particular, the attempt of the US government to reframe the practice of 'enhanced interrogation techniques' as being essentially different from torture – a form of proactive contestation – was met with criticism. Some commentators have thereby pointed to the similarities of such techniques to the interrogation practices of *Verschärfte Vernehmung* (which literally translates as 'enhanced interrogation') conducted by the Gestapo (The Atlantic 2007). A report by Amnesty International (2019) documenting the reactions of visitors of a Polish torture museum likewise draws a clear parallel from depictions of Gestapo interrogations to human rights violations in Abu Ghraib and Guantanamo. Columnist

Frank Rich stated that "[o]ur humanity has been compromised by those who use Gestapo tactics in the Iraq war. The longer we stand idly by, the more we resemble the 'Good Germans'" (Rich 2007). From this observation, the author draws the conclusion that "we must also examine our own responsibilities for the hideous acts committed in our name in a war where we have now fought longer than we did in the one that put *Verschärfte Vernehmung* on the map" (Rich 2007).

The drawing of these historic parallels evoke clear emotional images on the atrocities committed by the Nazi regime. This has a particularly high impact in the case of the United States, which has historically conceived its role as a spearhead for the persecution of war crimes during World War II and as a distinctive counterpart to human rights-violating regimes. The Center for Justice and Accountability (2010) states that "[f]ollowing the horrors of WWII, the United States championed the rights of prisoners of war as well as the rights of civilians during hostilities," specifically naming the leading role of United States in the implementation of the Geneva Convention. It contrasts this historical precedent with current practices, stating that "the United States' lead role in opposing torture ended as it began psychologically and physically tormenting detainees following the attacks of September 11, 2001."

The reaction of the US government to torture allegations has been twofold. Initially, the Bush administration attempted to legitimise the interrogation practices in question as not falling under the definition of torture. Thereby, the administration principally acknowledged the salience of the anti-torture norm in the broader framework of internationally recognised norms but declined that the specific interrogation practices used would fall in this category. Then-secretary of defense Donald Rumsfeld's statements on the incidents in Abu Ghraib are a case in point: He emphasised that "[w]hat has been charged so far is abuse, which I believe technically is different from torture … I'm not going to address the 'torture' word" (Hochschild 2004). This statement also demonstrates a second type of reaction to *shaming* attempts, namely excuses in the sense that torture incidents were framed as being unsystematic, isolated events being perpetrated by few individuals. It is important to note that the administration has indeed not shied away from acknowledging that the criticised incidents are generally perceived as *shameful* events. For example, President George W. Bush stated that "[u]nder the dictator [Saddam Hussein] prisons like Abu Ghraib were symbols of death and torture. That same prison became a symbol of disgraceful conduct by a few American troops who dishonored our country and disregarded our values" (New York Times 2004). Although the recurrence of emotions and a normative value system becomes apparent, the statement conveys the message that torture occurred systematically under the former Iraqi regime, whereas the human rights violations by American soldiers – albeit indeed being shameful – have been restricted to a small circle of individual perpetrators. In a similar vein, the Taguba report from 2004, which was launched to investigate the torture accusations, came to the conclusion that the occurrence of "numerous incidents of sadistic, blatant, and wanton criminal abuses [that] were inflicted on several detainees. This systemic and illegal abuse of detainees was intentionally perpetrated by several members of the military police guard force" (Taguba 2004). These examples corroborate the assumption that *shaming* attempts by international human rights organisations failed to yield collectively felt emotions of shame that pointed to the whole administration's liability.

The question of assuming responsibility for human rights violations thus appears to be of central importance. In the case of the US reaction to the torture allegations, we did see policy changes reflecting what the literature describes as *tactical concessions*. For example, after initially failing to redefine the concept of torture by declining the inclusion of the interrogation techniques under question, the Bush administration issued a principled condemnation of torture in a memorandum by the US Department of Justice (2004). Most prominently, the subsequent Obama administration banned the CIA interrogation techniques entirely and promised to close Guantanamo within a year after the new administration's assumption of office. Although these concessions may be interpreted as a shift towards the prescriptive status of the norm, both the Bush and Obama administrations circumvented the question of accountability and thereby showed a behaviour that was still at odds with their self-image as a guarantee power for human rights. Even in the longer run, a condemnation of the so-called enhanced interrogation techniques did not become universally shared in the sense that any attempt to legitimise this practice would lead to a strong emotional response (i.e., shaming). As a prominent example, then-presidential candidate Trump's remarks to "bring back a hell lot worse than waterboarding" (McCarthy 2016) were not met with a backlash to the degree that it became a significant issue in the run-up to the elections. The fact that this statement did not lead to a public outcry – a lack of a negative feedback loop – points to a further norm erosion (see also Winston, Chapter 9).

The example shows that the reason why the shaming attempts failed to bring about a renewed commitment to norm compliance was not because the norm itself was contested. We do in fact see that the US government reiterated the incompatibility of torture with human rights norms in general. However, the specific events that were deemed violations of the norm by human rights advocates failed to evoke emotional resonance on part of the target country – in this case the United States. The absence of this emotional resonance was reflected in a missing evaluation of the specific behaviour as not congruent with the norm's expectations. The administration's concern lay rather with the attempt to downplay the extent of the abuses to only a small circle and protect the personnel involved from legal persecution (Sikkink 2013). Therefore, there was no emotional resonance to the *naming and shaming* campaign.

Conclusion

In this contribution, we pointed to the significance of emotional resonance for explaining why actors sometimes comply with international norms, and sometimes not. We argued that we are more likely to see norm compliance if the respective norms evoke shared images, memories, and collective emotions among international actors. In those instances where norms fail to emotionally resonate, we expected non-compliance. Furthermore, we stated that the degree to which states are susceptible to emotional resonance or capable of withstanding emotional appeals hinges strongly on their relative status within the international system. We illustrated the salience of emotional resonance with regard to naming and shaming, a frequently used practice in international human rights enforcement to exert pressure on norm-violating states. We closed with the example of the US government's reaction to torture allegations in the course of the 'War on Terror'.

In line with the broader objective of this edited volume, our findings offer further implications for studying norm contestation. The current challenges to the global liberal order underline how much liberal international norms depend on emotional resonance. The inconclusive findings in the norms literature on the effectiveness of naming and shaming should thus not necessarily be seen as actual absence of evidence but may rather reflect a too narrow conception that fails to take the centrality of the emotionalisation process into account. We seek to push the theoretical agenda of norm research further by not taking emotions for granted but instead explicating their role within norm processes. Our findings suggest that when liberal norms lose their emotional resonance and are not adequately complied with by states assuming higher status, the liberal normative order may be threatened with being undermined in the long run as well.

7 Advancing Rights through an Accountability Norm?

The Case of Multilateral Development Banks

Susan Park

Introduction

In 2015, UN Special Rapporteur on Extreme Poverty Philip Alston stated that the World Bank treats "human rights more like an infectious disease than universal values and obligations" because of its understanding of what constitutes political interference outlined in its Articles of Agreement or constitution (UN 2015: 20, para 68). As a 'focal institution' in the development finance regime complex (Fioretos and Held 2019), the World Bank's interpretation has been replicated by the other Multilateral Development Banks (MDBs; Bratton 2016). It has also shaped how activists have tried to hold the banks to account for international human and environmental rights abuses separate from, and sometimes in addition to, legal processes. This chapter examines how the international accountability norm emerged through a process of contestation between activists and the World Bank before spreading throughout the regime complex to be taken as given for development finance. Such a norm emerged separate from international human rights and environmental elemental regimes with international laws at their apex. It then documents how activists engage in proactive contestation over procedural human and environmental rights with the banks to advance the norm (see Wiener 2018: ch. 1) with implications for the banks' culpability. This is a clear case of proactive contestation because activists continue to contest the norm to improve it. Although there is an increasing recognition of some rights such as free, prior, and informed consent and labour, the banks continue to view these as internal standards not legal obligations. The chapter then examines whether the implementation of the international accountability norm needs to be backed by hard law to be enforced, given legal claims as to the banks' role in human and environmental rights abuses.

This chapter proceeds in five parts. The first section outlines how the World Bank has refused to engage in responding to human rights and environmental conventions using its apolitical mandate as a defence for inaction despite increasing legal scrutiny of their contribution to environmental and social harm. It is original in seeking to bring together the legal status and obligations of the MDBs with norms research, particularly pertaining to human rights and the environment. The second section then examines how activists demanded compliance with the bank's internal social and environmental standards, which led to a 'policy norm' of accountability distinct from legal obligations evident in elemental human rights and environmental regimes.[1] The third section identifies the international laws and elemental regimes that exist to uphold human rights and protections for the environment. Section four then analyses the increasing convergence in the development finance regime complex of social and environmental standards that the MBDs are accountable for meeting. The final section concludes with an examination of whether the implementation of the international accountability norm needs to be backed by international law to ensure norm compliance in development finance.

MDB Immunity

The World Bank sits atop the apex of the development finance regime complex, comprising an increasing number of multilateral development finance institutions (Kellerman 2019; Faure et al. 2015). A regime complex is a "set of international institutions that operate in common issue area and the mechanisms that coordinate them" (Henning 2017: 19). MDBs such as the World Bank, International Finance Corporation (IFC), the African, Asian and Inter-American Development Banks, and the European Bank for Reconstruction and Development, are multilateral vehicles for donor states to channel international development assistance to developing states (OECD 2018).[2] The MDBs are similarly structured international organisations (IOs) with legal immunity operating to provide

[1] A policy norm is distinct from legal instruments in that it refers to "shared expectations for all relevant actors within a community about what constitutes appropriate behaviour, which is encapsulated in (Fund or Bank) policy" (Park and Vetterlein 2010: 3).

[2] Over the last decade there has been a push for 'One World Bank Group' to harness and synergise the activities of the International Bank for Reconstruction and Development (IBRD), the International Development Association (IDA), the International Finance Corporation (IFC), the Multilateral Investment Guarantee Agency (MIGA), and the International Centre for the Settlement of Investment Disputes (ICSID). However, in the 1990s when activists pushed to hold these institutions accountable there was a sharp delineation made by member states that an accountability mechanism should only cover the IBRD and IDA (the World Bank). The primary basis for the World Bank Group (IFC and MIGA) to have an international accountability mechanism was from transnational campaigns against the IFC (see Park 2010). ICSID is an arbitration body and is therefore excluded.

international financing and technical services to borrower member states in order to promote economic growth through project and programme financing, investments, and guarantees. As functionally similar IOs within the development finance regime complex, they tend to follow the norms, organising principles, and standards of the World Bank (see Orchard and Wiener, Chapter 1; on norm complexes, see Winston, Chapter 9).

While a source of vital credit and technical assistance for states, MDB actions can impact on human rights in three ways: violating human rights directly or indirectly through the projects and programmes they finance (through, e.g., loss of lives, livelihood, and land; or contributing to increased economic hardship and inequality); lending to governments who engage in human rights violations; and failing to uphold or promote human rights in their lending practices (Sarfaty 2012: 2). Development projects may also contribute to dramatic and irreparable damage to local ecosystems and the crossing of known ecological system boundaries globally, such as climate change, habitat loss, and species extinction (Lenton et al. 2019), despite the proliferation of international environmental agreements that states have established to counter such trends (Mitchell 2002–19). This is done primarily but not exclusively through project loans for infrastructure and natural resource extraction. The impact of international development financing is important not only because the MDBs' development mission is often couched in improving the plight of the poor (Weaver 2007), but also because the of broader considerations of not contributing to environmental harm and doing good (Wade 1997); both are now captured in the United Nations Sustainable Development Goals.

The following discussion situates the MDBs in international law and people's right to remedy for the violation of human rights and environmental procedural rights that result from development financing. Environmental procedural rights refer to having access to information regarding decisions that affect people's environment, being able to participate in decisions affecting their environment, and having access to justice in environmental matters. The World Bank, which the other MDBs emulate, has argued that human rights are beyond its technical apolitical mandate as outlined in its Articles of Agreement, which prohibits political interference in its member states (Article IV, section 10), especially pertaining to its lending decisions (Article III, section 5(b), see Sarfaty 2012: 3). Until recently, the MDBs have also ignored being beholden to international environmental agreements, which are signed and ratified by their member states.[3] Instead, the MDBs have established internal

[3] The World Bank's Environmental and Social Framework (2016, operationalised from 2018) now includes the statement that its borrowers must take "into account in an

standards such as social and environmental safeguard policies to protect people and limit their environmental impact in development project areas (Mares 2019; Park 2020).

The MDBs rely on their immunity as IOs in order not to become embroiled in human rights and environmental disputes (Wellens 2002). However, the legal basis IO immunity is not as clear as might be assumed. States have both absolute sovereign immunity (*acta jure imperii*) and restricted immunity pertaining to foreign commerce (*acta jure gestionis*) under customary international law. There are questions as to whether IO immunity refers to the treaty establishing the organisation, which pertains to meeting the functional requirements for undertaking its activities (and located at its headquarters), or whether contingent or restricted immunity exists in relation to the IO's commercial acts. While there have been different domestic legal cases accepting or rejecting the absolute immunity of IOs, US cases involving the MDBs have upheld the absolute immunity of these IOs based on functional necessity (Ringaert 2010: 123, 129).

This changed in February 2019, when the United States Supreme Court ruled that the IFC, the private lender and investor component of the World Bank Group, had only limited immunity in the *Jam v. International Finance Corporation* case. The basis for immunity was to protect IOs from the interference of member states in their operations (Bradlow 2019).[4] The supreme court ruled that there were limits to IO immunity, in the same way that states have limited immunity (*Jam v. IFC* 2019). The ruling was made considering environmental protections and human rights that exist to check states prerogatives. Opening the World Bank Group to legal claims thus expanded access to the process of contestation directly to those affected by its actions. The activities of IOs are increasingly recognised for impinging on human rights and the environment. In the *Jam v. IFC* case, local farmers and fishers in Gujarat, India, the area of the Tata Mundra power plant financed by the IFC, challenged the immunity of the IFC through the US courts given the air, water, and land pollution stemming from the plant. IFC was ruled to have restricted immunity in this case. The case not only has ramifications for the IFC but the development finance

appropriate manner all issues relevant to the project, including … obligations of the country directly applicable to the project under relevant international treaties and agreements" (World Bank 2017: 19).

[4] There are other recent legal challenges to the World Bank Group, see also *Juana Doe et al. v. IFC et al.*, US District Court for the District of Columbia, Case No. 1:2017cv00363 (9 March 2017); and *Zhan v. World Bank*, No. 1:19-CV-01973, 2019 WL 6173529 (20 November 2019) (Darrow 2021).

regime complex because all the MDBs have engaged in similar lending with consequences for people and place (Park 2020).

The *Jam v. IFC* case opens the door to discussions as to whether immunity should be further restricted if an effective remedy is not offered by the IO, where immunity precludes remedy by a court (Ringaert 2010: 132). While IO immunity is currently being debated on the merits of people employed by the IO having access to remedy, scholars have questioned the threshold for the provision of remedy for those outside the IO who are affected by its activities. For example, research on human rights abuses by United Nations (UN) peacekeepers recognise the locus of responsibility and recourse for those affected by peacekeepers lies with the troop-contributing member state (Wills 2013), which makes prosecution difficult (Odello and Burke 2016).[5] However, there has been a push to open UN peacekeepers to prosecution by the International Criminal Court (Vezine 2012), highlighting the need for further consideration of how immunity limits the right of remedy for people affected by the acts or omissions of IOs such as the MDBs.

The Accountability Norm for Upholding MDB Standards

Beyond domestic legal protections, people whose rights have been abused because of an MDB-financed project now have access to processes known as 'citizen driven accountability mechanisms'. These emerged from the critical engagement of affected stakeholders (Lewis 2012; McIntyre and Nanwani 2020).[6] Provided for by the MDBs, these international accountability mechanisms constitute a norm of accountability in that they seek to provide recourse for environmentally and socially damaging behaviour through a formal sanctioning process (Park 2022).[7] This section details how the international accountability norm emerged through a process of contestation in

[5] UN Security Council Resolution 2272 also gives the secretary general powers to repatriate and replace national contingents if states fail to hold their peacekeepers accountable (Whalen 2017).

[6] Some of the international accountability mechanisms preclude access to justice if people are engaged in domestic legal processes against the executing agent or the government or corporation undertaking the project with MDB financing (Park 2020).

[7] The formal sanctioning process refers to the IAMs ability to determine whether a bank's actions have been compliant with its environmental and social standards and whether this contributed to harm, which then enables member states to impose sanctions should those responsibilities have not been met (such as cancelling the loan, requiring remedial action to address the harm, or stopping any future lending in that sector, such as for palm-oil).

order to hold the MDBs to account for their environmental and social impacts. Pressure from transnational advocacy networks, backed by the United States, began with the World Bank, and then cascaded to the rest of the MDBs.

From the early 1980s, a process of proactive contestation emerged against the World Bank's environmental and social impacts. Through direct and indirect means, activists were able to gain access to the norm contestation process.[8] Activists coalesced into a transnational advocacy network primarily comprising US environmental NGOs: the Natural Resources Defense Council (NRDC), the Environment Defense Fund (EDF, now Environment Defense), Environment Policy Institute (EPI, now Friends of the Earth – US), National Wildlife Federation (NWF), International Rivers Network (IRN), and the Sierra Club (Gutner 2002: 55; Keck and Sikkink 1998). Strategic information and support was later provided by the Bank Information Center (BIC). These environmental NGOs worked with activists in project-affected areas to create transnational campaigns. This included against the Polonoroeste road project in the Brazilian Amazon, the Indonesian transmigration plan, and the Narmada Dam in India among others (Rich 1994).[9] Various actors constituted the network: local social movements, NGOs, members of IOs, members of government, the media, the academy, foundations, churches, trade unions, and consumer organisations. They were driven to challenge the World Bank, using 'boomerang politics' to directly pressure powerful World Bank shareholders such as the United States, Western European states, and Japan (Keck and Sikkink 1998: 12–14). These powerful shareholders in turn placed pressure on the World Bank (Lavelle 2011; Babb 2009) to stop the harm in the state undertaking the project. The dual aim of the network was therefore to stop harmful practices at development project sites in the Global South, while demanding policy improvements at the World Bank to prevent future occurrences (Wade 1997).

In response, it would take over a decade for the World Bank to agree to establish or improve specific environmental and social standards such as protecting Indigenous Peoples and using environmental assessments (see later). Taking proactive contestation further, in the 1990s, activists would then demand greater World Bank transparency and accountability (Blanton 2007; Clark et al. 2003) to ensure that these protection standards were being enforced (Table 7.1). The first accountability mechanism created was the World Bank Inspection Panel in 1994. Transnational advocacy networks pushed hard for such a mechanism

[8] This section unless otherwise stated is from Park (2010).

[9] Numerous bank projects aroused controversy at the time (Wade 1997: 637–57).

Table 7.1 *The MDBs and their accountability mechanisms*

MDB	The Accountability Mechanism
World Bank	Inspection Panel 1994; clarified 1996, 1999. Updated 2021
Inter-American Development Bank	Independent Investigation Mechanism (IIM) 1994–2009. Replaced in 2010 with the Independent Consultation and Investigation Mechanism (known as MICI from its Spanish acronym).
Asian Development Bank	Inspection Function 1995–2002. Replaced with the Accountability Mechanism in 2003.
World Bank Group (IFC/MIGA)	Compliance Advisor/Ombudsman (CAO) 1999
European Bank for Reconstruction and Development	Independent Recourse Mechanism (IRM) 2003–8. Replaced by the Project Complaint Mechanism (PCM) in 2009. Superseded by the Independent Project Accountability Mechanism (IPAM) in 2020.
African Development Bank	Independent Review Mechanism (IRM) 2004

using persuasion, social influence, and coercion (Park 2010). They provided evidence of environmental and social harm from the Narmada dam scheme in India to demand a mechanism to provide recourse to affected people (Udall 1997). The United States backed their demands and worked with activists to create the template for the Inspection Panel. The United States then threatened to withhold replenishment funds for the bank's soft-loan facility, the International Development Association (IDA), until such a mechanism was created. The World Bank board was split between developed and developing states over allowing people the right to air their grievances about development projects in their territory. Despite the controversy, the United States was able to broker a consensus on the need for such a mechanism (Fox 2000).

The Inspection Panel provides recourse for people harmed by World Bank-financed development projects (Clark et al. 2003). From 1994, the World Bank's Inspection Panel aimed to ensure the bank was held to account for meeting its protection standards.[10] People affected by a project financed by the World Bank could submit a claim to the Inspection Panel, who would then investigate if the harm resulted from the bank's compliance with its environmental and social safeguard policies. For

[10] The safeguard policies were: Environmental Assessment, Natural Habitats, Pest Management, Involuntary Resettlement, Indigenous People, Forests, Safety of Dams, Cultural Property, and Projects on International Waterways (Park 2020).

example, the Inspection Panel's very first investigation found that the World Bank had not met its own policies on Environmental Assessment, Involuntary Resettlement, and Indigenous Peoples in relation to the Arun III hydroelectric project in Nepal (Park 2010). The controversy led then-president of the World Bank James Wolfensohn to cancel the loan.

The United States would then become a norm entrepreneur, seeking to spread the norm to the rest of the MDBs. It used financial threats, incentives, persuasion, and its vote on the banks' boards to diffuse the accountability norm. Over a ten-year period, the Inter-American, Asian, and African Development Banks, the European Bank for Reconstruction and Development, and the World Bank Group would establish what would become known collectively as independent accountability mechanisms (IAMs, see Table 7.1, Park 2017). The accountability norm also spread beyond the US-dominated MDBs to be taken up by the new Chinese-led Asian Infrastructure Investment Bank (AIIB) (AIIB 2018), as well as by sub-regional development banks, bilateral development agencies, and private sector development financiers (Hujistee et al. 2016).[11]

The accountability norm therefore provides a formal mechanism for people to have their grievances heard because of a failure by banks to uphold their environmental and social protection standards. Owing to the structure of the MDBs, the norm is about the provision of recourse for environmental and social harms, not remedy. The provision of a remedy for harm lies with the management of the banks (the president and senior staff) and the Board of Executive Directors (member states) who oversee a bank's operations (Naude Fourie 2012). This creates an extra step in the provision of remedy. There are well-recognised failures in board oversight of bank management (Woods and Lombardi 2006), and where bank management has resisted being held to account for its actions (Naude Fourie 2012). The evolution of the accountability norm through proactive contestation raises questions as to how formal recourse processes fits within existing robust human rights and environmental elemental regimes in international relations.

Elemental Rights Regimes: Where Do the MDBs Fit?

While the accountability norm does provide some means of redress for people harmed by MDB-financed projects (Park 2020), the accountability mechanisms were not established to provide remedy nor were

[11] The take up of similarly styled IAMs by other development finance lenders indicates that the norm was widely accepted as requiring a specific style of mechanism although they vary in their details.

they given a mandate to determine if people were better off after seeking recourse. Indeed, there has been little investigation of the impact of the norm for improving people's plight. In one analysis it was revealed that little had changed at the project site after two World Bank Inspection Panel investigations in Brazil (Rodrigues 2003). However, the 2019 *Jam v. IFC* case has jolted the MDBs because it directly challenges their immunity in undertaking activities that abuse human rights and environmental procedural rights. The MDBs have been reticent in accepting obligations in recognising the rights of people (Braaten 2016; Naude Fourie 2012) and the impact of their activities on nature (Wade 1997; Park 2010). Scholars posit that the World Bank and the MDBs should be subject to human rights obligations under international law (Braaten 2016; Skogly 2001; Darrow 2003). This section details the elemental human rights and environmental procedural rights regimes to demonstrate how the accountability compares.

Failure of the World Bank and the MDBs to engage with human rights is evident in three ways: not having a policy to ensure staff mitigate the impacts of development projects and programmes on human rights; a failure to consider borrower member states international legal obligations when drafting country assistance strategies; and establishing guidelines to respond to situations when human rights standards have been violated (Sarfaty 2012: 2). Arguably, the MDBs should also be subject to environmental procedural law (access to information, the ability to participate in environmental matters that affect them, and access to justice for environmental matters), which are increasingly under threat from development under conditions of hyperglobalisation (Butt et al. 2019). Instead, the World Bank and the MDBs have established internal standards, or 'safeguard policies' that detail specific protections (Mares 2019; Park 2020). Many of these protections are non-binding although some argue that the World Bank's standards constitute global administrative law (Kingsbury et al. 2005).

The accountability norm in the development finance regime complex crosses two elemental regimes: the International Human Rights Regime and regional agreements that protect environmental procedural rights. An elemental regime is "an international institution, based on explicit agreement, that reflects agreed principles and norms and codifies explicit rules and decision-making procedures" (Raustiala and Victor 2004: 283). The locus for the International Human Rights Regime is the UN, whose founding principle is to encourage "respect for human rights and for fundamental freedoms for all" (UN 1948: Article I (3)). Human rights are promoted primarily through the Human Rights Council and the Office of the High Commissioner for Human Rights, and are protected through the International Criminal Court. Human rights, include but are not limited to the following: the right to life, liberty, work, social security, and freedom of privacy, thought, expression, and association (see the UN 1948). The UN is host to ten major human rights treaties and their secretariats. Regional bodies including courts also aim to ensure the protection of these rights.

The UN also has a Declaration on the Rights of Indigenous Peoples (UNDRIP). The declaration details that states should consult with Indigenous Peoples in managing resources including that no forcible relocation can occur without their Free, Prior, and Informed Consent; that Indigenous Peoples have rights to their traditional lands; and that they have the right to redress and to just, fair, and equitable treatment if their land has been taken without Free, Prior, and Informed Consent (Schrijver 2010: 72). Protections for human rights are upheld by states at the national level, through regional human rights bodies, and the UN treaties. Legal processes such as international courts and tribunals have increased in number (Alter 2014). Other IOs are also involved in adjudicating disputes over natural resources such as the International Court of Justice, and environmental and human health risks, such as the World Trade Organization's Dispute Settlement Mechanism (Foster 2011; Peel 2010).

Of relevance to the MDBs is the increasing human rights work being done by the UN in relation to business.[12] In 2011, the UN Human Rights Council endorsed the Guiding Principles for Business and Human Rights in relation to Human Rights and Transnational Corporations and other Business Enterprises. The principles are drawn from international customary laws and convention: the Universal Declaration of Human Rights (UDHR), the International Labour Organization's (ILO) Declaration on Fundamental Principles and Rights at Work, the Rio Declaration on Environment and Development, and the United Nations Convention Against Corruption. There are three UN Guiding Principles: to protect, respect, and remedy human rights abuses. The first stipulates that states have responsibilities to protect against human rights abuses by business enterprises. Second, corporations have responsibilities to respect human rights and address any human rights impacts of their activities. Third, both states and corporations should provide access to remedies when human rights are breached. State institutions for the provision of remedies may include: the courts, tribunals, Ombuds processes, and National Contact Points under the Guidelines for Multinational Enterprises of the Organisation

[12] This section, unless otherwise stated, is from Park (2020).

for Economic Co-operation and Development. A UN report into how business met their provision of access to remedy through activating non-judicial grievance mechanisms highlighted a lack of transparency and therefore data on their efficacy (Zagelmeyer et al. 2018; see also Lukas et al. 2016).

The protection of environmental procedural rights is more specific than those outlined in the UDHR and are not explicitly covered by the UN Guiding Principles (Park 2020). The idea that individuals and communities have rights to their environment appeared in the 1972 Stockholm Declaration (Principle 1), 1992 Rio Declaration (Principle 10), Agenda 21, and in the 1987 World Commission on Environment and Development report. Rio specifically "formulated the link between human rights and environmental protection in … procedural terms" including participation, access to information, and access to redress and remedy. Such procedural rights are beginning to be incorporated into international environmental agreements (Ognibene and Kariuki 2019: 176–7). However, procedural environmental rights are rarely codified on their own in international environmental law (Conca 2015: 74–5). Two exceptions to this are regional UN conventions. These are: the 1998 Convention to on Access to Information, Public Participation in Decision-Making, and Access to Justice in Environmental Matters, which is housed under the United Nations Economic Commission for Europe (the Aarhus Convention, Mason 2005); and the 2018 Escazú Agreement, a binding regional treaty for Latin America by the United Nations Economic Commission for Latin America and the Caribbean. Currently there are 47 parties to the Aarhus Convention, with states agreeing to provide their publics with these rights, while the Escazú Agreement entered into force in April 2021 with 24 signatories and 12 parties. International environmental agreements, the regional conventions, and the Declaration relate to how states should advance procedural environmental rights for their citizens. In 2018 the UN Special Rapporteur on Human Rights and the Environment reinforced the need for states to protect these rights (UN 2018). In contrast, the accountability norm within the development finance regime complex provides for access to justice in environmental matters through the accountability mechanisms of the MDBs.

The Merging of Global Standards

Given their immunity and apolitical mandates, it is not surprising that the World Bank and the MDBs do not have a comprehensive human rights policy (Sarfaty 2009; Fujita 2013). The MDBs resist discussing social protection standards as human rights on the basis that their Articles of Agreement preclude political interference in their member states activities (Clapham 2006). This is despite criticism that they are subject to human rights obligations under international law (Darrow 2003), and the identification of the harm World Bank policies can have (Abouharb and Cingranelli 2007). Nonetheless, specific human rights pertaining to Involuntary Resettlement and Indigenous Rights are included in the safeguards, and the World Bank Inspection Panel has specifically identified upholding them as a means of protecting human rights (Inspection Panel 2009). Meanwhile, procedural environmental rights, while not framed as rights, emerged over time in the World Bank and other development lenders' safeguard standards: access to information is provided for in the form of information disclosure policies from the 1990s. Access to participation is referenced in relation to meaningful consultation in Environmental Assessment policies, as well as in specific policies on poverty reduction, gender dimensions of development, as well as Involuntary Resettlement, Indigenous People (World Bank 1993: Annex I), and the later incorporation of Free, Prior, and Informed Consent. Access to justice in environmental matters is evident in the emergence of the accountability norm from 1994 onwards.

These protection standards first arose after the 1972 UN Conference on the Human Environment. The World Bank's policies expanded from the 1980s as the transnational environmental campaigns discussed earlier emerged to reveal how its development projects contributed to environmental and human harm (Clark et al. 2003; Fox and Brown 1998); as the 1987 Bruntland Report was published; and in preparation for the UN Conference on Environment and Development in 1992. By the late 1990s, the World Bank had a suite of safeguard policies in place (see footnote 7). Environmental Assessment (EA) is the overarching policy for the remaining environmental and social policies because it assesses the extent to which a project requires oversight. Each project goes through a screening process to determine the type and depth of EA required, and which of the safeguards apply. The application of the EA in the World Bank depends on whether the project is classified as a high environmental and social risk (category A), less risky (B), no risk (C), or pertaining to a project undertaken by a financial intermediary (FI). These operational policies are incorporated into borrowers' project loan agreements where required. The standards were institutionalised within the World Bank through the project cycle (the main vehicle for project lending) backed by monitoring and evaluation procedures.

The World Bank first developed specific policies, guidelines, and procedures to protect people and the environment whilst financing international development projects. All World Bank practices were governed by the organisation's internal operational policies (OPs) which were derived, where relevant, from the Bank's Articles of Agreement.[13] The operational policies cover activities including its business products, lending instruments, information disclosure, and social and environmental protection measures. Specific standards evolved over time for ensuring information is available and that people can participate in development projects affecting them, along with protecting Indigenous Peoples, and stopping the forcible movement of people. The safeguards are recognised benchmarks for how to mitigate negative environmental and social impacts by the World Bank, by its borrowers and contractors, and by other MDBs including the World Bank Group. This means that most of the international development financiers follow similar policies when considering the need to move people, or whether Indigenous Peoples will be affected, or whether local biodiversity will be irreparably harmed, when devising development projects such as dams, mines, railways, and roads. Moreover, the other MDBs standards revert to the more detailed World Bank standards where gaps remain.

A process of interpretive contestation took place from the early 2000s as the IFC tried to better incorporate the standards into private sector operations. From 2003 the IFC translated the standards from the World Bank into the Equator Principles for private sector financiers to manage their environmental and social risk in international project finance (Hunter 2008: 450). In 2006, the IFC then reworked its safeguard policies into a Sustainability Framework with performance standards. This translated external policies to hold the companies it lends and invests in to account, into an internal risk management framework for companies to use themselves (Wright 2007). This led IFC to include labour protections for the first time. IFC's most recent performance standards recognise that business must respect human rights in accordance with the UN Guiding Principles, and explicitly adopted Free, Prior, and Informed Consent for Indigenous Peoples in accordance with UNDRIP (IFC 2012: 5, 22; Razzaque 2019: 204). IFC has explicitly stated that human rights can be addressed through its environmental and social standards (IFC 2012b: 1; Mares 2019: 523).

After years of deliberation, in 2016 the World Bank established an Environmental and Social Framework (ESF) which came into effect

[13] In the World Bank these are now called Environmental and Social Standards (ESS) and Environmental Performance Standards within IFC and the EBRD.

in 2018. The ESF, like the IFC's Sustainability Framework, seeks to provide a risk management framework for borrower states to ensure their ownership over development. As noted previously, the ESF distinctly places the responsibility for meeting international environmental agreements with the borrower, while realising their human rights commitments (World Bank 2017: 7). The ESF was mandated by the bank's board to increase their coverage and harmonisation across the World Bank Group, to improve supervision and monitoring, and to "improve accountability and grievance redress systems and instruments" (World Bank 2017). NGOs have countered this by arguing the ESF has loopholes that allow the bank to avoid environmental and social protections (CIEL 2016), which may enable more opposition from bank management and borrowers to the Inspection Panel (Passoni et al. 2016).

What is noticeable is a trend towards recognising previously denied rights by the MDBs such as Free, Prior, and Informed Consent and labour protections: the World Bank has flagged its objective to respect human rights, including the adoption of Free, Prior, and Informed Consent in the ESF in 2016 in relation to Indigenous Peoples (World Bank, 2017: 76). This means that Indigenous People must consent for their land to be used for development projects. Previously it had only required borrowers to "engage in a process of free, prior, and informed *consultation*" (Razzaque 2019: 205; World Bank OP4.10, emphasis added). The World Bank (2017), IFC (2012), the Equator Principles (2013), and UNDRIP now align on Free, Prior, and Informed Consent (Mares 2019: 521).[14] Both the IFC (2006, 2012) and the World Bank (2017) also now include labour standards, as does the African Development Bank and the European Bank for Reconstruction and Development. The inclusion of Free, Prior, and Informed Consent and labour standards paves the way for a further recognition of these protections as rights backed by international law.

Upholding Global Norms: Do They Need to Be Codified?

The accountability norm provides access to a non-judicial means for recourse for the MDBs protection standards compared with access to legally mandated remedies. While the independent accountability mechanisms can document MDBs compliance with their protection standards when investigating a claim, they are unable to ensure a remedy. Over time the norm has strengthened with the independent accountability mechanisms becoming more independent in undertaking

[14] The OECD also follows Free, Prior, and Informed Consent (OECD 2017).

their investigations, gaining more power to make recommendations to address the harm not just findings of non-compliance, and being given monitoring powers by member state shareholders to ensure that bank management is rectifying the harm (Park 2022). We have evidence that the MDBs are found non-compliant primarily in relation to their Environmental Assessment, Involuntary Resettlement policies, and for their failure to disclose information (both human rights and procedural environmental rights).[15] The independent accountability mechanisms also undertake direct mediation to address the grievance, but only 18.2 per cent of those accepted for mediation lead to an agreement among the parties to address the problem (Park 2020: 49). Mediation processes highlight the issue of attempting to reconcile objective human rights to the subjective preferences of the parties in remediation (Thompson 2017). Overarchingly, we therefore do not know whether people are better off after accessing the provision for recourse.

This has implications for the accountability norm. Activists engaged in proactive contestation to change the MDBs policies to prevent harm. The emergence and strengthening of the norm highlights that they have been successful in having environmental and social standards backstopped by the independent accountability mechanisms. Yet this does not provide assurance that people have access to remedy, which lies with the banks' member states and management. There is little evidence to suggest that the independent accountability mechanisms are shaping the operations of the MDBs to reduce human rights and environmental procedural rights from being transgressed (Park 2022).

Do we therefore need international law to enforce remedies for human rights abuses and the failure to ensure environmental procedural rights in development finance? This goes beyond the limits of the accountability norm. On the one hand, legal protections can be enforced, while norms rely on the MDBs do the right thing. The MDBs are concerned that legal cases like *Jam v. IFC* limit their immunity for their operations and make them liable for human rights abuses and environmental devastation. This has direct implications for the accountability norm, because in the *Jam v. IFC* case litigants relied on the findings of the IFC's independent accountability mechanism that documented IFC's policy non-compliance contributing to harm (IFC 2020). This raised fears that member states and bank management would support the curtailing of the independent accountability mechanisms to prevent such findings being used in legal claims.

[15] The independent accountability mechanisms are only now beginning to document the actions of bank management in becoming compliant. Whether this constitutes an effective remedy has not been examined.

The Office of the High Commissioner for Human Rights has identified the need to ensure that states and corporations meet international standards for remedy as outlined by the UN Guiding Principles (Zagelmeyer et al. 2018) and identified how the MDBs could provide access to remedy through their operations (Darrow 2021). These recommendations go beyond the accountability norm, and they could provide a means for advancing ideas for the protection of human rights and environmental procedural rights within the MDBs. The prospect for upholding human rights and environmental procedural rights through international law is however limited (Darrow 2021; see Stimmer, Chapter 10), given the significant barriers for claimants in accessing justice, and little evidence of an appetite among member states for ensuring the MDBs meet international law. However, this accountability norm remains open to further proactive (and reactive) contestation.

Conclusion

As a 'focal institution' in the development finance regime complex, the World Bank has advocated that its apolitical mandate means that it should not engage with states over human rights or environmental impacts. This has led activists to press for specific protections through demanding both environmental and social standards, and a norm of accountability for people and their environments in development finance. Activists demanded compliance with the bank's internal social and environmental standards, which led to a norm of accountability distinct from legal obligations evident in elemental human rights and environmental regimes. This chapter documents how activists engaged in proactive contestation to create international accountability mechanisms for the MDBs as non-judicial processes with implications for the banks' culpability. However, there is an increasing convergence in the development finance regime complex of social and environmental standards the MBDs are accountable for meeting, raising questions as to how these protections can be upheld – through norm compliance for recourse or legal remedies.

8 Beyond Appropriateness

A Typology of Norm-Based Behaviour in World Politics

Sassan Gholiagha and Mitja Sienknecht

Introduction

People continued to wear masks to protect themselves and others, although current health regulations may not require such behaviour. Someone travelling by plane may use the option of offsetting CO_2, although it is not a legal requirement. A chief executive officer may ensure that the company hiring policy reflects diversity, although they are not obliged to do so. We can quickly point to norms guiding these actors' behaviour (the right to health, norms of environmental protection, norms about equal representation, respectively). While norms certainly matter, actors somewhat exceed what applicable norms in that situation require them to do.

Based on these observations, and given that actors sometimes go beyond what is required (and considered appropriate), we ask two related questions. First, how can we understand such behaviour that goes beyond appropriateness? Second, how can we understand the relationship between norms and actors' behaviour, more generally? To answer the first question, we suggest conceptualising such prima facie puzzling observation of pre-emptive or overly compliant behaviour as *responsible behaviour*. To answer the second question, we conceptualise such responsible behaviour as one configuration of different types of norm-related behaviour. Distinguishing between four ideal types – that is, appropriate, responsible, inappropriate, and irresponsible behaviour – we offer a novel typology of norm-related behaviour and illustrate its applicability to research on world politics.

Appropriate behaviour refers to situations of norm compliance where actors meet normative expectations. Responsible behaviour describes situations of norm-overfulfilment. The overfulfilment can manifest itself through a range of behaviours such as, first, actors exceeding appropriate behaviour, second, new actors displaying appropriate behaviour, or third, actors contributing to norm development. By contrast, inappropriate behaviour denotes situations where actors display norm-conflicting behaviour, either through norm violation/non-compliance or norm-underfulfilment.

And, finally, irresponsible behaviour refers to actors' non-action in situations of moral obligation. We argue that all four types constitute norm-related behaviour because all actors relate their respective behaviour to the norms which they consider as applicable in a given situation. This typology of norm-related behaviour contributes to norms research in three innovative ways for it allows us to, first, move away from a logic of appropriateness that dominated the 'first move' in norms research (compare Orchard and Wiener, Chapter 1), second, show how norms and responsibility are connected (compare also Ralph (Chapter 14), Liese (Chapter 4), and Rüland and Welsh Chapter 3), and third demonstrate how a relational understanding of responsibility can be used to study norms.

Our chapter provides insights into how norms develop following these different types of norm-related behaviour, arguing inter alia that certain types of norm-related behaviour can be linked to specific types of contestation. This argument connects our contribution to the edited volume's third argument about the 'norm-generative' effect of contestation (Orchard and Wiener, Chapter 1: 4). Furthermore, studying norm-related behaviour relates to all three moves in norms research identified in the introduction of this book (Orchard and Wiener, Chapter 1). First, our discussion of the concept of appropriateness relates to a core theme of the first move. Second, the focus on behaviour relates to the second move's central interest in norm adaptation. And third, as we illustrate later, our conceptualisation of different types of norm-related behaviour can be regarded as 'proactive and reactive contestation' which is a central element driving the third move (compare Wiener and Orchard, Chapter 15: Figure 15.1).

The remainder of this chapter is structured as follows. First, we locate our approach within the literatures on norms and responsibility in world politics (section 2). Second, we present the four types of behaviour in more detail and demonstrate how this distinction lets us fill a research gap in current norms research on the relationship between actor's behaviour and norms, and demonstrates how research on responsibility and norms can be connected in a novel way (section 3). Third, we then illustrate the added value of this distinction and conception with empirical situations (section 4). Finally, in conclusion (section 5), we outline avenues for future research and offer a reflection on our normative standpoint.

Research on Norms and Responsibility: State of the Art

We situate our approach in the broader context of norms research, following various scholars who have called for more normative theorising (Wiener 2018; Krieger and Liese 2019; Price and Sikkink 2021), and which has presented a lasting challenge to norms research (Erskine 2012; Havercroft 2018). We do this by bringing together relevant insights from the third move of norms research (Orchard and Wiener, Chapter 1: 8–12) and responsibility research (Sienknecht and Vetterlein 2022) to conceptualise behaviour that goes beyond appropriate behaviour but remains related to norms. We understand norms as shared understandings that also constitute a form of "*soft institutions*" (Orchard and Wiener, Chapter 1: 12, emphasis in original). Norms can be differentiated regarding their function (prohibitive, permissive, regulative, constitutive), their source (social or legal), or their moral reach and level of contestation (Wiener 2018: 62).

Irrespective of the type of norm, all norms entail normative expectations regarding actors' behaviour (Winston 2018: 641; Jurkovich 2020: 2–3). These normative expectations describe the "value-based" dimension of norms (Wiener 2020: 5). We assume that it is only against the backdrop of these values or normative expectations that we can assess and subsequently categorise actors' norm-related behaviour. To develop the typology of behaviour, we now discuss two core concepts from the first and second move of norms research that focuses on the behavioural dimension of norms: appropriateness and compliance. In the third section, we integrate the value-based dimension of norms. The separation of the interlinked value-based and behavioural dimension of norms reflects an analytical and not an ontological distinction.

Appropriateness and Compliance

With James March and Johan Olsen's suggestion of a logic of appropriateness that guides actors in world politics, the concept of appropriateness constitutes a central focus in norms research (March and Olsen 1989: 26). However, as Matthias Hofferberth and Christian Weber note, "[a]lthough notions of appropriateness help an actor to choose between different options, these decisions are by no means imagined as clear-cut and predictable reasoning in which unequivocal norms determine a certain behaviour" (Hofferberth and Weber 2015: 83). This observation already points to the need for actors to interpret a situation before choosing how to behave. But, of course, these interpretations vary between actors (Orchard and Wiener, Chapter 1: 15, 17).

Whether that behaviour is seen as appropriate depends on the interpretation of the situation and the norm by others. The intersubjective agreement may stem from iterated interactions between actors, which creates habitual or social validation (March and Olsen 1998; Wiener 2018: 44). What is seen as appropriate depends on shared normative expectations and an agreement on the meaning of a norm in a specific situation, that is, the norm's *meaning-in-use* (Wiener 2009). Appropriateness is, therefore, always intersubjectively constructed. But the concept of appropriateness tells us little about specifying divergent behaviour that goes beyond or below appropriateness.

Research on norm compliance offers a more nuanced understanding of what we identify as norm-related actors' behaviour by studying under which conditions and in which situations actors comply or do not comply with a norm (for a foundational work, see Chayes and Chayes 1993). More critical assessments of the compliance literature noted the need to focus on the meaning of norms and norm contestation to provide a more holistic picture of what norms are and how they work (Wiener 2004). Scholars studying compliance have also looked at legalisation as providing potentially stronger binding norms and better understanding when actors do or do not follow a prescribed behaviour (Abbott et al. 2000), with more critical assessments questioning this focus on legalisation (Finnemore 2000).

However, drawing on the logic of appropriateness and the concept of compliance does not enable scholars to conceptualise norm-related behaviour more nuancedly than to distinguish between compliance and non-compliance. To better grasp such situations, we now turn to third move norms research, looking at agency and contestation. This literature enhances our understanding of the development of norms based on actors' behaviour and their interpretation of norms.

Contestation and Agency

As Phil Orchard and Antje Wiener note, contestation "has the potential to be the primary theoretical framework through which norms are understood" (Orchard and Wiener, Chapter 1: 3). The research on contestation has questioned models of linear norm development and ideas about a fixed or fixable meaning of norms. Such scholarship is rather interested in questions about the structure of norms (Winston 2018), questions of contestation and normativity (Wiener 2018), and dynamic norm relations (Fehl 2018; Gholiagha et al. 2020). The literature on contestation tells us much about how actors interact with a norm, how a norm's meaning depends on its use (Wiener 2009), and whether actors only contest the norm's application or reject the norm more fundamentally (Deitelhoff and Zimmermann 2020). Furthermore, research that can be located within the third move has moved towards a stronger focus on the "agency of the governed" (Draude 2017; Wiener 2017a). Yet, even within such research, a research gap remains regarding "normative questions of ethics and moral *responsibility*" (Wiener 2018: 18, our emphasis). In aiming to close this gap, we turn to the literature on responsibility.

Responsibility in World Politics

Since normative shifts in world politics in the 1990s and accompanying changes in the political context, responsibility has become a reference point in many political debates and a subject of growing attention in International Relations (IR) literature (Erskine 2003b, 2008; Hansen-Magnusson and Vetterlein 2020, 2021; Sienknecht 2021a). Responsibility in norms research is commonly found in the study of specific norms. Perhaps the most well-known example is work on the Responsibility to Protect (Bellamy 2011). And there are other 'responsibility norms' such as the common but differentiated responsibility or corporate social responsibility. Wiener suggests defining these norms as "organizing principles" on the intermediary level (Wiener 2018: 62). This conceptualisation allows for distinguishing between different degrees of moral reach depending on the norm type. However, bringing in responsibility research enables us to substantiate the distinction between different forms of norm-related behaviour.

Regarding responsibility research, we build on studies that put questions about the role of responsibility and morality in global politics to the fore (Erskine 2003b; Hansen-Magnusson and Vetterlein 2020, 2021; Sienknecht and Vetterlein 2022). As no single agreed-upon definition of responsibility exists, scholars have focused on different aspects of responsibility. They have conceptualised it as a policy norm (Park and Vetterlein 2010: 4), accountability (critically Vetterlein 2018, see also Park, Chapter 7), moral agency (Erskine 2003a, 2008; Hoover 2012), capability or relationality (Bukovansky et al. 2012; Vetterlein and Hansen-Magnusson 2020: 9). Those studies have revealed the diversity of actors in world politics that can be held responsible for their actions (Erskine 2008; Mills and Karp 2015) and have focused on the constitution of responsibility of different political actors and the related practices of responsibility. Owing to its focus on actors and agency in relation to norms, such research provides a viable connection point for thinking about the responsibility dimension in norms research.

Responsibility is a relational concept constituted by the inner relations between a subject that takes responsibility for things or people (objects) on the ground of a norm (Zimmerli and Aßländer 1996; Sienknecht 2021a). *Norms* influence the behaviour of subjects (e.g., norm compliance or overfulfilment), and the subject's behaviour affects norms (e.g., reactive or proactive contestation, norm generation).[1] *Subjects* construct people and things as objects of responsibility. At the same time, subjects are also perceived as being responsible for certain objects due to the objects' importance or status; for example, oceans as the common heritage of humankind. Finally, norms 'translate' *objects* of responsibility into expectations about appropriate behaviour, while (new) responsibility objects might lead to norm generation (e.g., in the realm of new technologies).

In this chapter, responsibility is understood as a moral category for demanding and identifying responsible relationships between different (groups of) actors in the world (Vetterlein 2018: 3, see also Ralph, Chapter 14). It integrates an understanding of morality into the analysis of world politics by underlining that if an actor is capable of changing an unjust situation, even if not causally responsible for it, they are morally obliged to do so (Sienknecht and Vetterlein 2022), while also acknowledging that an actor's autonomy and capability to act responsible depends on the actor's social position and social context (Sondermann et al. 2018: 3).

In this section, we have demonstrated that norms research often focuses on behaviour with a dichotomous understanding: behaviour is appropriate or not, compliance is in place or not. But anything that defies such categorisation remains outside the conceptual reach. Second, we also demonstrated how third move constructivist research and responsibility research provide a viable pathway to include such behaviour within a norms research framework. In the following, we develop such a conceptual approach: in a first analytical step, we focus on the behavioural dimension of norms. We demonstrate that this provides us with novel insights into the normative dimension of norms, as we can infer from actors' behaviour how they understand norms and how they bring their values and beliefs in line with the behavioural requirements stipulated within the norm. In a second step, we (re-)integrate the value-based dimension of norms by connecting our behavioural focused typology with the different types of contestation (reactive, proactive, interpretive).

From Norms and Responsibility to Responsible Behaviour

In the following, we conceptualise different types of norm-related behaviour in world politics based on the distinction between responsible and appropriate behaviour. We take the relational understanding of norms

[1] This, of course, can also be phrased in terms of the dual quality of norms as "both structuring and socially constructed" (Wiener 2018: 28).

and responsibility as a starting point and carve out how the distinction between the two types of behaviour offers a pathway to understanding situations beyond (and also falling short of) appropriate behaviour. By introducing the negative foil of the two types – that is, inappropriate and irresponsible behaviour – we suggest a typology of four different types of norm-related behaviour: appropriate, inappropriate, irresponsible, and responsible. In the following, we spell out our core assumptions and conceptual suggestions regarding the distinction of behaviour in more detail.

Figure 8.1 outlines the four types of norm-related behaviour. Moreover, when actors move along the axis between appropriate and responsible behaviour, we expect more proactive contestation. In contrast, changes in actors' behaviour on the axis between irresponsible and inappropriate behaviour lead us to expect more reactive contestation of the norm. This connection between types of contestation and behaviour re-introduces the element of normativity into our typology that we had bracketed for analytical reasons in a first step. The arrows indicate that the types are co-constitutive of each other.

Appropriate behaviour: in line with existing norms research, we understand appropriate behaviour as norm-compliant behaviour of actors. We argue that an actor's behaviour is appropriate when the action of an actor is compliant with the shared understanding of the norm abiding. Let us take as an example the 'prohibition of the use of force' norm. This norm is explicated in Article 2(4) of the UN Charter and prohibits

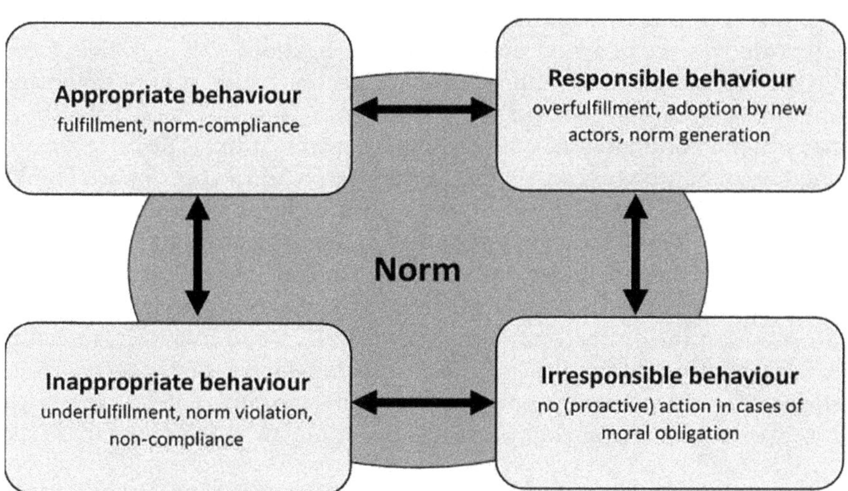

Figure 8.1 A typology of norm-related behaviour
Source: Authors

all UN member states "from the threat or use of force against the territorial integrity or political independence of any state, or in any other manner inconsistent with the purposes of the UN" (UN Charter, Article 2(4)). The charter explicitly defines which behaviour is deemed appropriate and can thus serve as a template for states to adjust their behaviour accordingly. If actors align their actions with the norm, meaning they do not use force or threat to use force against another state, the behaviour is defined as *appropriate*.

Inappropriate behaviour: we speak of inappropriate behaviour when the action of a political actor is norm conflicting. We distinguish two types of inappropriate behaviour: norm violation/non-compliance and norm-underfulfilment. An example of a norm violation would be committing mass atrocities, which violates norms in international criminal law. In cases of norm-underfulfilment, actors do not fully reach the requirements of a norm. Where this threshold lies depends on the shared understanding of what is acceptable in terms of compliance. For example, the 'Official Development Assistance' norm stipulates that states of the Global North should provide 0.7 per cent of their gross national income (GNI) as development aid for states of the Global South; in the case where states provide development aid, but less than 0.7 per cent of their GNI, we speak of norm-underfulfilment.[2] Both configurations of actors' behaviour are defined as *inappropriate*, thus, we expect to see either a reactive or interpretive contestation of the relevant norms (Orchard and Wiener, Chapter 1: 4).

Irresponsible behaviour: we talk of irresponsible behaviour when actors do not act in a situation of moral obligation, although they have the means to change an unjust situation. In this sense, it is not relevant whether there is a clear norm that stipulates the appropriate behaviour in that situation and identifies the responsible actor. What is decisive here is whether an actor who can change an unjust situation acts or not. Think, for example, about the 'rescue-at-sea-norm' that is enshrined in international law: There is "an obligation to render assistance to those in distress at sea without regard to their nationality, status or the circumstances in which they are found" (UNHCR 2015: 4). In the current situation in the Mediterranean Sea (see Liese Chapter 4), we are witnessing states pushing back migrants (ProAsyl 2013) and denying access to their ports to organisations that saved people in distress (Safety4Sea 2019). If actors do not take up action to change an unjust situation, although they can do so,

[2] Of course, whether it is a very strong or robust norm can be debated. However, actors refer to this norm when discussing whether the amount of develop aid is appropriate or not. On the question of norms strength see Michal Ben-Josef Hirsch and Jennifer M. Dixon, Chapter 2.

we speak of *irresponsible* behaviour. In doing so, we expect to see reactive contestation (Orchard and Wiener, Chapter 1: 4) of the relevant norms, objecting, for example, to the rescue-at-sea-norm or denying vessels entry to a port.

***Responsible behaviour*:** we define responsible behaviour as behaviour that goes beyond behaviour that is regarded as appropriate. The notion of going beyond appropriate behaviour reveals that we assume that norms reflect a shared understanding of appropriate behaviour. Yet, this shared understanding is neither pre-given nor fixed but context-specific and depends on actors' perception and the norms' *meaning-in-use* (Wiener 2009). When actors move towards responsible behaviour, we expect to see proactive contestations of the norms they draw on, given that in such cases, they "engage with norms in order to improve them" (Orchard and Wiener, Chapter 1: 4). Drawing on the previously introduced conceptualisation of responsibility as relational between norms, subjects, and objects, we suggest distinguishing three different configurations of responsible behaviour alongside the three responsibility dimensions.

Regarding the normative dimension, the overfulfilment of a norm is one configuration. An example of an overfulfilment is states of the Global North providing more than 0.7 per cent of their GNI as development aid to states of the Global South. Regarding the subject dimension, we identify situations in which new actors adhere to a norm who are not yet obliged to do so as another configuration of responsible behaviour. An example would be non-governmental organisations that adhere to the 'rescue-at-sea' norm because they believe that actors initially addressed by the norm violate it (e.g., push-back operations) or do not take appropriate actions (e.g., downsize or cancel rescue missions). Finally, regarding the object dimension, we identify behaviour leading to norm generation that stems from actors' convictions that a situation requires responses not expected but deemed appropriate by those actors. For example, NATO's intervention in Kosovo led to the development of the Responsibility to Protect, an example we return to later.[3] In sum, responsible behaviour either exceeds appropriate behaviour in its normative value (norm dimension), exceeds it regarding the scope of addressees (subject dimension), or leads to norm generation (object dimension).

We contend that there are many different reasons why actors choose to act responsibly. They may do so for moral reasons. They may also

[3] This example demonstrates that such behaviour can at the same time also constitute behaviour that is norm-violating, as in this case NATO violated the prohibition of the use of force.

do so because it enables them to participate in global politics and/or get recognised as legitimate actors. An example of such a rationale can be found in armed non-state actors' (ANSAs) behaviour who commit to international norms and treaties to signal their willingness to be part of a larger normative community (Sienknecht 2021b; Geis et al. 2021). Furthermore, actors may act responsibly because they have a specific self-interest. Think, for example, of pacific island states who will suffer existentially from rising sea levels sooner than anyone else. Hence, they take more proactive steps than other states and push for more robust climate protection measures in international negotiations (Carter 2021). It is not always possible to trace back an agent's rationale for acting responsibly. They may behave responsibly for different reasons and due to the general latency of intentions and ambitions. Thus, this chapter aims not to tease out actors' (hidden) motives but to offer an evaluation standard for assessing actors' behaviour.

There are several potential outcomes or possible effects of responsible behaviour. First, we argue that overfulfilment of a norm affects the norm. Concerning questions of robustness (Percy 2019; Deitelhoff and Zimmermann 2019) or strength (Ben-Josef Hirsch and Dixon, Chapter 2), it is imaginable that responsible behaviour leads to stronger and more robust norms, given that additional actors behave accordingly and contribute to the structuring role of norms. By displaying behaviour that exceeds appropriateness, a norm is strengthened. We may also observe norm change when a norm is regularly overfulfilled by a sufficient number of actors, which leads to a shift in what is deemed appropriate behaviour (akin to the development of international law through custom). Furthermore, actors may shift away from supporting a norm because other (perceived as illegitimate) actors start to support it, respectively starting to claim it for themselves; for example, governments with secessionist movements in their state territory downscale their support for ethnic minority rights. Finally, actors, by displaying responsible behaviour, may also contest the norm in question, and depending on the specific behaviour displayed, this could be conceptualised as interpretative or proactive contestation (Orchard and Wiener, Chapter 1: 4).

In sum, focusing on norms and responsibility when studying actors' behaviour allows us to identify different varieties of behaviour and assess whether they go beyond appropriateness. Responsibility research helps us to grasp the manifestations of different types of norm-related behaviour. This conceptual suggestion allows scholars to study the norm-related behaviour of actors more systematically and grasp behaviour that is more or less appropriate. Combining this with the analysis of different types of contestation, we bring the behaviour-dimension of norms together with the value-based dimension of norms. In the following section, we present in more detail what responsible behaviour entails as this type of behaviour constitutes the core of our novel contribution to both norms and responsibility literature.

Responsible Behaviour in World Politics

To assess situations of responsible behaviour, it is necessary to specify the relevant subjects, objects, and norms in each case. In order to identify responsible behaviour and distinguish it from appropriate behaviour, we zoom in on the characteristics of the respective norm. As we will demonstrate, the distinction between fundamental norms, organising principles, and standardised procedures or regulations (Wiener 2018: 62) helps us categorise the specificity of a norm, which in turn affects how easily one can determine if a behaviour goes beyond appropriateness. Another indication for responsible behaviour can be detected on the level of subjects. Thus, it is necessary to identify the relevant actors within a norm-related relationship. These actors are either addressed by a norm or influence the normative setting (e.g., contestation, norm generation). The actors can be distinguished according to their type (e.g. states or individuals) and if they are initially addressed by the norm (e.g., international human rights law initially only addressed states). Especially the latter aspect, whether the actors are initially addressed by a norm or act on their own helps us identify responsible behaviour by *new* actors. Finally, detailing the object of responsibility specifies whether there is already a norm that actors deem applicable to the situation or whether the situation requires the development of a new norm, based on moral obligations. In the remainder of this section, we provide examples for each of the three identified configurations – overfulfilment of a norm, new actors, norm generation – of responsible behaviour.

Configuration 1: Overfulfilment of a Norm

An example of an overfulfilment of a norm is the case of women's quotas. As a result of debates around gender equality, gender mainstreaming, and the need for more diversity in leadership positions in both the private and the public sector, several businesses and governments worldwide have agreed or signed up to implement women's quotas to increase the number of women in leadership positions.

On the level of fundamental norms, which are generally global, the prohibition of discrimination based on sex, codified in Article 2 of the International Covenant on Civil and Political Rights, is relevant (UN General Assembly 1966). However, whether a state acts responsibly cannot be easily ascertained. Fundamental norms, though morally unassailable, are not very specific about expected behaviour in a measurable way. In contrast, organising principles or standardised procedures *can* (and often do) entail a specific formulation of what is regarded as appropriate.

In the case of gender equality, the organising principle can be found in the *Convention on the Elimination of All Forms of Discrimination against Women* (CEDAW), which specifies gender equality in various articles and the preamble (UN General Assembly 1979). CEDAW addresses signatory states who are obliged to act in accordance and pass laws to ensure non-discrimination and strengthen gender equality. It is imaginable that states would agree, for example, on a quota for equal representation in leadership positions. Such an agreement would constitute an organising principle. In that case, a state, an international organisation, or a company could act responsibly by overfulfilling this quota compared with other states or international organisations. If there is no agreed-upon quota, the comparison on the state level would also reveal responsible behaviour; for example, when a state sets a higher quota than the average of other states. Norway, for example, has one of the highest legally enforcable quotas in Europe (Reuters 2023), making it act responsibly compared with other European states. This example demonstrates that responsible behaviour is always relational. In the absence of an internationally agreed-upon quota, we can identify responsible behaviour on the level of standardised procedures, which determines a quota for that state's public and/or private sector. If those actors then overfulfil the quota, they would be acting responsibly.

Another example of such an overfulfilment on the level of standardised procedures is the decision of the city of Paris to fill 11 of 16 leadership positions with women. In doing so, they reached a quota of 69 per cent. This would generally – and according to our approach – count as responsible behaviour. However, Paris was fined €90,000 by the ministry of civil services because the specific regulation asks that both women and men make up at least 40 per cent of leadership positions. With a quota of 69 per cent women, men were discriminated against. The mayor of Paris, Anna Hidalgo, called the decision 'irresponsible' in light of the century-old structural discrimination against women (ZEIT 2020). The rule within that law was later repealed (New York Times 2020).

Configuration 2: New Actors

An example for the second configuration of responsible behaviour, where we see new or additional actors declaring that they will behave in accordance with a norm although they may not (initially) be addressed by it, is the informal signing up of cities to the Paris Agreement on Climate Change (see Jakobi and Loges 2021 for the idea of cities as norm amplifiers). For example, the US-based Climate Mayors initiative asks its members to agree on standardised procedures such as specific emission reduction targets (Climate Mayors 2020).

Another example is the adherence of certain ANSAs to the ban on landmines, which constitutes an organising principle. Anti-personal landmines were banned in the 1997 Ottawa Convention, which entered into force on 1 March 1999. The convention obligates state parties to no longer use, produce, stockpile, or transfer anti-personal landmines (Ottawa Convention 1997). Non-state actors are neither signatories to nor bound by the convention. Nevertheless, numerous ANSAs have publicly and in written statements declared they will abide by the convention, binding themselves to the prohibition of anti-personal landmines (Geneva Call 2022), thus displaying responsible behaviour. Moreover, ANSAs have begun to commit themselves to the fundamental norm of environmental protection (McKay 2012; Somer 2015). Again, we see an increase of actors for a norm, thereby displaying responsible behaviour in an area where so far largely states and, in some cases, corporations and multi-national enterprises have been the primary addressees.

While the two illustrations of ANSA's behaviour qualify conceptually as responsible behaviour, it is necessary to stress that this conceptualisation does not mean that the actor in question is regarded as a responsible actor in general. As discussed in the previous section, the motives for actors to behave responsibly can be manifold. Thus, we do not suggest classifying an actor as responsible based on self-commitment. However, we argue to categorise such *behaviour* as responsible as it contributes to disseminating appropriate behaviour. Moreover, we argue that acting appropriately or overfulfilling appropriate behaviour is a value in itself.[4]

Configuration 3: Norm Generation

Our third configuration of responsible behaviour describes situations in which actors' behaviour leads to norm generation, that is the development of new norms for situations in which either existing norms were not

[4] It also must be noted that certain norms of international humanitarian law bind all actors involved in armed conflicts, irrespective of their status.

perceived as sufficient to provide guidance or in which actors hitherto had not agreed on a specific norm to guide their behaviour.

A good example of such a development is the 1999 intervention by NATO in Kosovo (NATO 1999). While there is little doubt that the intervention violated the prohibition of the use of force, given the absence of a UN Security Council Resolution, there have been arguments about the intervention's legitimacy (Independent International Commission on Kosovo 2000). Two things make this intervention relevant for us as an example of responsible behaviour. First, as an actor, NATO argued that fundamental norms such as preventing a potential genocide required that they intervene.[5] As Lothar Brock noted, this indicated that the conflict between fundamental norms of sovereignty and non-interference, on the one hand, and fundamental norms of mass atrocity prevention and human rights protection, on the other, came into the open (Brock 1999). Second, debates about the intervention and its effect on the functioning of the UN Security Council and its responsibility for maintaining international peace and security (Annan 1999) led to the development of a new norm, the Responsibility to Protect (Gholiagha 2022: ch. 6).

Parts of the norm constitute a fundamental norm about the protection of populations from mass atrocities. Other parts reflect organising principles that establish procedures for how populations can be protected from mass atrocities if states are unable or unwilling to do so themselves, while the norm also entails standardised procedures concerning the work of the UN Security Council acting under Chapter VII to authorise the use of force (United Nations 2005: §§138–9). As Jennifer Welsh notes, it is a complex norm with different normative expectations, as the failure of a state's individual responsibility triggers the responsibility of the international community (Welsh 2013: 384). In the case of Kosovo, the responsible behaviour displayed led to the development of R2P and hence constitutes a case of proactive contestation (Orchard and Wiener, Chapter 1: 4).[6] Another example can be found in the question of support for Ukraine in light of the Russian full-scale invasion. As we have demonstrated elsewhere, in the case of support for Ukraine, we have identified a norm generative moment, leading to a potential emergence of a norm, we suggest to call, *Responsibility to Support* (Gholiagha and Sienknecht 2023).

[5] There is doubt whether the violence in Kosovo at the end of 1998 and 1999 really amounted to genocide or at least acts of genocide, but this is of less interest here as we are concerned with how actors perceived the situation and how they related their behaviour to norms (Smith 2010: 197–207).

[6] We thank Phil Orchard for drawing our attention to this point.

Conclusion

We began our chapter with the observation that – compared with the abundance of research on norm conflicts (see Rüland and Welsh, Chapter 3), norm contestation, and most recently, norm collisions (see Liese, Chapter 4) – research on behaviour *beyond* norm compliance is less present. However, as we have demonstrated, such research is needed. We suggested in this chapter that the research in the context of the third move of constructivist norms research in conjunction with scholarly work on responsibility provides a useful framework for thinking about these instances. Discussing the existing literature in the second section, we identified a research gap in norms research regarding the conceptualisation of responsibility and presented a relational understanding of responsibility as developed in the responsibility literature. In the third section, we identified four types of norm-related behaviour: appropriate, inappropriate, responsible, and irresponsible. In line with our puzzle about norm-overfulfilment, we zoomed in to responsible behaviour, identifying three specific configurations. Configuration 1 manifests on the level of norms when actors overfulfil a norm. Configuration 2 manifests on the level of subjects when new actors not initially addressed by the norm decide to act in accordance with it. Configuration 3 describes situations of norm generation. In the penultimate section of the chapter, we provided empirical illustrations for all three configurations of responsible behaviour.

In our conclusion, we also want to address some obvious shortcomings of our approach. In some situations, it is difficult to assess responsible behaviour when we are lacking measurable things such as quotas. In such cases, it becomes methodologically challenging to validate whether an actor has gone beyond a norm with norms that do not contain a specific and measurable standardised procedure, such as a quota or a specific target, such as an emission level. Another conceptual shortcoming – and one that all typologies struggle with – is that while different types are distinguishable on the level of theory, empirics demonstrate that these ideal types might overlap in practice. Assigning an empirical case to a specific type always remains an exercise in interpretation. Further research might then identify more precise lines of delineation between the types, helping to clarify cases of ambiguity. Despite these shortcomings, the distinction between appropriate and responsible behaviour offers a conceptual approach to disentangle situations that cannot sufficiently be analysed by only looking at them through the lens of compliance or appropriateness.

Our typology also opens up avenues for further research. Such research may take up our suggested typology to study instances of different norm-related behaviours in more detail. What we offer here is a typology that norms researchers in IR can employ to study the norm-related behaviour of actors in world politics for state and non-state actors alike. Furthermore, by using a specific norm as the analytical departure point, scholars can then study how the norm manifests in different types of norm-related behaviour and thus evaluate and better understand the status of that norm in world politics. We have published an example of such research elsewhere, demonstrating the application of our typology on conceptualizing state behaviour in the case of states responding to the Russian war against Ukraine (Gholiagha and Sienknecht 2023).

Regarding the different types of contestation identified in this book's Introduction, we envision that future research will interrogate the links between contestation and norm-related behaviour in more detail. We have indicated earlier our assumption that we would expect proactive contestation when actors move towards responsible behaviour and reactive contestation when they move towards irresponsible behaviour (see also Wiener and Orchard, Chapter 15: Figure 15.1). Future work will hopefully be able to provide an empirical evaluation of that assumption. This, in turn, would help to further fine-grain the typology while at the same time providing additional empirical insights into different types of contestations. In sum, we argue that building on our initial contribution to the third move norms research will provide a way forward to strengthen normative theorising in IR norms research.

Our notion of responsible behaviour could also be employed as a concept to study other instances of behaviour beyond appropriateness. While this chapter was not concerned with why actors behave in a specific manner but only offers a typology of behaviour that we observe in world politics, the issue of motivation does raise additional questions on the causes of responsible behaviour; for example, recognition, social pressure or emotional factors (see Akhrif and Koschut, Chapter 6). In addition, our three configurations of responsible behaviour can be refined through empirical research and conceptual and theoretical discussions. Here, research may clarify the boundaries of these three configurations, identify additional configurations, and investigate whether or not alternative factors or conditions may also explain the observed behaviour.

Finally, we want to close with two necessary normative reflections. First, we have not discussed norms and norms research's 'dark side' (Heller et al. 2012; Wunderlich 2020). Our typology does not answer whether any type of responsible behaviour is normatively desirable and from whose perspective such an assessment ought to be made. We would refute that just because an actor displays responsible behaviour in a specific situation, they are generally a responsible actor. Yet, the question remains as to what effect the display of responsible behaviour has on an actor's identity and how they are perceived. Our second note of reflection concerns the normative standpoint visible in our examples and our normative positions. Obviously, our examples of responsible behaviour are primarily within the context of liberal norms, and the responsible behaviour we identify often relates to these norms. Of course, we accept that others may have a different perspective. We are cognisant that our normative standpoint has affected our examples to illustrate responsible behaviour. But we do not believe that assessing questions of norms and responsibility from an Archimedean or neutral standpoint is possible. Instead, reflecting on our normativity is the only way to conduct such research.

Part III

Meta-theorising, Linkages, and International Law

9 A Systems Approach to Norms Theory

Carla Winston

Introduction

Norms research has a broad epistemological ambit: some scholars investigate norm actors (Madokoro 2015; Bloomfield and Scott 2016), while others examine the processes of diffusion and adaptation (Acharya 2004, 2013; Bower 2015). Some chart the evolution and effect of specific norms themselves (objects) (Price 1998; Prantl and Nakano 2011), while others look for the pathways and networks through which norms arise and move (Carpenter 2014; Hadden 2018).

One piece of the puzzle, however, has been relatively under-theorised: the system. Systems thinking was an early and important part of the growth of constructivism (Wendt 1992; Kratochwil 1986; Albert 1999), and appears sporadically within the first 'move' in norms research. Work within the second 'move', however, has tended to prioritise the study of actors, processes, and objects in the quest to identify and understand the origins and effects of norms in the international system.

The third 'move' re-engages with some of these ideas. It has become common to refer to norms as embedded in larger structures of meaning and practice (Wiener 2018: 714; Deitelhoff and Zimmermann 2019: 3), but theoretical acknowledgement of the system which houses these structures, and how that system matters for norms research, remains rare (Crawford 2016; Hunt 2016). In addition, the question of *which norms* emerge, and from where, can be approached as a study of the system structure which enables, channels, or constrains their emergence in various ways (Carpenter 2011).

The function of this chapter is to highlight norms research which touches on how norms exist within and interact with systems: not just as objects for agents to build or encounter, but also as part of a larger structure which affects *how* those agents build or encounter them. Using challenges to the rule of law as an example, the chapter argues that systems thinking, particularly complex systems theory, can help to re-orient how we understand opportunity, risk, limits, and the possibility of change – both of norms themselves and of the system of which they form a part. The international system affects, and is affected by, the emergence, diffusion, contestation, and evolution of norms. As we grapple with a complex and changing international system, systems approaches can provide a valuable lens through which to understand the nature and function of international norms.

Systems and Systemic Theory

A system has a simple definition, but potentially complex implications. As Robert Jervis explains, "we are dealing with a system when (a) a set of units or elements is interconnected so that changes in some elements or their relations produce changes in other parts of the system, and (b) the entire system exhibits properties and behaviours that are different from those of the parts" (Jervis 1997: 6).

Systemic theory can be descriptive or explanatory. For the first, description, what does the system actually look like? What are its component parts, and how are they connected to one another? Explanatory forms of system theory treat the system as either the dependent or the independent variable (Donnelly 2019; Jervis 1997). Scholars investigating the system as the dependent variable are interested in how the system arises and comes to have the form that it does (Axelrod 1986; Cederman 1997). Those looking at the system as the independent variable search for the impact of *system effects* on the behaviour of actors, objects, structures, and processes within that system (Jervis 1997).

These forms of analysis fit within all three moves in norms research detailed in the introductory chapter: social facts and mutual agent-structure co-constitution as system-generative (move 1); adaptation and implementation varying according to system positionality and relationships (move 2); and the ways in which system structure facilitates or inhibits normative development from particular actors (move 3). However, finding systemic approaches in much of the existing norms literature often requires us to 'dig out' the system structure from within the explanatory theory which overlays it. As will be shown later, scholars of norms and of adjacent research areas have been implicitly acknowledging system effects for several decades, but have been less willing to explicitly describe the system which produces them. This limits our ability to see additional implications of that system, or to tie the various explanations together in a holistic way.

If we wish to truly understand how norms work, we should start with the best possible description of the system in which they work. This chapter argues that the best descriptor for today's international political system is that of a 'complex adaptive system' (Kavalski 2007; Miller and

Page 2007; Gunitsky 2013; Crawford 2016). While non-complex systems are easier to understand and analyse, their basic properties (closed to outside information, clearly organised patterns of interaction, linear effects, and the ability to reduce the whole to the sum of its parts) do not seem to accurately describe today's international system (Harrison 2006). Complex systems are characterised by the presence of a multitude of actors, of different types and capacities, which are connected through overlapping and varied forms of relationships, and which are open to information or other forces from outside the system (such as the environment) (Harrison 2006; Bousquet and Geyer 2011). The actors in today's international system are both numerous and varied. States and the international organisations they create interact in a non-hierarchical fashion with one another (in the UN General Assembly, for example). Some actors may cross the boundaries of other actors or systems (transnational organisations or companies), or work across multiple levels of analysis. Some actors operate within the bounds of formal relations (treaties between states) while others do not (terrorist groups); some relationships are bilateral and some are multilateral, and so forth.

Beyond descriptive accuracy, the processes which take place in complex adaptive systems, and the types of effects they produce, seem to fit many of our observations about what actually happens in today's international system. Causes can be multiple and spring from different levels of analysis; effects can be diffuse, unpredictable, and non-linear; we can swing between periods of stability and change; and, most importantly for norms scholars, we can see the emergence of new system properties (Jervis 1997; Bousquet and Curtis 2011; Cotsaftis 2009). The 'adaptive' part of the term 'complex adaptive system' refers to us as human beings: because the system is populated by agents which can adapt to changing circumstances in real time, the system is dynamic in a way that non-adaptive systems are not.

First, as actors can be connected to each other via multiple pathways, the effect of any particular action can either grow or diminish in non-linear fashion. Non-linear system effects include outcomes such as feedback loops (either negative or positive) and tipping points, producing the well-known 'S-curve' which charts the speed and extent of norm adoption. After a "tip," we might see cascades or bandwagoning (Petrova 2019: 589), which are both forms of positive feedback loops.[1]

[1] Not all of these are exclusive to complexity theory; for example, historical institutionalism also relies heavily on the existence of feedback loops. A major difference is that historical institutionalism examines politics from the starting point of institutions, whereas complexity theory starts from the system and views institutions as both producing and produced by systemic properties.

The causes of these tips, cascades, and bandwagons are rarely singular. Another potential system effect is multiple causality: there might be several ways to accomplish a goal due to the varying and dense nature of relationships. It might also be the case that outcomes tend to have multiple causes which interact (non-linear) rather than simply stack up (linear) (Rosert 2019: 23; Schmidt 2021; Orsini et al. 2020). In addition, because actors are so connected, effects are likely to be felt indirectly as well as directly (Jervis 1997; Garriga 2016). Sometimes this can be taken into account in the planning (and may be purposeful), but often this outcome is an 'unintended consequence' of failing to take the system, and this possibility, into account (Edwards 2020; Gunitsky 2013; Strezhnev et al. 2021).

This does not mean that today's system is 'perfectly' complex (Kim 2020). Some actors are more central than others in terms of how many relationships they have and who they can thus affect or be affected by (e.g., Britain vs. the Seychelles), while others have more or less power to produce specific outcomes (the United States vs. Honduras). There are also elements of order and hierarchy (Bially Mattern and Zarakol 2016), including common institutions for solving problems or resolving disputes (the UN Security Council), which reduces complexity. But in relative terms, to say that the contemporary international system is complex is no stretch of the imagination.

What are Norms within the International System?

Following from the previous section, if the international system is complex, what are norms within that system? As social facts, constructivists argue that norms form part of the 'social structure' of the international system, and that structure is both "irreducible and potentially unobservable" (Wendt 1987: 41). Such a description of norms as part of social structures also fits the definition of an emergent property of a complex system; an emergent property arises from the micro-level interactions of its agents but is not reducible merely to the characteristics of those agents (Gunitsky 2013: 39). In addition, structuration theory argues that structures and agents are mutually constitutive. Agents can create structure through their efforts to define and diffuse norms. In turn, those norms can constitute agents. Complexity theory suggests that emergent properties, although they arise from agents within the system, also have "autonomous causal power" to affect other parts of the system (Sawyer 2005: 71), which begins anew a cycle of micro-level actions.

Following both constructivists and complexity theorists, then, international norms are system properties. They and other system components are mutually constitutive. As discussed in Chapter 1, they are both "a thing and a process" (Onuf 1994: 1). They are objects in and of themselves and, in the case of widespread, formalised, or internalised norms, part of the system's intersubjectively created structure. As new system properties are created by the micro-level actions of the actors within that system, they are said to 'emerge'. Once they reach the status of systemic property, norms are more than the sum of their micro-level development: they may not resemble, and do more than just reflect, individual choices. They can also affect the behaviour of actors which disagree with their content. Norms theorists already use some of the language of complex systems; we refer to new norms as 'emergent' or 'emerging' (Daly 2008; Gillies 2010; Pratt 2018; Rosert 2019; Schmidt 2014); it seems only fair to make the theoretical link.

Thinking of norms as systemic properties also calls attention to the dual roles constructivists ascribe to norms: they both constitute and constrain (Checkel 1997). Constitution refers to the ability of norms to delineate actors and roles. For example, fundamental norms (Wiener 2008: 60), which play a constitutional role in today's international system, include the concept of the territorial state (Ruggie 1993), the meaning and importance of sovereignty (Schmidt 2014; Paris 2020), the use of international law as a way to regularise interaction, and so forth. A norm's constraining quality is the traditional formulation of "standard of appropriate behaviour" (Finnemore and Sikkink 1998: 891). Norms can not only shape states' conduct towards other states, but also towards their own populations and actors operating below the level of the state, such as NGOs or corporations. 'Constraining' norms are considered to be system properties because their adoption and compliance (or lack thereof) by any particular state engenders a reaction from other states in the form of positive reputational effects, shaming and sanction, or access to other forms of relation (such as trade). These effects are not strictly bilateral; they are general system rules which apply to actors beyond the action–reaction dyad, which is what makes them systemic properties.

Finding the System in Theories of International Norms

Norms research as a subfield of IR has a varied relationship with systems and systemic theorising: while relatively few scholars explicitly take a systems approach to norms, the language and concepts of systems infuse a good deal of scholarship across the field. This includes work across the three 'moves', in both descriptive and explanatory forms.

This section surveys several theories about norms to demonstrate the sometimes explicit, but often implicit, systemic approaches contained therein. It begins with two ways of describing the international system, moves to processes of contestation and system evolution, and finishes by discussing the ways in which some of our best-known theories of norm diffusion implicitly rely on system effects.

System Complexity: Problem or Opportunity?

Complexity theory has not yet firmly taken hold among norms researchers.[2] However, scholars working in the related subfield of regimes have coined the terms 'regime complex' and 'regime complexity'. This terminology has spilled over into norms research, with the growth of 'norm complexes' (Bernstein 2001; Simmons and Jo 2019) and 'norm complexity' (Fehl and Rosert 2020). Used as both a descriptive term and as an independent variable, regime and norm complexes indicate systemic thinking. A regime complex is "an array of partially overlapping and nonhierarchical institutions governing a particular issue-area" (Raustiala and Victor 2004). This is a system structure, characterised by a multiplicity of actors interacting with one another in a variety of institutionalised ways. Each regime complex looks and behaves differently due to its micro-foundations (Gehring and Faude 2013), but exhibits similar types of system effects on the behaviour of the actors within them.[3]

As norms are constituent parts of regimes, it follows logically that norms themselves can form complexes and display complexity (Fehl 2019; Fehl and Rosert 2020). Alternative terms for agglomerations of norms which interrelate in some way include 'clusters', 'sets', 'bundles', 'frameworks', and 'structures' (Finnemore and Sikkink 1998; Betts and Orchard 2014; Crocker 1999; Winston 2018; Lantis and Wunderlich 2018; True 2020). Navigating a norm or regime complex requires identifying and resolving 'interface conflicts' (Kreuder-Sonnen 2020), or disagreements which arise over norm meanings and behavioural implications. If and when these conflicts are resolved, elements of order may emerge: 'fundamental norms' (Wiener 2008: 60; Sandholtz and Stiles 2009: 17), 'metanorms' (Axelrod 1986), or 'metagovernance norms' (Pantzerhielm et al. 2022). These are all examples of norms as emergent system properties.

[2] Axelrod's use of agent-based modelling to capture the growth and persistence of norms remains the only serious treatment of norms through a complexity lens.

[3] Although there is much overlap between regimes theory and complexity theory in a descriptive sense, explanatory regime theory mostly takes on the regime complex as independent variable, with relatively little work on the systemic origins of regime complexes or the implications of co-constitutive processes.

The effects of norm or regime complexes are not fixed. Some scholars have found that such interconnection produces order by stabilising interactions and reducing competitive pressure (Gehring and Faude 2013: 120), but others have suggested that they can create greater opportunities for traditionally weaker challengers (Dreyling 2021) or other types of structural change (Krisch et al. 2020). Understanding how interface conflicts influence system structure allows the researcher to connect conflicts over specific norms to the broader make-up of the normative landscape.

Ecological and Biological Metaphors

Another form of systems-oriented norms research borrows directly from the biological sciences (Hunt and Orchard 2020: 16; Strand 2019; Ruhl et al. 2020). For example, Kirby and Shephard define a 'policy ecosystem' as "the field of activities, actors, and artifacts circulating in the name of the [Women, Peace and Security] agenda" (Kirby and Shephard 2020: 7). Their term differs from a normative framework in that it includes some rules and policies, and actors at all levels of international society, and does not imply that normative conflicts within the ecosystem have necessarily been resolved. In addition, the label of 'ecosystem' allows for, they argue, more fluidity and openness: the ability to redefine and broaden the types of units which populate that system as well as their relationships to one another. Lastly, they suggest that thinking of an ecosystem encourages (as does other systemic theorising) 'holistic' understandings, rather than concentrating on single types of information, "keeping the whole in mind even as we engage closely with its parts" (Kirby and Shephard 2020: 7). Wendt makes the same plea when discussing the co-constitution of agents and structures (Wendt 1999: 26–9); holistic thinking is a valuable tool for non-reductive (i.e., complex) systems.

Ann Florini (1996) takes an even more explicit biological approach, analogising norms as genes and the process of norm emergence and diffusion as 'genetic inheritance'. She suggests that the entry of new norms into the international system is akin to Darwin's theory of natural selection, where the success of a "mutation" (new norm) depends on both object and system factors, known as "fitness" (Florini 1996: 368). The concepts of fitness, cultural match or mismatch (Checkel 1999: 86; Börzel and Risse 2003: 58), and the local normative environment (Merry 2006: 38; Acharya 2004: 244) have been key ways of thinking about which norms diffuse where, and whether or not they diverge from existing meanings as they do so.

Contestation: Opportunity as Structural/Positional

Much has been written on contestation, principally by Antje Wiener (2017b, 2018). For example, this volume's introductory chapter details a nine-box 'cycle-grid model' (see Figure 1.1) which identifies sites and types of contestation in the temporal and spatial development and evolution of norms. Contestation has multiple systemic implications. When the system is treated as a dependent variable, norms generate system structure, so contestation may alter that structure. As the independent variable, the system channels contestation into specific sites, groups, relationships, and processes. Although the cycle-grid model refers to 'scales of global order' and 'stages of norm implementation', this can be viewed in a more granular fashion.

Where specifically in the structure of the international system is contestation occurring? What institutions or relationships serve as sites of proactive, interpretive, or reactive contestation? Who has access to these sites and by what processes do they enable contestation to occur? These questions are both empirical and normative.

The answers are not likely to be singular, either. Given the interaction of different 'scales' of global order, such contestation may occur between the three levels, and it may occur either sequentially or all at once. Systems thinking allows us to move back and forth between actors and the spaces in which they interact, tracing norm contestation wherever and however it might occur. This in turn enables norms researchers to think differently about the relationship between structure, agency, and effects.

Cascades, Spirals, and Boomerangs: The Impact of Systems on Actors' Behaviour

Most norms scholars are familiar with the work of Kathryn Sikkink and her collaborators on norm cascades, spirals, and boomerangs (Sikkink and Kim 2013; Risse et al. 1999, 2013; Keck and Sikkink 1998). All are, implicitly, theories about systems and how systems affect norm diffusion, adoption, and potential effects on behaviour. The norm life cycle (Finnemore and Sikkink 1998), with its descriptions of 'tipping points', 'cascades', and 'internalization', charts how new norms may become emergent system properties, and the effects that the system itself has on actors' motivations at different parts of the process. Tipping points are inflection points at which the forces attempting to block a norm change (a negative feedback loop) are no longer able to effectively compete against those pressing for the new norm (a positive feedback loop).

The system 'tips' from stable to unstable, and a new system property (the norm) emerges. This new system property affects actors in ways beyond its actual content, such as with the conferral of reputational benefits to adopters (Finnemore and Sikkink 1998: 902–4). Successful norm cascades are evidence of non-linear outcomes and indirect effects. This does not always happen (Krook and True 2012), but it *can*, because the system enables it.

However, spirals and boomerangs are about how the parts of the system interact with one another to affect norm adoption by any particular actor. Each theory requires different kinds of actors at multiple levels of analysis to not merely interact, but cooperate, across multiple relationships and potential causal pathways, in order to overcome a (domestic) negative feedback loop and alter the decisionmaking of the target state. This takes enormous effort and is certainly not always successful (Risse et al. 2013; Winston 2020), but if actors can create and sustain the spiral, the state's own systemic properties eventually settle into a new pattern which incorporates the norm in question (Ruggie 1993: 167; Colgan et al. 2012).

This section has demonstrated that much of our existing theory about international norms is already implicitly grounded in complex systems theory. We are able to effectively 'dig out' the descriptive markers of a complex adaptive system from well-known theories about the origins, dynamics, and implications of international norm emergence, diffusion, and evolution.

Thinking Systemically: Challenges to the Rule of Law

How does one employ systems thinking beyond description in order to evaluate the state of particular norms? This section will examine recent challenges to a fundamental norm – the rule of law – which is heavily embedded across multiple institutions as well as norm and regime complexes, and which enjoys broad legitimacy (Wiener 2008: 66; May and Winchester 2018). Specific kinds of challenges to the rule of law can create specific system effects, which are not captured by other forms of analysis. The focus will be to explore the relationship between norm contestation and the structure and properties of the international system.

Some recent examples of rule of law contestation include the attempt by the United States to redefine torture in order to make the Convention Against Torture inapplicable to their practice of waterboarding terrorism suspects (Birdsall 2016); US president Donald Trump's disregard of multiple international treaties (Panke and Petersohn 2017; Driesen 2019); the governments of Hungary and Poland pushing back on EU standards on judicial independence and human rights (Walker 2020); Russia's use of poison to kill dissidents abroad; and the increasing use of transnational repression, which is a violation of territorially based sovereign authority (Schenkkan and Linzer 2021). The collection of these activities, among other developments, has sparked concern for the robustness of the current Liberal International Order (LIO), of which rule of law is a foundational component.

Feedback Loops and Tipping Points

First, for any individual norm challenge, complexity may enable either increasing or decreasing (non-linear) effects over time. Negative feedback loops, in which the effect of a particular event diminishes over time and the system returns to the status quo, are more likely when the particular norms which are challenged are 'robust', or 'embedded' in multiple institutions (Lantis and Wunderlich 2018; Percy and Sandholtz 2022). Challenges are also more likely to take the form of interpretive, or applicatory, contestation (Zimmermann et al. 2018). This limits the amount of fallout from individual decisions; it may narrow the scope of a norm or law but does not undermine it completely. Negative feedback loops are sustained by the reaction of other actors; perceived violations or unacceptable potential changes to a norm are met with some form of sanction which discourages others from doing the same thing. It also forces others making the same decision to justify it, opening themselves up for scrutiny to see if that decision was legitimate, thus actually strengthening the remaining norm. As such, over time it becomes harder to deviate from the rule of law except in specific, accepted, and consistent ways.

One example would be the Bush administration's challenge to the legal definition of torture. Although initially some states took the US lead and began to use waterboarding, this has faded over time as the outraged reaction from other states, legal scholars, and non-state actors encouraged the United States to revert to its previous policy. The norm has mostly returned to its previous status quo (Foley 2021; McKeown 2009; Schmidt and Sikkink 2019; Birdsall 2016).

Conversely, the lack of sanction (or outright approval) of various forms of contestation can not only cement changes coming from one party, but also encourage others to do so as well. This carries the potential to create a positive feedback loop, which could be much more problematic as regards rule of law norms. A positive feedback loop occurs when an initial change leads to increasing effects over time. For norm entrepreneurs seeking alternatives to the rule of law, as well as for norm saboteurs (Schneiker 2020), this is the preferred outcome: that the rule of law becomes increasingly, and increasingly quickly, disregarded, and eventually loses its status as an international norm. If other actors see that rule of law contestation has been successful and imitate this behaviour, it becomes harder and harder for norm proponents to prevent these kinds of defections. If we reach a point at which the energy required to prevent defections is less than the energy required to sustain them, the rule of law norm will 'tip' into instability, and begin a cascade into a 'new normal' without the rule of law as a fundamental norm of international society.

Multiple Causality and Indirect Effects

All the challenges to rule of law mentioned earlier occurred in different forums, which are not officially connected to one another. They were initiated by different actors with different specific laws whose rule they were challenging. By themselves, non-systems theorists would not necessarily be worried about these challenges; a challenge to the rule of law in one domain should not necessarily impact its robustness in another. However, systems theorists would focus on learning and connection across different types of issues and relationships: actors are able to *see* each other act, even in different contexts, and learn from that new information on how and where to try again in the future. Each instance of contestation provides more information to others who might also wish to contest it, for whatever ultimate purpose. As noted earlier, multiple causality can come in two forms: multiple pathways towards a goal, or interacting, rather than summative, effects of different efforts. These diverse challenges provide the space for multiple potential causes of the destruction of the rule of law norm: any of these institutions could fail to robustly protect the norm, leading other challengers to act in the same way and exploit the same gap. This is why actors forum-shop: to take advantage of the variety of pathways available to get what they want (Busch 2007; Coleman 2013).

If initial 'successful' challenges embolden new challengers in other domains, the cumulative effect of many challenges in many places at once and the additional stress of tailoring reactions to each of these particular challenges might simply overwhelm the ability of actors to muster effective defences of the rule of law. The interaction effects of numerous challenges and numerous forums (each with its own procedures for responses) can make negative feedback loops harder to sustain and a 'tip' more likely.

Lastly, systems encourage thinking about indirect and delayed effects, and of how information moves across relationships. Challenging the rule of law, in any domain, has indirect effects: it is a source of information about how actors are likely to respond to those challenges and where they are more or less likely to be successful. Because the rule of law is so fundamental to the existing international order, challenges to it might come from nearly anywhere, but these same challenges might also indirectly affect respect for the rule of law nearly everywhere.

Unpredictability, Stasis, and Change

The rule of law is embedded in the broader LIO, which emerged with the end of World War II (Ruggie 1982) and became dominant after the end of the Cold War. For most of us, the fall of the Soviet Union and the end of the Cold War seemed to have come 'out of nowhere'. This rapid change to a new order was enabled by the complexity of the international system: things may appear stable from the outside, but eventually even seemingly stable systems will become unstable. Maintaining stability requires ever more energy to sustain negative feedback loops, and eventually a tipping point is reached: the system changes, and rapidly. Systems theorists, understanding the possibility for rapid change, are rightly concerned about what now seems to be a shift away from the LIO, including respect for the rule of law. The speed and intensity of that shift might increase unexpectedly, leading to either disorder or new forms of order which cannot be effectively predicted (Friedman 2012). Those who think that the rule of law is appropriate are no doubt pleased that it became so widely adopted, but that outcome was by no means certain. And it is entirely possible that the rule of law could either decay or disappear in a new period of major normative change.

Conclusion

This chapter has set out to revivify the study of systems as they relate to international norms. By reassessing several well-known aspects of norms theory and constructivism more broadly, we have seen that system descriptions and system effects have been sometimes explicitly, but more often implicitly, acknowledged across the three moves in norms research. The example of rule-of-law contestation has shown that paying attention to system contents, structure, and resulting effects can help us to understand the whole *and* the parts, as the one is not reducible to the other. It can also help us to identify spaces of contestation and conflict upon which to focus future theories about how norms emerge, diffuse, interact with one another, evolve, and are consolidated into larger structures of meaning and practice.

The methodological tools available to systems theorists are diverse, and most are already in use. Although agent-based modelling to investigate system effects is rare, there is exciting new work in this domain (Bloodgood and Clough 2017). Network analysis (as discussed by True, Chapter 12) is another promising avenue, as networks are system structures (Carpenter 2014; Hafner-Burton et al. 2009; Kim 2020). In the end, however, integrating a systems focus with other approaches is a valuable way for us to 'zoom in and out' between the forest and the trees.

10 The Interaction of Law and Politics in Norm Implementation

Anette Stimmer

Introduction

When states join international treaties, we expect that they will make efforts to implement their terms. This raises the question: What does a state's effort to implement a norm of international law tell us about its sense of obligation towards that norm? I propose that we can infer a state's sense of obligation by looking at the consistency and publicity of words and actions and the state's engagement with the international community. Obligation describes the sense of commitment towards a norm which can vary in strength (Finnemore and Sikkink 1998; Abbott et al. 2000). Depending on whether a state's discourse and behaviour exhibit low or strong levels of commitment, we can then identify weak normative influence, strong normative influence, and discursive or behavioural norm avoidance. I therefore add insights on norm implementation to the interpretation–contestation framework (Chapter 1: 14–18). I propose criteria for determining Orchard and Wiener's five outcomes of societal agents' norm interpretations and further refine them (Chapter 1: 16–18).

By implementation, I mean the application of general norms to particular cases. I focus on international legal norms. This definition is broader than Alexander Betts and Phil Orchard's (2014: 3) description of implementation as "the steps necessary to introduce the new international norm's precepts into formal legal and policy mechanisms." It encompasses any type of international legal norm and is not limited to devising formal legal and policy mechanisms. The definition also includes more informal mechanisms, such as press releases or speeches about the application of a norm to a particular case.

Studying norm implementation fills a blind-spot in Finnemore and Sikkink's seminal "norm life cycle": they do not discuss what happens after norm emergence and diffusion but before norm internalisation, when "conformance with the norm is almost automatic" (Finnemore and Sikkink 1998: 904). International Relations (IR) and International Law (IL) scholars from various theoretical backgrounds have sought to fill this gap by analysing how international law, once established, influences politics. International legal norms are a sub-set of norms or "standards of appropriate behavior" (Finnemore and Sikkink 1998: 891). International law's authority rests on being part of the body of international law. While there is little binding dispute-settlement or enforcement in international affairs, international legal norms come with distinct discourses, practices, and audiences. States are the primary subjects of international law and therefore this chapter focuses on norm implementation by states.

As Jeffrey Dunoff and Mark Pollack (2013: 10) note, IR and IL scholarship is deeply intertwined, with both sets of scholars using IR theories and methods. The dividing line in the norm implementation literature is not disciplinary background but the focus of analysis. One strand of the literature analyses state behaviour, and often relies on rational choice approaches to identify compliance levels and to what extent law caused behavioural change. Another strand prioritises discourse, namely how international law figures in the justifications of political actions. This group of scholars mainly uses constructivist insights and tends to analyse constitutive effects: how norms shape the way actors think about implementation or communicate it.[1]

I first discuss these different strands of the literature. I show that existing approaches tend to be ill-suited for assessing what implementation efforts tell us about a state's commitment to international law. They require a too static understanding of law and state preferences or do not primarily focus on individual implementation efforts. I suggest that we can identify a state's degree of commitment to a norm by looking at the publicity and consistency of actions and justifications and the state's engagement with the international community. Depending on whether the words and actions of a state display a strong or weak sense of obligation, norm implementation shows discursive or behavioural norm avoidance or weak or strong normative influence. I illustrate these four kinds of normative influence on implementation with case studies and conclude by discussing further usages of this framework.

Research on Compliance and Effectiveness (State Behaviour)

Research on compliance studies congruence between the behaviour of states and their international legal commitments. In the early 1990s,

[1] Some see discourse and behaviour as practices but do not analytically distinguish between the two. However, this distinction is important: actors often face a choice on whether to express their commitment to norms with words or actions and this choice has different implications (Stimmer and Wisken 2019).

Antonia and Abram Chayes (1993) developed a 'managerial approach' to compliance. They assumed that states are generally inclined to comply with international law (178), among others because treaty negotiation and ratification lead others to expect compliance (184). Non-compliance, which might be due to ambiguous language or lack of capacity, can therefore be managed with dispute-settlement, financial and technical assistance, and transparency (204). In their rejoinder, George Downs, David Rocke, and Peter Barsoom (1996) question whether widespread compliance is good news. They argue that most compliance is shallow because states only commit to international treaties that stipulate what states would have done even in their absence. When compliance is shallow, a state's sense of obligation towards treaty rules is also shallow. International law does not have a significant effect on decisionmaking when it merely reflects pre-existing preferences.

Lisa Martin (2013) finds that compliance scholars also commit the opposite mistake: they underestimate international law's influence when states are not technically 'in compliance' but more so than prior to entering legal commitments. To avoid these errors of commission and omission, Kal Raustiala (2000) and Martin (2013) have suggested to study effectiveness, or international law's causal effect: "A causal effect is stated as a counterfactual: how does state behaviour in the presence of an institution differ from the behaviour that would have occurred in the absence of that institution?" (Martin 2013: 605). However, establishing causality in this way is problematic. Scholars have to rely on a too static conceptualisation of state preferences and norm meaning.

It is difficult to establish with certainty whether states would have behaved similarly in the absence of law because state preferences may not have remained constant. While it may not have been costly to comply with a norm when signing a treaty, this may change over time as unforeseen circumstances can change state preferences. In addition, international law creates a new reality that is hard to discount. Take the UK's preferences regarding freedom of movement, one of four fundamental freedoms of the European Union (EU). Initially, immigration levels from the EU were low and compliance shallow as the income levels in most member states were similar. When Eastern European states joined the EU in 2004, unlike other EU members, the UK did not impose transitional controls, which led to significant migration from new member states (Watt and Wintour, 2015). When anti-immigration sentiments took hold, it became costlier to comply and the UK's preferences and commitment to this norm changed. This change in preferences contributed to a desire to change the law and Britain's relationship with the EU. It is difficult to know what would have happened in the absence of law as the events that changed the UK's commitment would not have happened.

Moreover, rational choice scholars often treat international law as fixed; for example, in large-N regression analyses. Judith Kelley and Beth Simmons (2015: 62) use criminalisation of outlawed behaviour as an indicator of compliance. As international law's meaning is not static but in flux (Krook and True 2012), such conceptualisations fail to adequately capture commitment to international law. To continue with the example of freedom of movement, the Cameron government tried to change the norm when preferences changed. Britain argued that only unemployed EU migrants with more than five years of residency in the UK should be entitled to welfare benefits. The commission claimed that discrimination based on nationality is forbidden but the European Court of Justice (2016) agreed that limiting welfare benefits is proportionate to the need to protect host state finances. This norm change took hold as, shortly after, Germany also implemented it (Connolly 2016). Hence, what states say and do affects norm meaning: dispute-settlement, treaty modification and changes in state practice and discourse can all change international law and make it harder to isolate its effect on implementation.

In sum, the literature on compliance and effectiveness tends to take a norm as given and assesses actor behaviour in relation to this fixed norm. If we accept that norms and state preferences are not static, it becomes difficult to identify normative influence with large-N studies and counterfactuals.

Research on Justificatory Discourse

To account for the changing nature of international law, constructivist norm scholars have turned to discourse. Norms can be ambiguous or in tension with each other, and so their application to particular situations can generate debates about their meaning.[2] If we accept that norms are subject to interpretation, the question arises how meaning (if at all) becomes established and how norms influence state behaviour.

Some question whether norms can ever truly reflect shared understandings and regard norms as "contested all the way down" (Niemann and Schillinger 2017). However, norms structure discourse by providing a reference point for debate, but also get constructed in the process, which Wiener (2004: 191) describes as their "dual quality." Thus, there can be different degrees of consensus when states implement norms. The

[2] For an analysis of interpretive difficulties, see Rüland and Welsh (Chapter 3) and Liese (Chapter 4).

more consistency and convergence of interpretations we see, the stronger the reference point and influence of law.[3]

Ian Johnstone (2011) illustrates how an interpretive community, consisting of decisionmakers, experts, and the public at large, judges the validity of interpretations and thereby refines international law. Knowledge of the rules and practices of interpreting international law, rather than material power, is what gives the interpretive community authority. When the interpretive community perceives a state's norm implementation to violate international law, this comes with social and material costs, even for the powerful. Take the 2003 Iraq War – the United States and UK had trouble getting military and financial assistance due to the widespread perception that the intervention was illegal (Sandholtz 2008: 108). Thus, this strand of the literature locates the influence of international norms in the justificatory discourse that surrounds their implementation.

Scholars who prioritise discourse tend to focus on how the exchange of arguments influences norm strength and norm change (Deitelhoff and Zimmermann 2019; Sandholtz 2008) or on how the use of legal discourse can commit states to consistently implement their legal obligations (Bower 2015). We lack indicators for assessing what a specific effort to implement an international legal norm tells us about the states' commitment to the norm. Furthermore, the prioritisation of discourse risks overestimating the effect of law on state behaviour. As Anette Stimmer and Lea Wisken (2019: 521) show, instead of engaging in discursive contestation, actors may engage in behavioural contestation: while stating their commitment to international norms, states may fail to introduce (adequate) implementation mechanisms.

In the following sections, I propose to explore the grey zone between empty words and purposive action. I suggest three indicators for identifying the degree of commitment to international norms in state behaviour and discourse. These indicators help us to evaluate a state's commitment to a norm of international law when we look at specific implementation efforts.

Conceptualizing Obligation

Obligation describes the sense of commitment towards a norm. Constructivists see obligation as a social and normative concept, rooted in intersubjective ideas of what 'ought' to be done. Such a normative

[3] I show elsewhere that contestation can affect precision, and thus norm strength, in four ways. It can lead to norm clarification, norm recognition, norm neglect, or norm impasse (Stimmer 2019a and Stimmer Forthcoming).

commitment can develop in various ways, ranging from socialisation and learning to argumentative practices (Finnemore and Sikkink 1998; Johnston 2001). Rational choice scholars trace commitment back to pragmatic considerations such as the interest in maintaining a reputation as good cooperation partner or mutual benefits from norm-following (Guzman 2010). Regardless of the source, when actors feel a sense of obligation towards a norm, we should see this commitment reflected in their discourse and behaviour.

Legal obligation is distinct because it involves a commitment to legal procedures, reasoning, and discourses. Some scholars infer the sense of obligation from whether states design hard or soft legal commitments.[4] Using norm type as an indicator is too static; it only provides us with a snapshot of how states felt about norms when entering legal commitments. Implementation provides an updated indicator.

International law's main sources are treaty norms and customary law. Examining how much commitment a state's discourse and behaviour displays takes seriously the two main elements of customary international law: *opinio juris* (expression of legal belief) and state practice. Both are hard to measure and therefore some scholars doubt the existence of customary law (D'Amato 1987) or exclusively focus on treaty norms (Abbott et al. 2000). More pragmatically, Kirgis (1987) argues that state practice and *opinio juris* are substitutes: long-standing, consistent state practice indicates commitment when clear expressions of *opinio juris* are absent, and vice versa. Hence, when we study discourse and behaviour to evaluate commitment to a norm, it is important to bear in mind that both can be substituted to a certain extent.

Obligation is difficult to pin down. Thus, the following indicators are not exhaustive but a starting point for analysis. I propose that there are three signposts of obligation in the words and actions that accompany a state's norm implementation: consistency, publicity, and engagement with the international community. These three indicators are all somewhat inter-related but distinct enough to be helpful analytical tools. The indicators rely on an understanding of international law as social fact. Those who practise it and are subject to it construct international law, and international law follows certain conventions (Sandholtz 2008; Johnstone 2011).

As Wayne Sandholtz (2008: 106–7) writes: "legal scholars recognise analogical reasoning, and the logic of fit, as central to legal systems and to the development of law … [w]ithout some fundamental level of consistency, rules cease to be rules.' Consistency is an important

[4] For a review of the literature on soft and hard law, see Shaffer and Pollack (2013).

indicator: it contributes to international law's legitimacy by making it less arbitrary and more predictable. However, as there are tensions and ambiguities in every legal framework and unexpected situations may arise, a state might be inconsistent when implementing norms (Wiener 2004, 2014; Krook and True 2012).

Inconsistency, therefore, is not a sufficient indicator for lack of normative influence. We need to look at the reactions of other members of the interpretative community to identify whether divergent actions and words are seen as a legitimate new way of implementing a norm or as a violation of legal obligations (Krisch 2005; Johnstone 2011).[5] The judgements of influential actors such as international courts or states who are crucial for the implementation of the norm are of particular relevance. The institutional position of states, for example as members of the United Nations Security Council, gives weight to their norm interpretations (Stimmer 2019a). When gauging a state's commitment to a legal norm, it is important how the state engages with the international community and reacts to criticism: is the state open to discussions and to changing its implementation?

Transparency and openness are also signs of normative commitment. 'Publicity' facilitates engagement with the international community and indicates a willingness to be scrutinised. However, we cannot rule out normative influence when we do not see publicity. A state may implement a norm in a way that differs from the international community's understanding without realising it (Stimmer and Wisken 2019: 524–5; Orchard and Wiener, Chapter 1: 15). Let us now look at the three indicators for obligation in greater detail.

Consistency

Behaviour: building on Frederic Kirgis (1987), consistent state practice signals commitment towards the norm. Thus, when the implementing action under study is consistent with prior practice, this indicates normative commitment. Following Downs et al.'s (1996) distinction between shallow and deep cooperation, the costs involved in implementing a norm give insights into the depth of the commitment. When norms are implemented despite great costs, this increases our confidence in normative influence.

Discourse: similarly, consistent arguments show that a state is clear on what norm is relevant and does not merely use any explanation that may receive support. Hence, the less different explanations a state uses and

[5] See also Liese (Chapter 4) and Ralph (Chapter 14).

the more quickly a state settles on a normative justification, the more likely is it that this justification reflects a sense of obligation. Similarly, it indicates commitment when states use justifications repeatedly in similar situations and show that the precepts of the invoked norm are met.

Publicity

Behaviour: when it comes to norm implementation, states sometimes hide their inadequate norm implementation to prevent reputational or material costs while paying lip-service to the norm (Stimmer and Wisken 2019). Therefore, it increases our confidence in their normative commitment when states are transparent about their implementing actions; for example, by allowing monitoring organisations into their country.

Discourse: states can develop international law further when other states approve of their interpretations of the law (or at least remain silent) (Sandholtz 2008: 103). Hence, when states publicly present legal justifications for their behaviour, these public statements contribute to the repertoire of a norm and thus signal a sense of commitment.

Engagement

As discussed, the more the international community converges on a legal interpretation, the clearer it becomes whether an implementing action conforms to it. When the international community clearly criticises a state for its norm implementation, the way a state engages with the international community can indicate normative commitment. For instance, we would expect a committed state to constructively engage in discussion in a timely manner and to be open to making changes. The verdict of the international community can take many forms. Other states can express their *opinio juris* with press releases and public statements. States can often resort to dispute-settlement when they differ on how to interpret and implement international norms. As dispute-settlement is law-governed, it signals commitment when states subject their norm implementation to the scrutiny of international courts or other dispute-settlement bodies and accept their verdict (Alter 2014; Abbott et al. 2000). Furthermore, whether a state considers the opinion of others is a particularly important indicator when a norm should be implemented collectively; for example, by the UN Security Council. A failure to consult others before the implementing action then strongly signposts a low sense of obligation.

* * *

In sum, the more consistent, public, and attuned to the reactions of the international community justifications are, the stronger the sense of commitment. The same holds for behaviour. Note that these indicators are only indicators of the degree of commitment. When scholars are interested in the legality of norm implementation, they should also study other factors such as the prevalence of legal justifications.

Classifying Norm Implementation

When we have identified the state's commitment to a norm in its behaviour and discourse, we can classify instances of implementation. When both state behaviour and justifications reflect a low sense of obligation, the norm has had a weak influence on decisionmaking. The opposite is the case when state behaviour and justifications reflect a strong sense of obligation. This configuration is a sign of strong normative influence. When the degree of obligation that is reflected in behaviour and discourse diverges, we may see attempts at norm avoidance – either behavioural (low obligation in behaviour/high obligation in discourse) or discursive (low obligation in discourse/high obligation in behaviour) (Figure 10.1). I will illustrate these different degrees of normative influence on decisionmaking in turn.

Weak Normative Influence

Norms weakly influence implementation when state behaviour and discourse display low levels of obligation. When the words and actions of a state are contradictory, ill-timed, clandestine, and dismissive of objections of others, we can infer that the cited legal norm does not have a strong influence on decisionmaking. These situations can fall

		Behavior	
		Low sense of Obligation	High sense of obligation
Discourse	Low sense of obligation	**Weak Normative Influence**	**Discursive Norm Avoidance**
	High sense of obligation	**Behavioral Norm Avoidance**	**Strong Normative Influence**

Figure 10.1 Different degrees of normative influence on implementation

under Orchard and Wiener's (Chapter 1) second outcome of how a societal agent can interpret norms, namely that the agent does not implement the norm.

Russia's involvement in Crimea's secession from Ukraine in 2014 serves as example. Russia invoked Crimea's right to self-determination to justify its actions, whereas Ukraine emphasised its right to territorial integrity. These rights are in tension with each other. The right to self-determination is enshrined in the United Nations (UN) Charter and international human rights treaties. Colonies have the right to secede from the colonial state but it is contested when communities within existing states can secede. In non-colonial cases, there is a presumption for protecting minority rights within a state (i.e., internal self-determination) because of the right to territorial integrity. If at all, then secession without permission of the host state (i.e., external self-determination) is seen as last resort, permissible only in the most extreme cases of human rights violations (Borgen 2009: 8–9; Grant 2015). What does Russia's support for such a remedial right to self-determination for Crimea tell us about the norm's influence on Russia's decisionmaking?

Remedial self-determination requires that sustained efforts of a long duration were made to find another solution to protect human rights (Grant 2015: 77). Instead of engaging in negotiations, for instance through the UN or Organization for Security and Cooperation in Europe (OSCE), Russia decided to first create facts on the ground. In late February 2014, shortly after the Ukrainian parliament removed Russian-backed President Yanukovych from power and banned Russian as second official language, unidentified gunmen seized control of key infrastructure in Crimea. They raised the Russian flag in the Crimean parliament and pro-Russian lawmakers voted for a referendum on greater autonomy from Ukraine, against Ukrainian wishes (Gumuchian et al. 2014; BBC News 2016). In early March 2014, referring to its right to have up to 25,000 troops at its Black Sea fleet base, Russia deployed thousands of troops to Crimea, which seized and blockaded military bases and pressured Ukrainian soldiers to leave (Isachenkov 2014). The Crimean parliament converted the referendum into a referendum on joining Russia or remaining part of Ukraine (Karmanau and Baetz 2014). In the UN Security Council, Russia portrayed the new Ukrainian government as undemocratic and illegitimate, referring to its historical attachment to Crimea and saying that "the right-wing forces in Ukraine are very strong. They cannot stand Russian citizens or ethnic Russians ... with 1.5 million of them in Crimea" (UNSC S/PV.7125 2014: 17; UNSC S/PV.7134 2014: 14–16). Approximately

60 per cent of the population of Crimea are ethnic Russian. On 16 March, it was reported that 96.77 per cent voted for joining Russia (Grant 2015: 69). President Putin then publicly endorsed the referendum result and framed the incorporation of Crimea as compatible with self-determination in a much-publicised speech in the State Duma two days later (President of Russia 2014).

Regarding publicity, Russia resorted to a show of military might rather than to extended discussions and negotiations over human rights in Crimea before the referendum. In addition, Russia did not emphasise systematic and widespread human rights violations in the run up to the referendum. These actions indicate a lack of commitment to the precepts of the self-determination norm and imply a lack of confidence that other states would accept this norm implementation. Indeed, the United States, European Union, and Ukraine argued that Ukraine's territorial integrity and sovereignty take priority.

Regarding consistency, Putin referred to the 'Kosovo precedent' when justifying his acceptance of the referendum result (President of Russia 2014). He criticised inconsistency of the West as the United States and European Union supported Kosovo's independence, saying: "this is not even double standards; this is amazing, primitive, blunt cynicism" (President of Russia 2014). However, Russia's support for Crimea's right to self-determination contradicts its opposition to Kosovo's independence. In the Kosovo case, Russia rejected the applicability of the right to self-determination and instead emphasised Serbia's sovereignty and territorial integrity (Borgen 2009; Grant 2015: 72–3). This inconsistent application casts further doubt on whether the right to self-determination played a role in Russia's decisionmaking.

If the self-determination norm strongly influenced Russia's actions, we would have expected constructive engagement with criticism from the international community and perhaps behavioural change. This has not been the case. The West and Ukraine sharply criticised the referendum in Crimea, rejected the result and issued sanctions (Laughland et al. 2014). International monitoring bodies have found no evidence of widespread and systemic violations of the rights of ethnic Russians in Crimea (Grant 2015: 75). Moreover, the UN General Assembly passed a resolution affirming Ukraine's territorial integrity and called for non-recognition of the referendum result on Crimea's status with 100 votes in favour, 11 against, and 58 abstentions, whereby the abstentions were largely due to issues with specific wording rather than doubts about the annexation's illegality (Grant 2015: 90–1). Despite these criticisms, President Putin has maintained that "[t]he referendum was fair and transparent, and the people of Crimea clearly and convincingly expressed their will" (President of Russia 2014). Hence, all indicators point to the right to self-determination only weakly influencing Russia's decisionmaking regarding Crimea.

Discursive and Behavioural Norm Avoidance

Sometimes there is a mismatch in the level of obligation that words and actions reflect. When we see norm avoidance, states circumvent some normative obligations. They say one thing and do another. There are two types of norm avoidance. Behavioural norm avoidance occurs when states display a low level of commitment in behaviour but a high level of commitment in discourse. Discursive norm avoidance is the mirror opposite. States display a low level of commitment in discourse but a high level of commitment in behaviour. As I will show, both forms of norm avoidance can be the flipside of the same coin when there is a tension between two norms that affects implementation. Others have described behavioural norm avoidance as 'decoupling' (Zimmermann 2016: 102). Despite rhetorical acceptance, norms are at the same time decoupled from implementation. Discursive norm avoidance or decoupling from discourse has not yet been studied to the same extent.

When two norms conflict, a state might seek to implement one norm while not damaging the other. We may therefore see discursive commitment to one norm while state behaviour conforms to another norm. Thus, we see both types of norm avoidance: behavioural norm avoidance of one norm and discursive norm avoidance of the conflicting norm. The norm avoidance by the United States when recognising Kosovo's statehood serves as an example (Stimmer Forthcoming). The norm conflict was also between the host state's right to sovereignty and territorial integrity and a possible right to remedial self-determination of the entity that seeks to secede. While the United States first pushed for collective approval of Kosovo's statehood in the Security Council, when it became clear that Russia would not agree, preparations for Kosovo declaring independence unilaterally ensued. The United States recognised Kosovo's statehood, and thereby its behaviour in this concrete case is consistent with the remedial self-determination norm and inconsistent with Serbia's sovereignty and territorial integrity. However, the United States did not justify its recognition with the self-determination norm. The justificatory discourse by the United States displayed low commitment to remedial self-determination and high commitment to state sovereignty. The United States went to great lengths to portray Kosovo as a one-time exception and affirmed its commitment to sovereignty and territorial integrity.[6] The United States argued that Kosovo was a *sui generis* or 'special case', among others due to the history of ethnic cleansing and UN administration, that "cannot be seen as a precedent for any other situation in the world today" (Rice 2008). Hence, we see discursive norm avoidance of remedial self-determination and behavioural norm avoidance of territorial integrity.

There is a risk of 'entrapment' when states voice commitment to a norm interpretation at one point in time because changing their mind in the future would call into question the state's reliability as cooperation partner and commitment to community norms (Schimmelfennig 2001: 64; Krebs and Jackson 2007: 44–7; Johnstone 2011: 210–11). Thus, norm avoidance indicates that states generally feel an obligation towards one norm and do not intend to weaken it vis-à-vis a conflicting norm and incur obligations to that norm in future situations. However, the particularities of a case make it difficult to follow the norm the state is more committed to in that instance.

We can also see norm avoidance when the implementation of a single norm is contested. For instance, behavioural norm avoidance occurs when a state consistently voices commitment to a norm in public and denies wrongdoing, while failing to adequately implement the norm.[7] We are likely to see such norm avoidance when a state can implement a norm domestically on its own as this allows for cover-ups and secrecy. For instance, from 2001 to 2004 the Bush administration publicly signalled its commitment to the prohibition of torture – a norm which the United States had previously upheld consistently and publicly – and was able to allay concerns of others (Keating 2014). During this timeframe, George W. Bush and the White House denied accusations of torture and voiced commitment to legal obligations. Bush stated, for example, that '[t]he values of this countries are such that torture is not part of our soul and being' (Bush 2004) and a White House spokesperson affirmed that "we believe we are in full compliance with domestic and international law, including domestic and international law dealing with torture" (quoted in Cooperman 2002). However, at the same time, the United States engaged in waterboarding of terror suspects (Ward 2008), which is widely considered to be a form of torture. Notably in later years of the Bush administration, we see more public acknowledgement of inconsistent practices that amount to torture such as waterboarding and less commitment to the prohibition of torture in

[6] I have called this 'overt exceptionalism' elsewhere (Stimmer Forthcoming).
[7] I have called this 'covert exceptionalism' elsewhere (Stimmer Forthcoming).

discourse (Keating 2014; Stimmer 2019a). Thus, we see a change from behavioural norm avoidance to weak normative influence.[8]

Generally speaking, norm avoidance indicates that a state is trying to avoid the obligations that come with a norm in a specific situation but seeks to signal general commitment towards the norm. Unlike when we see weak normative influence, when norm avoidance occurs, either what states say or do is consistent with prior commitments or practices, public and responsive and thus corresponds to a high level of obligation. However, the state also displays low commitment on the other dimension, that is, either in its actions or words, and thereby reveals that despite a general commitment to the norm, in the concrete situation, it attempts to avoid normative obligations. Both discursive and behavioural norm avoidance therefore add nuance to Orchard and Wiener's third outcome of norm interpretation, where the agent's interpretation differs from the established consensus, but the agent does not engage in contestation of the consensus (Orchard and Wiener, Chapter 1: 16).

Strong Normative Influence

We see strong normative influence when states show a high sense of obligation in their discourse and behaviour. Strong normative influence comes in different guises, and at the far end of it, we may see internalisation or norm implementation that is almost automatic (Finnemore and Sikkink 1998: 904). As discussed, identifying whether implementation signals strong normative influence is challenging because not all norm-conforming behaviour goes back to a sense of obligation towards the norm (Martin 2013). For instance, the United States granted women the right to vote and started to destroy chemical weapons stockpiles long before international obligations existed. While the United States is honouring its international legal commitments in those cases, international norms are not the main influence on norm implementation. An additional obstacle is that norm meaning is not always clear-cut. Tensions and ambiguities in international law sometimes make it difficult to ascertain how to implement a norm or which norm should be implemented (Sandholtz 2008; Krook and True 2012).

Some types of cases increase our confidence in strong normative influence. Initial reluctance to join a treaty, followed by consistent and transparent implementation, indicates that a sense of obligation developed because of international norms. Studying a state's reaction to

[8] For further discussion of how this case relates to the interpretation–contestation framework, see Winston (Chapter 9), Ralph (Chapter 14), and Akhrif and Koschut (Chapter 6).

the interpretive community's judgement of a contested norm implementation allows us to address norm ambiguities and tensions. As the engagement indicator captures, if a state is open to changing the way it implements a norm after an adverse verdict from a dispute-settlement body or overwhelming criticism from other states, we see an intention to honour legal obligations. The same applies if, after initial contestation, the international community accepts the state's interpretation and implementation (Byers 2003; Stimmer 2019a). The following examples serve as illustration.

Initial reluctance to sign, followed by consistent and transparent implementation, characterises several countries' relationship with the mine ban treaty (MBT), also known as the Ottawa Treaty. Japan, for example, was hesitant to accede to the MBT due to its complete prohibition of anti-personnel mines (APLs) (Adachi 2005). The influential Japanese Defence Agency and Foreign Minister Ikeda saw APLs as an important defensive deterrent and argued that Japan's export ban on APLs meant that civilians in other countries would not be harmed (Adachi 2005: 399). In June 1997, Japan withdrew from the Ottawa Process due to national security concerns (Adachi 2005: 407). Adachi (2005) shows how domestic dynamics led to a change in Japan's attitude: there was sustained pressure from non-governmental organisations (NGOs), lawmakers, and the media, and a cabinet reshuffle brought about a pro-ban foreign minister. As a result, Japan signed the MBT and it entered into force for Japan on 1 March 1999. Since then, Japan has been transparent and consistent in its implementation: Japan has fulfilled reporting requirements, destroyed its mines, and provided assistance to other countries (Eiichiro 2021; MBT Website 2021). Thus, we see strong normative influence of the MBT on Japan that is equivalent to Orchard's and Wiener's (Chapter 1: 16) first outcome of norm interpretation as Japan has fully endorsed the existing international understanding of the norm.

We also see a strong normative influence if a state accepts the verdict of the interpretive community on a contested norm implementation. This verdict can take many forms but is most law-governed when it is a formal ruling of a dispute-settlement body (Abbott et al. 2000; Alter 2014). Up until 2019, when the United States rendered the Appellate Body (AB) inoperative by blocking the appointment of judges, the World Trade Organization (WTO) dispute-settlement mechanism (DSM) was one of the most used and effective. The DSM has several stages, starting with a request for consultations, which can lead to the establishment of a panel and a possible appeal of the panel report at the AB. If the dispute-parties disagree on whether compliance with the DSM decision has been achieved by the end of the implementation period, the aggrieved party can initiate further proceedings which may culminate in retaliation. There has been a high level of acceptance of DSM decisions. In only 37 of the 598 cases, arbitration proceedings were initiated to determine a permissible level of retaliation (WTO 2021a). When states implement DSM decisions, strong normative influence is at play: states lay open their reasoning during dispute-settlement, engage with criticism, and ultimately act consistently with legal obligations. The 'Canada – Term of Patent Protection' dispute over patents that were filed prior to the Agreement on Trade-Related Aspects of Intellectual Property Rights (TRIPS) entering into force illustrates this. On 12 October 2000, the AB upheld a panel report that rejected Canada's argument that 17-year protection is equivalent to the 20-year protection TRIPS mandates if informal and statutory delays are taken into account. Within the implementation period, Canada passed a bill that brought its patent laws in conformity with those rulings and TRIPS on 12 July 2021 (WTO 2021b). While Canada might have deliberately endorsed a different understanding of the norm initially (Orchard and Wiener's fourth outcome of norm interpretation), we eventually see full endorsement of the international norm understanding and thus the first outcome of norm interpretation.

Legal ambiguities and tensions sometimes make it difficult to ascertain how norms should be implemented. The verdict of the interpretive community, whether rendered by courts or more informally by other states, public opinion, and NGOs, then plays an important role. When states are open to discussions, to changing implementing practices, and to clarifying norms, we see strong normative influence. The contestation over TRIPS and access to HIV-medication illustrates this. TRIPS is ambiguous on patent protection of medicines. Article 33 requires WTO members to grant patent rights for 20 years but there are exceptions. For instance, Article 31 allows states to issue compulsory licences to make patented drugs available at an affordable price during health emergencies. Compulsory licences allow the government or third parties such as generic drug manufacturers to produce and sell the drug without the patent owner's consent. They can only be issued after genuine negotiations with the patent-holder for reasonable commercial terms (Joseph 2011: 221–3). There are also tensions between TRIPS patent rights and human rights, particularly the right to health (Article 12 ICESCR) and to life (Article 6 ICCPR). These tensions and ambiguities led to disputes over implementing practices. Brazil threatened to introduce compulsory licences for HIV-medication and consequently was able to negotiate significant price cuts with drug manufacturers, which halved the number of

HIV deaths and reduced the rate of infection. The United States initiated a complaint against Brazil in the WTO, claiming it had breached TRIPS (Joseph 2011: 223). At roughly the same time, in 2001, 39 pharmaceutical companies invoked TRIPS and sued South Africa in the High Court in Pretoria over legislation that they worried would facilitate the issuing of compulsory licences and the import of generic drugs. After a wave of global outrage over companies trying to stop the provision of cheap HIV-medication, the pharmaceutical companies dropped the lawsuit a few weeks later (Joseph 2011: 224). As a result, developing states campaigned for the clarification of compulsory licensing provisions within the WTO. The United States backed away from its case against Brazil and in November 2001 the Declaration on the TRIPS Agreement and Public Health was adopted. Among others, the Doha Declaration reaffirmed the right of states to issue compulsory licences in "public health crises, including those relating to HIV/AIDS, tuberculosis, malaria and other epidemics" (Joseph 2011: 224–5).

The actions and words of host states of pharmaceutical companies who benefit from patent rights indicate that they may not have intended the negative effect of TRIPS on the right to healthcare. Orchard and Wiener describe this as the fifth outcome of norm interpretation (Chapter 1: 17). Political leaders (e.g., of the United States and European countries) repeatedly stressed that the right to healthcare and patent rights are not only compatible, but also mutually supportive (European Commission (DG1) 1998). The complaint by the United States against Brazil might have merely been a routine practice: at the time, the United States routinely issued complaints against states even though their policies were possibly compliant with TRIPS (Joseph 2011). When the apparent contradiction between its behaviour and its pledges to support health norms was called out, the United States and European Union acknowledged the possible detrimental implications of TRIPS on the right to healthcare and quickly adopted the Doha Declaration (Haugen 2007). As a result of the Doha Declaration, 52 developing states issued compulsory licences, which predominantly related to HIV/AIDS-medication. Hence, the declaration had the intended effect of clarifying the law and increasing access to drugs, when it comes to HIV/AIDS-medication (Joseph 2011: 225–8). Thus, even when norms give unclear guidance, we can see strong normative influence when contestants engage with each other, try to be transparent and consistent with prior commitments, and attempt to clarify norms.

* * *

In sum, depending on whether the words and actions of a state display a strong or weak sense of obligation, we can characterise implementation as showing weak or strong normative influence, discursive or behavioural norm avoidance.

Conclusion

This chapter has studied the process of norm implementation and suggested three indicators for identifying normative commitment: whether a state is transparent about its implementation efforts in public; whether a state's actions and justifications are consistent over time; and whether a state engages with the international community. After classifying whether a state's actions and words display high or low levels of obligation, we can then draw conclusions on the extent to which norms have influenced implementation in a particular situation. Doing so avoids the attribution problems of the existing literature.

I would like to conclude by noting that the four different degrees of normative influence on implementation can change over time. For instance, while the United States engaged in norm avoidance regarding the prohibition of torturing terror suspects during the Bush administration, afterwards controversial decisions and legal opinions were retracted or reversed, paving the way for strong normative influence.

Future research on international law's influence on norm implementation could therefore focus on analysing a state's norm implementation over time: under what conditions does a certain kind of implementation (e.g. behavioural norm avoidance) get protracted? When do we see change? What increases or decreases normative influence over time? By helping us to identify international norms' role in decisionmaking, this framework can assist scholars in gaining a richer understanding of the interaction of law and politics in norm implementation.

11 International Lawyers, Legal Norms, and Contestations of Legal Validity

Jakob v. H. Holtermann, Mikael Rask Madsen, and Nora Stappert

Introduction

International Relations (IR) norms research has grown into a rich research field over the past three decades. However, when compared with the discipline of law, which for centuries has explored different features of legal norms, it is still relatively nascent. Norms have been the central objects of enquiry within legal scholarship since the advent of the first law faculty in Bologna in the thirteenth century, and the questions pertaining to the concepts of validity, legitimacy, and justice have continuously, yet in different ways, been at the heart of the discipline. In contemporary legal studies, national and international, particularly doctrinal legal approaches have made the analysis of valid law and its contents the very core of legal science. In legal philosophy, there is also an extensive history of systematic reflection on how to study law's normativity and how a science of legal norms may be possible. Within international law scholarship, these legal philosophical debates have again resurfaced in recent years following its alleged 'empirical turn', which has challenged the traditional prevalence of doctrinal approaches (e.g., Shaffer and Ginsburg 2012).

Given these rich debates, there is in our view considerable promise for norms research in IR in using an interdisciplinary approach that stretches across IR, Legal Philosophy, and the Sociology of International Law to study legal norms. Specifically, in this chapter, we propose a practice-oriented approach to make visible theoretically, and trace empirically, one type of normative contestation: the day-to-day contestations of legal validity by groups of legal professionals. While part of their daily work, such legal contestations are important, as they may lead to normative legal change in practice (Brunnée and Toope 2018; Stappert 2020; Venzke 2012). This group of professionals can be understood as one – or

Authors are listed alphabetically and have contributed equally to this chapter.

more accurately, several overlapping – Bourdieusian fields or communities of legal practice. In this chapter, we argue for the promise of both approaches to further advance norms research's second move related to norm adaptation as one option for a practice-oriented take on legal norm contestation (Orchard and Wiener, Chapter 1: 6–7). Specifically, both approaches allow us to examine how norms change not through policymaking processes or adaptations to domestic legal systems (Orchard and Wiener, Chapter 1: 6–7), but through processes of legal contestation enacted by transnational groups of legal professionals. We thus contribute to norms research by utilising not only insights from IR practice theory,[1] but also Bourdieu-inspired work within the Sociology of International Law and recent debates on legal realism in International Legal Theory. Different from Stimmer's (Chapter 10) proposal to study legal norms by focusing on states as agents of contestation, our approach concentrates on groups of legal professionals (and in some cases, more loosely-associated 'semi'-professionals).

Ultimately, our approach calls attention to normative contestation specifically concerning the legal validity of norms, and how such contestations may lead to normative legal change in practice. In line with what the editors call "interpretive contestation," international lawyers frequently have "interpretive variance on how they understand a given norm" (Orchard and Wiener, Chapter 1: 15; Figure 15.1). Legal norms are not only contested during the negotiations of treaties, or in the context of policy implementation. Instead, enacting and contesting the validity of legal norms is part of the day-to-day practice of a group of individuals specialising in international law, ranging from legal counsel, international judges, and legal scholars, to legal officers working for non-governmental organisations (NGOs) and international courts. Beyond more visible contests about the validity of legal norms by, for instance, legal counsel for opposing parties, such day-to-day instances of enacting and contesting legal validity can be less apparent as well.

For example, in some of our earlier work (Stappert 2018: 971–5), we found that scholarly writings are referred to surprisingly frequently by international criminal courts, even though such scholarship formally is only a "subsidiary means for the determination of rules of law" (Article 38(1)(d) of the Statute of the International Court of Justice). At the

[1] After all, important theorisations of norm contestation have in part been inspired by reflexive sociology and the work of Bourdieu (Wiener 2004: 200), and have sought to build bridges between both (Wiener 2018: 33–37; on international law, also Liste 2020: 11–27).

same time, legal academics in turn regularly comment on and thereby scrutinise the validity of recent judgements of international courts. In addition to the inadvertent and implicit forms of interpretive contestation outlined by Orchard and Wiener (Chapter 1: 15–16), day-to-day interpretive legal contestations can therefore be both explicit and deliberate. Furthermore, as part of the day-to-day practices of international lawyers, such interpretive legal contestations thus extend beyond what Wiener called formal validation practices taking place during initial negotiations of legal provisions by "high-level representatives of states" at the "constituting stage" of norms (Wiener 2014: 29; see also Figure 1.1, Orchard and Wiener, Chapter 1: 10).

To paraphrase Pierre Bourdieu (1987: 817), the battle over the meaning of law is thus at the heart of the legal field. The main promise of making such legal interpretive contestations among legal professionals visible empirically is that it accentuates specifically how legal validation and contestation are shaped by, and reflect, underlying power dynamics (Dezalay and Madsen 2012). In Wiener's (2018: 1) words, it asks "whose practices count" and whose voices are excluded within normative contestation in and surrounding international law. What is more, it might exactly be the, at times, more technical, legal character of these contestations that obscures such power dynamics and ultimately restricts access of 'lay' stakeholders to such contestation. By not subsuming legal validity contestation under other, broader types of contestations, our approach allows for contestation to be researched empirically specifically within social contexts dominated by (competing forms of) legal expertise.

Therefore, to practice law invariably involves contesting the contents and validity of laws and legal principles. However, in line with Orchard and Wiener's invitation to conceptualise contestation as a "neutral process" (Orchard and Wiener, Chapter 1: 14), such legal interpretive contestation does not undermine law but rather affirms its existence (Madsen et al. 2018: 202). For example, for lawyers advising specific clients, such as government lawyers or defence counsel, it is part of their professional responsibility to propose a view of the law that is most favourable to their clients. Regardless, by doing so, they draw on shared professional assumptions on how to interpret international law (see also, e.g., Brunnée and Toope 2010, 2011; Johnstone 2011).

Consequently, focusing on legal norms, legal validity, and the actors that enact and contest them also provides a distinct perspective on legal norms' legitimacy and normativity, and thereby also contributes to norms research's third move. After all, as David Beetham (2013: xiii–xiv,

16) highlighted, there is an assumption that legal rules are legitimate, leading him to conceptualise legality as a "*prima facie*" element of legitimacy. Equally, among international lawyers, legitimacy may, at least partially, become equated with legality (e.g., Collins 2017). Regarding legal norms' normativity, at least within the legal philosophical tradition of natural law, for example, what 'ought' to be law is necessarily what 'is' law. As a result, attempts to evaluate norms' normative legitimacy as central to the third move in norms research (Orchard and Wiener, Chapter 1: 7–8) arguably apply differently to law, while raising questions about how to research legal norms empirically without losing sight of international law's inherent normativity. Drawing on long-standing debates within legal philosophy on how to study law's normativity, and specifically around different forms of legal realism, this chapter also seeks to make some of these important and often epistemological discussions useable for IR norms research.

The remainder of this chapter proceeds in two steps. First, we lay the foundations of our approach by clarifying this chapter's epistemology, drawing on legal philosophical debates on legal realism and how to study law's normativity that have rarely found its way into IR norms research so far. Second, we outline how such a research approach can be implemented within empirical studies, specifically via Bourdieu-inspired approaches and the concept of communities of practice. We use normative contestations in and around climate change law to illustrate the promise of such an approach.

Epistemological Foundations: Axiological and Empirical Legal Validity

Before turning to how to research interpretive legal contestations among groups of legal professionals empirically, in our view, it is crucial to first clarify the epistemological foundations of such an approach. After all, how to research legal validity empirically has been the subject of long-standing debates within legal philosophy, and specifically around legal realism. Compared with natural law and legal positivism, legal realism has often been dismissed in legal philosophy as the outlier that fails to address the foundational challenges facing the scholarly study of law. The long-standing, legal philosophical objection against this empirical approach is that legal realists fail to appreciate the fundamental distinctness of law and legal norms as social phenomena and instead reduce law to that which it is not (e.g., habitual behaviour, legal institutions). Within IR, such preferences are indirectly reflected in recent contributions that draw on legal philosophy; for example, while Jutta Brunnée and Stephen Toope (2010: 20–55) built on Lon Fuller's (1969) procedural version of natural law, Silviya Lechner and Mervyn Frost (2018: 58–60) partly drew on HLA Hart's (1961) version of legal positivism.

However, the strength of legal realism, at least in the version we consider here,[2] lies precisely in the way it provides conceptual resources rich enough to fully investigate and understand the distinctive normative field that is (international) law without abandoning a social scientific outlook. Specifically, to clarify the epistemological foundations of our approach, we revisit a specific strand of legal realism that we previously introduced as European New Legal Realism in the context of recent debates in International Legal Theory (Holtermann and Madsen 2015). It has been a key contribution of this approach to trace a longstanding distinction within a distinctive European strand of legal realism between two types of legal validity: a) axiological legal validity as indicating juristic truth; and b) empirical legal validity, which focuses on the actual beliefs about axiologically valid law held by actors in the legal field (Holtermann and Madsen 2015). With the following discussion, we seek to make this key epistemological distinction usable for IR norms research. We thus clarify the distinction between norms and their normativity central to norms research's third move (Chapter 1: 7–8), specifically as applicable to legal norms. Such epistemological foundations are significant, given that they entail two fundamentally different approaches to what 'counts' as valid law, who is involved in constructing and contesting it, and how to research such interpretive legal contestations empirically.

In most general terms, what we called European New Legal Realism builds on a combination of the work of sociologist Max Weber and so-called Scandinavian legal realism, represented by Danish legal philosopher Alf Ross, and which we demonstrated to be continuous with the legal sociology of Pierre Bourdieu (Holtermann and Madsen 2015). Unlike the two other main schools of thought in legal philosophy – natural law and legal positivism – legal realism consistently emphasises a strong methods continuity thesis in law: there can be no exceptions from the epistemological tenets underlying general empirical social science, and any attempt to conduct norms research in the legal field must observe this desideratum (Weber 1977; Ross 2019: 81). This approach led both Weber and Ross to reject the classical doctrinal study of law,

[2] This is not to imply that IR has entirely overlooked legal realism's promise. For example, Philip Liste (2020: 11–27) recently fruitfully used key insights from (American) legal realism and critical legal studies to highlight the promise of building links between practice theory and norms research.

which aims to identify valid legal norms, that is, the rights and obligations of legal subjects in any given legal system.

This promise is particularly evident in the conception of legal validity, originally developed by Weber and Ross. Both authors developed a distinction between two kinds of validity – so-called axiological and empirical, respectively – to perform empirical research on legal norms without *becoming* doctrinal lawyers who seek to establish what (axiologically) valid law is using the traditional doctrinal method.[3] The key feature of this distinction is that it allows the social scientific researcher of legal norms to manage the intricate balancing act between being internal in a sense that allows understanding of what doctrinal lawyers see as valid law and remaining external by not sharing the participants' beliefs about valid law. Ultimately, the difference as applied to norms research is between a researcher citing, for example, a treaty provision as part of their empirical evidence, thereby themselves implicitly providing an assessment of what a 'right' legal interpretation of this treaty might be, and empirically researching how this treaty provision is interpreted by different legal professionals, such as by authors of legal commentaries or international judges.

Weber introduces axiological legal validity as follows:

> [C]onsider the 'validity' of a legal maxim in … the 'ideal' sense. From the standpoint of the scholarly conscience of the person who wants to establish 'juristic truth', it is constituted by a rigorous logical relationship between concepts. … [I]t is constituted by the 'axiological validity' which a certain logic has for the legal mind. (Weber 1977: 128)

The person who aims to establish juristic truth or axiologically valid law thereby aims to establish it through the use of the doctrinal legal method that determines which legal rights and obligations objectively bind the legal subjects in a given jurisdiction at any given time.[4] For both Weber (1977: 115) and Ross (2019: 80–1), the problem with axiological validity and thereby with juristic truth is epistemological. For epistemological reasons, both deny the possibility of establishing sound empirical legal science based on 'juristic truth', since any assertions about the ideal axiological validity of legal rules – of the objective existence of specific rights and obligations – are in principle unverifiable.

[3] In the English translation of Ross's (2019: ch. II) main work, the two kinds of validity are referred to as "valid law" ("*gyldig ret*") and "scientifically valid law" ("*gældende ret*"), respectively.

[4] For a traditional legal positivist, axiologically valid law is constituted by the set of legal rules that can be deduced from a presupposed basic norm. For a natural lawyer, it would be the set of legal rules that can be deduced from, for example, an underlying social contract or the fundamental idea of justice.

However, this scepticism regarding axiological validity does not exclude an empirical understanding of normative legal practices.[5] On the contrary, it is perfectly possible to observe a widespread wish to establish 'juristic truth' among the participants of a legal practice without participating in this enterprise oneself, that is, without searching for 'juristic truth' or generating corresponding beliefs on axiological validity. As Weber observes, the collective enterprise aiming at 'juristic truth' and at generating beliefs of axiological validity is itself an empirical phenomenon amenable to empirical study:

> *In general,* actual persons who *want* to establish 'juristic truth' are *disposed* to infer 'axiological validity' of a certain 'legal maxim' from certain verbal relationships. This fact is obviously not without empirical consequences. On the contrary, it is of the greatest conceivable empirical-historical significance. Simply consider the fact that a 'jurisprudence' exists. And consider the 'intellectual habits' which are actually governed by this 'jurisprudence', habits which develop in an empirical-historical fashion. This fact is of tremendous practical-empirical significance for the actual organization of human affairs. … Within empirical reality there are 'judges' and other 'officials' who are in a position to influence human behaviour by employing certain physical and psychological instruments of coercion. They have been educated in such a way that they *want* to establish 'juristic truth'. And – actually, with very different degrees of consistency – they conform to these 'maxims'. (Weber 1977: 128)

The distinction between axiological and empirical validity is easily overlooked, and examples of a conflation of both abound in both empirical research and in legal philosophy. One reason may be that 'validity' as a stand-alone term is ambiguous and can be used correctly in both contexts. However, the two phenomena are fundamentally different both ontologically and epistemologically. The question whether a legal right or an obligation exists as a matter of 'juristic truth' is fundamentally different from the question whether certain people in a given legal practice are disposed to infer its 'axiological validity' and to act accordingly. Correspondingly, the two kinds of legal validity invite different research methodologies:

> [T]he empirical 'existence' of 'law' [is] completely different from the legal idea of the '*axiological* validity' of law. 'Empirical' validity can be ascribed to both 'juristic truth' and 'juristic error' in exactly the same degree. Consider the question: *What* is 'juristic truth'? That is to say, in view of certain 'objective' principles of jurisprudence as a scholarly discipline, what logically *should* be 'valid', or what should *have been* 'valid'? The logical import of this question is entirely different

[5] This is denied by Lechner and Frost (2018: 28), who assert that "[a]ccording to practice internalism, understanding epitomises knowledge internal to the … practice" (as also poignantly critiqued by Maren Hofius (2020)).

from the import of the following question: In a concrete case or in a plurality of cases, what in fact *followed* as the empirical, causal 'consequence' of the 'validity' of a certain 'paragraph'?" (Weber 1977: 129–30)

The categorical difference between axiological and empirical validity highlights the importance of observing this crucial distinction, including for IR norms research. By introducing it, Weber and Ross offer a unique tool to disambiguate this otherwise deceptive term. In sum, by researching legal norms, outlining 'what the law is' by referring to treaties, negotiation documents, or even to authoritative interpretations by international courts, is epistemologically in line with how doctrinal lawyers approach this question (axiological legal validity). Instead, such an approach is distinct from the empirical study of how, whether, and by whom such legal texts, interpretations, and judgements are socially constructed as valid, and how they might be contested (empirical legal validity).

Researching Empirical Legal Validity Empirically

How can this distinction between axiological and empirical legal validity be used for the empirical study of legal norms? In our original outline of how to operationalise our European New Legal Realism (Holtermann and Madsen 2015: 222–7), we introduced Bourdieu's sociology of law (Bourdieu 1987; Dezalay and Madsen 2012) as a means for further theorising our attempt at an integrated perspective on law that combines internal and external perspectives, and for putting this theory into action. However, distinguishing between axiological and empirical legal validity also has implications beyond Bourdieu-inspired studies of international law and can be used as a starting point for other approaches at the intersection between IR practice theory and norms research. Specifically, a promising alternative approach is to use the concept of communities of practice (and, relatedly, interpretive communities). Both approaches share a focus on a relatively close-knit social setting, be it legal fields (in a Bourdieusian sense) or communities of international lawyers. Moreover, both approaches have an interest in making change visible, as new legal fields may emerge or normative meaning may develop through the day-to-day practices of international lawyers. We discuss each approach in turn.

To begin with, the idea of double reflexivity found in Bourdieusian sociology offers one option for articulating a way forward for studying a normative phenomenon – valid law – without falling prey to the normativity of the phenomenon itself (Madsen 2011: 260). Bourdieu provides specific tools for how to go about this analysis – something missing in the work of both Weber and Ross. Specifically, Bourdieu helps us understand law as a double construction through a 'double bataille': a battle within the legal field over the meaning of law and a battle over the place of law in society in competition with other fields, for example, politics and economics. A brief conceptual clarification is warranted here regarding the central Bourdieusian "thinking tools" (Leander 2008) of field, habitus, and symbolic power, including how they apply to international law specifically, a key analytical dimension rarely subject to Bourdieu-inspired approaches in IR.

Bourdieu (here with Wacquant 1992: 97) defines a field as a:

> network, or a configuration, of objective relations between positions. These positions are objectively defined, in their existence and in the determinations they impose upon their occupants, agents or institutions, by their present and potential situation (*situs*) in the structure of the distribution of species of power (or capital) whose possession commands access to the specific profits that are at stake in the field, as well as by their objective relation to other positions (domination, subordination, homology, etc). (Bourdieu and Wacquant 1992: 97)

For our purposes, particularly interesting are the relative structuration of international fields and with that the emergence of increasingly specific legal discourses on what are the axiologically valid legal concepts and interpretations. However, this battle over form and meaning is not open to everyone, which is where the notions of capital and symbolic economies enter the picture. Owing to their particular combinations of capital, some agents are better situated to influence what makes legal arguments appear axiologically valid and thereby become empirically valid. Therefore, in addition to struggling over meaning and form, agents also struggle over what capitals qualify them to speak in the name of axiologically valid law. Capital is accumulated through an agent's social trajectory. Through the same social process, the agent is also developing a certain worldview, what Bourdieu terms 'habitus'. Habitus is the internalised ideas and schemes that guide behaviour and creates a practical sense of what is right or wrong in specific contexts (Bourdieu 1980). Legal education is illustratively a form of symbolic violence forcing a certain mind-set that is often shared in legal fields as common maxims (Madsen 2018). But variations in such legal education, for example, including across legal traditions, generate not only competition, but also conceptual uncertainty and confusion – an outcome that can be observed across several international courts and transnational fields (e.g., Dezalay and Garth 1996). Law is at the end of the day a highly specialised form of symbolic power. Different from physical power, symbolic power is the ability to introduce and impose categories that steer perception and judgement and thereby, ultimately, divisions of the social world (Bourdieu 1987).

Law is a limited language game, not only on its own participants but also on the social world, that reduces social complexity into simple formulas and solutions. But since these formulas are never entirely clear-cut, those with the power to speak the law have a disproportionately large influence on articulating more precisely what the meaning of the law is (see also Liste 2020: 18–25). The force of law is, however, ultimately based not only on the recognition of law among powerful actors within the legal field, but also in relevant adjoining fields. Therefore, the empirical study of the making of legal validity necessarily implies an analysis of the specific battles of the legal field in conjunction with their interface with other fields.

Especially within the Sociology of Law, the outlined Bourdieusian tools have in various ways been used to explore the production of law as fields of contestation over normative change. Such scholarship typically studied specific fields of international law, often new or emerging fields. A classic in this regard is the analysis of the transformation and expansion of the field of international commercial arbitration by Yves Dezalay and Bryant Garth (1996). Focusing on battles over form and associated expertise, they demonstrated how expertise and interest in legal form correspond to different social positions (i.e., European academic law and American-style Wall Street law) and ultimately competing transnational elites. Similarly, John Hagan (2003) focused on the making of the International Criminal Tribunal for the former Yugoslavia resulting from the interplay and competition of a host of actors from various backgrounds, including prosecutors and investigators. Antoine Vauchez (2010) analysed the social and legal processes behind the *Van Gend en Loos* decision of the European Court Justice, one of the pivotal judgements leading to the construction of an autonomous order of European law. He demonstrated how the judgement only later was turned into a landmark decision in a series of post-judgement socio-legal processes that gave the decision its prominent standing.

Except for Vauchez's analysis, these studies are mostly concerned with the broader structural space influencing the production of law and its associated professional battles. We instead suggest studying the legal battles over international legal norms alongside the standing of those legal fields in the respective societies. For example, Madsen provided an analysis of how the European Court of Human Rights and its jurisprudence has gained its standing in European society through entering the legal fields of member states. Examining the decades-long processes of import and acceptance of decisions by the European Court of Human Rights (ECtHR) in legal and political circles beyond the inner circles of the Court, the analysis highlights how contestations of legal validity influence the standing of legal norms in both law and politics (Madsen 2010, 2021).

Beyond Bourdieusian approaches, another option to study the construction and contestation of perceived axiological, that is, empirical legal validity is to use the concepts of communities of practice or, relatedly, interpretive communities. Within IR, communities of practice approaches have emerged as one of the main strands loosely associated with international practice theory (Bueger and Gadinger 2018: 51–9). Such work is inspired by Jean Lave and Etienne Wenger's (1991) early study of apprenticeship training to understand how learning occurs in social contexts defined by a shared sense of identity, which was further refined by Wenger's (1998) 'communities of practice' (see also, e.g., Adler 2019; Hofius 2016; Stappert 2020). International legal scholarship has also used the concept of interpretive communities, developed by Stanley Fish (especially 1990) within literary theory (e.g., Bianchi 2009; Johnstone 2011; Rajkovic et al. 2016).

Despite some differences (e.g., D'Aspremont 2016: 15–21), both concepts share a focus on meaning that is established and negotiated within a social process carried out interactively by a community that shares common assumptions about how such a process should be conducted. For Fish (1990: 1–17), the main point has arguably been that the interpretation of literary texts is a social process enacted by a community of interpreters that draw on shared approaches on how to (authoritatively) interpret such texts. For Wenger (1998: 55–7), and drawing on his earlier work with Lave on what they called *legitimate peripheral participation* (Lave and Wenger 1991: 29–37, 91–117), communities of practice form the social context in which meaning is negotiated through mutual recognition among community members, accountability when upholding shared standards, and the construction of a shared identity.

When applied to international law, a common denominator between both concepts is that they see legal meaning as negotiated within a community of lawyers assessing the axiological legal validity of proposed interpretations (D'Aspremont 2016: 17–22; Johnstone 2011; Stappert 2020: 44–5). Similar to Bourdieu-inspired approaches, and reminiscent of Oscar Schachter's (1977) "invisible college of international lawyers," international legal communities span organisational contexts and may include, among others, government lawyers, international judges, and legal academics (Johnstone 2011: 41–4; Hernandez 2017; Roberts 2017; Stappert 2018).

One key strength of using such an approach is that it directs attention towards normative change as meaning is negotiated in practice

(Adler 2019; Brunnée and Toope 2010, 2018, 2019; Stappert 2020). Understanding change in international law, despite its arguably stabilising function within international relations, has been an almost classic challenge within international legal (and IR) scholarship. Normative change may occur through formal treaty-making mechanisms, and thus resulting from normative contestation that is likely to occur during the treaty negotiation phase (and in line with contestations of norms' formal validity (Wiener 2009, 2014, 2018). Beyond such contestations, normative change in international law is often less formalised and may be driven by international organisations, and especially international courts (e.g., Venzke 2012; von Bogdandy and Venzke 2012). Such avenues for change coincide with increased reliance on non-legal mechanisms, including unilateral action (Krisch 2014). Within international law, normative change is typically gradual, as legal interpretations that are accepted as axiologically valid (as 'juristic truth') are required to remain within the bounds of what is seen as permissible from a legal perspective (Brunnée and Toope 2018; Johnstone 2011: 50; Stappert 2020: 37). Despite such constraints, however, normative change in international law through interpretive practices has the potential to be substantial (Stappert 2020; Venzke 2012; von Bogdandy and Venzke 2012). Approaches tracing how normative meaning is contested within legal communities can make this change visible within empirical studies.

Nevertheless, the concept of both interpretive communities and communities of practice arguably have a key weakness, namely that it may entail an implied assumption of homogeneity and coherence (see also Stappert 2020: 44; Vauchez 2014: 662–3). To counteract such a – likely misleading – tendency, we suggest that it is crucial to enrich such a perspective with a research strategy that emphasises contestations within and among different members and subgroups of international (and transnational) legal communities (see, e.g., Bianchi 2009; Roberts 2017; see also the Bourdieusian works quoted earlier).

One way to do so is to take inspiration from recent attempts to reintroduce a focus on struggles within IR practice theory (Martin-Mazé 2017). Other promising avenues are the proposals by Maren Hofius (2016) for analysing how communities' boundaries are constructed and enacted in practice, or suggestions by Leonie Holthaus and Jens Steffek (2020) to concentrate on the "trading zones" between scholarly theory and different types of practice. Moreover, previous suggestions to focus on overlapping interpretive communities (Rajkovic et al. 2016) can be enriched with the finding that it is especially those individuals who gained experience across different fields who are able to assume prominent positions, including as international judges (Madsen 2014: 333–4). Regardless of which approach is taken, such a focus promises to make visible how different members of potentially overlapping legal communities may compete for the ability to authoritatively interpret international law, and how some groups and individuals may be excluded from this process altogether. After all, as Shashank Kumar and Cecily Rose (2014) have shown, for example, lawyers conducting oral proceedings before the International Court of Justice have been overwhelmingly male and from the Global North.

We illustrate our proposed research approach by using the example of legal interpretive contestations in international climate change law, as well as international environmental law more broadly (for an overview, see, e.g., Bodansky et al. 2017). Climate change governance is an area of global governance that is comparatively less legalised, as it does not include a specialised international court and is in large parts governed by mechanisms that are not legally binding. At the same time, climate change is often addressed, including through court cases, as part of domestic legal orders in legal fields ranging from environmental law to tort law, human rights, and constitutional law (see, e.g., Dellinger 2017). Recent years have seen a considerable increase in domestic climate litigation, broadly understood, reflected by growing scholarly interest (see, e.g., Setzer and Vanhala 2019; Peel and Lin 2019; Peel and Osofsky 2020). At the international level, legal developments concerning climate change similarly have tended to spill over into adjacent legal fields. One example is a recent decision by the United Nations Human Rights Committee that, in general, the principle of non-refoulement in international refugee law can be applied to circumstances in which the consequences of climate change may entail the risk of life-threatening circumstances or of cruel, inhuman, or degrading treatment (McAdam 2020; Human Rights Committee, *Teitiota v. New Zealand*, UN Doc. CCPR/C/127/d/2728/2016 (Oct. 24 2019)). Another example are recent attempts to criminalise ecocide as part of the Rome Statute of the International Criminal Court (e.g., Minha 2020; Mwanza 2018). As a result, there has been growing scholarly interest in (international) environmental law and how it is treated by (international) courts and quasi-judicial bodies (see also, e.g., Bodansky 2017). However, much of this work has been confined to doctrinal perspectives (see also Setzer and Vanhala 2019: 5–6).

To trace the construction and contestation of axiological validity (i.e., empirical validity) in and surrounding climate change law, future studies may investigate how these instances of (proposed) change in normative meaning have been situated at the intersection between fields (understood in Bourdieusian terms). Another fruitful avenue is to trace the emergence of a field of climate change law in the first place. Such studies could investigate how far the elites and legal professionals proposing these changes have benefited from gaining expertise, and thereby capital, across different fields, and how the boundaries of their communities are constructed and enacted in practice. Furthermore, such studies may ask which role different groups, including NGOs and legal scholars, have played in advocating for legal changes, and whether differences in shared understandings across different legal communities may have led to contestations in legal interpretations (see e.g., Murcott and Webster 2020: 162). In the long run, such a research approach could analyse how the recent decision by the Human Rights Committee in *Teitiota v. New Zealand*, for example, is endorsed or challenged by other domestic and international judicial and quasi-judicial bodies, thus tracing how axiological validity is constructed and contested in practice (i.e., empirical validity).

Conclusions

This chapter sought to contribute to IR norms research by introducing an interdisciplinary, practice-oriented approach that combines IR with Legal Philosophy and the Sociology of International Law. To study contestations of legal norms specifically, we drew on legal philosophy to outline a key, but in our view within IR norms research overlooked, epistemological distinction between axiological and empirical legal validity. We operationalised our approach by combining it with Bourdieusian and community of practice approaches. By doing so, this chapter proposed a research strategy to make contestations of axiological legal validity visible without remaining confined to doctrinal legal approaches, which may inadvertently be reproduced by analyses of legal norms and norm contestation. Instead, it offered two possible options for making visible as an object for empirical study the internal construction and contestation of axiological legal validity that such doctrinal work itself is part of, that is, as empirical legal validity.

Such an epistemological distinction, and the research approach we outline based on it, is significant because it has fundamental implications for how to think about contestation and where to look for it, as well as its theoretical relationship with (legal) interpretation. One theoretical expectation that has been proposed is that contestation occurs once norms move across social contexts, as a shared cultural and social context is theorised to provide shared interpretations of norms (Wiener 2004: 200; 2014: 30; 2009: 181). Regarding international law specifically, Wiener correctly observed that contestation may occur due to differences among legal traditions (Wiener 2009: 185). Even beyond crucial differences across legal traditions, however, our approach underlines how contestation is at the heart of the legal profession, as proposing and contesting legal arguments is a core part of what lawyers 'do' on a day-to-day basis, both within and beyond the courtroom. Beyond formal validation during the drafting of a treaty, for example (Orchard and Wiener, Chapter 1: 10; Wiener 2014: 29), we thus seek to also make visible the contestations of legal validity that occur within a treaty's subsequent interpretation and its passage into the practice of law. Such contestations over how to interpret international law and which legal interpretations are considered as axiologically valid are important, as they may lead to change in normative meaning, and ultimately allows us to understand the power of legal norms in politics.

Consequently, this chapter encourages further research that concentrates on, and empirically traces, how and with what consequences the axiological validity of norms is established and contested within the context of law specifically. Such research would focus on (international) lawyers and their practices, and how perceptions of axiological legal validity are constructed, re-constituted, and contested through them within the social context of a specific social (legal) field or community of lawyers. Potentially equally interesting questions emerge on how such expertise-driven, legal contestation may exist alongside, reflect, or even be shielded from broader societal contestation, and with what normative (ethical and empirical) consequences (e.g., Kennedy 2016). Finally, a further research avenue may be to examine the roles that international lawyers may play within norm implementation. Drawing on Betts and Orchard's (2014: 22) conceptualisation of norm implementation as a process through which a "new international norm's precepts [are introduced] into formal legal and policy mechanisms within a state or organization," such research could examine how (potentially overlapping) transnational and national communities of lawyers specifically may contest and develop normative meaning as part of this process.

Part IV

Dimensions of Norm Contestation

12 Of Norms and Networks

Theorising the Vital Link between Norm Contestation and Network Globalisation

Jacqui True

The globalisation of advocacy and policy networks, including the dynamics of power that shape them, are integral to the emergence and evolution of norms, as seen in cases such as sustainable development and the 'rights of nature' (Kauffman 2017), the prevention of violence against women (Keck and Sikkink 1998), and the prohibition of sexual violence in conflict (Davies and True 2017). Yet the relationship between norms and networks has hardly been theorised.[1] How far and in what ways do changes in network structures affect the dynamism and diffusion of norms? Despite the cross-over empirically, and the early scholarship on the role of advocacy networks in diffusing norms, the scholarship on international norms and that on transnational networks (Tarrow 2005; Moghadam 2005; Stone and Maloney 2019) have subsequently developed largely their own. This chapter bridges the gap between transnational networks and norm contestation by studying the spread and localisation of the Women, Peace and Security (WPS) norm bundle. Like Cecilia Jacob (see Jacob, Chapter 13), this chapter focuses attention on the micro-agentic processes and power relations that enable norm contestation, here networked advocacy rather than the decisionmaking processes in the design of regulation. The chapter also shares with Jason Ralph (see Ralph, Chapter 14) a concern with the normativity of norms and the importance of mapping pro-active contestations which sustain the legitimacy of norms, in this case of gender inclusion in protection, rights, peace, and security decisions.

Networks that span different political spaces and jurisdictions as conveyed by the adjective 'transnational' are not merely transmission belts that serve to spread norms, as illustrated in the case of the WPS norm bundle explored in this chapter. Rather, networks are integral to the

[1] For exceptions, see Wiener (2018) on transnational litigation networks, which has been used to analyse norm(ative) change with regard to the torture prohibition norm, and on climate justice see Murcott and Webster (2020).

construction of international politics and to the legitimacy of normative orders through processes of norm contestation. This chapter aligns with the second and third arguments put forward by the editors of this volume regarding the import of norm contestation, therefore. Networks are key actors and part of the political opportunity structure that gives rise to new norms. They shape their evolution through processes of norm emergence, change, and replacement as well as diffusion and localisation through contestation (see Tarrow 2005; Joachim 2008). Importantly, networks also create novel spaces for contestation that enhance the validity and legitimacy of the norm. They enable greater access to contestation from the bottom up, for actors who are most affected by them, but who have least access to organisational or political sites for socially and culturally validating these norms. This access increases the robustness of norms because networks promote the relevance and meaningfulness of a norm at various levels and spaces in global society – which no one single, even powerful, actor can achieve (alone).

The transnational network spawned by UN Security Council Resolution 1325 established a process to keep building the 'norm bundle' (True and Wiener 2019) and the dialogue surrounding it. Just as "'norms as processes' are works in progress," which I have argued in previous contributions to the 'third move' in norms research (Krook and True 2012: 104; True 2019) highlighted by the editors, so too are the networks that purport them. Thus, this chapter argues and adds to the norms scholarship that more attention needs to be focused on the changing nature of networks, the agents of global and local contestation, and the content of the evolving norms themselves in discerning their legitimacy or relative success.

This chapter introduces an empirical exploration of the impact of network changes on norm diffusion in the context of the bundle of norms sustaining the WPS agenda. Underpinned by UN Security Council Resolution 1325 (2000) and nine subsequent resolutions to date, the WPS agenda is the major international normative framework addressing the gendered impacts of conflict on women and girls. It establishes the critical role of a gender perspective in peace and security processes, which recognises that women and girls experience conflict differently from men and that women can and should meaningfully participate in conflict prevention and peace and security decisionmaking (see Hill et al. 2003; Cohn 2006). While the WPS agenda has evolved into four main pillars of focus – protection, participation, prevention, and relief and recovery – the uneven development of the respective pillars over the last two decades has resulted in varied meanings and practices in the WPS agenda. The relative broadness and ambiguity of this international normative framework supports the dynamic theory of norms as processes – that WPS norms are neither linear nor fixed in their form and content. The WPS agenda is therefore an ideal site to examine the impact of changes in agency and network structure upon the evolution and proactive and interpretive contestation of norms in particular.

This chapter consists of three sections. The first section reviews the traditional constructivist approach to norm diffusion and contestation popularised in theoretical debates at the end of the twentieth century. It then explores scholarship addressing the limitations of this early non-normative agenda about norms and policy transfer, and the growth of gender and post-colonial scholarship aligning the theorisation of gender norms with new understandings of transnational networks. The second section applies these ideas to the spread and localisation of the WPS norm bundle instigated by UN Security Council Resolution 1325. By examining two key historical moments informing the diffusion of these norms – namely, the international women's peace movement during World War I and the modern linkage of women peace activists from the Global South and North in support of the WPS agenda – this section explores how certain gender-related norms have evolved through the agency of transnational actors in the WPS network. The third section considers contemporary challenges to post-1325 WPS diffusion in light of current normative contestations of the WPS agenda and the context of the COVID-19 pandemic. Analysis of this situation reveals the tensions in advocacy for the internalisation of international gender-related norms and how crucial transnational networks are to sustaining the relevance of WPS norms and the prospect of political as well as normative change.

Theorising Norm Diffusion and Contestation

The initial 'first move' theorisation of norms in the IR constructivist research agenda was a largely state-centric activity. Notwithstanding the theoretical contributions of constructivists, first and second move studies on norms and norm localisation pursued a largely empirical research agenda, which did not address the normativity of the norms themselves and their contribution to the legitimacy of the international order, which characterises the 'third move' in norms research. Norms were thought to arise through the actions of purpose-oriented actors who sought to drive moral progress and international normative change. In the first move of norms research, scholars highlighted the agency of non-state actors and transnational advocacy networks in supporting target states in their normative uptake by linking domestic policymakers with international frameworks, movements and resources, as argued by Jacqui True and Michael Mintrom with regard to gender mainstreaming (True and Mintrom 2001). However, they did not interrogate the dynamics of the networks themselves and/or the impact of these dynamics on the domestic or local adaptation of the norms (Sikkink 1993; Klotz 1995; True and Mintrom 2001). Notably, though, scholars first pursued research on norm diffusion by examining feminist non-state networks prior to applying their models to other areas of international relations (Keck and Sikkink 1998 on violence against women; Finnemore and Sikkink 1998 on women's suffrage).

The second and third theoretical moves on international norms towards understanding how norms are adapted to reconcile with prior normative histories and identities (Acharya 2004) and how they are continually evolving through contestations (Wiener 2004, 2009, 2014, 2018; Krook and True 2012) was reinforced by the empirical conclusions reached by IR feminist scholars. Susanne Zwingel (2012, 2015) found that state acceptance of the international norms contained within the *Convention on the Elimination of All Forms of Discrimination against Women* (CEDAW) was ultimately the product of the linkages built by transnational feminist advocates between the CEDAW text and domestic situations and values, reflecting the view that the global regime for gender equality is fundamentally a "story of debate, contestation and dissent in norm development" (Kardam 2004: 91; see also Klotz, Chapter 5). Considering this scholarship, the 'first move' of constructivist theorisation of norms can be seen to contain a level of linearity and determinism that did not capture the complex impacts of localisation, identity, the salience of the domestic context, and the discursive construction and contestation of a norm's meaning which the second and third move conceptualisations respectively achieved. This scholarship, including my own (True and Mintrom 2001; Krook and True 2012), however, has yet to capture the dynamism in the agency of networks and their role in norm contestation, which generates enhanced legitimacy of international norms especially those relating to gender equality and women's rights.

Theorising Network Globalisation

In addition to their theorisation of the dynamic meanings of norms, feminist scholars have been among the group pioneering the study of transnational networks. By recognising the distinct agency of these networks and the feminist principles of governance that have evolved within them, gender researchers have established a field of study that demonstrates how Transnational Feminist Networks (TFNs) are powerful mechanisms for the transformation of gender-related norms (Sawer et al. 2023). This literature encompasses the evolution and promotion of several core international norms regarding gender equality and women's rights, including universal suffrage, state institutions for gender mainstreaming, gender quotas, and the prevention of violence against women (Paxton et al. 2006; True and Mintrom 2001; Krook et al. 2015; Htun and Weldon 2012).

Looking beyond the individualist lens of norm entrepreneurs in 'first move' constructivist frameworks, feminist researchers have reinterpreted transnational networks as agents of norms 'in progress' that work across jurisdictions localising international norms to bring about domestic change (see Moghadam 2005). By treating norms as dynamic and unfinished, this approach recognises how networks can shape and contest normative content and meaning through their own advocacy and internal transformations. Just as the content and meaning of norms change over time, transnational networks frequently embark on "trial-and-error processes in the nexus between theory and practice" (Krook and True 2012: 117).

Networks are not just engaged in the agenda-setting stage of norm emergence or issue prioritisation (Carpenter 2005, 2007), but also their professionalism, expertise and connection to governments and advocacy organisations are critical to the recognition and institutionalisation of norms by state and non-state actors. When this process occurs across borders, networks can transform the content and meaning of the norms that they are advocating for, while at the same time overcoming domestic and international political obstructions to their causes. Through their exploration of the agency and dynamism of TFNs, feminist scholars have highlighted how networks undertake critical knowledge-building activities to reach solutions. TFNs have a long history, starting with organisations such as the International Council of Women (ICW), formed in 1888, the International Alliance of Women (IAW), founded in 1904 as the International Woman Suffrage Alliance (Sluga and James 2015), and the Women's International League for Peace and Freedom (WILPF), which emerged from women's peace activism during World War I (WWI) and was founded in 1919 (Confortini 2012). Since their inception over a century ago, feminist advocacy networks have constructed a reflexive dialogue process to challenge existing social relations and build the momentum for normative change. Critically, this dialogue includes opportunities for contestation and critique and occurs within highly politicised environments, leading some scholars to view feminist advocates themselves as cross-cultural theorists of norm diffusion (Ackerly 2003).

TFNs navigate their own political agendas and membership bases to translate desirable norms into concrete policy (Zwingel 2013: 113). In this sense, they are not simply transmission belts for international norms, but also operate as mechanisms of norm emergence, contestation, transformation, and impact. Analysing four decades of efforts to enact new laws to reduce and prevent violence against women, Htun and Weldon (2012) found that the critical factor in the institutionalisation of international anti-violence norms within countries was the continued presence and activism of feminist networks. Transnational networks do not necessarily operate homogeneously, however. Rather, their divergent values and agendas can both proactively contest and/or undermine certain international norms. Feminist research, for example, observes how norms are rendered less useful as a result of exclusionary or closed network trends or behaviour (Basu 2016). Liberal women's rights agendas during the UN Decade for Women (1975–85) were limited in their global import, for instance, because they excluded women's movements in the Global South focused on poverty and structural inequalities, in part, resulting from Global North economic policies and proxy conflicts during the Cold War (Moghadam 2005). Hughes, Krook, and Paxton (2015) also found that women's transnational organising is constituted by diverse and often confronting agendas that sometimes reactively contest the adoption of new norms, such as gender quotas, despite the international support for them.

The Case of Women, Peace, and Security

The WPS agenda as a case study allows us to explore how norms evolve and contestation occurs in the context of changes in the structure and dynamics of networks. This is visible in the agency of new actors in the network – representing greater global diversity – and the network's capacity to forge new spaces for contestation open to these actors. Following Wiener's (2014, 2019) theory of norm contestation, both dynamics impact upon norm legitimacy. WPS is the result of dynamic encounters between women's rights and peace activism across myriad contexts and the channelling of this activism through transnational networks (Tryggestad 2009). These networks are responsible for the spread and localisation of the WPS norm bundle which comprises several norms expressed within ten UN Security Council (UNSC) resolutions that together form an international framework to promote and protect women's rights in peace and security policies. The following analysis examines two historical moments in the evolution of this norm bundle to explore how the membership, structure, and agency of networks change as both a cause and an effect of changes in norms.

The Women's Peace Congress Network

The first moment is the emergence of anti-militarist women's peace activism across Europe and America culminating in the 1915 International Congress of Women (ICW). From the middle of the nineteenth century, women across Europe and North America had been forming suffrage organisations and peace groups, with some of their leaders undertaking international visits. An alliance was formed between British and European women activists and American women leaders, led by Jane Addams, the founder of Hull House in Chicago, during one of these visits to the United States to promote a peaceful solution to the incipient WWI. Together they established the Women's Peace Party and began organising the inaugural ICW at The Hague in the Netherlands to put forward their plans to end the war to state leaders.

The transnational network that met at The Hague in 1915 set forth a new normative vision for international peace. Supported by the Women's Peace Party meeting shortly prior, Addams brought to her position as chair of the ICW a platform that stressed the importance of international cooperation over balance of power politics and promoted women's interests within the evolution of global post-war consciousness (Tickner and True 2018; Addams 2007). Alongside more than 1,500 women from twelve nations, the ICW produced twenty resolutions to bring about a peaceful and constructive end to WWI. Up until the outbreak of WWI, the suffrage and peace movements were heavily linked. However, many suffragettes did support the war, and the International Woman Suffrage Alliance did not support the Congress at The Hague (see Marshall et al. 1987; Berkman 1990). As a result, the establishment of the network caused a split within national and international women's suffrage movements (New York Times 1915); the division among suffragists involved a conscious delinking of the universal suffrage norm – women's citizenship right to vote within states – from the anti-war norm.

The quest to resolve conflict through inclusive peacemaking among states, however, depended on the equal political rights and representation of women and men within democratic states. The first resolution to come out of the Congress challenged the idea that women were protected in conflict, instead noting their entrenched vulnerability to "horrible violation[s]" during all wars (Addams et al. 2015). As such, there was a need to increase women's roles in decision-making in both conflict prevention and conflict resolution. Crucially, another of the peace principles to emerge from The Hague entailed that the foreign policies of all states be subject to democratic control through the establishment of equal rights and political participation for women. Thus, as Tickner and True (2018: 222) argue, "the women's peace principles were prospective international norms interconnected with, but also predating, the full realization of the international suffrage movement." Yet a new norm that aligned social, economic, and gender justice within states – with peace between them – required a new network.

While the resolutions of the ICW did not prevail over the ardent militarism of state leaders during WWI, they nevertheless strongly influenced later peace and security developments. As the American chair of the International Congress of Women at a time when the United States was still neutrally positioned in the war, Jane Addams led the delegation that met with President Woodrow Wilson to propagate the anti-war norms developed at the ICW and advocate for American leadership of mediation to resolve disputes between belligerent nations. Although President Wilson was ultimately committed to a policy of military preparedness at the time, many of the anti-war norms espoused in the ICW resolutions were later reflected in his Fourteen Points statement for peace in 1918 (Tickner and True 2018: 223). Moreover, the ICW resolutions arguably pre-empted the establishment of the League of Nations and subsequent international systems of post-war multilateralism (Elshtain 2002: 255).

In the wake of a devastating war, and following the International Women's Congress at The Hague, the Women's International League for Peace and Freedom (WILPF) was established in 1919 to further the peaceful anti-war vision of TFNs. WILPF's advocacy during the interwar period emphasised the importance of economic and social justice including women's roles in preventing future wars (McCarthy et al. 2015). WILPF developed as a federation, with national units as well as an international secretariat, and gradually assumed feminist anti-militarism as its overarching mandate frame. It engaged with the new multilateral organisation, the League of Nations, in line with the principles that emerged at The Hague in 1915 to establish delegations of women to travel and communicate anti-war and democratic ideas to belligerent states to bring about 'a just and lasting peace' (Addams et al. 2015). Indeed, the early humanitarian work of the League of Nations and its democratic reform to improve organisational representation, notably women's organisations, is largely attributable to the advocacy and contestation of transnational networks of feminist activists in the interwar period (Cochran 2017: 157).

The feminist anti-war network that arose from the ICW and subsequent post-war activism operated as a dynamic and intelligent agent for the establishment of a normative WPS agenda on the international stage. The inherent dynamism of the network – visible in its ever-adapting structures, activities and membership base in the face of new contexts for peace activism from WWI to the League of Nations and World War II (WWII) – impacted upon the emergence of early WPS norms as well as their socialisation and interpretive contestation within and across post-war politics and institutions. At the same time, internal dialogue and reactive contestation of the normative agenda in the post-WWII period by feminists in protracted conflicts who did not experience a neat alignment of gender equality and peace created reflexive changes within the network itself (Confortini 2012). A mutually transformative process ensued for both norm and network in the pursuit of gender-sensitive peace.

The UNSCR 1325 Network

The second moment considers the linking up of women's peace activism across the Global South and North to lobby for greater recognition of the specific impacts of war on women and their roles in conflict resolution, culminating in United Nations Security Council Resolution (UNSCR) 1325 in 2000. UNSCR 1325 constitutes the foremost international instrument formally recognising women's unique experiences of conflict and providing a normative framework for the protection of women and girls, for women's meaningful engagement in conflict prevention and peacebuilding, and for the inclusion of a gender perspective in peace and security policy and decisionmaking (see Hill et al. 2003). The global expansion of women's peace networks enabled proactive contestation of the emergent WPS norm bundle, through new spaces and increased access for women activists from the Global South and especially from contexts of protracted conflict.

WPS has a far longer history than the immediate run-up to the adoption of UNSCR 1325 – a history that relates to the forging of transnational solidarities across women's movements with violence against women, equality, justice, and conflict as the first moment highlighted. Following the interwar efforts of women's peace movements and the establishment of the United Nations and the international liberal order, a new wave of TFNs emerged in the mid-1980s. Taking stock of the North–South political divisions and reactive contestations that challenged earlier international feminist and peace movements, these networks undertook significant bridge-building across regional, religious, and ideological divides to expand their reach. Activist women in developing and developed countries created the second generation of women's transnational networks to combat the rise of neoliberalism and fundamentalist movements, now with explicitly 'feminist' framings: for example, MADRE, DAWN, WEDO, WIDE, Women Living Under Muslim Laws, and in 1995 the World March of Women (Moghadam 2005).[2] This globalisation of TFNs well preceded the UNSCR 1325 norm bundle and was critical to its successful adoption and subsequent dynamism.

Despite an optimism for peace in the post-Cold War era, the 'new wars' of the late twentieth century saw global women's movements gain traction. Gendered violence perpetrated across a multitude of conflicts in the Global North and South established a universality to women's experiences of conflict and provided a renewed opportunity for TFNs to critique state failure to stem conflict and advocate for women's involvement in conflict resolution efforts (Chinkin 2019). While the international community was receptive to norms regarding the protection of women from gender-based violence, the absence of feminist advocates from the 1995 Dayton negotiations revealed resistance towards women's full and equal participation in peace processes. Nevertheless, networked advocacy efforts persisted; in the late 1990s, CSOs led a conference on women's experiences of conflict and peacebuilding attended by women from fifty conflict-affected countries, established an NGO Working Group on WPS and formed a Women in Armed Conflict Caucus comprising sixty organisations from conflict-affected countries to demand a UNSCR on WPS (Anderlini 2019). Where their ideas failed to receive routine recognition, TFNs latched onto the shifting political opportunity structure – with the emergence of the human security discourse and the international community's legal obligation to protect civilians – to infiltrate mainstream institutional dialogue with a gender perspective on sustainable peace.

The normative agenda that emerged with the adoption of UNSCR 1325 at the end of the twentieth century reflected significant Global South participation among state and non-state feminist actors not previously seen or achieved before – certainly not when compared with the whitewashed first wave of international feminist mobilisation at the ICW in 1915. Global South actors were instrumental to the uptake of early WPS norms; as president of the UNSC in early 2000, Bangladesh made the first formal statement linking international peace and security with gender equality and undertook significant engagement with feminist networks regarding the framing, strategy, and tactics to socialise and diffuse WPS norms. Likewise, non-permanent UNSC member

[2] DAWN: Development Alternatives with Women for a New Era; WIDE: Women in Development Europe; WEDO: Women's Environment and Development Organization.

Namibia adopted the Windhoek Declaration and a specific Plan of Action to mainstream gender perspectives within its peacekeeping operations. This advocacy set the stage for Namibia to introduce the text of 1325 into the UNSC during its presidency in late 2000 (Anderlini 2019). As Soumita Basu (2016: 370) argues, while the Global North may make itself out as the material and institutional home of UNSCR 1325, "the conceptual underpinnings of UNSCR 1325 have a broader base, with involvement of gender advocates from across the world. The Global South has been engaged in the 'writing' of UNSCR 1325 and can also claim ownership of the WPS resolutions."

The expansion of the wide-ranging WPS network can be observed both prior to and alongside the development of the WPS norm, reinforcing their mutually transformative relationship. During the UN Decade for Women (1975–85) and especially culminating in the Fourth World Conference on Women in Beijing (1995), a key mechanism of network influence in shaping gender equality norms, including the norm recognising the impact of armed conflict on women and women's roles in conflict resolution, was the inclusion of non-government organisations (NGOs) in government delegations to UN conferences on women. Such mixed delegations enabled internal networking among state and non-state actors and normative socialisation and diffusion as a result. True and Mintrom (2001) compiled a list of fifty-two women's international NGOs (constituting those with offices and membership in several countries and present at the 1995 Beijing Women's Conference and one previous UN women's conference in the NGO Forum since 1975), cross-checking the conference registrations with the Yearbook of International Organizations, which lists country membership and headquarter presence. Revising this analysis since 1998 concomitant with the rise of the UNSCR 1325 network, they noted significant growth in transnational networking. The list of organisations now meeting sightly updated criteria[3] has since increased to ninety-five organisations (True 2017).

The networking of women's peace movements across the Global South and North at the end of the twentieth century reflects the power of transnational solidarity and mobilisation in pursuit of normative change recognising the gender-differentiated impacts of war and conflict and enabling women's roles in conflict-resolution and prevention.

[3] An additional criterion replaced the presence at UN Decade for Women conferences for the 1998–period, that is, the explicit mention in the UN Security Council WPS Presidential Statements, Open Debate minutes or resolutions and 2015 Global Study on the Implementation of 1325 (UN Women 2015).

The breadth and depth of their networked advocacy shifted perceptions of the UNSC's role in the maintenance of international peace and security towards the protection of individuals and their fundamental rights, thereby fostering an environment that was conducive to the socialisation and institutionalisation of WPS norms via UNSCR 1325. Moreover, by advocating for a normative vision of WPS in UNSCR 1325 that extended beyond conflict settings to include prevention, peacebuilding, and reconstruction, global women's movements ensured that WPS norms would remain dynamic in the face of new environments for norm emergence, contestation, and transformation.

Contemporary Challenges to WPS

Over the last century, the WPS norm bundle has evolved through distinct networks and practices of contestation as state and non-state actors have competed to identify, define, and apply emergent norms. Reactive contestation of normative alignment of gender equality and peace by suffragist movements during WWI and later by women activists in Global South contexts led to the formation of a transnational women's network that created new spaces and access for proactive contestation of international peace and security. The articulation of an emergent norm, women's right to equal participation in peace, and security decisionmaking was subsequently developed through interpretative contestations of what this norm entailed within different national settings (via WPS National Action Plans) and in actual peace processes. Subsequent to the adoption of UNSCR 1325, different norms in the norm bundle have taken priority and received greater endorsement over others. In previous research, engagement in transnational advocacy networks and membership in an intergovernmental organisation that has committed to implementing the WPS agenda were both found to matter significantly for WPS normative change (True 2016: 319). This is precisely because TFNs enable the enhanced access to proactive contestation of WPS. In particular, the expansion and transformation of the networks that advocate for the prohibition norm against the use of sexual violence in conflict have been highly influential in the implementation of local documentation practices by grassroot organisations and standarised investigation procedures by states, as well as the cases of international prosecutions at the International Criminal Court and ad hoc criminal jurisdictions (Davies and True 2017; Chappell 2016).

New mechanisms for network influence have also evolved following the proactive contestations of UNSCR 1325 in particular. These mechanisms, such as, 'Friends of WPS', a group of WPS supporting activist states, and the NGO Working Group on WPS (NGOWG) constituted new resources for WPS normative change. They have garnered greater legitimacy for WPS because they are the product of proactive contestations by grassroots and non-state actors as well as states. Whereas the inclusion of women CSOs was previously limited to invite-only government delegations or UN conferences on women, the formation of NGO coalitions and caucuses has resulted in growing advocacy for WPS norms in previously impenetrable spaces. Anderlini (2019: 45) describes how the early advocacy of NGO caucuses at the UN Commission on the Status of Women resulted in government representatives and UNSC delegations mixing with TFNs at campaign events for the first time, marking a 'generational shift' in network mobilisation and relationship-building that greatly enhanced the international diffusion of WPS norms.

Nowadays, coalitions such as the NGOWG – which comprises nineteen international NGOs whose members operate in over fifty conflict-affected countries and partner with over 275 NGOs, and civil society activists – hold access to the highest peace and security decisionmaking spaces. Between 2004 and 2022, the NGOWG has brought civil society representatives from Global South conflict zones to brief Security Council member states at open debates on WPS. This has included briefings speakers from Afghanistan (3x), Democratic Republic of the Congo (2x), Iraq (2x), Colombia (2x), Côte d'Ivoire, Burundi, Timor-Leste, Somalia, Uganda, Senegal, Central African Republic, Libya, South Sudan, Palestine, and Sudan. Civil society representatives have also briefed the UNSC open debate on sexual violence in conflict since its inception in 2012, hailing from Libya (2x), Mali, Uganda, South Sudan (2x), Nigeria, Iraq, Myanmar (2x) and Central African Republic.

As Taylor (2019: 74) reflects, "[i]t is difficult to overemphasise how unusual this [civil society briefing arrangement] is, as Council members are traditionally only briefed by UN representatives." Yet thanks to the tenacious advocacy of TFNs to cement WPS matters on the UNSC agenda, it is an arrangement that has evolved within subsequent UNSC open debates on sexual violence in conflict and on the protection of civilians, revealing how the expansion of WPS networks has broadened the contexts in which norm emergence, contestation, and diffusion occurs. This mechanism for network influence also pushes back against the conceptual supremacy of Global North over the WPS normative agenda, given the increasing global diversity of the CSO representatives who provide briefings and the NGOWG-aligned CSOs themselves (Cook 2016). Moreover, the inclusion of CSO representatives has placed a welcome emphasis on women's agency and participation in peace and security dialogue – a clear shift from the pre-UNSCR 1325 attitudes of the UNSC mentioned earlier (True and Wiener 2019). As a result, despite its vacillating engagement with the WPS agenda over the past two decades, "the Council is now regularly briefed on women's participation in peace talks, on the impact of conflict related sexual violence, of the need for accountability" (Taylor 2019: 74).

Shifts in the breadth and depth of transnational networks can also lead to significant norm changes. In the WPS context, contrasting with the relative silence of the UNSC and international community between 2000 and 2008, conflict-related sexual violence has received extensive (if not disproportionate) attention by both the UNSC and UN member states. Between 2008 and 2022, eight resolutions have been adopted by the UNSC regarding conflict-related sexual violence, and a further resolution was introduced in 2016 regarding sexual exploitation and abuse perpetrated by UN peacekeepers.[4] Some CSOs and women's networks have contended that the over-emphasis on protecting women from sexual violence redirects attention onto the victimisation rather than the agency of women in conflict situations; consequently, normative contestation regarding the prioritisation of protection over participation has been ongoing in the WPS agenda since 2008 (see Jansson and Eduards 2016; Kreft 2017; Kirby and Shepherd 2016).

Network contestation of the WPS norm has also resulted in challenges to certain assumptions around sex within UNSCR 1325 and later resolutions. Over the last two decades, WPS resolutions have moved away from a binary conception of sex to recognise increasing diversity and intersectionality in the category of women (by recognising youth, ethnicity, disability and so on) while also recognising that men and boys are victims of sexual and gender-based violence. In leading this change, advocacy networks have not only added to the normative content of the WPS agenda by expanding its application to more groups, but also reshaped the norm by growing the meaning of gender compared with its previously narrow binary conception in peace and security dialogue.

Similarly, internal dynamism in the WPS normative agenda is visible across global regions in the way in which domestic actors reject dominant 'protection' and 'development' frames and instead adopt different frames to adapt the WPS agenda to their own local and regional contexts. In certain states in Africa, for instance, the WPS 'development' frame is predominantly employed to localise WPS as a women's empowerment issue in the context of conflicts incited and influenced by underdevelopment and poverty (see Reiling 2017). The WPS norm has had to adjust to a

[4] Resolutions 1888 (2008), 1889 (2009), 1920 (2013), 2122 (2014), 2242 (2015) Security Council resolution 2272 (2016) March 11, 2016, S/RES/2272.

raft of threats to peace and security and gender equality issues, including armed conflict, violent extremism, domestic and international terrorism, migration, and displacement. Consequently, the focus of the WPS norm – being protection against conflict-related sexual violence and women's capacity to prevent and resolve conflict – has been reshaped and reapplied to fit different issue areas (see UN Secretary-General 2015), and the networks that propagate and diffuse this norm have broadened and deepened as a result. Following the financial crisis of 2007–8, gender equality norms in political and economic governance have also affected the broader global WPS normative environment. Similar to women's inclusion in corporate leadership, women's inclusion in peace processes has received growing endorsement, with mounting evidence of the investment returns from women's inclusion in governance and decisionmaking.

However, in recent UN debates and member state policies, the inclusion of women in peace processes has become focused on increasing the numerical representation of women rather than changing gender relations (Stone 2015). To date, only the Colombian peace process "has addressed gender concerns (including sexual violence) in a systematic manner that exemplifies the aims of the Security Council resolutions 1325 (2000) and 1820 (2008)" (UN Secretary-General 2016: 5/34). Failed peace talks in Afghanistan, Myanmar, and Syria barely engaged with women, especially beyond those affiliated with armed groups (see Olivius et al. 2021; Rivas and Safi 2022; Alsaba and Kapilashrami 2016). Key normative issues – including asking *which* women should sit at the peace table and *what agendas* they bring to their position – have generally been excluded from discussion by states despite being the focus of advocacy by women's networks. These activists campaign for women's full and meaningful participation by asking how societies can be reconstructed in a manner that guarantees sustainable peace and recognises women's agency, particularly in peace mediation and conflict resolution (see Paffenholz et al. 2016; WILPF 2017; Turner 2019; Aggestam 2019; UN Women 2018). Often, this involves creating parallel mechanisms to official peace processes to serve as a normative counterweight; in 2019, for instance, a global network of women mediators formed from regional networks to increase the visibility and participation of women mediators appointed to peace processes by the United Nations and other groups (True and Wiener 2019: 561).

As the preceding discussion shows, changes to the normative content of the WPS agenda are inseparable from the diversification and globalisation of the transnational networks who seek to challenge gendered norms and act as agents of peace and security. Since the 1990s, global efforts to constrain civil society participation coupled with women's exclusion from political participation has led to coordinated advocacy efforts by WPS networks to secure women's involvement and influence peace and security policy. By lobbying and sharing entry points to official policy-making spaces, facilitating parallel consultations and peace discussions, and mobilising non-violent civic resistance, networks of women peace activists have been able to generate feedback loops between advocacy spaces and official peace processes (Susskind and Duarte 2019: 792–3). These strategies were visible at the Women Lead to Peace forum in 2014, where in retaliation to the exclusion of women CSOs from the Geneva II Conference for Syrian peace discussions, activists convened women peacebuilders and international allies to share their conflict prevention experiences and advocacy tactics, thus bolstering pressure for the inclusion of Syrian women peacebuilders at future negotiations (Susskind and Duarte 2019; Gambale 2016). At the same time, women's networked advocacy and leadership in community and informal spaces are just as critical to normative change in peace and security processes. For example, Colombian CSOs offering community storytelling and survivor-centred care to women impacted by conflict-related sexual violence have produced critical social norm change towards peace by de-normalising sexual violence as a mode of social control and destigmatising survivors' post-war identities (Susskind and Duarte 2019: 800).

Studying the impact of transnational network agency and structure on the emergence, contestation, transformation, and diffusion of WPS norms remains in its early stages. Yet transnational networks, which are dynamic and ever-changing, can be readily seen as part of the authorising environment for norm evolution and contestation, as well as the well-recognised agents crucial to the initial formulation and emergence of the WPS norm bundle. It is important therefore to sociologically study the transnational network dynamics within and across institutions and problem settings (e.g., on and in conflict-affected areas) in order to trace the evolution of international norms-as-processes. In the twenty-three years since UNSCR 1825s adoption, the UNSC remains deeply concerned about "persisting barriers … and the frequent under-representation of women" in national and international peace and political processes and "the resulting detrimental impact on the maintenance of international peace and security" (UNSG 2493 2019). TFNs are key influencers of global policy discourse on WPS through their engagement in ongoing norm creation, debate, and contestation. Moreover, these networks are major players in the localisation and diffusion of WPS norms on the ground, working closely with the UN peacebuilding missions to implement the WPS agenda (Dönges and Kullenberg 2019). This practical implementation is critical to the dynamism of WPS norms by providing myriad opportunities for transformation through alignment and cooperation within the external norm environment. Networks of women's CSOs and activists help to evolve and align WPS norms with their unique local settings by drawing connections between WPS and other cross-cutting peace and security agendas, including children in armed conflict, arms control, violent extremism, and the protection of human rights (Acheson and Butler 2019). This networked advocacy ensures that the WPS agenda is free from co-optation by security apparatuses and state interests and that the normative objectives of non-violent peace and gender equality are maintained as the objectives against which all WPS operational achievements are assessed.

COVID-19 and the New Normative Agenda of TFNs

Normative change and transnational network development are inextricable as can be seen in the current contestation of the WPS agenda in certain contexts; namely, the advent of the COVID-19 pandemic. COVID-19 emerged and expanded at a time of increased global tensions, which the United Nations and other peace and security institutions appeared ill-equipped to alleviate. Some of these pressure points were well established by 2019 – for instance, the internationalised conflict in Syria and subsequent European refugee crisis – while others remained fresher and less certain in their consequences, including escalating economic tensions between the United States and China, diplomatic standoff between the US and Russia (that have now escalated as a result of Russia's war in Ukraine), and also the US and Iran following US withdrawal from the nuclear non-proliferation deal and the rise of right-wing populist leaders in several democratic elections. In light of multiple sources of global unease, TFNs had to adapt and mobilise against social, economic, health, and conflict-related pressures that threatened to roll back many of the hard-fought normative gains of the WPS agenda.

In many ways, the advent of COVID-19 within this turbulent environment pushed TFNs and the norms they propagate to new, more radical heights. Rather than retreat into local and nationally oriented advocacy streams – a lesson learnt from the missteps of their second-wave predecessors following WWII – international women's movements utilised the pandemic as an opportunity to strengthen their network linkages and broaden the WPS normative framework. By drawing connections between the impacts of intersecting economic, political, environmental, and health crises on gender equality and sustainable peace, transnational feminist activists have reconfigured

WPS norms to fit the evolving peace and security context. In 2020, for example, the Global Network of Women Peacebuilders (GNWP 2020) launched its COVID-19 and Women, Peace and Security database to document the leadership of local women and youth peacebuilders in conflict-affected countries during the pandemic. Feminist scholars at the same time gathered data on the impact of COVID-19 on gender equality, peace, and security, women's rights/peacebuilding organisations, and women-led humanitarian and conflict prevention responses (see Johnston et al. 2021). These efforts assisted in the development and implementation of gender- and conflict-sensitive pandemic response and recovery strategies.

TFNs have also used the advent of COVID-19 to emphasise the long-term impacts of COVID-19 on democratic governance and human rights, as well as women's employment and economic security, thereby renewing the focus on the relevance of the WPS agenda. Civil society groups have reported the weakening of democracy and human rights in at least eighty countries since 2020, finding an acceleration of authoritarian agendas, social unrest, disinformation, and the curtailing of civil and political rights (see Freedom House 2020). The impact of the pandemic has been particularly acute for women, who have experienced exponentially higher rates of gender-based violence, significant burdening of unpaid care work, and compounded economic impacts from lost, informal, or insecure employment (UN Secretary-General 2020a). Cognisant of the well-documented trend of women experiencing increasing gendered discrimination in times of disaster, conflict, and economic recession (Wenham et al. 2020), TFNs have worked to redefine normative perceptions of gender-based violence during the pandemic as not simply discrimination, but evidence of misogyny and a 'war on women' that threatens social, economic, and political peace and security. This framing was reflected in the UN Secretary-General's (2020b) call for a 'ceasefire' on violence against women (VAW) and against girls, akin to that on armed conflict, and urged "all governments to make the prevention and redress of VAW a key part of their national response plans for COVID-19" (Mintrom and True 2022: 147).

Networked advocacy focused on anti-militarism, resource reallocation, and social justice has been critical to proactive contestation of WPS during times of global insecurity. As WPS norms sit in direct contestation with the escalating military spending of the UNSC permanent members, advocates have pushed for a 'feminist UNSC' that implements its mandate consistent with the WPS agenda and shifts its approach from aggressive crisis response to upstream conflict prevention and sustainable peace centred on women's participation, protection, and rights

(WILPF 2018). WILPF's #MoveTheMoney campaign, for example, encourages the United Nations, international financial institutions and national governments to divest from a political economy of war, discrimination, and violence and invest in a political economy of gender justice and peace (WILPF 2016). COVID-19 provided the external conditions to facilitate the uptake of WPS norms as TFNs pushed their own vision of 'building back better', in which gender equality, social justice, and sustainability are the basis for post-pandemic recovery and transformation (UN Women 2021). So far, this has included the rollout of multiple national and regional feminist foreign policy movements bringing together women civil society organisations, scholars, and advocates seeking to make gender equality a central goal of foreign policy given it is the foremost predictor of more peaceful and prosperous societies (Aggestam and True 2023; IWDA 2021; ICRW 2019; CFFP 2020).

This brief snapshot of networked advocacy and significant norm contestation demonstrates that in the most recent period of global unrest, TFNs have not just enhanced WPS normative claims and their institutional and mobilised capacity at the same time, but also become more diverse, inclusive, and intersectional – as have the norms that they avow. This amounts to an incremental normative transformation in both the content and the purpose of WPS.

Conclusion

This chapter has examined constructivist approaches to norm contestation and feminist approaches to the globalisation of advocacy and policy networks. As the first section has shown, feminist constructivism provides a compelling discursive analytical approach to norms while also appreciating the power of networks in the identification and interpretation of norms and their policy translation. Contrary to criticism that norms research treats norms as structures or is excessively agent-focused, feminist research has highlighted the tensions between agency and structure by analysing both the dynamic process of norm diffusion and the fluidity of network globalisation. However, the relationship between international norms and transnational networks is not well understood despite their early connection in the 'first move' of IR norms research. Yet the chapter argued that we cannot understand the processes of normative change and contestation without understanding the dynamism and globalisation of networks.

This chapter contributes to 'third move', norm contestation scholarship by bridging the theoretical gap between the dynamics of norm contestation and network globalisation analysed in IR feminist research. It reveals how new forms of networking both shape and are shaped by distinct practices of norm contestation and enable new mechanisms for proactive contestation. The chapter's analysis of two historical moments in the evolution of WPS highlights how TFNs have been crucial to the dynamic and contested WPS norm bundle both as social mechanisms of norm dynamism and as intelligent and multifaceted agents themselves. Reactive contestation by suffragists and Global South women activists were crucial to the network delinking and transnational expansion that led to WPS norm emergence during WWI and to its institutionalisation at the UNSC almost a century later. Interpretative contestations primarily socialised WPS meaning-in-use within national and local settings, especially crisis and conflict-affected settings. Proactive contestations, however, have been instrumental in expanding state and civil society participation in WPS, which has, in turn, enhanced the legitimacy and soft power of the normative agenda. The significant network activity of women's movements in the two decades following UNSCR 1325 attests to their dynamic compositions and capacities as they seek to shape and contest dominant state security agendas in local, national, and international spaces, and within institutional settings beyond the UNSC. In this sense, WPS norms and the networks that purport them are ongoing works 'in progress'.

In light of their co-constitution, norm contestation and network globalisation would benefit from increased attention by IR scholars. In the cases analysed in this chapter, network dynamism provides access to proactive contestation by forging new paths of participation in WPS for activists and citizens including women affected by conflict. In this way, transnational networks are not merely mechanisms of norm diffusion or issue linkage, they also create more legitimate forms of norm diffusion. The WPS agenda is an ideal site for greater analysis given that its relatively broad and non-binding normative framework has undergone significant growth and change since its formal inception in 2000. Moreover, the advent of numerous intersecting global crises in the two decades since provides ample opportunity to explore the limitations and successes of networked WPS advocacy and norm contestation in diverse political, social, and economic contexts. Further study in this area should seek to adopt a feminist or gender-informed approach for its attention to the discursive origins and contestation trajectories of international norms and their transnational networks, thereby moving beyond norm emergence and agenda-setting. From this basis, TFNs will cement their position as critical mechanisms for reflexively evolving the WPS norm bundle and driving political as well as normative change in international peace and security.

13 Regulatory Contestation and the Creation of Transnational Legal Orders

Cecilia Jacob

Introduction

This chapter presents the concept of *regulatory contestation*, a form of proactive contestation that occurs within a given regulatory context to advance analysis of the role of norms in the development of transnational legal orders (TLOs). As international law has become increasingly specialised, indeed 'fragmented' (Study Group of the International Law Commission 2006), TLOs now serve an integral role in regulating actors across the international–domestic divide, shaping the character of global governance and the evolving constitution of international order (Halliday and Shaffer 2015; also Kingsbury 2010; Krisch and Kingsbury 2006).

This chapter conceptualises the regulatory function of norms in order building, it views 'regulation' through a socio-legal lens that is broader than the prevalent definition of regulation that operates in the discipline of International Relations (IR). IR characterises certain norms as 'regulatory', namely those norms that "order and constrain" behaviour (Finnemore and Sikkink 1998: 891), or in other words, those that have "regulatory or restrictive effects" on actor behaviour (Price 2006: 258). This conceptualisation narrows understanding of the regulatory function of norms once initial contestation over norm validity has settled. Regulation, as conceptualised in this chapter, includes purposive, generative, and creative agency of those with decisionmaking authority/influence in global governance institutions to negotiate the mechanisms through which routinised, or more consistent, implementation of norms can be governed. Regulatory contestation is proactive and occurs as a distinct process during the stage of implementation. It engages

The author thanks the editors of this volume and the participants at the workshops "Norm Research in Theory and Practice" on March 24, 2020, and 1 April 2021 for valued feedback on this chapter. Parts of the chapter were also presented at the Department of International Development, Oxford University, on December 16, 2019 and the European Centre for the Responsibility to Protect, Leeds University, on December 19, 2019, and the Australian Political Science Association Annual Meeting, September 20, 2021. Special appreciation is due to Terry Halliday for guidance on the broader project from which this chapter is drawn.

legal mechanisms and logics for realising a more permanent functioning of norms in global governance; however, it involves diverse agency that interacts with different layers of social, legal, and political ordering through which regulatory reach can be established.

The definition of regulation employed in this chapter is "efforts to steer or influence the flow of events towards specified governance outcomes" (Jacob 2021a). Regulation is understood as a social practice that is process-oriented, responsive to contingency, and inherently normative. As this chapter will show in the case of human protection in the United Nations (UN), there is a bias in the regulatory mindset of actors to move problem solving out of the ostensibly unpredictable and inconsistent domain of politics towards technocratic, legal, and juridical solutions. Consequently, analysis of regulatory contestation draws the IR norms literature into debates within international law regarding the promises and pitfalls of global regulatory governance, and attests to the political and social character of international law-making that contributes to bringing politics (back) into norms research (Orchard and Wiener, Chapter 1).

This chapter applies this approach to studying norms to a case study of the development of the prevention and human rights agenda in the Human Rights Council (HRC) in Geneva. The recent proliferation of juridical and institutional mechanisms to prevent, protect, and prosecute mass violations of human rights is indicative of an emergent transnational human protection order that draws direct connections to the wider UN reform process that employs prevention as a guiding logic (Jacob 2021b). Developments in the UN Human Rights Council (HRC) show a preference for improving the legal administration of accountability for atrocities where political bodies of the UN have faltered. Contestation over the actual form of the regulatory design for implementing the prevention agenda reveals the normative values and principles that shape actors' choices when designing regulation frameworks. These contours include divergent normative assumptions regarding the nature of accountability for mass violations of human rights and its value in promoting 'just' outcomes at the international level.

The Emergence of a Human Protection Transnational Legal Order

Over the past seventy-five years, a TLO (Halliday and Shaffer 2015; Teitel 2011) on human protection[1] has emerged, regulating the governance

[1] Most notable of these are the Protection of Civilians and the Responsibility to Protect (R2P); see Bellamy (2016: 119–25) for a discussion of the 'eight streams' of the international human protection regime.

of humanitarian crises at the global level and bringing legal order to a problem of international significance. A TLO is defined as 'a collection of formalised legal norms and associated organizations and actors that authoritatively order the understanding and practice of law across national jurisdictions' (Halliday and Shaffer 2015: 475). The socio-legal TLO framework analyses the way in which actors 'conceive' and 'order' social problems, employing a recognisable legal form of problem solving (even if norms themselves are not officially legalised) through engagement with governance institutions and legal bodies. Finally, TLOs are concerned with the transnational character of order building that integrates analysis of the domestic–global interactions in issue-specific areas (Halliday and Shaffer 2015: 476) that transcends traditional state-international divisions that have long been eroding in international law and global governance (Sieber 2010).

The norms literature in IR has explored the emergence, contestation, and institutionalisation of international norms to protect civilian populations during episodes of violent conflict and mass atrocity (Acharya 2013; Deitelhoff 2019; Welsh 2013). The human protection TLO (HPTLO) integrates these norms within an innovative legal and institutional configuration at the international level that has been consolidated over the past thirty years, although its origins go back much further. The HPTLO is shaped by intertwining logics of prevention, protection, accountability, and human rights. These logics promote deeper integration of international human rights law (IHRL), international humanitarian law (IHL), and international criminal law (ICL) in prevention and protection (Alexander 2015; Meron 2000; Teitel 2011), and has promoted new institutional linkages between the UN Security Council, Human Rights Council (HRC), International Criminal Court (ICC), International Court of Justice (ICJ), and other legal mechanisms that address impunity for mass atrocities (Hunt 2017; Meron 2018; Rapp 2016: 11–13).

The contestation over the meaning of specific human protection norms (Deitelhoff 2019; Paddon-Rhoads and Welsh 2019; Welsh 2013), the strength of international norms, and their institutionalisation has been theorised in the international norms literature (see Ben-Josef Hirsch and Dixon, Chapter 2). However, less attention has been paid to the conceptualisation of regulation itself and the process of regulatory design in the study of international norms (Berliner and Prakash 2012; Camacho and Glicksman 2021). Varied actors hold different normative and conceptual understandings of regulation itself that feeds into contestation over the regulatory design and functions that are agreed upon in the process of norm implementation.

By paying attention to the conceptualisation of regulation, and researching the contours of its contestation in the process of norm implementation, the norms research field is opened to new empirical sites of research to investigate *how* and *where* different actors are realising their normative and strategic visions of international order. Actors may accept the underlying premise of a settled international norm and yet hold different positions on the normative dimensions of a regulatory system, such as transparency, accountability, the rule of law, or the primacy of human rights by negotiating these values through the design of the regulatory regime itself. Methodologically, this approach engages socio-legal emphasis on assessing, "the 'gap' between the 'law on the books' and the 'law in action'" (Pound 1910, cited in Menkel-Meadow 2019: 35; see also Stimmer, Chapter 10) to show the functioning of norms in practice. This perspective also opens the norms research agenda to further engage with a central research problem in the field of international law, namely what are the implications of the increasing fragmentation and specialisation of norms on international order (Cogan 2011; Koskenniemi 2007)? The increased regulatory governance of atrocities signals deeper institutionalisation, and therefore wider socialisation and internalisation of international norms to influence actor behaviour in ways that are norm-consistent.[2] From an IR perspective, this outcome is an indicator of a norm's success in transforming the repressive or deviant behaviour of actors in line with important international norms that have a significant global bearing in areas such as human rights, nuclear disarmament, or climate change.

To what extent does the success of issue-specific orders have on the broader international order? Scholars of the international legal order are concerned with fragmentation and the toll that specialisation exacts on the broader political ideals that sustain the normative project of international law, as expressed through the growing body of literature on global constitutionalism and the global rule of law (Klabbers et al. 2011). In the case of the prevention and human rights agenda examined in this chapter, diplomats have questioned the benefit that the fast-rising accountability agenda has on global politics, questioning whether it is instead a sign of weakened political institutions, such as the UN Security Council, to govern international peace and security issues effectively in the current geopolitical environment. In this scenario, devolving responsibility for mass atrocities and humanitarian crises from the Security Council to bodies such as the Human Rights Council and independent investigatory mechanisms may be seen as the

[2] For a conceptual discussion of norm consistency, see Crossley (2020).

Security Council defaulting on its responsibilities. The emphasis on accountability has been interpreted by some as a sign of significant failure in key institutions of the multilateral order in the area of peace and security (Jacob 2021a). Further this trend points to a shift in global politics to deal with crises through increased expediency (Karlsrud 2019; Wiuff Moe and Stepputat 2018), that is, "moving from liberal templates towards more pragmatic forms of intervention" (Riis Andersen 2018: 343) that also has bearing on the normative foundations of global order.

The study of norms and their implementation is enhanced through a TLO lens that positions the analysis of issue-specific normative orders in relation to the broader dynamics in the international legal and political order. The next section explains the contributions that the concept of regulatory contestation brings to studying norms before applying this lens to the case of the accountability and prevention agenda in the UN system.

Conceptualising Regulation

As briefly touched on earlier and detailed at length in the introduction to this volume, the IR norms contestation literature has spawned a scholarly field that is attuned to the political constitution of global norms. The critical constructivist approach attends to the changing dynamics in global power and creates theoretical space to account for diverse actors in shaping areas of international legal and normative order (Wiener 2008). In terms of the *normativity* of norms, scholars in this tradition conclude that deliberative processes increase access to shape the meaning of a norm, therefore only those norms that have been contested can be 'good' (Orchard and Wiener, Chapter 1: 19). This chapter employs a critical constructivist conception of norms, understanding both social and legal norms as socially constructed, contested, and rendered meaningful through social practice (Brunée and Toope 2011).

By focusing on the regulatory function of norms that are largely settled[3] in global politics, this chapter situates norms of human protection within the structural context of the human protection TLO. It pays attention to the changing institutional environment in which these norms are implemented, including the transformation of international law as an increasingly fragmented institution of global order. The consolidation of a TLO further contributes to the increasing

[3] While recognising that the meaning of norms-in-use remains contested and fluid, norms can become stable in their meaning when there is a broad consensus over the substantive contents of a given norm and agreement on the parameters of its application.

specialisation of international law into administrative and juridical modes of global governance. In this chapter's case study, I find that states, the UN Security Council, and the UN General Assembly 'pass the buck' to other actors for prevention and protection of populations in situations of dire humanitarian crisis, and legally oriented advocates seek to use law to 'fill the gap' (Farrall and Rubenstein 2009) left from this political void.

Mainstream conceptualisations of regulation in IR and international law tend to be very narrow, understanding regulatory norms in a more traditional, legalistic understanding of regulation as those that "order and constrain" (Finnemore and Sikkink 1998: 891), and therefore not inclusive of those that are generative of new modes of governance. Instead, I advance a broader definition of regulatory governance from the socio-legal literature on responsive regulation: "regulation means influencing the flow of events" (Parker and Braithwaite 2005: 119). This approach "is concerned with a broad array of practices and institutions that seek to alter or redirect a trajectory of events" (Jacob 2021a: 10) with the objective of improving the governance of settled, or stable, norms. This definition includes the governance functions of "steering, as opposed to providing, distributing, running, or voting" (Braithwaite et al. 2007: 6) that both creates more precision in terms of the actions and processes being studied and defines a mode of governance that is salient for imbuing an ethic of "regulatory cosmopolitanism" at the global level (Braithwaite 2021: 6).

In contrast to more traditional regulatory governance that emphasises legalism, efficiency, and compliance, the concept of responsive regulation challenges the idea of regulation as enforcement and control. Rather, it is a dynamic framework that understands social conflict as relational. Responsive regulatory governance is geared towards tailoring responses to social contexts and the actors being regulated (Westerman 2013), according to Drahos and Krygier, 'regulators should understand the context and motivations of those whose conduct they were regulating and then choose a response based on that contextual understanding' (Drahos and Krygier 2017: 5). Law is at the heart of regulatory governance, however, responsive regulation works on the premise that law in and of itself is insufficient to change actor behaviour. Rather, it is necessary to mediate legal and ethical principles into diverse social and political contexts in order to influence behaviour and to steer the flow of events towards alternative pathways (Charlesworth and Farrall 2016).

This definition allows for the analysis of the creative and generative function of regulation and shows that the process of regulatory contestation – focusing on the decisionmaking process in the design of regulatory mechanisms (as opposed to the underlying norm itself) – facilitates the mediation of international norms into varied social and political contexts. In other words, this approach shows how law "interacts with other forms of regulation or normative ordering" (Parker et al. 2004: 3) that is applicable in the context of multilateral engagement with the operational, political and legal dimensions of human protection and prevention.

Studying regulatory contestation provides insight into the power dynamics that are shaping fundamental institutions of international order at a micro-level. It departs from a conceptualisation of regulation as control mechanisms that limit individual and collective freedoms (Orbach 2012: 4) to one that acknowledges the creative and generative function of international norms in governing problems of international significance and actions that build order at the international level. Drawing insight from socio-legal studies on responsive regulation, this broader conception of regulation holds a *normative* commitment to the reduction of tyranny in the world and to restorative justice that resonates with pluralistic legal systems (Braithwaite and Pettit 1992; Braithwaite 2002). Responsive regulation encourages the design of regulatory mechanisms that promote these normative values, and is consistent with the normative commitment in critical constructivist IR to increasing diverse access and participation in the creation of normative orders both within and beyond the state level. The reduction of tyranny provides a benchmark against which the normativity of regulatory contestation may be evaluated. This is, however, an ideal type, and as discussed later, power imbalances persist in the formation of TLOs through regulatory contestation as it is an inescapably political process.

Situating Regulatory Contestation

The *process* of norm contestation moves through stages of constituting, negotiating, and implementing (Orchard and Wiener, Chapter 1: 18); regulatory contestation is a form of proactive contestation situated at the stage of implementation. Regulatory contestation follows initial validity contestation through which the legitimacy of norms are established. Validity is confirmed at this stage, as the "core normative claims" (Deitelhoff and Zimmerman 2020: 63) of norms are not challenged through regulatory contestation. Rather the collective – although not universal – decision to deliberate on appropriate regulatory mechanisms to routinise the implementation of a norm is a measure of both validity and legitimacy of norms, and a generalised understanding of the broad contexts in which given norms apply.

At the stage of validity contestation, deliberation is expressed through established institutions, albeit through ad hoc decisionmaking, and without a discernible or reliable pattern of behaviour. In the schema of this volume, once validity of a norm has been determined in relation *to a given regulatory environment*, regulatory contestation is a subsequent stage of contestation that defines the scope and usage of norms in that given environment. Regulatory contestation is a deliberate practice of shaping norm implementation that is oriented to the scope and mandate of the implementing body. Accordingly, regulatory contestation is likely to follow the institutional logic of the implementing body and operates on pre-existing templates for implementation. Regulatory contestation is a contingent process and is repeated as parallel processes in a vertical direction, at all levels of implementation from the micro-, to the meso- and macro-levels where implementing bodies have determined the relevance of the norm to their own mandates. Regulatory contestation also occurs in parallel in a horizontal direction *across* institutions, such as international organisations (IOs), regional organisations (ROs), and states, where there are multiple institutional sites with a mandate that is relevant to one or more aspects of norm implementation (Jacob 2018). Human rights is a clear example of a norm that transcends vertical and horizontal implementation sites, as the mechanisms for compliance and implementation varies across thematic and geographic scope. In this case, the contours of regulatory contestation is contingent on the rationale and mandate of the implementing body and the particularities of the given regulatory context (Jacob 2018).

Regulatory contestation also speaks to one of the core problems addressed in this volume, namely global power relations, or more precisely, "North–South and regional power biases that have existed in norms research" (Orchard and Wiener, Chapter 1: 8). The particular dynamics operating at each of these levels will reflect the context-specific power relations among actors within a given field. In global governance, access and decisionmaking authority in IOs remains skewed towards like-minded caucuses of states, dominated by powerful members with superior technical capability and political capital. At the global level, these power relations are those between the state actors involved in negotiating the structure and scope of a regulatory regime, and experts, IO bureaucrats, and non-governmental organisation (NGO) actors that form a community of practice around a norm or norm cluster. Consequently, the powerful few retain unequal influence in the design of global regulatory systems (Halliday et al. 2013). Transnational regulatory mechanisms perpetuate imbalances in representation of values and political objectives that are instantiated in these mechanisms. Accordingly, analysis of regulatory contestation facilitates empirical research into power imbalances in the construction of institutions of global order.

Regulation need not be synonymous with *legal* regulation, as explained earlier. For norms that are culturally validated at the micro-level, most regulation occurs outside of legal institutions, through social and political orders that are salient to the relevant audiences. In global governance, however, regulatory contestation finds legal expression in IOs, international law, and negotiated documentation/statements produced through formal decisionmaking forums. Although inherently political, regulatory contestation operates along a legalised logic for law-making and institutional building that includes a normative preference for increasingly prescriptive governance (Cogan 2011). Finally, in returning to the schema of this volume, regulatory contestation is *proactive* (Orchard and Wiener, Chapter 1: 16), aimed at strengthening the consistency and legitimacy of a norm by embedding its implementation through a permanent or concretised regulatory framework. It may also generate reactive contestation: conflicts may occur in relation to the scope, character, and governing principles of the regulatory framework. However, the process itself builds on a collective agreement as to the objective of formalising structures to shore up consistent implementation of the norm/s in question. Reactive contestation sets political parameters for what is possible in regulatory governance.

The value added to the field from this approach is twofold. First, opening analysis to regulatory contestation provides deeper empirical insight into the process of order building in international politics, illuminating how the norm implementation process works in reality and how diverse actors translate norms into governance outcomes. As demonstrated in the case of the accountability and prevention agenda later, states have consistently supported human protection norms in UN bodies across the New York–Geneva divide. However, the reform process has created new opportunities for actors to reconfigure parts of the system that have a bearing on the prevention capacity of the UN. Consequently, the normative premise for promoting prevention (improving the protection of civilian lives) remains intact while other liberal underpinnings of the UN have become exposed to new sites of contestation. This renewed contestation has resulted in the sidelining of human rights and conflict prevention in key areas of implementation (Jacob 2021b, 2021c), and divergent advocacy on the accountability agenda (Jacob 2021a). As new actors have opportunity to engage in proactive and reactive contestation, new values are being institutionalised into the reformed structures of the UN. Regulatory contestation provides a window into the normative commitments of influential actors that are reshaping the multilateral institutions that form a bedrock of international order, and therefore provides further insight into the processes through which these actors are reconstituting global order from within.

Second, regulatory contestation draws attention to the normativity of regulatory choices and the politics of norm implementation. The decisionmaking process to design and implement international norms through international institutions is not value neutral; it entails principled judgements around the nature and desirability of key dimensions of governance regimes, such as accountability, transparency, the rule of law, and rights. Further, the objectives of global governance are shaped by particular understandings of global justice and how to best achieve it. These macro-value systems determine the contours of regulatory contestation within a given TLO, and embed the politics of TLO creation into broader foundational questions of international legal order that were raised in the first section of this chapter.

Regulatory Contestation at the Human Rights Council: Pursuing Atrocity Prevention through Accountability

The UN human protection agenda has developed primarily in New York around thematic areas such as conflict prevention, protection of civilians, and R2P, and are addressed within the context of the UN Security Council (UNSC) and UN General Assembly, the operational functions of peacekeeping, political affairs, and peacebuilding, and the strategic leadership function of the UN Secretariat. However, the creation of the ICC and major reforms to the human rights system have prompted increased attention to the role of these bodies in promoting the protection of civilian populations from mass atrocities through accountability processes (D'Alessandra 2017; Pramendorfer 2020).

As the politics of the UNSC has hindered preventive and protection functions of the UN's peace and security bodies, this section describes the evolution of the human rights and atrocity prevention agenda, with a focus on the HRC in Geneva and the rapid growth of international accountability mechanisms. Specifically, diplomats, UN bureaucrats with specialised legal expertise, and civil society actors have made explicit connections between the Secretary-General's prevention agenda (United Nations Secretary-General 2017) and the mandated functions of the HRC, particularly in the area of accountability, to fill gaps in atrocity prevention and human protection. In doing so, they evidence a regulatory mindset in: (a) the way that they have conceptualised the relationship between human rights and atrocity prevention;

and (b) how they have articulated an interconnected, phased response to mobilise human rights accountability to steer towards improved prevention outcomes.[4]

Within this regulatory mindset, these actors turn to legal solutions to the problem of atrocities as international crimes,[5] evidencing a faith in international law and juridical processes to redress the deficiencies of political institutions for more consistent and less selective implementation of human protection norms. I provide two illustrations here to demonstrate how regulatory contestation is integral to international efforts to build legal order in the area of human protection. First is the development of the human rights and prevention agenda at the HRC. Second is the rapid growth in the number and mandate of accountability mechanisms, including the speed at which they are created, to develop more consistent responses to serious atrocities in the absence of UNSC leadership. This development has also generated reactive contestation in the HRC, with certain states resisting greater scrutiny powers by UN bodies. This section highlights proposals for the creation of a new standing mechanism to build capacity and fill gaps in the international accountability system to shore up consistency and effectiveness in the human protection TLO.

The development of the human rights and prevention agenda in Geneva was a response by diplomats and civil society groups to both the shortcomings of the UNSC when responding to situations of mass atrocity and a growing awareness of the relevance of the HRC to the wider prevention functions of the UN. These initiatives come from three different caucuses. First, a Ukraine-led caucus that first drew attention to preventive mandate of the HRC and its potential for addressing grave human rights violations. However, to draw in wide consensus, it now also promotes the widest definition of 'prevention' to not only include the most serious violations of human rights, but also extend the concept of prevention to a range of thematic areas, including education, governance, and livelihoods. Second, a Swiss–Norwegian-led caucus restricts the scope of prevention in its agenda to serious violations of human rights such as torture, genocide, mass atrocities, incitement to hatred, violent extremism, and discrimination (Human Rights Council 2015: 4). The third caucus is the R2P Group of Friends that insists

[4] For example, the Glion Human Rights Dialogue, see Universal Rights Group (2017); Jane Connors, presentation at the High-Level Event 'Implementing R2P in the Geneva Context – A Focus on Prevention', Palais des Nations, Geneva, 19 November 2015 (text with author).

[5] For a 'crimes based approach' to prevention, see Reike et al. (2015); also Jacob (2020).

on the most restrictive definition of rights violations to be included in the prevention agenda, namely, genocide, war crimes, crimes against humanity, and ethnic cleansing (Pramendorfer 2020).

Despite the disagreements over the scope of violations to be included,[6] these caucuses agree on the normative premise of the prevention agenda, which is grounded in General Assembly Resolution 60/251 (2006) that established the HRC. Prevention is included in the mandate of the HRC in Article 5(f), stating that the HRC should "[c]ontribute, through dialogue and cooperation, towards the prevention of human rights violations and respond promptly to human rights emergencies" (United Nations General Assembly 2006). There is also agreement that existing mechanisms such as the Universal Periodic Review (UPR), special procedures, commissions of inquiry, and fact-finding missions are integral to the UN's early warning and early response capacity. If fully realised, these mechanisms carry immense potential for identifying patterns of systematic human rights violation, including instances where specific population groups are being targeted and where violations are escalating in scale and intensity. This information would be invaluable for providing early warning of potential mass atrocity situations. Combined, these caucuses have been promoting prevention as a separate agenda item in the HRC.[7]

Conflicting views among the diplomatic caucuses on the scope and design of prevention mechanisms were debated in three intersessional seminars on the contribution of the HRC to the prevention of human rights violations in 2019: two in Geneva, and one in New York. The authors of the outcome report from the seminars (United Nations Human Rights Council 2020) reiterated areas of agreeance across the caucuses, namely that the HRC serves a crucial preventive role in monitoring situations at risk and early warning to the rest of the UN system through its mechanisms and personal representations by the High Commissioner for Human Rights to the UNSC. The HRC also facilitates in promoting accountability for past atrocities to help prevent recurrence (United Nations Human Rights Council 2019). The authors addressed the crucial area of contestation over the regulatory scope by endorsing the position of the Like-Minded Group (LMG) states[8] that

[6] For detail see Jacob (2021a: 11–13).
[7] Discussion in this section is based on interviews by author conducted in Geneva, December 2019, and New York in April 2018 and April 2019 with diplomats, NGOs and UN officials (anonymised).
[8] This group is comprised primarily of member states from the African Group, the Organisation of Islamic Cooperation, the Arab Group, and the Non-Aligned Movement that constitutes a significant majority in the UNHRC. See Essam (2016).

favour upstream, structural approaches to prevention while reassuring these states that developing stronger early warning and early action mechanisms would not risk undue intervention in the domestic affairs of states (United Nations Human Rights Council 2020: 3). Strong reactive contestation did feature in this process, particularly from LMG states, ensuring that the most radical proposals were removed from the final text of the OHCHR report. As a result, key changes required to empower the High Commissioner for Human Rights and the HRC to initiate early action within the UNSC on the most serious mass atrocity situations were omitted.

The second example of regulatory contestation that is proactively advancing international human protection norms is the proliferation of investigative mechanisms in response to situations of mass atrocity. Not only has there been an increase in the number of accountability mechanisms such as fact-finding missions and commissions of inquiry[9] to investigate cases of war crimes and crimes against humanity, but these mechanisms are being given more robust mandates to identify perpetrators and gather evidence that could be used to determine criminal accountability (D'Alessandra 2017). The logic animating this development is that legal solutions to the problem of international crimes redresses the deficiencies of political institutions for more consistent and less selective implementation of human protection norms, thereby advancing international justice.

The Independent International Commission of Inquiry (COI) on Ukraine was established only nine days after the Russian invasion on 24 February 2022, indicative of the upward trajectory of this accountability turn given the speed at which the HRC mobilised. In this case, the mandate of the COI included the collection, consolidation, and analysis of evidence of violations of human rights and international humanitarian law, "and to systematically record and preserve all information, documentation and evidence, including interviews, witness testimony and forensic material, consistent with international law standards, in view of any future legal proceedings" (A/HRC/RES/49/1 2022, para 11(b)). Russia was expelled from the HRC following its invasion of Ukraine. Further efforts to launch accountability efforts to counter Ukraine's aggression early on in the hostilities were the decision by the ICC prosecutor (ICC 2022) to open an investigation into the situation in Ukraine on 28 February (four days following the invasion), followed by the

[9] The UN created thirty-six commissions of inquiry and fact-find mandates in the sixteen-year period from 2006 to 2022. By way of comparison, before this the UN created a total of thirty-one such missions in its entire history.

referral of the situation to the ICC by forty-four states. Wider action has been taken to counter international crimes committed by Russia through international law; Ukraine instituted proceedings against Russia in the ICJ three days after the invasion (ICJ 2022), and several proposals were advanced for the creation of a Special Tribunal for Ukraine on the Crime of Aggression (Heller 2022).

In the case of Ukraine, we see the linking up of accountability measures across various international legal contexts, "bridging the divide" (Rapp 2016) between existing mechanisms and generating novel approaches to advancing justice as an accelerated response to mass atrocities. Indeed, since 2016, the UN has created a new type of investigative body to address war crimes, crimes against humanity and genocide in situations where the UNSC has failed to mobilise effective responses. These include the International, Impartial and Independent Mechanism for Syria, the United Nations Investigative Team to promote Accountability for the crimes committed by Da'esh, and the International, Independent Mechanism for Myanmar that have "geographically limited mandates with quasi-prosecutorial powers" (Oxford Institute for Ethics Law and Armed Conflict n.d.).

The expansion in both the number and the mandate of these investigative mechanisms pushes the formal roles of fact-finding and independent monitoring into the field of international criminal justice for which traditional human rights mechanisms have not been equipped. To build capacity and fill gaps in the international accountability system, several proposals have been made for the creation of a new standing mechanism. (D'Alessandra et al. 2022; International Commission of Jurists 2022). The mechanism would provide the HRC and investigative bodies with legal capacity and expertise to fulfil the increasingly demanding requirements of their mandates with formal international criminal law functions, and facilitate the ICC and other international judicial processes (such as universal jurisdiction) with access to evidence that meets the standards of court proceedings.

The developments described here speak to the significance of the current push among advocate states, lawyers, and civil society groups to formulate a regulatory system that has clearly identified processes and mechanisms for disseminating early warning and triggering early action on atrocities. It also speaks to the faith of the actors in the human rights system as a more reliable, systematic and impartial channel to advance prevention due to its legal character. Although yet to be empirically proven, the relationship between prevention, human rights, and accountability (including strengthened linkages to the ICJ and ICC) is understood to redress the deficits of the UNSC and other political bodies in

New York to respond in a coherent and consistent fashion to human protection crises.[10] To this end, regulatory contestation has prompted the development of law and institutions to advance the implementation of important human protection norms.

While proactive in nature, regulatory contestation in this space has also generated reactive contestation and shows the limits that politics places on the law in human rights promotion. A resolution calling on the HRC to hold a dialogue on the HRC report on the situation of the Uighurs in China, which provides evidence of crimes against humanity, was voted down in September 2022. China's resistance to the accountability agenda at the HRC (Jacob 2021c) has been evident in its influence over member states that have adapted voting patterns in the HRC in recent years (Human Rights Watch 2017). As regulatory logics seek to circumvent politics and advance consistency in norm implementation, divergent normative commitments among actors will continue to drive contestation in the design of regulatory regimes and render these processes deeply political.

Conclusion

As international law and norms settle and merge into defined TLOs, their role in governing specific issue areas becomes increasingly regulatory in character. This feature of international law prompts IR and IL scholars to deepen the conceptualisation of regulation in their respective fields. This chapter positioned its analysis within the critical constructivist account of norms as socially validated through contestation and legitimacy. It built on this literature by adopting a socio-legal understanding of regulation to further study the way that actors employ norms in the process of designing regulatory frameworks and mechanisms. To this end, I argue that studying regulatory contestation adds new insight into studies that examine the contestation over norms themselves to understand the contested processes through which international norms are employed with reference to specific regulatory logics to shape and create institutional and legal mechanisms for their implementation. In short, regulatory contestation studies the agential processes that occur between norm meaning creation and compliance, and situates the logics of the regulatory design within the political and social orders in which they are implemented.

Regulatory contestation contributes theoretically to the existing norms research by demonstrating the way in which actors contribute

[10] Author interviews with diplomats in Geneva.

to international order building at the micro-level, adopting a regulatory mindset towards transnational problems that is generative of TLO building and consolidation. In doing so, actors are making new connections between evolving norms and institutions, and employing new logics that are driving institutional reform. It draws attention to the creative and generative practices of not only shaping international norms, but also deploying them with a normative and strategic purpose to materialise them into the fabric of international order. These insights have implications for understanding micro-processes of order building during a period of power transition that is occurring, a fragmented process of steering outcomes through regulatory design.

Regulatory contestation also opens new sites for studying contestation whereby actors may endorse specific norms in principle while simultaneously resisting the broader normative structure underpinning the norms through institutional design and reform processes. Importantly, therefore, regulatory contestation is a value-laden practice that illuminates conflicting visions of the normative structure of international order and how these are expressed institutionally.

This chapter illustrated this process through a case study of the development of the human rights and prevention agenda at the HRC in Geneva. In the case of reform, efforts spearheaded by the UNSG to institutionalise prevention through improved coordination and strengthened mechanisms (Guterres 2016) speak to the desire to improve the regulatory function of the UN system to deliver on human protection norms in a more consistent and accountable way. Where the concept of prevention serves as an aspirational purpose of the UN from its creation, this was the most ambitious effort to operationalise prevention as both a political and a technical function of the UN system. Developments in the HRC to institutionalise prevention are situated in the context of the recent proliferation of juridical and institutional mechanisms to prevent, protect, and prosecute mass violations of human rights. Diplomatic caucuses, UN staff, and civil society groups have formulated an agenda on human rights and prevention that makes novel connections with the UNSG's agenda in New York. These actors have articulated a framework for mobilising and expanding the functions of the HRC for prevention in a way that identifies substantive regulatory functions to realise Article 5(f).

These efforts contribute to grounding the emergent transnational HPTLO through concrete regulatory mechanisms and functions that are an expression of the purposive and normative commitments of its chief architects. Yet these regulatory outcomes are deeply contested throughout and present a lowest common denominator scenario whereby global governance of human protection through TLOs are burdened with sub-optimal designs to accommodate a diverse set of actors. Regulatory contestation may result in improved access and legitimacy of a given TLO, yet it also illuminates the corrosive effect on broader international order to the extent that it erodes fundamental global justice norms such as human rights and accountability in the process. These outcomes characterise concrete challenges that fragmentation presents to international order as these trends intensify.

14 Norms, Normativity, and Pragmatist Justification

Advancing the Third Move in Norm Research

Jason Ralph

My aim in this chapter is to build on the argument (Ralph 2018) that classical American Pragmatism can contribute to what this volume calls the *third move* in International Relations (IR) norm studies. Norm studies has yet to fully embrace a research agenda that explicitly addresses the legitimacy of the norm being studied. The emphasis remains on the study of social 'logics' rather than normative questions about 'appropriateness' (see Wiener 2014, 2018; Price 2008; Erskine 2012 for exceptions). Those questions inevitably centre on how normative criteria can be grounded when constructivist norm research has demonstrated the historical and social contingency of standards. Acknowledging contingency does not necessarily lead to the paralysis of moral relativism (Friedrichs and Kratochwil 2009). A view informed by a Pragmatist disposition sweeps aside abstract concerns about foundations in favor of an 'evolutionary epistemology' (Haas and Haas 2002). Put differently, Pragmatism commits to open-ended enquiry for the purpose of ameliorating the lived experience by mitigating the social problems that emerge from practice. This is the basis of a norm's claim to legitimacy. A norm based on the learning that emerges from reflection and contestation can command an epistemic authority.

Epistemic authority here simply means that we know our norm-enabled practices are justified because a community of enquiry, having deliberated, has accepted that the consequences flowing from that practice are the best that can be hoped for in a given circumstance. The norm that enables that practice can lay claim to being a 'good' norm, at least to the extent deliberative enquiry judges otherwise. Given the centrality of enquiry and learning to the process of establishing epistemic authority, Pragmatists both embrace and qualify theories of norm contestation (Wiener 2014, 2018). A Pragmatist disposition means arguing: first (and last) that 'epistemic agonism' (Talisse 2007) is required to guard against the danger that pre-reflexive practice and taken-for-granted norms will lead to maladapted behaviours; second, that while contestation is good, contestation all the way down can be unhelpful, especially when society is confronted by material problems (e.g., pandemics, climate change) that demand action. Some norms and their associated practices can thus be defended *against* contestation because learning experiences have demonstrated their value in analogous situations. This does not mean opposing contestation as a practice, it means only that a norm need not necessarily change because it is contested. And third, that epistemic authority itself is contingent on the scope of the community of enquiry. The exclusion of the affected erodes epistemic authority. This should inspire a commitment to democracy as a means of continuous social learning.

To elaborate on how classical Pragmatist thought contributes to the third move in IR norm studies, I make five points. The first situates the chapter in the third move of IR norm studies by noting how previous moves focused on the *social logic* of appropriateness rather than the *normative claim* of appropriateness. I argue that Antje Wiener's theory of norm contestation only addresses this in part, for it does not tell us *what we should argue for* when a particular norm is contested (cf. also Gholiagha and Sienknecht, Chapter 8). The second and third sections speak to this problem by drawing on work inspired by the classical Pragmatists Charles Peirce and John Dewey. I draw on Robert Talisse's (2007) Peirceian-inspired concept of 'epistemic agonism' to explain why the Pragmatist commitment to democratic enquiry is an appropriate response to the normative problems created by pluralism and contingency. I argue in this section, however, that Talisse, like Wiener, potentially overvalues contestation. In so doing, he undervalues the progressive – in an epistemic, social, and political sense – aspect of Deweyan-inspired Pragmatism. This progressivism is necessary for the third move in norm studies because without the sense that indeterminacy or contestation can be resolved (even temporarily) we forego the possibility that norms work as accepted social facts. I set out what this means for norm analysis in the fourth and fifth sections where I draw out the links between a Deweyan conception of democracy and the deliberative democracy literature before briefly applying that to critique norms of global health governance.

Norms, Normativity, and Contestation

The language of 'generations', 'waves', 'turns' or 'dimensions' – in this volume we use 'moves' – is often used to describe the evolving nature of 'norm studies'. The lines are never distinct, and indeed Orchard and Wiener (Chapter 1) argue that such 'moves' are often overlapping rather than clearly consecutive. That said, such language can be helpful. Following Orchard and Wiener, we can identify a first move in norm studies, which analyses the role of norms as 'social facts', as well as a second move, which focuses on how the meaning of norms are adapted in the process of diffusion and localisation. I am interested in what Orchard and Wiener call the third move, which focuses on contestation as a societal practice that helps establish normativity. The limitations of this focus on *the logic* of appropriateness, rather than *the normative claim* to know what is appropriate, were noted as the first two moves progressed. For instance, Richard Price asked what constructivism could tell us about the normative direction of norm change. Upon what basis, Price (2008: 192) asked, "are accounts of moral change, which are presumed to be good, to be accepted as desirable and evidence of claims of progress?" The challenge for constructivist-inspired norm research, Price continued, was to engage normative theory. Toni Erskine (2012) also noted that if this engagement was to be consistent with constructivist social theory, then norm theorists had to find a normative theory that did not challenge the contingent character of values.

Some have resisted this move to forge a synthesis between constructivist social theory and political/normative theory (Barkin and Sjoberg 2019). From this perspective, what constructivism, including norm theory, tells us about the construction of social facts has no clear political affordance. "New Constructivism," David McCourt (2022) tells us, is politically "agnostic." Others have suggested, however, that the anti-essentialism and anti-foundationalism of the constructivist approach is more prescriptive. Indeed, Price answered his own question by suggesting a possible synthesis between its social theory and Pragmatist normative theory, a link that was also being highlighted by Matthew Hoffmann (2009).

For Price, a synthesis of constructivism and Pragmatism meant realising the fallibility of norms in social and political context (Price 2008: 193–4). Referring to Molly Cochran's (1999) IR Pragmatism for instance, Price wrote: "there seems to be very much in common in spirit between such an approach and an appreciation of the practical judgements that might flow from understanding how moral norms work." I sought to build on this line of enquiry on in my 2018 article 'What should be done?' (Ralph 2018). I argued there for a Pragmatist evaluation of a norm, or more specifically, the meaning of a norm in discursive use, based on the consequences that flowed from the actions or practices it enabled. In this way, I criticised the Responsibility to Protect (R2P) norm to the extent its meaning during the early Syria crisis enabled a policy of political and criminal accountability ('Assad must go'), which was practically useless in protecting Syria's vulnerable (compare also Rüland and Welsh, Chapter 3, Liese, Chapter 4, as well as Gholiagha and Sienknecht, Chapter 8).

There is a risk here that Pragmatic Constructivism amounts to little more than a situational ethic or indeed a prudential ethic of responsibility (see Gholiagha and Sienknecht, Chapter 8). It is my contention here, however, that Pragmatism offers norm theory much more. It is not only useful in understanding *when* (i.e., in what context) a norm is appropriate, but it can also tell us something more substantive about *why* a norm is appropriate. More specifically, for the Pragmatic constructivist, the epistemic fallibilism that emerges from the realisation that norms are historically and socially contingent leads to an openness to norm contestation, but that process must be for the purpose of learning how to improve the lived experience. To be clear, this process is not (to paraphrase Dewey) a quest for moral certainty. That is futile given the contingent character of knowledge. Contestation can only be for the purpose of ameliorating the lived experience by mitigating the social problems that emerge from actual practice. Furthermore, acknowledging that moral 'truths' are in fact constructed by 'communities of enquiry' enables norm theorists to remain loyal to their constructivist approach while interrogating the constitution of those communities and how well their learning processes establish epistemic authority by improving lived experiences. I shall now show how the classical Pragmatists settled on this as a method of 'fixing' a belief (or norm) starting with the thinking of Charles Peirce.

A Peirceian View of Justification

"Norms research must by definition entail research on the normativity of norms" (Wiener 2014: 2; see also 2018: 6–7). The third move in norm studies makes this explicit and engages with normative questions about the value of norms (and not simply their influence or robustness). Wiener's approach to engaging these issues leads her to focus on contestation not only as a social fact but also as a political value that should be encouraged. She distinguishes "*re*active contestation, or the practice of objecting to norms" from "*pro*active contestation, or the practice of critically engaging with norms" (Wiener 2018: 2). Contestation is to be valued and encouraged because it enables diverse views, especially those 'touched' by the norm (the *quod omnes tangit* principle), to engage in a 'multilogue'. This enhances legitimate governance.

There is much here that overlaps with the Pragmatist approach. But Wiener's 'agonistic' (Havercroft 2018) approach to norm studies potentially gives a different significance to pluralism. For Wiener (2018: 38–9, 61–79), access to proactive contestation is important as a means of recognising difference. For Pragmatists, contestation is valuable as a method for discerning the authority of truth claims, including those that underpin norms. That does not mean the Pragmatist is dismissive of what Wiener calls "the diversity principle," especially when it is paired with the concept of "sustainable normativity," which implies the possibility that stabilised (if not fixed) norms can emerge from diversity (Wiener 2018: 70). The Pragmatist emphasis, however, is on finding ways to reconcile as well as to open disputes. The purpose of contestation from this perspective is to (re)establish faith in a practice and to (re)constitute a norm's meaning so that it can alleviate lived problems. Taken to its extreme, contestation can unfix everything leading to an "uneasy and dissatisfied state" (Peirce 1877) of doubt and to the "epistemic insecurity" (Adler 2019) of post-truth politics. For Pragmatists, we should "struggle to free ourselves" from this "and pass into the state of belief," because there is "a calm and satisfactory state which we do not wish to avoid" (Peirce 1877).

Of course, norm contestation can be motivated by a variety of reasons, but it always involves knowledge claims about something; in this instance, knowledge about what constitutes appropriate behaviour. It is rare, for instance, for someone to defend or contest the appropriateness of an action by claiming they are *uncertain*. It is much better to claim that they, and everyone else, *knows* that the action is the right or wrong thing to do. That claim might give way to another argument when it is exposed to practice and reflective enquiry, but it is this recourse to *knowledge* as the source of authority (i.e., epistemic authority) that makes Peirceian Pragmatism a compelling response to scepticism. As Talisse (2007) puts it: "all doctrines aspire to get things right, and getting things right requires access to the processes and institutions that facilitate proper inquiry" (see also Misak 2000, 2004).[1]

That does not mean human beings are necessarily reasonable creatures. Peirce (1877) adds that we "are, doubtless, in the main logical animals, but we are not perfectly so. Most of us, for example, are naturally more sanguine and hopeful than logic would justify." It is often more advantageous to have our minds "filled with pleasing and encouraging visions, independently of their truth," only to be disappointed by their impracticality. Alternatively, we tend to limit ourselves "wholly to

[1] Or as Festenstein (2004: 299) describes Misak's (2000) Peirceian view: "This argument rests on a claim that is conditional but thought to be fairly uncontroversial: that we value the truth, and so value the conditions under which we can arrive at true beliefs."

practical subjects, and whose activity moves along thoroughly-beaten paths" only to lose 'orientation' when confronted by the unfamiliar experience. But the commitment to truth does mean that knowledge has a particularly compelling claim to authority, especially if it reorients practice in ways that enable us to understand and control change and to realise visions of an improved lived experience.

For Peirce, it is the scientific method that best produces this kind of knowledge and he establishes this by dismissing other commonly used methods of fixing belief. Each of these methods produces knowledge that is consequential because believers will act on it but unlike the scientific method they are flawed as a means of settling contestation and resolving doubt. The first method is what Peirce calls 'tenacity'. A "steady and immovable faith yields great peace of mind," and while it may give rise to inconveniences, "this method will not allow that its inconveniences are greater than its advantages." But for Peirce, "the method of tenacity, will be unable to hold its ground in practice" because "[t]he social impulse is against it." Tenacity makes 'hermits' of us, but as social animals we "necessarily influence each other's opinions." The problem is thus "how to fix belief, not in the individual merely, but in the community." This leads Peirce to consider the second method for fixing belief, what he calls 'authority', which enlists the 'passions' of the ignorant or indoctrinated so that unusual opinions are met with 'hatred and horror', and those who reject the established belief are 'terrified into silence' (Peirce 1877).

While accepting its 'proportionately greater' success, the authoritarian method ultimately fails to fix belief because "no institution can undertake to regulate opinions upon every subject." Possession of "a wider sort of social feeling," including a sense of those "in other countries and in other ages," reveals the arbitrary character of this method and inspires a feeling among people that knowledge "is the mere accident of their having been taught as they have, and of their having been surrounded with the manners and associations they have." An understanding of this kind of contingency is sufficient to reintroduce doubt, contestation and (ideally) enquiry. Peirce's third method for fixing belief suffers the same weakness. The a priori reasoning of philosophers is rarely able to silence the doubts of those who value practical experience because it is developed in abstraction and thus "extraneous to the facts." That this kind of knowledge has "never come to any fixed agreement," and is "more or less a matter of fashion," suggests to Peirce that it too is the product of power and practice. Again, realising this introduces the uneasy feeling of doubt and contestation. That can only be resolved through further enquiry.

The fourth method Peirce considers then is scientific contestation. This involves accepting that beliefs, and the habits they help constitute, are 'hypotheses'; they have to be tested in terms of the practical consequences that follow when acted upon. "The force of habit" will sometimes cause us to take beliefs for granted, but the scientific method insists that "reflection upon the state of the case will overcome these habits." Doubt is not as fatal to this method as it is to the authoritarian, for example. This is because scientists are committed to *a method*, rather than a particular truth claim, and they are able to revise their beliefs/ hypotheses (norms) when exposure to practice reveals unanticipated or unwanted consequences.[2] For as long as experimental practice confirms the hypothesis, belief within the community of enquiry is settled. This requires deliberation and the exercise of judgement, or a practice that weighs the significance of the evidence before making a truth claim. This approach more than any other, Peirce concludes, "has had the most wonderful triumphs in the way of settling opinion." But what does this mean for the third move in IR norm studies? The implication is that our faith in the appropriateness of a norm is only as strong as the evidence that acting upon it will work in practice to improve lived experiences. Contradictory evidence should lead to the contestation of a norm that might unjustifiably be taken-for-granted.

An example from contemporary norm studies helps to illustrate the point. By accepting the norm-generative function of multilogue, and advocating 'regular' (Wiener 2014) rather than constant critique, Wiener acknowledges the importance of resolving the indeterminacy created by contestation. By arguing it is possible to evaluate norm change, in terms of how it "takes diverse affected stakeholders into account" (Wiener 2018: 31), she also adopts a Pragmatist concern for practical consequences. Beyond that, however, there is little guidance on how contestation is resolved to fix (or stabilise) the meaning of a norm. Does a theory of contestation necessarily mean a norm should change to meet the objections of its critics? Should, for example, the torture prohibition have changed because the Bush administration, as an affected stakeholder, considered waterboarding to be an appropriate response to the terrorist threat? What would be the reason for defending this norm *against* contestation? Wiener's (2018) treatment of this particular case seeks to demonstrate the value of contestation

[2] Peirce (1878) called the idea that meaning was found in practice the 'pragmatic maxim': "Consider what effects, that might conceivably have practical bearings, we conceive the object of our conception to have. Then our conception of these effects is the whole of our conception of the object."

by focusing on the strategic litigation networks that contested Bush's interpretation, but again it does not tell us why one should support the work of such networks.

Taking the Pragmatist approach one step further, Wiener could defend torture prohibition by pointing to what Dewey (1915: 266) called a "stock of learning." This usually sits within the background knowledge of a normative regime and acts like the 'story' (Tilly 2002: 9) that we draw on to tell us "what forms of action and interaction are possible, feasible, desirous and efficacious."[3] But again the emphasis here is on *knowledge* and the deliberative process that distinguishes it from a mere story. That process is best characterised as 'learning' and it inspires faith in a norm because we know that the claims it makes have been tested by experience and are not merely reflecting the preferences of a story-teller. Norms are worth defending when they can draw on a 'stock of learning' because we know that such a resource has been produced by the deliberative and inclusive enquiry that "*made* it 'knowledge' (that which gives it a right to the title)" (Dewey 1915: 266). Only then should a story "function in the guidance and handling of future inferences" (Dewey 1915: 266). In this instance, the defence of the norm *against* the Bush administration's contestation could have pointed to evidence that cruel interrogation techniques are counterproductive. Indeed, faith in the torture prohibition was restored when the Obama administration noted how US actions under Bush in fact acted as a recruiting agent for terrorist enemies (Ralph 2013: 114–36).

Deweyan Pragmatism and Justification

Peirceian Pragmatism was developed further by John Dewey. The argument that beliefs (or, in our case, the meaning of norms) maintain authority when they are stabilised by a social process involving an inclusive community of enquiry – which was ideally constituted by deliberative stakeholders – ran through all aspects of his thought. Indeed, Dewey's political thinking evolved from the premise that the pursuit of epistemic authority involved an understanding of the direct consequences that norm-inspired practice had for those observing and practising it, as well as an appreciation of the indirect consequences such practice had on others. There was no other way of knowing:

> If a notion or a theory makes pretense of corresponding to reality or to the facts, this pretense cannot be put to the test and confirmed or refuted except by causing it to pass over into the realm of action and by noting the results which it

[3] I thank Antje Wiener for leading me to the comparison.

yields in the form of the concrete observable facts to which this notion leads. … A theory corresponds to the facts when it leads the facts which are its consequences, by the intermediary of experience. (Dewey 1925a [1998]: 8; see also 1925b [1998]: 100).

This emphasis on the everyday lived experience is important. We cannot properly know the appropriateness of a norm without including the experiences of the affected in the deliberations of the scientific community. Or put differently, the 'stock of learning' cited earlier is only valuable to the extent it includes these experiences. Dewey added that we cannot communicate or understand those experiences without recourse to the humanities, an important point that qualifies Peirce's emphasis on scientific method. In humanising Pragmatism in this way, Dewey saw 'experimentalism' as the means by which the humans coped with the problems created by a changing world. It was an evolutionary mechanism, a means of learning that led to the growth of expanded personalities and social identities. This was encouraged through an engaged and deliberative pedagogy in the classroom, and it involved activism in wider society on behalf of those whose experiences had been 'eclipsed' by practice (Ralph 2023). Dewey called eclipsed experiences 'publics', and their involvement in communities of enquiry was necessary if the otherwise technocratic practices of insiders were to claim epistemic authority.

Deweyan experimentalism and what it means for verifying standards of appropriate behaviour is not without controversy within Pragmatist circles. Robert Talisse, for instance, argues that Dewey offered a substantive moral view that is too far removed from the proceduralist emphasis of Peirceian Pragmatism. The idea of the expanded personality or 'growth', and its association in Deweyan thought with 'human flourishing', is – for Talisse – too prescriptive. It is, he argues, insufficiently sensitive to 'value' and 'epistemic' pluralism. He sees Dewey's insistence that democracy is "a way of life," which should influence social relationships, as something that is 'oppressive'. Returning to the 'epistemic agonism' of Peirce's Pragmatism is, for Talisse, a safer way to accommodate pluralism. Separating Peirce from Dewey in this way helps us to locate Weiner's 'agonistic constructivism' within the Pragmatist approach. Both Wiener and Peirceian Pragmatism stress the value of contestation as a means of recognising diversity, and both emphasise the risk that diversity is overlooked in the processes that negotiate change and reconstitute the meaning of norms.

Talisse's argument is helpful. Yet it seems to me that by separating Peirce from Dewey in this way he exaggerates the extent to which Dewey is committed to substantive concepts of the good, a reading I share with Melvin Rogers (2009).[4] Deweyan democracy is hardly dismissive of pluralism. The difference lies in the value that is given to the 'stock of learning' that emerges from the method of enquiry that *both* Dewey *and* Peirce were committed to. An emphasis on pluralism and contestation is important but it should not take diverse identities and preferences as given and fixed in a way that is antecedent to enquiry.[5] There is nothing about pluralism (and its components) that means it (and they) do not evolve.

Contestation as enquiry means diverse preferences and identities change as communities reach useful conclusions about good norms in the context of lived problems; but if contestation is only about constituting diversity, then it risks reifying the present and limiting the future in ways that do not address those problems. The norms and practices that emerge from contestation as enquiry might not have existed in the past, and they might not be sustained in the future, but they can ameliorate the lived experience by finding common solutions to the problems of the present. As a Pragmatist, Dewey was not for setting those norms and practices in stone, but for deepening the process of enquiry so that established norms could prove themselves in practice and new norms could emerge when that process exposed problems. Contestation had to be an ongoing process, but if a normative claim continued to prove itself by bettering lived experiences, then people would and could have faith that they were acting appropriately by following and defending that norm.

Contestation, Pragmatism, and Deliberative Democracy

Richard Posner's (2003) 'everyday pragmatist' account of democracy offers another angle from which to explore the question of how a norm's meaning can be fixed by contestation. He refers to 'concept 1' and 'concept 2' democracy. Concept 1 democracy, or 'deliberative democracy', mirrors the Deweyan commitment to social enquiry and learning. Democracy in this sense is a method for the "pooling of different ideas and approaches and the selection of the best through debate and discussion" (Sullivan and Solove 2013: 334). Posner dismisses the value of this approach because '[o]rdinary people simply don't have the expertise or time to be engaged in a robust political life." It is thus utopian. His

[4] I thank Molly Cochran for alerting me to this debate.

[5] On Deweyan relational approach, and denial of "the notion of a self that is antecedent to its interactions," see Pappas (2012: 60–1). This theme was of course developed by Mead, who would later influence constructivist IR especially through Wendt (1992).

'everyday pragmatism' takes people as they are. To define democracy by wishing people were more educated and more civic minded is, Posner argues, inconsistent with the Pragmatist temperament. The commitment to enquiry as a means of establishing epistemic authority instead lends itself to a technocratic form of government that is subject to electoral checks (Talisse 2007: 100–9; Sullivan and Solove 2013).

The implication for global norms, where of course electoral checks are not easily available, is that epistemic authority is akin to expert opinion. This is something that Dewey addressed. His most political text, *The Public and Its Problems*, emerged in response to similar arguments, notably Walter Lippman's view that the new political associations of the twentieth century were so large, and the interdependencies so complex, that it was impossible for citizens to engage in politics from an informed position. In these circumstances, Lippman argued, governments should be guided by expert opinion for only they could understand the consequences of novel practices within new associations. In this way, the citizen would be consulted on the general direction of government through regular elections, but they would not be involved beyond that.

Dewey did not ignore the difficulties of deliberation in this new era, but he did not accept Lippman's (and by extension Posner's) reading of the implications. Technocracy could easily fail as a means of government because it could not fully understand the complexity of social problems if those experiencing them were not part of the relevant community of enquiry. Publics in the associations created by material change may be 'inchoate', Dewey argued, but that was not an excuse for ignoring these experiences, which were themselves a form of knowledge (Dewey 1927: 207). Rather, it was an argument for political organisation within and across different publics. Deweyan politics is certainly more engaged, therefore. It involves a thicker and more solidaristic concept of democracy, but that followed directly from the Pragmatist's commitment to social enquiry and learning and the need to mobilise publics that were otherwise excluded from communities of enquiry.[6] Cheryl

[6] It should be noted that Talisse (2007: 99–100, 109–10) rejects what he calls Posner's 'democratic realism' as 'pragmatically untenable' because "pragmatism is opposed to ostentatious theorizing, academic abstraction and detached speculation" (111). Posner's realism "is every bit as invested in contestable moral, psychological and metaphysical claims as the substantive views he dismisses" (99). Indeed, Posner's criticism of Dewey's deliberative form of democracy can be turned on itself. As Sullivan and Solove note, Posner's "claims to adhere to a neutral pragmatic method without political valences" is in fact "deeply ensconced in ideology" (Sullivan and Solove 2013: 338). By "ring-fencing" (Festenstein 2004: 292) interests and identity and dismissing the participatory capacities of publics, Posner takes a very static view of human nature and a conservative

Misak (2004: 15) nicely captures this when she writes that "deliberative democracy in political philosophy is the right view, because deliberative democracy in epistemology is the right view." John Dryzek further helps us establish the connection. Pragmatism, he writes:

> provides a congenial philosophical basis for deliberative democracy, whose essence is the idea that the legitimacy of any collective decision should be sought in reflective acceptance on the part of those subject to the decision. The best way to ensure such acceptance is to define the relevant public as those affected, and to allow these individuals access (directly or indirectly) to consequential deliberation about the content of the decision at hand. Thus it is no surprise to find that pragmatism is recognized by some contemporary deliberative democrats (notably Habermas) as part of their intellectual ancestry. (Dryzek 2004: 72)

But the literature makes important distinctions here too. The assumption that the end of deliberation is consensus – or that the truth of a knowledge claim is found in the consensus established by the ideal community of enquiry – is contested. Dryzek (2004: 74), for instance, warns that "in a world of irreducible plurality of experience, the kind of world we live in, consensus may only be achievable at the expense of erasing particular kinds of voices" (see also Wiener 2014: 39, 2018: 32). Indeed, Dryzek notes that everyday political deliberation rarely takes on the forensic character of scientific deliberation. Deliberation "*in practice* is often more about telling stories than it is about making arguments."

Others such as Dmitri Shalin (1992: 254) distinguish the 'disembodied reason' of Habermasian pragmatics with the 'embodied reasonableness' of Deweyan Pragmatism. The latter's emphasis on learning through 'experience' (and the role the humanities play in articulating that) helps to address Dryzek's concern that the emphasis on scientific judgement and forensic deliberation may be too demanding for the everyday. Taking this into account, Dryzek (2004) argues by citing Noëlle McAfee's (2004b) 'quasi-Deweyan' model of deliberative democracy, that Pragmatism is less interested in what deliberation does to establish truths. It does not necessarily aim for consensus. Rather it is interested in revealing what works to solve the problems thrown up by associated living. Scientific enquiry of norms as hypotheses is still valued, but experiences and emotions, as expressed through the arts and humanities, provide the subject matter to be tested and the tools to be deployed.

This emphasis on deliberation among a plurality of views, and emotions, might be criticised for "opening the door" (Pappas 2012: 62) to

view of its potential. In doing so, Posner "recommends our acquiescence to the status quo," an "affirmation of the present than a demonstration that improvement is not possible" (Sullivan and Solove 2013: 342).

populist opinion, which has little respect for the better argument or factual evidence, and looks to authoritarian leaders who tenaciously share their beliefs. As Pappas (2012: 62) puts it: "[o]ne need not adopt a 'stiff' rationalism to be concerned about the consequences of some forms of rhetoric." But Deweyan democracy acts as a check on this kind of trajectory also. The scientific expert's respect for everyday experience should be reciprocated so that expert knowledge is also properly weighted in the deliberation on what works. Hilary Putnam (2004) captures this when recalling Dewey's "epistemological justification for democracy": in a deliberative democracy, he argues, "learning how to think for oneself, to question, to criticise, is fundamental. But thinking for oneself does not exclude – indeed it requires – learning when and where to seek expert knowledge" (quoted by Hilde 2012: 904; see also McAfee 2004a: 149–50). In fact, as is often the way with Deweyan philosophy, it persuades us to collapse the expert/everyday binary, in favour of a norm that values good judgement in the face of an indeterminate situation.

Justifying Global Health Norms

The COVID-19 pandemic exposed the deliberative shortcomings of modern polities, including Western democracies, especially the United States. This was in part because President Trump's beliefs were seemingly fixed by the method Peirce described as 'tenacity', and disseminated through media that did not enable effective deliberation. This cast doubt on scientific expertise and institutions, including the World Health Organization, in ways that were unwarranted in the context of a real problem. It is not a surprise, therefore, that Trump's defeat in the 2020 presidential election was described as a victory for science (Steinbrook 2020). But how does the Pragmatist approach to norm studies discussed here inform the discipline's analysis of global health norms?

I offer two suggestions. The first is that Pragmatism directs constructivist norm studies not only to consider the manner in which global norms such as International Health Regulations (IHRs) are 'localised', but also to assess whether that process is the result of a deliberative process and whether the practical consequences that follow address the problem by actually improving public health experiences. The second suggestion is that Deweyan Pragmatism in particular steers norm studies into a 'vocational' (Abraham and Abramson 2015) commitment to construct the kind of publics that contribute to deliberative processes and give norms their epistemic authority. I elaborate on the first point by referencing the work of Garrett Brown and look to the work of Owain Williams and Simon Rushton to illustrate the latter.

Brown does not locate his work within the Pragmatist tradition but his interest in deliberative democracy and its application to global health resonates with my approach. He is interested in deliberation because it "denotes a process of public reasoning geared toward generating decisions or opinions about how to resolve shared problems" (Brown 2010: 513). Furthermore, deliberation is valued because it can make "public policy more efficient, effective and legitimate by including multisectoral input and creating a sense of policy ownership" (Brown 2010: 513). He applies this thinking to the 'glocalisation' of global health norms and ethical codes of practice regarding the international recruitment of health care workers, which he subjects to what he calls "deliberative participation criteria" (Brown 2014: 878).

The point here is not just to *note* local input in the development of such criteria, but to *insist* on it as a requirement of epistemic authority. Again, Brown does not use Pragmatist language, but his interest in what deliberation does for solving a problem amplifies the common chord. Drawing on Hayley Stevenson's (2013) idea of "normative congruence building," he argues for analysis that is "less concerned with either confirming or denying the diffusion of a norm" but aims at normatively assessing the process of "intersubjective negotiation" (Brown 2014: 885). On this basis, Brown normatively critiques South Africa's localisation of global HIV/AIDS norms and denialism. This improved when, under Zuma's government, it adopted deliberative processes that allowed for "greater intersubjectivity, reinterpretation [and] participation."

Owain Williams and Simon Rushton (2011) focus on the increased influence of private actors in global health governance, and the concern that the norms of 'global health partnerships' (GHPs) serve an interest in profit. This also resonates with the Deweyan argument that without a critical, engaged, and activist approach to knowledge construction certain experiences are 'eclipsed', leading to a distorted conception of the public interest. GHPs can provide a new source of knowledge and expertise to address the state's failures, but Williams and Rushton argue, "it would be a mistake to assume that this knowledge is value neutral. Particular forms of knowledge are often privileged, and they are organised and channelled in specific directions" (Williams and Rushton 2011: 14).[7] They offer the example of the international emphasis on biomedical and technological/pharmalogical solutions, which was at

[7] On the epistemic and normative power of moral claims in global health, and the need to investigate "under what circumstances they are justly derived," see Shiffman (2014: 297). See also Brown (2015: 111) who adds that this "is, and always will be, deeply political." A better focus on "health politics can … facilitate deliberations that can, although imperfectly, help legitimate sources of influence and power."

the expense, at least initially, of support for robust national systems (Williams and Rushton 2011: 14). For Williams and Rushton, the diffusion of global health norms is inextricably linked to wider questions of the neo-liberal commitment to privatisation, where the interests of 'big pharma' are protected at the World Trade Organization (Williams and Rushton 2011: 20–1).

One should not draw from this critique of private interest a conclusion that confuses the state with 'the public' interest. In the context of the response to the COVID-19 pandemic, for instance, the concern around 'vaccine nationalism' illustrates how the practices of states can also lead to consequences where the experiences of some are overlooked. Weeks after the announcements of the successful COVID-19 trials, for instance, Oxfam (2020) noted that wealthy nations representing just 13 per cent of the world's population had already cornered more than half of the promised doses of leading COVID-19 vaccine candidates.

The issue from the Pragmatist perspective need not be interpreted in terms of a priori conceptions of rights or justice. Rather, the issue is how such practices emerge as a consequence of an 'inchoate' public that is unable to articulate, let alone implement, the global public interest in the face of private- and state-driven interests. The implication for the third move of norm studies is, I suggest, twofold: first, it reaffirms the importance of deliberative democracy to the processes that constitute what it means to act in the public interest, and that can be used to normatively assess the norms and practices that emerge from the pandemic; and second, it involves a normative commitment to engaging and supporting 'publics' whose experiences are otherwise eclipsed so that they themselves can engage in the deliberative processes that bestow epistemic authority on new norms.

Conclusion

My aim in this chapter has been to contribute to the third move of IR norm studies; a move that engages normative theory to address otherwise unwarranted claims about the progressive character of norm studies. To meet that aim, I drew on the ideas of classical American Pragmatism and the idea that progress is what emerges from the learning that emerges from scientific (in its widest sense) enquiry. This is not a linear view of progress. It does not start with an ideal end point, nor tell us how far we are from realising it. Rather, it lets us know whether we can have faith in what we currently believe we know about appropriate behaviour. It insists that we test that knowledge by deliberating about its lived consequences in a community of enquiry that includes experts *and* the affected.

After discussing the difference among Pragmatists on the question of what is required to properly constitute such a community, I linked the Pragmatist conception of democracy to the literature on deliberative democracy, including those such as Brown, who uses this deliberative lens to make a normative judgement on the process of global health norm diffusion. I also noted how a Deweyan understanding of 'publics', and the role they play in democratising communities of enquiry, can supplement the work of those such as Williams and Rushton who are concerned that global health norms lack legitimacy because they are dominated by private and/or state interests and because they leave others vulnerable. These examples are offered here merely as illustrations of a research agenda that can speak across empirical fields, and to demonstrate how the third move in norm studies can contribute to the normative assessment of practice.

15 Social in Practice, Contested in Principle

Future Norm Research

Antje Wiener and Phil Orchard

Over the past two decades, we have seen a significant shift in norms literature away from the idea that a norm reflects a fixed and universally accepted shared understanding to notions that any norm – even those which appear to be widely institutionalised in international organisations of global governance – remains subject to *contestation* and *interpretation* at multiple sites in world politics. Given that all norms are *per se* social, that is, a norm's existence depends on prior interaction in a social context, norms are always in principle contested. The fact that this observation of a norm's source (i.e., practices of social construction) and its flexible status (i.e., expected contestation) matters has been addressed by the surging field of norm contestation research. Yet how it matters and what this means for IR theory has remained largely underestimated so far. To address that research gap, this book has invited leading norms researchers to address cases of norm contestation. The result are the previous thirteen chapters which offer novel insights into norm contestations with reference to the three moves which have marked progress of norms research over the past three decades. This concluding chapter begins by recalling the shift of research focus from a norm's stability to its contestedness with reference to the field's three moves and illustrates the importance of 'contestation' with vignettes focusing on the Bush administration's efforts to contest the norm against torture and on the forced landing of Ryanair Flight 4978 by the government of Belarus. It then identifies the contributing chapters' use of the concepts of norm contestation and/or interpretation in norm conflicts, and presents the approaches in a contestation matrix. By doing so, the book confirms the contestedness of norms (in principle) and demonstrates how distinct contestations work out (in practice).

We have described the shift from studying stable norms to analysing norm contestations as developing over a time period that encompasses three moves. The first move brought a focus on the 'social' into global politics, examining the role of social facts as structural elements – including norms, standards, regulations, rules, and ideas – and moving away from an agent-centred perspective to one that examined agents and structures existing in a mutually constitutive manner. But, underpinning this move was also an underlying assumption of stability: that norms, in particular, can achieve a fixed, unquestioned status. This led to the second move, one which challenged this stability assumption by focusing on the adaptation or implementation of norms in processes of policymaking in which individual actors – particularly at the domestic level – were able to alter norms to fit their own cultural and institutional contexts. But this move, too, introduced its own issues by inadvertently leading to an 'ontologisation' of norms which focused on structural effects of norms as "ontologically primitive units" (Wiener 2007: 54, 66, citing other examples of ontologisation such as Melluci 1989: 330 on social movements, and Wendt 1987 on the state) rather than their socially constructed quality – agents were viewed as shaping the norms, rather than engaging with their underlying legitimacy. The third move – which we have suggested norm research is now in – seeks to remove this bracketing by focusing on both the normalcy (taken-for-grantedness) of norms as well as their normativity (value-based meaning). In so doing, this third move seeks to bring back in questions of politics and agency by focusing on norms as processes which are subject to ongoing contestation. This third move creates its own questions both on the role of 'contested' fundamental norms, and on how 'contestations' impact on the meaning of norms and the larger structural context in which norms work. It is these questions that this volume has wrestled with.

Each of these moves have weight and merit; each has sought to explain why norms matter; and each has treated norms as having a greater magnitude of complexity. Thus, we have argued that these three moves together have led to a three-layered theoretical advancement, which included the identification of norms, then working with and applying norms, and finally bringing in critical questions of order, legitimacy, and normativity. In this sense, exploring an instance of norm conflict through only the prism of the first move is not 'wrong', but it has less explanatory potential than exploring that same norm conflict through the second and third moves. By developing these latter moves and detailing how they contribute to understanding, explaining, and engaging with norm conflicts, we therefore improve our take on the role and effect of norm conflicts as organic parts of a contested world. Notably, when we speak of norm conflicts here in line with the three moves and against the backdrop of the contributions to this volume, we see these ranging from contested norm implementation, compliance with norms, and norm collisions, to contested norm violations. As this volume has demonstrated, the practice of norm contestation has been conceived both as an indicator pointing to an impeding local conflict which needed addressing before expanding and developing into a full-blown global conflict (e.g., by politics or policymaking) and as a necessary component in the process of generating legitimacy which required further detailed attention (e.g., by legal, political, or constitutional procedures).

The moves have thus triggered renewed emphasis at a general level on conceptual and normative questions about the role of 'contested' fundamental norms, and more specifically on how 'contestations' impact on the meaning of norms and the larger normative context in which norms work. Here, norms research has generated important new perspectives and methods to capture the changes generated through contestation as an interactive practice involving a diversity of societal agents at multiple sites in the world. The innovations include both a systematic assessment of discursive and behavioural elements and how norms' internal structures operate. Contestations can also mean that individual actors understand and interpret individual norms in different ways – that each norm may have a varying interpretative scope through which they are understood by actors. And yet some international norms do clearly have a relatively fixed nature, clearly understood by most if not all actors including those who may be engaging in violation.

Let us illustrate this with two brief vignettes. A number of the chapters in this volume have focused on the Bush administration's efforts to contest the norm against torture. This is a useful case, both because it was high profile and, with the time that has now passed, we have a relatively clear picture of the events. Akhrif and Koschut (Chapter 6) describe this as a case of reactive contestation, with the US administration seeking to argue that enhanced interrogation techniques did not constitute forms of torture, in spite of the views of international organisation and human rights advocates. For Ben-Josef Hirsch and Dixon (Chapter 2), this rhetoric demonstrated an effort by the administration to change the content of the norm, in particular its boundaries of coverage, which could in turn lower the overall strength of the norm. Akhrif and Koschut focus particularly on the emotional resonance of the violation, the efforts by actors to shame the US administration through evocative imagery and reverse the violation. While they find emotional resonance was not evoked in this case, this was because of the administration's efforts to downplay the events. But, as Winston (Chapter 9) finds in examining this same case, this reaction was important because it forestalled the creation of a positive feedback loop which would have led to ongoing reactive contestations and violations and the potential undermining of the norm itself.

As this vignette shows, while norm contestations can be complex, the exploration from different standpoints in this subdiscipline matters because it reveals distinct layers of 'the social'. Given that a 'norm is always contested', these distinct assessments are vital for policymaking, political decisionmaking, and theory-building alike. This is shown by another vignette, one of a more recent norm conflict, not covered elsewhere in the volume, but which nonetheless the tools we introduce can be used to understand.

In May 2021, Ryanair Flight 4978 travelling between Athens and Vilnius was forced to land in Minsk by the government of Belarus under the pre-text of a bomb threat. Once the plane landed, a Belarussian opposition activist, Roman Protasevich, was removed from the aircraft and arrested. Belarussian authorities claimed they had received the text of a bomb threat from Hamas; however, Hamas denied any knowledge or connection and German chancellor Angela Merkel quickly noted "We have seen a forced landing that led to the arrest ... all other explanations for the landing of this Ryanair flight are completely implausible"(Reuters 2021; DW 2021). The government's actions violated two conventions on civil aviation, which prohibited the use of weapons against civil aircraft in flight and unlawfully and internationally communicating information which is known to be false, "thereby endangering the safety of an aircraft in flight."[1]

These actions received widespread international condemnation. European Commission president Ursula von der Leyen stated that "the judgement was unanimous: This is an attack on democracy. This is an attack on freedom of expression. And this is an attack on European sovereignty. And this outrageous behaviour needs a strong answer"(European Commission 2021). US president Joe Biden called the action "a direct affront to international norms"(The White House 2021). The European Union, Canada, the United Kingdom, and the United States then responded by adopting a series of sanctions against forty-six Belarusian government officials, in order to "promote accountability for the Lukashenka regime's transnational repression and its affronts to international norms"(US Department of State 2021; European Union External Action Service 2021).

If we examine these events through the first move, this appears to be a clear violation of an institutionalised norm which trigger immediate

[1] The conventions are the 1944 Chicago Convention on International Civil Aviation and the 1971 Montreal Convention for the Suppression of Unlawful Acts Against the Safety of Civil Aviation. A number of sources quickly noted the illegality of Belarus' actions in international law (see Miles 2021; Wise 2021). Both conventions have large numbers of signatories – the 1944 Chicago Convention has 193 state parties, while the 1971 Montreal Convention has 188.

consequences, suggesting this is a robust or strong norm. But looking at it through the interpretation–contestation framework we propose in the volume's Introduction presents a significantly more complex picture, one in which different forms of contestation were attempted simultaneously by different sets of actors. That framework brings together three types of contestation (reactive, proactive, and interpretive) and notes that contestations can focus on norm validity or alternatively primarily on norm application (for the former, see Wiener 2018: 29, 38–49, and Orchard and Wiener, Chapter 1; for the latter, see Deitelhoff and Zimmermann 2020: 56–7).

To begin with, how did the European Union determine its response? The 1944 Chicago Convention notes only that the Council of the International Civil Aviation Authority can undertake and investigate "any situation which may appear to present avoidable obstacles to the development of international air navigation" and then issue a report.[2] Instead, the use of sanctions by the European Union appears to have simply been an example of grafting (Price 1998: 628–30), adding individuals to the existing sanctions against Belarus for human rights violations. But, in so doing, these countries also appear to be engaging in a form of proactive applicatory contestation, framing the response of this violation of international civil aviation law as similar to violations of international human rights law by using the similar tool of sanctions. Their rhetoric also sought to generate emotional resonance in line with Akhrif and Koschut's findings in Chapter 6, linking these events to attacks on democracy and sovereignty.

But this was not the only contestation at play. The government of Belarus sought to engage in a form of reactive applicatory contestation of this norm rather than in simply a straight violation of it, arguing that the threats required them to take action and seeking to delink the seizure of Protasevich from the landing of the plane. Belarusian president Alexander Lukashenko claimed that the actions were legal, noting "don't blame me. I was acting legally to protect my people. That's how it will continue to be"(The Moscow Times 2021). The government then took the position at the International Civil Aviation Organisation (ICAO) that "if we had not acted on these two letters with threats, the entire international community could have been completely justified in accusing us of criminal inaction!"(Belta 2021). The Russian government lent its support to this position, noting to the ICAO that the "the Belarusian side acted in full compliance with the Chicago Convention" (TASS 2021). And Russian president Vladimir Putin also attempted a linkage to other

[2] 1944 Chicago Convention, Art 55(e).

issues, arguing that other states had engaged in similar actions. He suggested the Western governments had responded "with an outburst of emotion," and that the landing was very similar to the forced landing of Bolivian president Evo Morales plane in 2013: "At one time they forced the Bolivian president's plane to land and took him out of the plane and nothing, silence" (Euronews 2021).[3] The Russian ambassador to the United Nations (UN), Dmitry Polyanskiy, also argued for the need for further investigations before actions were taken: "to say from the outset," he argued, that it was "a forced landing, to condemn it and to introduce sanctions without any investigation; this kind of behaviour is absolutely irresponsible" (Unifeed 2021).

The Chinese Ministry of Foreign Affairs made a similar claim to investigate the situation first. "The facts about the relevant incident is not yet clear. Before getting to the bottom of facts and truth, relevant sides should exercise restraint and avoid an escalation of the situation"(Ministry of Foreign Affairs of the People's Republic of China 2021) And there were certainly grounds to pursue this course of action rather than the immediate imposition of sanctions. In January 2020, the Iranian government accidentally shot down Ukraine International Airline Flight PS752, killing all 176 people on board. In spite of the government initially claiming it had been a crash caused by a fire before admitting culpability and monitoring the ICAO investigation, no sanctions have so far been imposed by any other governments.[4] This is in spite of the UN Special Rapporteur on Extrajudicial, Summary, or Arbitrary Executions concluding that – like Belarus – Iran had breached both the Chicago and the Montreal conventions by failing to "respect and protect the lives of these innocent civilians and failed to investigate their killing"(United Nations Mandate of the Special Rapporteur on extrajudicial, summary or arbitrary executions 2020).

Finally, we cannot view this specific norm conflict in a vacuum. The sanctions were connected to the wider human rights violations the government of Belarus has engaged in since the 2020 election. While the pressure was enough to have Protasevich released from prison, he was moved to house arrest rather than allowed to leave the country. There

[3] In that case, a number of European states had denied access to their airspace for the plane under the suspicion that Edward Snowden was on board. The pilots of the aircraft then requested an emergency landing in Austria due to concerns over fuel, and Austrian officials engaged in a search of the plane. A number of the governments subsequently apologised for the incident (Fisher 2013).

[4] A total of 138 of the 176 people on board the plane had ties to Canada. Following their own investigation, in June 2021 Canadian prime minister Justin Trudeau stated that the Canadian government would pursue reparations and a potential recourse to the International Court of Justice (Government of Canada 2021).

are concerns as well that the international condemnation may have simply led to the government adopting more clandestine methods for dealing with exiles outside of the country, with reports that one activist living in exile, Vitaly Shishov, was found hanged in Kyiv, and other exiles note they had been warned by Ukrainian security officers of threats including kidnapping and assassination from the Belarusian KGB (BBC 2021). The ICAO investigation concluded that Belarus did deliberately issue a false threat. However, their responses have been limited, and triggered only a condemnation of the Belarusian government for committing "an act of unlawful interference" as an offence against the Montreal convention (ICAO 2022). This led to a UN Security Council debate on 31 October 2022, in which the US representative noted that "we have a responsibility to put on record our denunciation of state actors who flagrantly violate their responsibilities and put their own ulterior interests ahead of international peace and security" but the council did not take further action (United States Mission to the United Nations 2022; United Nations 2022).

Like with the torture vignette, this vignette demonstrates a relatively simple norm conflict, one which appears to be a clear case of norm violation (from the perspective of the first move). But underpinning even this simple conflict, one in which the validity of the norm itself does not appear to be openly questioned, we can see multiple contestations occurring, contestations which focus on the application of the norm and how violations should be treated. The vignette provides instances in which both form and type of contestations are linked together. Thus, the European Union engaged in a proactive applicatory contestation, seeking to link Belarus' violation with sanctions as punishment, reflecting its own earlier efforts to punish wider human rights violations through a similar mechanism. Belarus and Russia engaged in their own contestation in the form of reactive applicatory contestation, arguing Belarus' actions were legal and similar in scope to other cases. But both the Russian and the Chinese governments also appeared to be engaging in a different form of contestation, arguing that more information was needed before an international response was taken. Here, it is difficult to disentangle the motivations behind such public utterances, but these types of responses could be another form of reactive applicatory contestation – seeking to delay or minimise the international response – or they could also mark interpretive contestations as different states put forward their own understandings of the process to examine norm violation.

There are questions left unanswered in both vignettes. In both, we have violations which take on similar forms: both the Bush administration and the Belarusian and Russian governments used similar acknowledgement and denial approaches. And yet, to fully understand this contestation, we would need to look deeper into both cases. We have not, for instance, demonstrated norm robustness beyond using international law as a shorthand, citing two conventions with significant numbers of signatories. Nor have we explored how individual states have implemented these norms. Such claims alone, Anette Stimmer (Chapter 10) suggests, are problematic because state signatures by themselves do not establish that those states have a sense of obligation towards these treaties. And neither vignette, while providing clear evidence of contestations occurring, have provided evidence that these contestations have changed either norm. As Michal Ben-Josef Hirsch and Jennifer M. Dixon have argued in Chapter 2, norm development and change are driven by two constitutive elements: changes in norm strength and norm content. But here, as of yet at least, we see no such change having occurred in the overall norm.

Against the background of these recent developments in norms research, in this concluding chapter we take up the challenge of studying these diverse types of norms and their meaning, use, and role in practice. It is important to note that, as the chapters demonstrate, as a social process norm implementation is always deeply contingent. And as this book has shown, while contingency does imply unknown obstacles for norm implementation, it also implies a largely unexplored sociocultural and normative baggage with potential for novel policy options. As we know by now, a norm's meaning-in-use differs across communities, social groups, cultural boundaries, political regimes, and policy levels. Yet, societal agents move across all these boundaries with their individual normative baggage in tow. It follows that ultimately the ongoing interaction with and about normative meaning-in-use both reflects and maintains that, as social constructions, norms are always in principle contested. While this contestedness may be perceived as a *vice* from a standpoint that aims to preserve a status quo, it is also to be understood as a virtue from a standpoint of societal change. Mindful of the dual quality of norms, therefore, this book's contributions have shed light on a range of distinctly different contexts in which contested and varied interventions about norms took place, and which are part of the larger process of re-ordering the global as a result from the co-constitution of structure and agency (cf. also Adler 2019). From a 'global IR' perspective (Acharya 2014, 2016; Anderl and Witt 2020) contestation is a *sine qua non* for change along the dimension of plural and critical dynamics. As a societal practice, it is therefore clearly more a virtue than a vice for achieving justice in global society.

Thus, we flag norm interpretation and norm contestation as two central concepts that represent an emerging interface for fruitful interdisciplinary research programmes, bringing together especially – if not exclusively – international relations and international law as both Stimmer (Chapter 10) and Holtermann, Madsen, and Stappert (Chapter 11) explore. To demonstrate the concept's elevated role for research in theory and in practice, in the remainder of this concluding chapter we elaborate on how the chapters in this volume have used the interpretation–contestation framework in three ways. The first is how they have helped to better understand an actor's relationship with a given norm (the A–N1 relationship from the Introduction). The second is to explore how the interpretation–contestation framework's three types of contestation (reactive, proactive, and interpretive) alongside different foci on norm validation or application have been used by the chapters to better understand processes of norm generation and change. The third is to then open up two questions for further exploration. This includes how norms are embedded in wider sets of structures and how this can help to clarify how a norm is specifically understood (or how we can introduce the interpretative scope that a range of individual actors may have around a given norm). We end by arguing that research on norm *contestation* offers an important dimension for the literature on the 'contested liberal international order' (Lake et al. 2021; Boerzel and Zürn 2021) because it offers largely under-researched potential for studying these contestations and their constitutive effects on global (re)ordering form later (Adler 2019; Wiener 2018). The following sketches this potential with reference to a brief genealogy of the concept of contestation in norms research.

Contestations in Norms Research

The initial conventional constructivist work of the 1990s significantly improved on prior understandings both by equalising the importance of ideational and material factors and by introducing the concept of mutual constitution. But this work still sought to "bracket" agents and structures (Finnemore 1996: 25), focusing on the effects one had on the other. Thus, the norm life cycle model culminates with a norm that has a fixed identity, a "stability assumption" in other words (Wiener 2014: 23). Rather than focusing on the norm, the focus was on the effects the norm had and how varied actors either accepted or challenged it. This focus on the effects of a fixed norm created two problems. The first was that it removed the capacity of societal agents to understand, challenge, and re-create a given norm in different forms rather than just being norm takers. The second is that it introduced the problem of 'cryptonormativism'. As Havercroft has noted, "focus on demonstrating that norms exist and shape the behaviours of states necessarily brackets the international ethics question of whether or not a norm is 'good' or 'bad,' 'just' or 'unjust'" (Havercroft 2018: 117). Observing the contestation of norms as a practice addresses both of these issues while revealing and changing the normative quality of international relations.

Over the past decade, the concept of contestation has become increasingly central for International Relations (IR) norms scholarship (Niemann and Schillinger 2017; Wolff and Zimmermann 2016; Zimmermann 2017; Stimmer and Wisken 2019; Deitelhoff and Zimmermann 2019; Johansson-Nogués et al. 2020; Wiener 2004, 2008, 2014, 2018) and beyond (Börzel and Zürn 2021). While conventional constructivism has continuously centred on examining the effect that norms have on behaviour, or the effect that norm dynamics have on robustness, critical constructivists begin their research from the practice. As norms research developed, moving on from the constructivist turn in IR (Checkel 1998), the novel interest in examining situations of "contested compliance" as "interventions on the normative structure in world politics" (Deitelhoff and Zimmermann 2019; see also, e.g., Wiener 2004: 12) marked a decisive shift in the field. Instead of focusing on changing (state) behaviour in relation with a given norm, this research suggested studying norms as embedded in normative structures of meaning-in-use that were re-enacted through practice (Byers 2003; Wiener 2004; Brosig 2012). This change in research objective was triggered by the recurrence of contestation "driven by acts of non-compliance" (Deitelhoff and Zimmermann 2019: 3, fn. 3). The local sites of contestation and contingent conditions of norm implementation gained in importance (Acharya 2004; Hofius et al. 2014; Zimmermann 2017).

Against this background, contestation allows us to understand norms in two key ways. The first is that contestation highlights the importance of conceiving of norms as both indicators of *normality* (i.e., indicating standards of appropriate behaviour) and of *normativity* (i.e., indicating moral principles that ought to be applied). The second is that it highlights the "dual quality of norms" (Wiener 2007) as both socially constructed through the practice of societal agency and, at the same time, entailing the potential to structure behaviour based on a norm's role within a given context and the effect of this dual quality. Focusing on this dual quality has enhanced our understanding of how socio-cultural background experience and everyday practices shape norm recognition, validation and meaning (Brunnee and Toope 2011; Deitelhoff and

Zimmermann 2019; Finnemore and Toope 2001; Havercroft 2018; Hofius et al. 2014; Niemann and Schillinger 2017; Orchard 2018; Stimmer and Wisken 2019; Krook and True 2012). This growing body of scholarship has generated a range of distinct approaches to studying contestatory practices including contesting compliance (Puetter and Wiener 2009), as practising dissent (Stimmer and Wisken 2019), as negotiating validity (Deitelhoff and Zimmermann 2019), or as engaging with values (Wiener 2018).

This conceptual development has advanced a concise toolkit which emphasises the importance of a practice-based approach to norm emergence, contestation, and constitution. The benefits of this perspectives include first of all novel ways of accounting for norm-change and normative change against, taking account of the wider socio-cultural environment of norm emergence and change, including distinct practices of norm validation, uneven access to norm contestation and cultural background experience (Krook and True 2012; Hofius et al. 2014; Engelkamp and Glaab 2015; Niemann and Schillinger 2017; Martin de Almagro 2018; Stimmer and Wisken 2019; Wiener 2014, 2018). Subsequently, the research agenda shifted from the effects of norms and how to enhance them (e.g., by learning, internalisation and/or diffusion) towards new practices in relation with norms (e.g., translation, interpretation, and contestation). The leading contention that is central to the third move regards the *effect of contestation* in a global context that is marked by a multiplicity of societal agents and a plurality of political orders. If and when this pluralist frame is considered a shared point of departure for norms research, a systematic and in-depth studies of instances of contestation, and which follow the conflict to the sites of conflict, will reveal novel insights on the effect of practices of contestation and the normative impact of contested fundamental norms. This perspective centres on the leading assumption that contestation is a virtue for world ordering from the bottom up. And, therefore,

> the point is not to start with some general thesis about cultural diversity versus equality … but to examine actual cases to see what the conflict is about. This implies *listening* to the people engaged in the struggles over the prevailing norms of recognition in their own terms, taking the dialogical step, and accepting the maxim of *audi alteram partem* (always listen to the other side) as integral to a political approach to issues of recognition. (Owen and Tully 2007: 284; emphasis in original text)

Against the backdrop of the current state-of-the-art of norm contestation research, the central constructivist claim that as social facts norms matter for international relations remains vital for IR theory. However, the leading research question has shifted. Three decades ago, constructivists sought to demonstrate why and how norms matter both for international relations (i.e., as standards of behaviour for global agents interacting beyond the regulatory setting of nation-states) and for IR theory (i.e., as a novel concept that allowed for theorising 'the social'). At the time, norm dynamics mattered for explaining the changing behaviour – predominantly, if not exclusively – of states in international relations (Finnemore and Sikkink 1998). In turn, today's norms researchers are especially interested in practices of norm contestation and ask: how does contestation contribute to norm-generation and change? They are especially interested in how contestation affects norm-change or stability, and if so, they also ask: how does contestation affect normative order and who has access to contestation? These questions are approached by a research operationalisation that distinguishes between practices of contestation and validation, and which begins by identifying norm conflicts to follow the conflict to local sites of contestation, then identify the involved societal agents, and their opportunities of access to contestation. With reference to this book's contributions, the following sections offer examples of how this approach is applied. Here we first turn to the practice of interpretation about norms and norm conflict, and then address practices of contestation.

Interpreting Norms and the Role of Norm Conflict

In the Introduction, we argued that there are two takes of how agents interact among each other with respect to specific norms. The first produces a specific understanding of that norm for that agent (the A–N1 relationship), a relationship that may be repeated but that is always between one or more agents and that given norm. The second takes place between a variety of agents (A1, A2, and so on) who are part of a conflictive encounter during which norms are challenged and changed. The A–N1 relationship is also about exploring *how states understand norms*. Several of the volume's authors focus on how these understandings emerge and, in particular, how the concept of norm compliance may be too narrow.

Anette Stimmer argues that understanding should not be focused on compliance or effectiveness, both of which become difficult to measure when norms and state preferences are treated as not being static. She instead proposes a sense of obligation as a measure by looking at how states have implemented a norm. Focusing on legal obligation, she suggests three signposts exist: consistency, publicity, and engagement with the international community, with each identifiable through both behaviour and discourse. And, for her, it is this form of obligation, including both self and relational factors, which can be used to a create a converging interpretation of a given norm. As she notes, "the more the international community converges on a legal interpretation, the clearer it becomes whether an implementing action conforms to it" (Chapter 10: 171).

Michal Ben-Josef Hirsch and Jennifer M. Dixon focus on when a norm becomes a norm and how it changes and develops. Like Anette Stimmer, they find compliance to not be a useful measure: "full compliance is extremely rare" (Ben-Josef Hirsch and Dixon, Chapter 2: 34). They suggest instead an understanding of a norm based on two distinct elements: norm strength (defined as the extent of collective expectations related to a principled idea) and content (defined as the behaviours that are prescribed or proscribed, for whom, and under what conditions). Contestations can see norm content get re-defined in terms of its applicability, what falls within and outside of its purview, and even flipped entirely from one norm to another related, yet distinct norm. And strength reflects how widely a norm's collective expectation are shared.

Carla Winston takes a systemic view to norms emergence, arguing that which norms emerge, and from where, can be understood as much as system properties as from the qualities of any particular norm. She sees the international system as a structure that enables, channels, and constrains their emergence and as such she recommends that norms be views as 'emergent properties' of the system, arising "from the micro-level interactions of its agents" but which are not reducible down to the "characteristics of those agents" (Winston, Chapter 9: 154).

For Halima Akhrif and Simon Koschut, emotional resonance is crucial for both the maintenance and enforcement of international norms: "we are more likely to see norm compliance if the respective norms evoke shared images, memories, and collective emotions among international actors" (Akhrif and Koschut, Chapter 6: 114). In their chapter, they focus on the capacity of emotional resonance is a mechanism to respond to reactive contestations, allowing the "evocation of emotional images, memories, and feelings puts the targeted actor into the position to also react with an emotional assessment of the norm's value" (Chapter 6: 106). When these images and feelings are absent or weak, by contrast, this connection cannot be created, and non-compliance can be expected.

Sassan Gholiagha and Mitja Sienknecht similarly note issues with the concept of compliance, suggesting like Stimmer that it is difficult to assess but also both that non-compliance may not always be deliberate, reflecting issues of interpretation, and that compliance may be more of a continuum with acceptable standards allowed below "strict compliance." Such a continuum leads them to suggest the concept of responsible behaviour, behaviours that overfulfills what should be expected as 'appropriate' behaviour for shared understandings of a given norm, and conversely irresponsible behaviour where actors fail to act in situations of moral obligation. They suggest that such behaviours are practices of contestation affecting a given norm: "it is imaginable that responsible behaviour leads to stronger and more robust norms" (Gholiagha and Sienknecht Chapter 8: 140).

Audie Klotz echoes the volume's Introduction of norms as soft institutions that are both value and fact bases by exploring racial discrimination. For her, too often "our analyses of norms in the world 'out there' are also embedded within a professional normative fabric derived from that world: the liberal imaginary," an imaginary that can sideline critical questions (Klotz Chapter 5: 87). Thus, devoting attention to specific episodes of contestation can actually challenge a "norm against noticing" by revealing practices that are otherwise omitted in conventional meta-narratives. This is a "reminder that taken-for-granted interpretations may be hidden in plain site" (Klotz Chapter 5: 96).

Situations become even more complex when multiple norms may be applicable and if their normative directives are inconsistent or not uniquely action-guiding. As Anchalee Rüland and Jennifer Welsh note, in such situations of norm conflict "neither norm is applicable without seeming to conflict or 'collide' with the other" (Chapter 3: 44). Actors seeking to resolve such conflicts may well appear to be in violation of one of the norms, leading to potential social costs. Thus, they propose a consequentialist framework of five possible strategies that such actors can adopt in order to manage the potential costs to legitimacy and reputation that they face from consistent norm prioritisation through denial or reconciliation to full scale norm replacement.

Liese focuses on the converse situation, where crises can destabilise extant balances or hierarchies between potentially colliding norms. Such collisions, she argues, may actually be quite ubiquitous in different policy domains and affect even legally codified norms which would appear to have well defined boundaries. And collisions can affect contestations in different ways. They may trigger proactive contestations as new actors may be empowered, but they can also trigger reactive contestation as actors argue for the necessity of exceptional measures (Liese, Chapter 4).

Researching Contestation

In addition to the practice of interpretation, we now offer an overview of how the individual chapters explored contestation. To recall, the book worked with the premise that norm(ative) change is constituted through societal agency in which agents engage in distinct practices of contestation. And it was argued that to uncover these practices, we address both the empirical reconstruction of the constitutive (i.e., behaviourally induced) and the constructive (i.e., normatively induced) generation of norms. While both generative processes are social constructions, the third move literature in particular highlights that the former brackets normativity, while the latter addresses it expressly. It argues that if 'all practice is normative',[5] it follows that norms research needs to be able to take account of, and account for, both the normality and the normative effects of contestation. The putative definition of the legitimacy of a given normative order is therefore viewed as depending on whether those governed by this order have access to contest the norms of governance: the higher the potential for engagement with norms, the more legitimate becomes the order of which they are part. To facilitate this engagement, institutional pathways that enable stakeholders to partake in processes of norm validation are required.

Under the regulatory conditions of global governance, access to norm validation is not equally distributed among the involved stakeholders who are governed by international law. In this context, a set of political and legal institutions facilitate and mediate the implementation of norms, and, in addition, the social environment in which norms are interpreted plays a crucial role (Finnemore and Toope 2001). However, the focus on a given norm's effect, such as the prohibition of torture or the ban on landmines (Liese 2009; Price and Sikkink 2017), brackets the generation of fundamental norms through the practice of contestation and therefore we have relatively little data or theory on norm generation through practice. The effect of a dialogical relationship depends on the conditions under which involved stakeholders obtain access to regular contestation (Laden and Owen 2007: 19). But unpacking contestation requires us to focus on methodological distinct practices of contestation in both form and type.

To that end, the introduction introduced two forms of contestation: validity contestations which focus on the specific normative claims being made by a norm; and applicatory contestations which focus primarily on whether a given norm is appropriate for a given situation. We also suggested that three types of contestations could occur. Reactive

[5] This shared dictum reflects a summary comment by Emanuel Adler when discussing norm contestation with an interdisciplinary group of norm researchers attending the seminar on "The Cycle of Contestation" at the Munk School of Global Affairs, University of Toronto, Ontario, 27 March 2017. For the recent move on behalf of practice theorists towards a more rigorous engagement with normativity, see, for example Bueger and Gadinger (2018).

contestations are being indicated primarily as an objection to norms. Proactive contestations are being indicated primarily by efforts to engage with a norm, seeking to improve it. Interpretive contestations, by contrast, reflect instances in which agents have different interpretive understandings of a norm which may not be readily apparent, and which may be inadvertent rather than deliberate (compare Orchard and Wiener, Chapter 1: Figure 1.1). Thus, as with the preceding Ryanair example, it is possible to indicate contestations take on both a form and a type, that is, *reactive-validity contestation.*

Several authors across the volume have focused on specific form and type contestations either in terms of specific cases or in terms of how contestations are understood (Figure 15.1). As an example of a specific case, and as noted in the earlier vignette, the anti-torture norm was one that was frequently examined. Halima Akhrif and Simon Koschut saw the Bush administration engaging in a reactive contestation against the anti-torture norm, a contestation gradually undermined by both

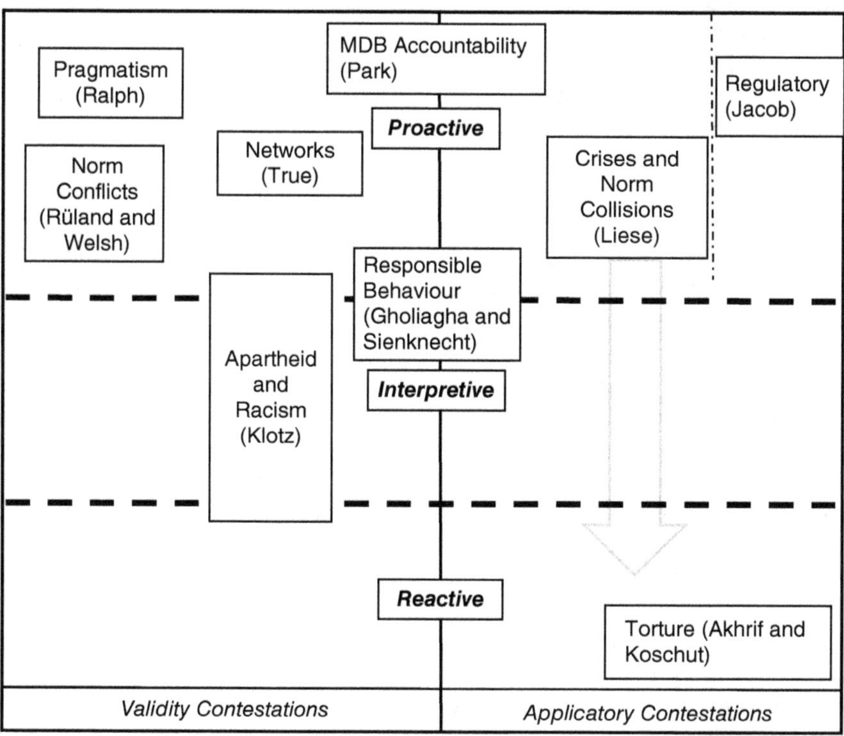

Figure 15.1 The process of contestation

international and domestic actors by using emotional resonance to link these abuses with historical instances of torture including the tactics of the Gestapo. They find as part of this process that the US government also engaged in applicatory contestation, seeking to reframe the practice of 'enhanced interrogation techniques' as being essentially different from torture which helped to buttress criticisms against them. Susan Park points to two forms of proactive contestation in terms of how multilateral development banks (MDBs) accepted an accountability norm: first, transnational advocacy groups successfully pushed for the need for accountability with respect to the World Bank's environmental and social impacts; but, second, as the World Bank and other MDBs accepted this, they engaged in applicatory contestations, shaping a very specific interpretation of the norm even while supporting it (Park, Chapter 7).

Other authors advanced how the framework can be understood. Cecilia Jacob argues that a specific form of proactive contestation, regulatory contestation, can follow validity and applicatory contestation. For her, this is a social, process-oriented practice focused around "efforts to steer or influence the flow of events towards specified governance outcomes." This type of contestation is proactive because it is aimed "at strengthening the consistency and legitimacy of a norm by embedding its implementation through a permanent or concretised regulatory framework" (Jacob, Chapter 13: 227).

For Audie Klotz, hidden norms, can play as much a role within international normative debates as at the domestic level. Focusing on apartheid and racism, she notes how a "norm against noticing" has meant that the IR community has been too silent on the role contestations around both of these concepts played in creating our modern conception of human rights (Klotz, Chapter 5: 87).

Finally, Jason Ralph argues that contestation can both reconcile as well as open disputes because its purpose under a pragmatist emphasis "is to (re)establish faith in a practice and to reconstitute a norm's meaning so that it can alleviate lived problems" (Ralph, Chapter 14: 240). Thus by proactively building norms in his view, contestations always involve knowledge claims about what constitutes appropriate behaviour. This is an important claim in two senses. First, through his use of a pragmatist approach, he notes the importance of a stock of learning, or background knowledge within a normative regime, that can be used to adjudicate between different contestations. Second, is the need to include the everyday lived experience: "we cannot properly know the appropriateness of a norm without including the experiences of the affected in the deliberations of the scientific community" (Ralph, Chapter 14: 244).

This links into the important question of how 'good' norms are created. This question is vital for third movers who no longer eschew normativity and place norms within a larger societal context of which norms form a constitutive part and echoes Havercroft's critique that bracketing the normative in order to pursue the empirical creates a kind of cryptonormativism (Havercroft 2018: 117). In accepting that dual quality of norms as indicators of both normalcy and normativity, the quasi-ontological status of norms as 'good' norms that is taken-for-granted fundamental norms that lie at the core of Western liberal communities has become increasingly questioned by third movers who have come to distinguish normative meanings-in-use with reference to degrees of moral reach and the expected contestation of norms at sites of norm contestation (Wiener 2004, 2018). As argued in the Introduction, contestation as a process of norm generation needs to be seen as having both behaviourally (or constitutive) and normatively (or constructive) proprieties, ensuring not only that actors follow a given norm, but also that norm possess a widely shared and legitimate understanding (and thereby becoming robust). But legitimacy relies on access, and hence the more access that stakeholders have – across the macro-, meso-, and micro-levels – the more they are included and able to be included within contestation, and the more likely a norm is to possess this legitimacy. This said, it is important to stress that while we do agree with the Tully-inspired dictum that "only a contested norm can ever be considered a good norm" (Wiener 2020: 197; Tully 2002), we also note that not all contested norms are necessarily good norms. That is, contestation is considered a necessary however not a sufficient condition for a norm's legitimacy. And as Jason Ralph argues in his chapter, there might be situations where norms need to be "defended against contestation" in the sense of objecting to norms without offering access to proactive engagement (Ralph, Chapter 14: 237).

Hence, how stakeholders are included within contestation processes is a critical issue across the volume's chapters. For instance, Susan Park documents how a transnational advocacy network comprised primarily of US environmental NGOs sought to challenge the World Bank in the early 1980s around its environmental and social impacts. They used transnational campaigns, linking with activists in project areas, to pressure both the bank and its governmental shareholders for reform leading to clear accountability mechanisms. But while the bank responded to this pressure by adopting clear accountability mechanisms, evidence that suggests a proactive contestation leading to norm generation, it was also able to shape the norm to preserve its own immunity and thereby create a distinct interpretation of a wider normative commitment, an interpretation that other multilateral development banks then adopted in turn. For Jacqui True, networks are important for contestation because they can improve access. Examining the development of the Women, Peace and Security agenda, she argues that initially reactive contestations during earlier movements led to the formation of a truly transnational women's network that represented greater global diversity and hence created new spaces and access for proactive contestations.

Stakeholders matter in a different sense as well. Both Anette Stimmer and Jakob Holtermann, Mikael Madsen, and Nora Stappert point to the roles of "interpretive communities" and "communities of practice," respectively, to create senses of shared understandings of norms. Both of their chapters focus on legal norms. For Stimmer, inconsistency in norm following alone is not enough to suggest a lack of normative influence. Instead, we need to examine how the state reacts to the judgements of others, particularly influential actors (such as powerful states or international courts) within those communities. For Holtermann, Madsen, and Stappert, legal validation is shaped by and reflects underlying power dynamics, with international lawyers potentially serving a key role in processes of norm implementation.

The Role of Other Structures

The Introduction also raised the question of the role played by other structures with respect to norms: how a specific norm is embedded or fits together and is nested within other norms and international structures. Norm content, as Ben-Josef Hirsch and Dixon note in Chapter 2, can vary significantly in reflecting a range of prescriptive or proscriptive behaviours. This content can directly reflect how complex the specific behaviour required by an individual norm is (Orchard 2018: 27–8). A proscriptive norm forbids a certain pattern of behaviour (Price 1997; Percy 2007). As this norm is in the form of an injunction, the action required by the norm is clear: the individual actor must not engage in the action which is prohibited. A prescriptive norm, by contrast, requires a positive duty or action on part of states; the norm requires for the individual actor not only to not engage in the injuncted behaviour, but also to sanction in some way other actors if they do so (Glanville 2006: 154–6). This means that norms with prescriptive elements will be more complex: they create a responsibility within the group of actors who share that norm. As an example of these issues, Ralph has noted that with respect to the Responsibility to Protect, its prescriptive element "which insists that states as members of an international community have a responsibility to protect foreign populations, is less clear, and from a pragmatic constructivist perspective this indeterminacy is useful given the problem R2P addresses" (Ralph 2018: 186). This means that prescriptive norms will be subject to significantly greater interpretive variation than proscriptive norms. And the more complex a norm is, the more likely it connects to other norms and structures.

While such structures have been referred to by a variety of different terms,[6] one approach is to view a regime existing which bundles together what might otherwise be disparate norms. In so doing, it provides a clear sense of the scope of international behaviour required and how states and other actors *should* deal with a particular problem. Thus, regimes provide a mechanism through which the appropriate standards of behaviour suggested by the individual norms are linked together to create a response within the complexity of the issue area. Since a regime provides this linkage, it brings an increased regularity to state practices than would otherwise be the case; they "frame the nature and scope of a given problem and provide potential response scripts" (Orchard 2014: 241). Linkages between norms can also increase resilience, particularly when norms are clustered together that "originate and develop in a cohesive manner, and that are embedded in or backed up by a dense institutional network and legal structures" (Lantis and Wunderlich 2018: 580).

Such structures are a key component for Susan Park. She explores the development of the international accountability norm which emerged within the World Bank and was then replicated by the other Multilateral Development Banks. These banks sit within a specific development finance regime complex, and because of this they have been able to develop a separate understanding of accountability from that of international human rights law, one focused on a view of them as internal standards rather than legal obligations, and a system that does not create a clear legal remedy. This is although actions by the banks can impact directly and indirectly on human rights through the project and programmes they finance; their lending to human rights violating governments; and their own failures to uphold or promote human rights in their lending practices. In essence, the regime complex as a structure has allowed discrete and differing interpretations of norms to develop.

[6] These include "norm complexes" (Finnemore and Sikkink 1998: 891; Bernstein 2000), "norm clusters" (Lantis and Wunderlich 2018: 571), and "regimes" which Orchard (2014: 20) uses in other work following Goertz's argument that regimes can be understood as structures of norms and rules, with norms and rules being counterparts for most purposes (Goertz 2003: 15).

But this is a structure that relies on the banks' immunity as international organisations, a claim of immunity that has now been challenged by the US Supreme Court.

Jakob Holtermann, Mikael Madsen, and Nora Stappert similarly point to how, in the case of climate change, legal developments frequently cover a range of different but adjacent legal fields. Thus, changes in normative meaning, they note, "have been situated at the intersection between fields" (in a Bourdieusian sense; Chapter 11: 194). And Carla Winston sees norms as constituent parts of regimes and regime complexes, and notes that these structures generate 'interface conflicts' driven by disagreements over norm meanings and behavioural implications. When resolved, it is the outcome of these conflicts that can create elements of order, clarifying the norm and increasing its robustness.

Hence, together these works suggest that structures (in an international relations sense) can and do interact with norms during processes of contestations. This can trigger distinct norm interpretations to emerge within some regime complexes (as Park shows), but it can also see norm understandings transmitted across different issue areas.

Outlook: Contestations and International Orders

As this book demonstrated, the three moves of norms research reveal distinct preferences regarding where to allocate their research object (i.e., is the norm contested at the macro-, meso-, or micro-scale of global society?) and how to theorise it (i.e., is norm-change an opportunity or a threat?). These distinctions show the conceptual limits of theorising at the middle-ground. For example, some would consider norm contestation a threat to norm 'robustness' (Deitelhoff and Zimmermann 2019) while others would consider norm contestation as an opportunity for norm-followers and norm-entrepreneurs alike (Stimmer and Wisken 2019). Against this background it could be argued that extant epistemological and ontological differences draw the field apart, given that "the presuppositions about the 'reality status' (ontology) of the subject of study and about its 'knowability' (epistemology) that are enacted through research procedures of various sorts" (Haverland and Yanow 2012: 401) do not converge. This book sought to demonstrate that the distinct approaches which have been developed by norms research over the past three decades do speak to one another in meaningful and innovative ways. And, as Figures 1.1 and 15.1 show, over time the three moves have contributed to constitute a conceptual grid with reference to the *practices* and *types* of contestation and their respective impact on the changing world order.

Against this background, and with a view towards future contributions of norms research within the subfield as well as for the wider discipline of IR, we contend that this grid has analytical potential. This matters especially with regard to addressing the important question of the 'contested liberal international order' (LIO) which has recently been flagged by the seventy-five-year birthday issue of *International Organization* (2021).[7] Notably, none of the contributions to this special issue understands the practice of contestation as constructive and with normative potential (i.e., as a necessary if not sufficient for legitimacy) for this order. And as one of the special issue editors commented in a personal discussion "we did ourselves a bit of disservice by taking contestation to mean decay" whereas they had now learned that "contestation can also be constructive."[8] In turn, this book's contributions focus on practice allows for a more detailed assessment of the potential of 'bottom-up' dynamics of norm(ative) change that matters for research that seeks to understand and explain the contested liberal international order.

In a nutshell, we argue that in contrast to the quickly growing literature addressing the 'contested liberal order' or 'contestations of the international liberal order' which is spurred by an interest in repairing that order's parts to re-instate its stability, research on norm contestation shifts the analytical perspective and approaches the constitution of order(s) from the bottom-up. The rationale for this opposing perspective lies in the question of where theories allocate normative meaning, value, and change. While the contested order literature allocates these virtues within the order itself, and therefore aims to restore order based on repairing selected parts, the literature on norm contestation begins from the contested values and meanings of the part. As this book suggests, therefore, rather than in each order, the virtue lies in the practices and types of contestation that contribute to the construction of the constitutive norms of any order. Applying the norms research grid, it becomes possible to identify the needs for 'repair' which are indicated by reactive contestation, following the location of norm conflicts to local sites of contestation. And subsequently, these needs can be addressed by establishing

7 Compare the theme of the special issue on the liberal international liberal order (LIO) in *International Organization* 2020: www.cambridge.org/core/journals/international-organization/firstview; see also the rather different perspectives that were presented at the #LSECOVID19 series event *World on the Edge: The Crisis of the Western Liberal Order* featuring Ikenberry (LIO is worth striving for), Mearsheimer (LIO is not desirable), and Jahn (democratic norms and values must be re-negotiated locally): www2.lse.ac.uk/Events/2021/02/202102161800/World-on-the-Edge-the-Crisis-of-the-Western-Liberal-Order.

8 Antje Wiener in conversation with David Lake and Thomas Risse, 16 October 2021.

and/or enhancing pathways which enable affected stakeholders' access to proactive contestation and/or interpretation. Where the liberal order literature considers the liberal order an uncontested virtue and, relatedly, contestation a malfunction, we would suggest that leading questions for prospective norm research 'contesting the world' are instead: How do norms and their meanings change through interaction? And how does that effect order(s) in world society? Norm contestation, viewed as both a vice and a virtue, helps us to understand norms not only in a unique way but also how they fundamentally constitute the world.

References

Abbott, Kenneth W., Keohane, Robert O., Moravcsik, Andrew, Slaughter, Anne-Marie, and Snidal, Duncan 2000. 'The Concept of Legalization.' *International Organization* 54(3): 401–419.

Abdelal, Rawi 2007. *Capital Rules: The Construction of Global Finance*. Cambridge, MA: Harvard University Press.

Abouharb, Rodwan M., and Cingranelli, David L. 2007. *Human Rights and Structural Adjustment*. Cambridge: Cambridge University Press.

Abraham, Kavi J., and Abramson, Yehonathan 2015. 'A Pragmatist Vocation for International Relations: The (Global) Public and Its Problems.' *European Journal of International Relations* 23(1): 26–48.

Acharya, Amitav 2004. 'How Ideas Spread: Whose Norms Matter? Norm Localization and Institutional Change in Asian Regionalism.' *International Organization* 58(2): 239–275. https://doi.org/10.1017/S0020818304582024.

2013. 'The R2P and Norm Diffusion: Towards a Framework of Norm Circulation.' *Global Responsibility to Protect* 5(4): 466–479.

2014. 'Global International Relations (IR) and Regional Worlds: New Agenda for International Studies.' *International Studies Quarterly* 58: 647–659.

2015. *Indonesia Matters: Asia's Emerging Democratic Power*. Singapore: World Scientific Publishing.

2016. 'Advancing Global IR: Challenges, Contentions, and Contributions.' *International Studies Review* 18(1): 4–15.

Acheson, Roy, and Butler, Maria 2019. 'WPS and Arms Trade Treaty.' In Davies, S. E., and True, J. (eds). *The Oxford Handbook of Women, Peace, and Security*, 690–703. New York: Oxford University Press.

Ackerly, Brooke A. 2003. 'Women's Human Rights Activists as Cross-Cultural Theorists.' *International Feminist Journal of Politics* 3(3): 311–346.

Adachi, Kenki 2005. 'Why Japan Signed the Mine Ban Treaty: The Political Dynamics behind the Decision.' *Asian Survey* 45(3): 397–413.

Addams, Jane 2007. 'The Newer Ideals of Peace.' In Ely, R. T. (ed). *The Citizen's Library of Economics, Politics, and Sociology*, 209–238. New York: Macmillan.

Addams, Jane, Balch, Emily G., and Hamilton, Alice 2015. *Women at The Hague: The International Congress of Women and Its Results*. New York: Macmillan.

Adler, Emanuel 1997. 'Seizing the Middle Ground: Constructivism in World Politics.' *European Journal of International Relations* 3(3): 319–363.

2019. *World Ordering: A Social Theory of Cognitive Evolution*. Cambridge: Cambridge University Press.

Adler, Matthew D. 2012. 'Interpretive Contestation and Legal Correctness.' *William & Mary Law Review* 53(4): 1115–1136.

Adler-Nissen, Rebecca 2014. 'Stigma Management in International Relations: Transgressive Identities, Norms, and Order in International Society.' *International Organization* 68(1): 143–176.

Adler-Nissen, Rebecca, and Pouliot, Vincent 2014. 'Power in Practice: Negotiating the International Intervention in Libya.' *European Journal of International Relations* 20(4): 889–911.

Aggestam, Karin 2019. 'WPS, Peace Negotiations and Peace Agreements.' In Davies, S. E., and True, J. (eds). *The Oxford Handbook of Women, Peace, and Security*, 815–828. New York: Oxford University Press.

Aggestam, Karin, and True, Jacqui 2023. 'Foreign Policy and Feminist Governance.' In Sawer, M., Banaschak, L., True, J., and Kantola, J. (eds). *The Handbook of Feminist Governance*, 203–215. London: Edward Elgar Publishing.

AIIB. 2018. 'Policy on the Project-affected People's Mechanism.' 7 December. www.aiib.org/en/policies-strategies/_download/project-affected/PPM-policy.pdf.

Albert, Mathias 1999. 'Observing World Politics: Luhman's Systems Theory of Society and International Relations.' *Millennium – Journal of International Studies* 28(2): 239–265.

Alexander, Amanda 2015. 'A Short History of International Humanitarian Law.' *European Journal of International Law* 26(1): 109–138.

Alsaba, Khuloud, and Kapilashrami, Anuj 2016. 'Understanding Women's Experiences of Violence and the Political Economy of Gender: The Case of Syria.' *Reproductive Health Matters* 24: 5–17.

Alter, Karen J. 2014. *The New Terrain of International Law*. Princeton: Princeton University Press.

Alter, Karen J., and Meunier, Sophie 2009. 'The Politics of International Regime Complexity.' *Perspectives on Politics* 7(1): 13–24.

Amnesty International. 2004. 'USA: Pattern of Brutality and Cruelty. War Crimes at Abu Ghraib.' Amnesty International Press Release, 7 May.

2008. 'Myanmar Briefing. Human Rights Concerns a Month after Cyclone Nargis.' 5 June. www.amnesty.org/es/wpcontent/uploads/2021/07/asa160132008eng.pdf.

2019. 'Coming Face to Face with Torture.' www.amnestyusa.org/coming-face-to-face-with-torture/.

2022. 'Israel's Apartheid against Palestinians: Cruel System of Domination and Crime against Humanity.' Released 2 February, https://amnesty.org.

Anderl, Felix and Witt, Antonia 2020. 'Problematising the Global in Global IR.' *Millennium* 49(1): 32–57.

Anderlini, Sanam N. 2019. 'Civil Society Leadership in Adopting 1325 Resolution.' In Davies, S. E., and True, J. (eds). *The Oxford Handbook of Women, Peace, and Security*, 38–52. New York: Oxford University Press.

Anderson, Christopher G. 2013. *Canadian Liberalism and the Politics of Border Control, 1867–1967*. Vancouver: University of British Columbia Press.

Anelay, Joyce (The Minister of State, Foreign and Commonwealth Office) 2014. 'Mediterranean Sea Question Asked by Lord Hylton.' UK Parliament. www.publications.parliament.uk/pa/ld201415/ldhansrd/text/141015w0001.htm.

Anievas, Alexander, Manchanda, Nivi, and Shilliam, Robbie (eds). 2015. *Race and Racism in International Relations: Confronting the Global Colour Line*. Abingdon: Routledge.

Annan, Kofi 1999. 'Two Concepts of Sovereignty.' *The Economist*, 18 September.

2004. 'Secretary-General's Address to the General Assembly.' United Nations Secretary-General. www.un.org/sg/en/content/sg/statement/2004-09-21/secretary-generals-address-general-assembly.

Arnold, Magda B. 1960. *Emotion and Personality*. Irvington: Columbia University Press.

Aust, Helmut P. 2015. 'The UN Human Rights Due Diligence Policy: An Effective Mechanism against Complicity of Peacekeeping Forces?' *Conflict and Security Law* 20(1): 61–73.

Axelrod, Robert 1986. 'An Evolutionary Approach to Norms.' *American Political Science Review* 80(4): 1095–1111.

Azuma, Eiichiro 2019. 'Japanese Agricultural Labor Program: Temporary Worker Immigration, US-Japan Cultural Diplomacy, and Ethnic Community Making among Japanese Americans.' In Marinar, M., Hsu, M., and García, M.C. (eds). *A Nation of Immigrants Reconsidered: US Society in an Age of Restriction, 1924–1965*, 161–186. Champaign: University of Illinois Press.

Babb, Sarah 2009. *Behind the Development Banks*. Chicago: Chicago University Press.

Badescu, Cristina G., and Weiss, Thomas G. 2010. 'Misrepresenting R2P and Advancing Norms: An Alternative Spiral?' *International Studies Perspectives* 11(4): 354–374.

Bailey, Jennifer L. 2008. 'Arrested Development: The Fight to End Commercial Whaling as a Case of Failed Norm Change.' *European Journal of International Relations* 14(2): 289–318.

Barkin, Samuel J., and Cronin, Bruce 1994. 'The State and the Nation: Changing Norms and the Rules of Sovereignty in International Relations.' *International Organization* 48 (1): 107–130.

Barkin, Samuel J., and Sjoberg, Laura 2019. *International Relations' Last Synthesis? Decoupling Constructivist and Critical Approaches*. New York: Oxford University Press.

Basham, Victoria M. 2015. 'Waiting for War. Soldiering, Temporality and the Gendered Politics of Boredom and Joy in Military Spaces.' In Ahall, L., and Gregory, T. (eds). *Emotions, Politics and War*, 128–140. New York: Routledge.

Basu, Soumita 2016. 'The Global South Writes 1325 (Too).' *International Political Science Review* 37(3): 362–374.

BBC. 2021. 'Vitaly Shishov: Head of Belarus Exiles Group Found Dead in Ukraine.' 3 August. www.bbc.com/news/world-europe-58065313.

BBC News. 2016. 'Ukraine Crisis: Timeline.' *BBC News*, 24 February. www.bbc.co.uk/news/world-middle-east-26248275.

Beauregard, Philippe 2019. 'Beyond Cold Monsters: A Cognitive-Affective Theory of International Leadership.' Dissertation. Université de Laval. https://corpus.ulaval.ca/jspui/bitstream/20.500.11794/36238/1/35290.pdf.

Beetham, David 2013. *The Legitimation of Power*. 2nd ed. Houndmills: Palgrave Macmillan.

Beirlaen, Mathieu 2011. 'A Unifying Framework for Reasoning about Normative Conflicts.' In Pelis, M., and Puchocar, V. (eds). *The Logica Yearbook*, 1–14. College Publications. www.clps.ugent.be/sites/default/files/publications/logica2011_proceedings.pdf

Belich, James 2009. *Replenishing the Earth: The Settler Revolution and the Rise of the Anglo-World, 1783–1939*. Oxford: Oxford University Press.

Bellamy, Alex J. 2010. 'The Responsibility to Protect – Five Years On.' *Ethics & International Affairs* 24(2): 143–169.

2011. *Global Politics and The Responsibility to Protect: From Words to Deeds*. Oxford and New York: Routledge.

2016. 'The Humanisation of Security? Towards an International Human Protection Regime.' *European Journal of International Security* 1(1): 112–133.

Bellamy, Alex J., and Drummond, Catherine 2011. 'The Responsibility to Protect in Southeast Asia: Between Non-Interference and Sovereignty as Responsibility.' *The Pacific Review* 24(2): 179–200.

Belta. 2021. 'Belarus Participates in ICAO Council Session on Ryanair's Flight FR4978 Incident.' 29 June. https://eng.belta.by/society/view/belarus-participates-in-icao-council-session-on-ryanairs-flight-fr4978-incident-141272-2021/.

Ben-Josef Hirsch, Michal. 2009. 'And the Truth Shall Make You Free: The International Norm of Truth-Seeking.' Ph.D. diss., Massachusetts Institute of Technology.

2014. 'Ideational Change and the Emergence of the International Norm of Truth and Reconciliation Commissions.' *European Journal of International Relations* 20(3): 810–833.

Ben-Josef Hirsch, Michal, and Dixon, Jennifer M. 2021. 'Conceptualizing and Assessing Norm Strength in International Relations.' *European Journal of International Relations* 27(2): 521–547.

2024. 'Rethinking Norm Change: Content and Strength in Norm Development.' In Orchard, P., and Wiener, A. (eds). *Contesting the World. Norm Research in Theory and Practice*, 29–42. Cambridge: Cambridge University Press.

Berger, Thomas U. 1996. 'Norms, Identity, and National Security in Germany and Japan.' In Katzenstein, P. (ed). *The Culture of National Security: Norms and Identity in World Politics*, 317–356. New York: Columbia University Press.

Berkman, Joyce 1990. *Feminism, War, and Peace Politics: The Case of World War I*. Savage: Rowman & Littlefield.

Berkovitch, Nitza, and Gordon, Neve 2016. 'Differentiated Decoupling and Human Rights.' *Social Problems* 63(4): 499–512.

Berliner, Daniel, and Prakash, Aseem 2012. 'From Norms to Programs: The United Nations Global Compact and Global Governance.' *Regulation and Governance* 6: 149–166.

Bernstein, Steven 2000. 'Ideas, Social Structure and the Compromise of Liberal Environmentalism.' *European Journal of International Relations* 6(4): 464–512.

Bernstein, Steven 2001. *The Compromise of Liberal Environmental Norms*. New York: Columbia University Press. https://doi.org/10.7312/bern12036.6.

Betts, Alexander, and Orchard, Phil 2014. 'Introduction: The Normative Institutionalization-Implementation Gap.' In Betts, A., and Orchard, P. (eds). *Implementation and World Politics: How International Norms Change Practice*, 1–26. Oxford: Oxford University Press.

Bewarder, Manuel, and Walter, Lisa 2017. 'Rettungseinsätze vor Libyen müssen auf den Prüfstand – Interview mit Frontex Direktor Fabrice Leggeri.' *Die Welt Online*, 27 February. www.welt.de/politik/deutschland/article162394787/Rettungseinsaetze-vor-Libyen-muessen-auf-den-Pruefstand.html.

Bhabha, Jacqueline 2014. *Child Migration and Human Rights in a Global Age*. Princeton: Princeton University Press.

Bhana, Surendra 1997. *Gandhi's Legacy: The Natal Indian Congress, 1894–1994*. Scottsville: University of Natal Press.

Bially Mattern, Janice 2011. 'A Practice Theory of Emotion for International Relations.' In Adler, E., and Pouliot, V. (eds). *International Practices*, 63–86. New York: Cambridge University Press.

Bially Mattern, Janice, and Zarakol, Ayşe 2016. 'Hierarchies in World Politics.' *International Organization* 70(3): 623–654. https://doi.org/10.1017/S0020818316000126.

Bianchi, Andrea 2009. 'The International Regulation of the Use of Force: The Politics of Interpretive Method.' *Leiden Journal of International Law* 22(4): 651–676.

2016. 'But We Don't Call It "Torture"! Norm Contestation during the US "War on Terror".' *International Politics* 53(2). https://doi.org/10.1057/ip.2015.42.

Birkenkötter, Hannah 2020. 'International Law as a Common Language across Spheres of Authority?' *Global Constitutionalism* 9(2): 318–342.

Black, David 1999. 'The Long and Winding Road: International Norms and Domestic Political Change in South Africa.' In Risse, T., Ropp, S., and Sikkink, K. (eds). *The Power of Human Rights: International Norms and Domestic Change*, 78–108. Cambridge: Cambridge University Press.

Blanton, T. 2007. 'The Struggle for Openness in the International Financial Institutions.' In Florini, A. (ed). *The Right to Know: Transparency in an Open World*, 243–278. New York: Columbia University Press.

Bleiker, Roland, and Hutchison, Emma. 2008. 'Fear No More: Emotions and World Politics.' *Review of International Studies* 34: 115–135.

Bloodgood, Elizabeth A., and Clough, Emily 2017. 'Transnational Advocacy Networks: A Complex Adaptive Systems Simulation Model of the Boomerang Effect.' *Social Science Computer Review* 35(3): 319–335. https://doi.org/10.1177/0894439316634077.

Bloomfield, Alan 2016. 'Norm Antipreneurs and Theorising Resistance to Normative Change.' *Review of International Studies* 42(2): 310–333.

Bloomfield, Alan, and Scott, Shirley V. (eds). 2016. *Norm Antipreneurs and the Politics of Resistance to Global Normative Change*. London: Routledge. https://doi.org/10.4324/9781315707341.

Bodansky, Daniel 2017. 'The Role of the International Court of Justice in Addressing Climate Change: Some Preliminary Reflections Symposium: The Forefront of International Law.' *Arizona State Law Journal* 49(Special Issue): 689–712.

Bodansky, Daniel, Brunnée, Jutta, and Rajamani, Lavanya 2017. *International Climate Change Law*. Oxford: Oxford University Press.

Boekle, Henning, Rittberger, Volker, and Wagner, Wolfgang 1999. 'Norms and Foreign Policy: Constructivist Foreign Policy Theory.' *Tübinger Arbeitspapiere zur Internationalen Politik und Friedensforschung* 34a: 1–46.

Bogdandy, Armin von, and Venzke, Ingo (eds). 2012. *International Judicial Lawmaking*. Berlin: Springer.

Borgen, Christopher J. 2009. 'The Language of Law and the Practice of Politics: Great Powers and the Rhetoric of Self-Determination in the Cases of Kosovo and South Ossetia.' *Chicago Journal of International Law* 10: 1–34.

Börzel, Tanja A. and Risse, Thomas 2000. 'When Europe Hits Home: Europeanization and Domestic Change.' *European Integration Online Papers* 4(15). http://eiop.or.at/eiop/texte/2000-015a.htm.

2003. 'Conceptualizing the Domestic Impact of Europe.' In Featherstone, K., and Radaelli, C.M. (eds). *The Politics of Europeanization*, 57–81. Oxford: Oxford University Press.

Börzel, Tanja A., and Zürn, Michael 2021. 'Contestations of the Liberal International Order: From Liberal Multilateralism to Postnational Liberalism.' *International Organization* 75(2): 282–305.

Bourdieu, Pierre 1980. *Le Sens Pratique*. Paris: Minuit.

1987. 'The Force of Law: Toward a Sociology of the Juridical Field.' *Hastings Law Journal* 38(5): 814–853.

Bourdieu, Pierre, and Wacquant, Loic 1992. *An Invitation to Reflexive Sociology*. Chicago: Chicago University Press.

Bousquet, Antoine, and Curtis, Simon 2011. 'Beyond Models and Metaphors: Complexity Theory, Systems Thinking and International Relations.' *Cambridge Review of International Affairs* 24(1): 43–62. https://doi.org/10.1080/09557571.2011.558054.

Bousquet, Antoine, and Geyer, Robert 2011. 'Introduction: Complexity and the International Arena.' *Cambridge Review of International Affairs* 24(1): 1–3. https://doi.org/10.1080/09557571.2011.558713.

Bower, Adam 2015. 'Arguing with Law: Strategic Legal Argumentation, US Diplomacy, and Debates over the International Criminal Court.' *Review of International Studies* 41(2): 337–360. https://doi.org/10.1017/S0260210514000217.

Braaten, Daniel B. 2016. 'Ambivalent Engagement: Human Rights and the Multilateral Development Banks.' In Park, S., and Strand, J. (eds). *Global Economic Governance and the Development Practices of the Multilateral Development Banks*, 99–118. London: Routledge.

Bradlow, Daniel 2019. 'Mulilaterals Must Earn the Right to Limited Immunity.' *Financial Times*, 28 March. www.ft.com/content/2512aa84-515d-11e9-9c76-bf4a0ce37d49.

Braithwaite, John 2002. *Restorative Justice and Responsive Regulation*. New York: Oxford University Press.

2021. 'Glimmers of Cosmopolitan Criminology.' *International Criminology*. Online First. 1–8.

Braithwaite, John, and Pettit, Philip 1992. *Not Just Deserts: A Republican Theory of Criminal Justice*. Oxford: Oxford University Press.

Braithwaite, John, Coglianese, Cary, and Levi-Faur, David 2007. 'Can Regulation and Governance Make a Difference?' *Regulation and Governance* 1(1): 1–7.

Brock, Lothar 1999. 'Normative Integration und kollektive Handlungskompetenz auf internationaler Ebene.' *Zeitschrift für Internationale Beziehungen* 6(2): 323–347.

Brosig, Malte 2012. 'No Space for Constructivism? A Critical Appraisal of European Compliance Research.' *Perspectives on European Politics and Society* 13(4): 390–407.

Brown, Garrett W. 2010. 'Safeguarding Deliberative Global Governance: The Case of The Global Fund to Fight AIDS, Tuberculosis and Malaria.' *Review of International Studies* 36: 511–530.

2014. 'Norm Diffusion and Health System Strengthening: The Persistent Relevance of National Leadership in Global Health Governance.' *Review of International Studies* 40(5): 877–896.

2015. 'Knowledge, Politics and Power in Global Health.' *International Journal of Health Policy and Management* 4(2): 111–113.

Brunnée, Jutta, and Toope, Stephen J. 2010. *Legitimacy and Legality in International Law: An Interactional Account.* Cambridge: Cambridge University Press.

2011. 'Interactional International Law: An Introduction.' *International Theory* 3(2): 307–318.

2012. 'Constructivism and International Law. In Dunoff, J. L., and Pollack, M. A. (eds). *Interdisciplinary Perspectives on International Law and International Relations: The State of the Art*, 119–145. Cambridge: Cambridge University Press.

2018. 'International Law and the Practice of Legality: Stability and Change.' *Victoria University of Wellington Law Review* 49(4): 429–445.

2019. 'Norm Robustness and Contestation in International Law: Self-Defense against Nonstate Actors.' *Journal of Global Security Studies* 4(1): 73–87.

Bueger, Christian, and Gadinger, Frank 2015. 'The Play of International Practice.' *International Studies Quarterly* 59: 449–460.

2018. *International Practice Theory*. 2nd ed. Basingstoke: Palgrave Macmillan.

Buitelaar, Tom, and Hirschmann, Gisela 2021. 'Criminal Accountability at What Cost? Norm Conflict, UN Peace Operations and the International Criminal Court.' *European Journal of International Relations* 27(2): 548–571.

Bukovansky, Mlada, Clark, Ian, Eckersley, Robyn, Price, Richard, Reus-Smit, Christian, and Wheeler, Nicholas J. 2012. *Special Responsibilities: Global Problems and American Power.* Cambridge: Cambridge University Press.

Burke, Roland 2010. *Decolonization and the Evolution of International Human Rights.* Philadelphia: University of Pennsylvania Press.

Busby, Joshua W. 2007. 'Bono Made Jesse Helms Cry: Jubilee 2000, Debt Relief, and Moral Action in International Politics.' *International Studies Quarterly* 5(2): 247–275.

Busch, Marc L. 2007. 'Overlapping Institutions, Forum Shopping, and Dispute Settlement in International Trade.' *International Organization* 61(4): 735–761. https://doi.org/10.1017/S0020818307070257.

Bush, George W. 2004. 'Remarks Following Discussions with Prime Minister Peter Medgyessy of Hungary and an Exchange with Reporters.' www.presidency.ucsb.edu/documents/remarks-following-discussions-with-prime-minister-peter-medgyessy-hungary-and-exchange.

Butt, Nathalie, Lambrick, Frances, Menton, Mary, and Renwick, Anna 2019. 'The Supply Chain of Violence.' *Nature Sustainability* 2: 742–747.

Búzás, Zoltan I. 2021a. *Evading International Norms: Race and Rights in the Shadow of Legality*. Philadelphia: University of Pennsylvania Press.

2021b. 'Racism and Antiracism in the Liberal International Order.' *International Organization* 75(2): 440–463.

Byers, Michael 2003. 'Preemptive Self-Defense: Hegemony, Equality and Strategies of Legal Change.' *Journal of Political Philosophy* 11(2): 171–190.

Camacho, Alejandro E., and Glicksman, Robert L. 2021. 'Designing Regulation Across Organizations: Assessing the Functions and Dimensions of Governance.' *Regulation and Governance*. Early View, 3 July.

Cameron Miles. 2021. 'Belarus and the Hijacking of Ryanair Flight FR4978: A Preliminary International Law Analysis.' *Lawfare*, 24 May. www.lawfareblog.com/belarus-and-hijacking-ryanair-flight-fr4978-preliminary-international-law-analysis.

Capie, David 2012. 'The Responsibility to Protect Norm in Southeast Asia: Framing, Resistance, and the Localization Myth.' *The Pacific Review* 25(1): 75–93.

Cardenas, Sonia 2007. *Conflict and Compliance: State Responses to International Human Rights Pressure*. Philadelphia: University of Pennsylvania Press.

Carpenter, Charli R. 2005. '"Women, Children and Other Vulnerable Groups": Gender, Strategic Frames and the Protection of Civilians as a Transnational Issue.' *International Studies Quarterly* 49(2): 295–334.

2007. 'Setting the Advocacy Agenda: Theorizing Issue Emergence and Nonemergence in Transnational Advocacy Networks.' *International Studies Quarterly* 51(1): 99–120.

2011. 'Vetting the Advocacy Agenda: Network Centrality and the Paradox of Weapons Norms.' *International Organization* 65(1): 69–102. https://doi.org/10.1017/S0020818310000329.

2014. *Lost Causes: Agenda Vetting in Global Issue Networks and the Shaping of Human Security*. Ithaca: Cornell University Press.

Carraro, Valentina, Conzelmann, Thomas, and Jongen, Hortense 2019. 'Fears of Peers? Explaining Peer and Public Shaming in Global Governance.' *Cooperation and Conflict* 54(3): 335–355.

Cartan, Brian 2008. 'Thai Ties Bind Myanmar Cyclone Relief.' *Asia Times*, 24 May.

Carter, George 2021. 'Pacific Island States and 30 Years of Global Climate Change Negotiations.' In Klöck, C., Castro, P., Weiler, F., and Blaxkejaer, L. (eds). *Coalitions in the Climate Change Negotiations*, 73–90. Oxon: Routledge.

Cederman, Lars-Erik 1997. *Emergent Actors in World Politics: How States and Nations Develop and Dissolve*. Princeton: Princeton University Press.

Center for Justice and Accountability. 2010. 'Human Rights Abuses in the USA.' *Center for Justice and Accountability.*

CEPAL, UNICEF, and Office of the Special Representative of the Secretary-General on Violence against Children. 2020. *Violence against Children and Adolescents in the Time of COVID-19.* COVID-19 Report. New York: United Nations.

CFFP. 2020. *A Feminist Foreign Policy for the European Union.* Belgium: The Greens/EFA in the European Parliament.

Chaiken, Shelly, Wood, Wendy, and Eagly, Alice H. 1996. 'Principles of Persuasion.' In Higgins, E. T., and Kruglanski, A. W. (eds). *Social Psychology: Handbook of Basic Principles*, 702–742. New York: Guilford.

Chappell, Louise 2016. *Gender Justice and the International Criminal Court.* New York: Oxford University Press.

Charlesworth, Hilary, and Farrall, Jeremy 2016. 'Regulating the Rule of Law through the Security Council.' In Charlesworth, H., and Farrall, J. (eds). *Strengthening the Rule of Law through the UN Security Council*, 1–10. Abingdon: Routledge.

Chayes, Abram, and Chayes, Antonia H. 1993. 'On Compliance.' *International Organization* 47(2): 175–205.

Checkel, Jeff T. 1997. 'International Norms and Domestic Politics: Bridging the Rationalist-Constructivist Divide.' *European Journal of International Relations* 3(4): 473–495. https://doi.org/10.1177/1354066197003004003.

1998. 'The Constructivist Turn in International Relations Theory.' *World Politics* 50(2): 324–348.

1999. 'Norms, Institutions, and National Identity in Contemporary Europe.' *International Studies Quarterly* 43(1): 83–114.

2001. 'The Europeanization of Citizenship?' In Cowles, M. G., Caporaso, J., and Risse, T. (eds). *Transforming Europe. Europeanization and Domestic Change*, 180–197. Ithaca, NY: Cornell University Press.

2005. 'International Institutions and Socialization in Europe: Introduction and Framework.' *International Organization* 59(4): 801–826. www.jstor.org/stable/3877829.

Chinkin, Christine M. 2019. 'Adoption of 1325 Resolution.' In Davies, S. E., and True, J. (eds). *The Oxford Handbook of Women, Peace, and Security*, 26–37. New York: Oxford University Press.

Cholvy, Laurence, and Cuppens, Frédéric 1995. 'Solving Normative Conflicts by Merging Roles.' In *Proceedings of the 5th International Conference on Artificial Intelligence and Law*, 201–209.

Chongkittavorn, Kavi 2007. 'Time for Thailand to Revisit Its Policy on Burma.' *The Nation*, 29 October.

CIEL. 2016. 'NGO Response: Proposed World Bank Safeguards Represent Dangerous Set-Back to Key Environmental and Social Protections,' Press Release 22 July. 19 December. www.ciel.org/news/safeguard-policy-endangers-rights/.

Clapham, A. 2006. *Human Rights Obligations of Non-State Actors.* Oxford: Oxford University Press.

Clark, D., Fox, J., and Treakle, K. 2003. *Demanding Accountability: Civil-Society Claims and the World Bank Inspection Panel.* Lanham: Rowman and Littlefield.

Climate Mayors 2020. 'Climate Mayors.' https://climatemayors.org/.

Cloward, Karisa 2016. *When Norms Collide. Local Responses to Activism Against Female Genital Mutilation and Early Marriage.* Oxford: Oxford University Press.

Cochran, Molly 1999. *Normative Theory in International Relations. A Pragmatic Approach.* Cambridge: Cambridge University Press.

2017. 'The "Newer Ideals" of Jane Addams's Progressivism: A Realistic Utopia of Cosmopolitan Justice.' In Cochran, M., and Navari, C. (eds). *Progressivism and US Foreign Policy between the World Wars*, 143–166. New York: Palgrave Macmillan.

Cogan, Jacob K. 2011. 'The Regulatory Turn in International Law.' *Harvard International Law Journal* 52(2): 322–372.

Cohn, Carol 2006. 'Motive and Methods: Using Multi-Sited Ethnography to Study US National Security Discourses.' In Ackerly, B. A., Stern, M., and True, J. (eds). *Feminist Methodologies for International Relations*, 91–107. New York: Cambridge University Press.

Coleman, Katherine P. 2013. 'Locating Norm Diplomacy: Venue Change in International Norm Negotiations.' *European Journal of International Relations* 19(1): 163–186. https://doi.org/10.1177/1354066111411209.

Colgan, Jeff D., Keohane, Robert O., and Van de Graaf, Thijs 2012. 'Punctuated Equilibrium in the Energy Regime Complex.' *Review of International Organizations* 7(2): 117–143. https://doi.org/10.1007/s11558-011-9130-9.

Collins, Richard 2017. 'Sources and the Legitimate Authority of International Law: A Challenge to the "Standard View"?' In Besson, S., and D'Aspremont, J. (eds). *The Oxford Handbook on the Sources of International Law*, 703–723. Oxford: Oxford University Press.

Conca, Ken 2015. *An Unfinished Foundation: The United Nations and Global Environmental Governance.* Oxford: Oxford University Press.

Confortini, Catia C. 2012. *Intelligent Compassion: Feminist Critical Methodology in the Women's International League for Peace and Freedom.* New York: Oxford University Press.

Connolly, Kate 2016. 'German Government Approves strict Limits on EU Migrant Claiming Benefits.' *The Guardian*, 12 October. www.theguardian.com/world/2016/oct/12/german-government-approves-bill-to-stop-eu-migrants-claiming-benefits.

Cook, Sam 2016. 'The 'Woman-in-Conflict' at the UN Security Council: A Subject of Practice.' *International Affairs* 92(2): 353–372.

Cooper, Frederick 2005. *Colonialism in Question: Theory, Knowledge, History.* Berkeley: University of California Press.

Cooperman, Alan 2002. 'CIA Techniques Called into Question: A Human-Rights Group Said Interrogation Methods Used on al-Qaeda Detainees Might Be Torture.' *Philadelphia Inquirer*, 29 December.

Cortell, Andrew P., and Davis, James W. 2000. 'Understanding the Domestic Impact of International Norms: A Research Agenda.' *International Studies Review* 2(1): 65–87.

2005. 'When Norms Clash: International Norms, Domestic Practices, and Japan's Internalisation of the GATT/WTO.' *Review of International Studies* 31(1): 3–25.

Cotsaftis, Michel. 2009. 'What Makes a System Complex? – An Approach to Self Organization and Emergence.' In Aziz-Alaoui, M. A., and Bertelle, C. (eds). *From System Complexity to Emergent Properties*, 49–99. Berlin and Heidelberg: Springer. https://doi.org/10.1007/978-3-642-02199-2_3.

Cowles, Maria Green, Caporaso, James, and Risse, Thomas (eds). 2001. *Transforming Europe: Europeanization and Domestic Change*. Ithaca, NY: Cornell University Press.

Crawford, Neta C. 1993. 'Decolonization as an International Norm: The Evolution of Practices, Arguments, and Beliefs.' In Reed, Laura E., and Kaysen, Carl (eds). *Emerging Norms of Humanitarian Intervention: A Collection of Essays from a Project of the American Academy of Arts and Sciences*, 37–61. Cambridge, MA: American Academy of Arts and Sciences.

2002. *Argument and Change in World Politics: Ethics, Decolonization, and Humanitarian Intervention*. Cambridge: Cambridge University Press.

2016. 'Studying World Politics as a Complex Adaptive System.' In Booth, K., and Erskine, T. (eds). *International Relations Theory Today*. 2nd ed., 263–267. Cambridge and Malden: Polity Press.

Crawford, Neta, and Klotz, Audie (eds). 1999. *How Sanctions Work: Lessons from South Africa*. Basingstoke: Palgrave MacMillan.

Crocker, David A. 1999. 'Reckoning with Past Wrongs: A Normative Framework.' *Ethics & International Affairs* 13(1): 43–64.

Crossley, Noele 2020. 'Conceptualising Consistency: Coherence, Principles, and the Practice of Human Protection.' *Global Responsibility to Protect* 12(4): 440–463.

Cusumano, Eugenio, and Villa, Matteo 2021. 'From "Angels" to "Vice Smugglers": The Criminalization of Sea Rescue NGOs in Italy.' *European Journal on Criminal Policy and Research* 27(1): 23–40.

D'Alessandra, Federica 2017. 'The Accountability Turn in Third Wave Human Rights Fact-Finding.' *Utrecht Journal of International and European Law* 33(84): 59–76.

D'Alessandra, Federica, Rapp, Stephen, Sutherland, Kirsty, and Ashraph, Sareta 2022. *Anchoring Accountability for Mass Atrocities. The Permanent Support Needed to Fulfil UN Investigative Mandates*. Oxford: Oxford Institute for Ethics, Law, and Armed Conflict.

Daly, Erin 2008. 'Truth Skepticism: An Inquiry into the Value of Truth in Times of Transition.' *The International Journal of Transitional Justice* 2(March): 23–41. https://doi.org/10.1093/ijtj/ijn004.

Damasio, Antonio 1994. *Descartes' Error: Emotion, Reason, and the Human Brain*. New York: G.P. Putnam's Sons.

D'Amato, Anthony 1987. 'Trashing Customary International Law.' *The American Journal of International Law* 81(1): 101–105.

Darrow, Mac 2003. *Between Light and Shadow: The World Bank, the International Monetary Fund and International Human Rights Law*. Oxford, Portland and Oregon: Hart Publishing.

2021. 'Up the Stream without a Paddle: Human Rights Challenges in Mega-infrastructure Finance and Investment.' In Bhuta, N. (ed). *The Struggle for Human Rights: Essays in honour of Philip Alston*. Oxford University Press, online first.

D'Aspremont, Jeanne 2016. *Epistemic Forces in International Law: Foundational Doctrines and Argumentation.* Cheltenham: Elgar International Law.

Davies, Sara E., and True, Jacqui 2017. 'Norm Entrepreneurship in International Politics: William Hague and the Prevention of Sexual Violence in Conflict.' *Foreign Policy Analysis* 13(3): 701–772.

De Maizière, Thomas 2014. 'Rede von Bundesminister Dr. Thomas de Maizière anlässlich der ersten Beratung des Bundeshaushaltes 2015.' www.bmi.bund.de/SharedDocs/reden/DE/2014/09/haushaltsrede-2015.html.

Deitelhoff, Nicole 2009. 'The Discursive Process of Legalization: Charting Islands of Persuasion in the ICC Case.' *International Organization* 63(1): 33–65.

2019. 'Is the R2P Failing? The Controversy about Norm Justification and Norm Application of the Responsibility to Protect.' *Global Responsibility to Protect* 11(2): 149–171.

Deitelhoff, Nicole, and Zimmermann, Lisbeth 2019. 'Norms under Challenge: Unpacking the Dynamics of Norm Robustness.' *Journal of Global Security Studies* 4(1): 2–17. https://doi.org/10.1093/jogss/ogy041.

2020. 'Things We Lost in the Fire: How Different Types of Contestation Affect the Robustness of International Norms.' *International Studies Review* 22(1): 51–76.

Dellinger, Myanna 2017. 'See You in Court: Around the World in Eight Climate Change Lawsuits.' *William & Mary Environmental Law and Policy Review* 42 (2): 525–552.

Dellmuth, Lisa, and Schlipphak, Bernd 2020. 'Legitimacy Beliefs towards Global Governance Institutions: A Research Agenda.' *Journal of European Public Policy* 27(6): 931–943.

DeMeritt, Jacqueline H. R. 2012. 'International Organizations and Government Killing: Does Naming and Shaming Save Lives?' *International Interactions* 38(5): 597–621.

Dessler, David 1989. 'What's at Stake in the Agent-Structure Debate?' *International Organization*, 43(3): 441–473.

Dewey, John 1915 [1998]. 'The Logic of Judgments of Practice', first published in *Journal of Philosophy, Psychology and Scientific Methods* 12, 505–523, 533–543. Republished in Hickman, L. A., and Alexander, T. M. (eds). *The Essential Dewey. Volume 2. Ethics, Logic,* Psychology, 236–271. Bloomington: Indiana University Press.

1925a [1998]. 'The Development of American Pragmatism', first published in Department of Philosophy, Columbia University (ed). *Studies in the History of Ideas.* Republished in Hickman, L. A., and Alexander, T. M. (eds). *The Essential Dewey. Volume 1. Pragmatism, Education, Democracy,* 3–13. Bloomington: Indiana University Press.

1925b [1998]. 'Existence, Value and Criticism', from *Experience and Nature.* In Hickman, L. A., and Alexander, T. M. (eds). *The Essential Dewey. Volume 2. Ethics, Logic, Psychology,* 84–101. Bloomington: Indiana University Press.

1927. *The Public and Its Problems.* London: George Allen and Unwin.

Dezalay, Yves, and Garth, Bryant G. 1996. *Dealing in Virtue: International Commercial Arbitration and the Construction of a Transnational Legal Order.* Chicago: University of Chicago Press.

Dezalay, Yves, and Madsen, Mikael R. 2012. 'The Force of Law and Lawyers: Pierre Bourdieu and the Reflexive Sociology of Law.' *Annual Review of Law and Social Science* 8(1): 433–452.

Diez, Thomas, and Wiener, Antje 2018. 'Introducing the Mosaic of Integration Theory.' *KFG Working Paper Series No. 88* (Online). Freie Universität Berlin, FB Politik- und Sozialwissenschaften, Otto-Suhr-Institut für Politikwissenschaft KollegForschergruppe 'The Transformative Power of Europe.' https://nbn-resolving.org/urn:nbn:de:0168-ssoar-57752-1.

Dixon, Jennifer M. 2017. 'Rhetorical Adaptation and Resistance to International Norms.' *Perspectives on Politics* 15(1): 83–99.

Dönges, Hannah E., and Kullenberg, Janosch 2019. 'What Works (and Fails) in Protection.' In Davies, S. E., and True, J. (eds). *The Oxford Handbook of Women, Peace, and Security*, 161–177. New York: Oxford University Press.

Donnelly, John 1986. 'International Human Rights: A Regime Analysis.' *International Organization* 40(3): 599–642.

2012. 'The Elements of the Structures of International Systems.' *International Organization* 66(4): 609–643.

2019. 'Systems, Levels, and Structural Theory: Waltz's Theory Is Not a Systemic Theory (and Why That Matters for International Relations Today).' *European Journal of International Relations* 25(3): 1–27. https://doi.org/10.1177/1354066118820929.

Dosch, Jörn 2014. 'Mahathirism and Its Legacy in Malaysia's Foreign Policy.' *European Journal of East Asian Studies* 13(1): 5–32.

Doty, Roxanne L. 1993. 'The Bounds of "Race" in International Relations.' *Millennium* 22(3): 443–461.

2004. 'Maladies of Our Souls: Identity and Voice in the Writing of Academic International Relations.' *Cambridge Review of International Affairs* 17(2): 377–392.

Downs, George W., Rocke, David M., and Barsoom, Peter N. 1996. 'Is the Good News about Compliance Good News about Cooperation?' *International Organization* 50(3): 379–406.

Drahos, Peter, and Krygier, Martin 2017. 'Regulation, Institutions and Networks.' In Drahos, P. (ed). *Regulatory Theory: Foundations and Applications*, 1–24. Canberra: ANU Press.

Draude, Anke 2017. 'The Agency of the Governed in Transfer and Diffusion Studies.' *Third World Thematics: A TWQ Journal* 2(5): 577–587.

(ed). 2019. *The Agency of the Governed in the Global South: Normative and Institutional Change*. London: Routledge.

Dreyling, Justus 2021. 'Institutional Complexity and Opportunity Structures: Weaker Actor Influence in International Intellectual Property Regulation.' *Global Policy* 12(S4): 37–46. https://doi.org/10.1111/1758-5899.12897.

Drezner, Daniel W. 2009. 'The Power and Peril of International Regime Complexity.' *Perspectives on Politics* 7(1): 65–70.

Driesen, David M. 2019. 'President Trump's Executive Orders and the Rule of Law.' *UMKC Law Review* 87(Spring): 489–524.

Dryzek, John S. 2004. 'Pragmatism and Democracy: In Search of Deliberative Publics.' *The Journal of Speculative Philosophy* 18(1): 72–79.

Dudziak, Mary L. 2000. *Cold War Civil Rights: Race and the Image of American Democracy*. Princeton: Princeton University Press.

Dunoff, Jeffrey L., and Pollack, Mark A. (eds). 2013. *Interdisciplinary Perspectives on International Law and International Relations: The State of the Art*. Cambridge: Cambridge University Press.

1982. *The Rules of Sociological Method: And Selected Texts on Sociology and Its Method*. London, Basingstoke: Macmillan.

DW. 2021. 'Angela Merkel says Belarus' story "completely implausible".' 24 May. www.dw.com/en/angela-merkel-says-belarus-story-completely-implausible/a-57639025.

Eckel, Jan, and Moyn, Samuel 2014. *The Breakthrough: Human Rights in the 1970s*. Philadelphia: University of Pennsylvania Press.

Edwards, Pearce 2020. 'Why No Justice for Past Repression? Militaries and Human Rights Organizations in Post-Authoritarian States.' *Journal of Conflict Resolution* 65(4): 759–787. https://doi.org/10.1177/0022002720957068.

Eiichiro, Washio 2021. 'Statement by H.E. Mr. Washio Eiichiro, State Minister for Foreign Affairs of Japan at the Sixth Annual Pledging Conference for the Implementation of the Anti-Personnel Mine Ban Convention.' www.disarm.emb-japan.go.jp/files/100174366.pdf.

Elhag, Abdullatif A.O., Breuker, Joost, and Brouwer, Bob W. 2000. 'On the Formal Analysis of Normative Conflicts.' *Information & Communications Technology Law* 9(3): 207–217.

Elshtain, Jean B. 2002. *Jane Addams and the Dream of American Democracy*. New York: Basic Books.

Elster, Jon 1989. 'Social Norms and Economic Theory.' *Journal of Economic Perspectives* 3(4): 99–117.

Engelkamp, Stephan, and Glaab, Katharina 2015. 'Writing Norms: Constructivist Norm Research and the Politics of Ambiguity.' *Alternatives* 40(3–4): 201–218.

Engerman, Stanley L. 2009. 'Apologies, Regrets, and Reparations.' *European Review* 17(3–4): 593–610.

Erskine, Toni (ed). 2003a. *Can Institutions Have Responsibilities*. Houndsmill: Palgrave Macmillan.

2003b. 'Making Sense of 'Responsibility' in International Relations.' In Erskine, T. (ed). *Can Institutions Have Responsibilities*, 1–16. Houndsmill: Palgrave Macmillan.

2008. 'Locating Responsibility: The Problem of Moral Agency in International Relations.' In Reus-Smit, C., and Snidal, D. (eds). *The Oxford Handbook of International Relations*, 699–707. Oxford: Oxford University Press.

2012. 'Whose Progress, Which Morals? Constructivism, Normative IR Theory and the Limits and Possibilities of Studying Ethics in World Politics.' *International Theory* 4(3): 449–468.

Essam, Amr 2016. 'The Like Minded Group (LMG): Speaking Truth to Power.' *Universal Rights Group*, 10 May. www.universal-rights.org/blog/like-minded-group-lmg-speaking-truth-power/.

Euronews. 2021. '"Putin Supports Lukashenko Amid Outcry over Ryanair Flight Diversion".' 29 May. www.euronews.com/2021/05/28/putin-supports-lukashenko-amid-outcry-over-ryanair-flight-diversion.

European Commission (DG1). 1998. 1/D/3/BW D (98) – Note on the WHO's Revised Drug Strategy.

European Commission. 2021. 'Opening Remarks by President von der Leyen at the Joint Press Conference with President Michel Following the Special Meeting of the European Council of 24 May 2021.' https://ec.europa.eu/commission/presscorner/detail/en/statement_21_2661.

European Court of Justice. 2016. Press Release No. 63/16.

European Union External Action Service. 2021. 'Belarus: Joint Statement by Canada, the European Union, United Kingdom, and United States.' 21 June. https://eeas.europa.eu/headquarters/headquarters-homepage/100402/belarus-joint-statement-canada-european-union-united-kingdom-and-united-states_en.

Evangelista, Matthew 1999. *Unarmed Forces: The Transnational Movement to End the Cold War*. Ithaca: Cornell University Press.

Evans, Gareth, and Thakur, Ramesh 2013. 'Correspondence: Humanitarian Intervention and the Responsibility to Protect.' *International Security* 37(4): 199–207.

Evers, Miles M. 2017. 'On Transgression.' *International Studies Quarterly* 61(4): 786–794.

Farrall, Jeremy, and Rubenstein, Kim 2009. 'Filling or Falling between the Cracks? Law's Potential: Introduction.' In Farrall, J., and Rubenstein, K. (eds). *Sanctions, Accountability and Governance in a Globalised World*, 1–24. Cambridge: Cambridge University Press.

Faure, Raphaëlle, Prizzon, Annalisa, and Rogerson, Andrew 2015. *Multilateral Development Banks: A Short Guide. Overseas Development Institute (ODI)* Report. London: Overseas Development Institute.

Fearon, James D. 1997. 'Signaling Foreign Policy Interests: Tying Hands versus Sinking Costs.' *Journal of Conflict Resolution* 41(1): 68–90.

Fehl, Caroline 2018. 'Navigating Norm Complexity: A Shared Research Agenda for Diverse Constructivist Perspectives.' *PRIF Working Papers* 41. Frankfurt/Main: Peace Research Institute Frankfurt.

2019. 'Bombs, Trials, and Rights: Norm Complexity and the Evolution of Liberal Intervention Practices.' *Human Rights Quarterly* 4(4): 893–915. https://doi.org/10.1353/hrq.2019.0066.

Fehl, Caroline, and Rosert, Elvira 2020. 'It's Complicated: A Conceptual Framework for Studying Relations and Interactions between International Norms.' *PRIF Working Papers* 49. Frankfurt/Main: Peace Research Institute Frankfurt. https://doi.org/10.1287/mnsc.21.5.608.

Festenstein, Matthew 2004. 'Deliberative Democracy and Two Models of Pragmatism.' *European Journal of Social Theory* 7(3): 291–306.

Fierke, Karin M. 2013. *Political Self-Sacrifice: Agency, Body and Emotion in International Relations*. New York: Cambridge University Press.

Fierke, Karin M., and Jørgensen, Knud E. (eds). 2001. *Constructing International Relations: The Next Generation*. New York: M.E. Sharpe.

Finnemore, Martha 1996. *National Interests in International Society*. Ithaca: Cornell University Press.

2000. 'Are Legal Norms Distinctive?' *NYU Journal of International Law and Politics* 32(3): 699–705.

Finnemore, Martha, and Sikkink, Kathryn 1998. 'International Norm Dynamics and Political Change.' *International Organization* 52(4): 887–917.

Finnemore, Martha, and Toope, Stephen J. 2001. 'Alternatives to "Legalization": Richer Views of Law and Politics.' *International Organization* 55(3): 743–758.

Fioretos, Orfeo, and Heldt, Eugénia C. 2019. 'Legacies and Innovations in Global Economic Governance Since Bretton Woods.' *Review of International Political Economy* 26(6): 1089–1111.

Fish, Stanley 1990. *Is There a Text in This Class? The Authority of Interpretive Communities*. Cambridge, MA: Harvard University Press.

Fitzgerald, David S., and Cook-Martin, David 2014. *Culling the Masses: The Democratic Origins of Racist Immigration Policy in the Americas*. Cambridge, MA: Harvard University Press.

Flonk, Danielle, Jachtenfuchs, Markus, and Obendiek, Anke S. 2020. 'Authority Conflicts in Internet Governance: Liberals vs. Sovereigntists?' *Global Constitutionalism* 9(2): 364–386. https://doi.org/10.1017/s2045381720000167.

Florini, Ann 1996. 'The Evolution of International Norms.' *International Studies Quarterly* 40(3): 363–389. https://doi.org/10.2307/2600716.

Foley, Frank 2021. 'The (De)Legitimation of Torture: Rhetoric, Shaming and Narrative Contestation in Two British Cases.' *European Journal of International Relations* 27(1): 102–126. https://doi.org/10.1177/1354066120950011.

Foster, Caroline E. 2011. *Science and the Precautionary Principle in International Courts and Tribunals*. Cambridge: Cambridge University Press.

Foot, Rosemary and Walter, Andrew. 2013. 'Global Norms and Major State Behaviour: The Cases of China and the United States.' *European Journal of International Relations* 19(2): 329–352.

Fox, J. 2000. 'The World Bank Inspection Panel: Lessons from the First Five Years.' *Global Governance* 6(3): 279–318.

Fox, Jonathan, and Brown, David L., (eds). 1998. *The Struggle for Accountability: The World Bank, NGOs and Grassroots Movements*. Cambridge, MA: MIT Press.

Franklin, James C. 2008. 'Shame on You: The Impact of Human Rights Criticism on Political Repression in Latin America.' *International Studies Quarterly* 52(1): 187–211.

Freedom House. 2020. *Democracy under Lockdown: The Impact of COVID-19 on the Global Struggle for Freedom*. Washington, DC: Freedom House.

Friedman, Jeffrey 2012. 'System Effects and the Problem of Prediction.' *Critical Review* 24(3): 291–312. https://doi.org/10.1080/08913811.2012.779806.

Friedrichs, Jörg, and Kratochwil, Friedrich 2009. 'On Acting and Knowing: How Pragmatism Can Advance International Relations Research and Methodology.' *International Organization* 63(4): 701–731.

Friman, Richard (ed). 2015. *The Politics of Leverage in International Relations*. London: Palgrave Macmillan UK.

2019. 'An "Untrammeled Right"? The McCarran Immigration Subcommittee and the Origins of Presidential Authority to Suspend and Restrict Alien Entry under §1182(f).' *Journal of Policy History* 31(4): 433–463.

Frost, Mervyn 1996. *Ethics in International Relations: A Constitutive Theory*. New York: Cambridge University Press.

Fujita, Sanae 2013. *The World Bank, Asian Development Bank and Human Rights*. Cheltenham: Edward Elgar Publishing.

Fuller, Lon 1969. *The Morality of Law*. New Haven: Yale University Press.

Gallagher, Anne T., and David, Fiona 2014. *The International Law of Migrant Smuggling*. Cambridge: Cambridge University Press.

Gambale, Maria L. 2016. 'How Syrian Women Landed at the UN Peace Talks and What It All Means.' *PassBlue*, 10 May. www.passblue.com/2016/05/10/how-syrian-women-landed-at-the-un-peace-talks-and-what-it-all-means/.

Garriga, Ana C. 2016. 'Human Rights Regimes, Reputation, and Foreign Direct Investment.' *International Studies Quarterly* 60(1): 160–172. https://doi.org/10.1093/isq/sqw006.

Gehring, Thomas, and Faude, Benjamin 2013. 'The Dynamics of Regime Complexes: Microfoundations and Systemic Effects.' *Global Governance* 19(1): 119–130. www-jstor-org.ezp.lib.unimelb.edu.au/stable/pdf/24526245.pdf.

Geis, Anna, Clément, Maeve, and Pfeifer, Hanna (eds). 2021. *Armed Non-state Actors and the Politics of Recognition*. Manchester: Manchester University Press.

Gelpi, Christopher 1997. 'Crime and Punishment. The Role of Norms in Crisis Bargaining.' *The American Political Science Review* 91(2): 339–360.

Geneva Call. 2022. 'Their Words: Directory of Armed Non-State Actor Humanitarian Commitments.' https://theirwords.org/.

Gholiagha, Sassan 2022. *The Humanisation of Global Politics: International Criminal Law, the Responsibility to Protect, and Drones*. Cambridge: Cambridge University Press.

Gholiagha, Sassan and Sienknecht, Mitja 2023. 'Between (ir)Responsibility and (in)Appropriateness: Conceptualizing Norm-related State Behaviour in the Russian wçar against Ukraine.' *Global Constitutionalism*: 1–22.

Gholiagha, Sassan, Holzscheiter, Anna, and Liese, Andrea 2020. 'Activating Norm Collisions: Interface Conflicts in International Drug Control.' *Global Constitutionalism – Human Rights, Democracy and the Rule of Law* 9(2): 290–317.

Gillies, Alexandra 2010. 'Reputational Concerns and the Emergence of Oil Sector Transparency as an International Norm.' *International Studies Quarterly* 54(1): 103–126.

Glanville, Luke 2006. 'Norms, Interests and Humanitarian Intervention.' *Global Change, Peace and Security* 18: 153–171.

GNWP. 2020. 'COVID-19 and Women, Peace and Security Database.' In *GNWP Resources*. https://gnwp.org/resources/covid-19-wps-database/.

Goertz, Gary 2003. *International Norms and Decisionmaking: A Punctuated Equilibrium Model*. Lanham, MD: Rowman & Littlefield.

Goldstein, Judith., and Keohane, Robert O. 1993. 'Ideas and Foreign Policy: An Analytical Framework.' In Goldstein, J., and Keohane, R. O. (eds). *Ideas and Foreign Policy: Beliefs, Institutions, and Political Change*, 3–30. Ithaca and London: Cornell University Press.

Gorman, Daniel 2006. *Imperial Citizenship: Empire and the Question of Belonging.* Manchester: Manchester University Press.

Government of Canada. 2021. 'The Downing of Ukraine International Airlines Flight 752: Factual Analysis.' June. www.international.gc.ca/gac-amc/assets/pdfs/publications/flight-vol-ps752/factual_analysis-analyse_faits-en.pdf.

Graf-Brugère, Anne-Laurence 2013. 'A Lex Favorabilis? Resolving Norm Conflicts between Human Rights Law and Humanitarian Law.' In Kolb, R., and Gaggioli, G. (eds). *Research Handbook on Human Rights and Humanitarian Law*, 251–270. Cheltenham: Edgar Elgar Publishing.

Grant, Thomas D. 2015. 'Current Developments – Annexation of Crimea.' *American Journal of International Law* 109(1): 68–95.

Gready, Paul 2011. *The Era of Transitional Justice: The Aftermath of the Truth and Reconciliation Commission in South Africa and Beyond.* Oxon: Routledge.

Grillot, Suzette R. 2011. 'Global Gun Control. Examining the Consequences of Competing International Norms.' *Global Governance* 17(4): 539–555.

Grovogui, Siba N. 2001. 'Sovereignty in Africa: Quasi-Statehood and Other Myths in International Theory.' In Dunn, K., and Shaw, T. (eds). *Africa's Challenge to International Relations Theory*, 29–45. London: Palgrave.

Gumuchian, Marie-Louise, Smith-Spark, Laura, and Formanek, Ingird 2014. 'Gunmen Seize Parliament in Ukraine's Crimea, Raise Russian Flag.' *CNN*, 27 February. https://edition.cnn.com/2014/02/27/world/europe/ukraine-politics/index.html.

Gunitsky, Seva 2013. 'Complexity and Theories of Change in International Politics.' *International Theory* 5(1): 35–63. https://doi.org/10.1017/S1752971913000110.

Gurowitz, Amy 1999. 'Mobilizing International Norms: Domestic Actors, Immigrants, and the Japanese State.' *World Politics* 51(3): 413–445.

Guterres, António 2016. *Challenges and Opportunities for the United Nations.* Secretary-General Vision Statement, Lisbon, 4 April.

Gutner, T. 2002. *Banking on the Environment: Multilateral Development Banks and Their Environmental Performance in Central and Eastern Europe.* Cambridge: MIT Press.

Guzman, Andrew T. 2010. *How International Law Works: A Rational Choice Theory.* New York: Oxford University Press.

Haas, Ernst B. 1980. 'Why Collaborate? Issue-Linkage and International Regimes.' *World Politics* 32(3): 357–405.

Haas, Peter M., and Haas, Ernst B. 2002. 'Pragmatic Constructivism and the Study of International Institutions.' *Millennium. Journal of International Studies* 31(3), 573–601.

Hadden, Jennifer 2018. 'The Relational Sources of Advocacy Strategies: Comparative Evidence from the European and U.S. Climate Change Sectors.' *Policy Studies Journal* 46(2): 248–268. https://doi.org/10.1111/psj.12217.

Hadden, Jennifer, and Seybert, Lucia A. 2016. 'What's in a Norm? Mapping the Norm Definition Process in the Debate on Sustainable Development.' *Global Governance* 22(2): 249–268.

Hafner-Burton, Emile M. 2005. 'Trading Human Rights: How Preferential Trade Agreements Influence Government Repression.' *International Organization* 59(3): 593–629.

2008. 'Sticks and Stones. Naming and Shaming the Human Rights Enforcement Problem.' *International Organization* 62: 689–716.

Hafner-Burton, Emile M., and Tsutsui, Kiyoteru 2005. 'Human Rights in a Globalizing World: The Paradox of Empty Promises.' *American Journal of Sociology* 110(5): 1373–1411.

Hafner-Burton, Emile M., Kahler, Miles, and Montgomery, Alexander H. 2009. 'Network Analysis for International Relations.' *International Organization* 63(3): 559–592. https://doi.org/10.1017/S0020818309090195.

Hagan, John 2003. *Justice in the Balkans. Prosecuting War Crimes in The Hague Tribunal.* Chicago: Chicago University Press.

Hall, Peter A., and Taylor, Rosemary R. 1996. 'Political Science and the Three New Institutionalisms.' *Political Studies* 44(5): 936–957.

Halliday, Terrence C., and Shaffer, George 2015. 'Researching Transnational Legal Orders.' In Haliday, T. C., and Shaffer, G (eds). *Transnational Legal Orders*, 475–528. Cambridge: Cambridge University Press.

Halliday, Terrence C., Pacewicz, Josh, and Block-Lieb, Susan 2013. 'Who Governs? Delegations in Global Trade Lawmaking.' *Regulation and Governance* 7: 279–298.

Hansen, Lene 2015. 'How Images Make World Politics: International Icons and the Case of Abu Ghraib.' *Review of International Studies* 41(2): 263–288.

Hansen-Magnusson, Hannes, and Vetterlein, Antje (eds). 2020. *The Rise of Responsibility in World Politics*. Cambridge: Cambridge University Press.

2021. *Responsibility in International Relations Theories*. London: Routledge.

Hari, Kurniawan 2013. 'Indonesia to Promote Reconciliation in Rakhine.' *The Jakarta Post*. 9 January.

Harlan, Chico 2018. 'The Retreat of Rescue Ships from the Mediterranean is a Sign of Changing Odds for Migrants.' *The Washington Post*, 16 June (Washington, DC). www.washingtonpost.com/world/europe/the-retreat-of-rescue-ships-from-the-mediterranean-is-a-sign-of-changing-odds-for-migrants/2018/06/15/099b74f0-6e61-11e8-b4d8-eaf78d4c544c_story.html.

Harrington, Joanna 2017. 'The Working Methods of the United Nations Security Council: Maintaining the Implementation of Change.' *International and Comparative Law Quarterly* 66(1): 39–77.

Harrison, Neil E. 2006. *Complexity in World Politics: Concepts and Methods of a New Paradigm*. Albany: SUNY Press.

Hart, H.L.A. 1961. *The Concept of Law*. Oxford: Oxford University Press.

Haugen, Hans M. 2007. 'Patent Rights and Human Rights: Exploring Their Relationships.' *The Journal of World Intellectual Property* 10(2): 97–124.

Havercroft, Jonathan 2017. 'Introduction. Symposium on Contestation and International Relations.' *Polity* 49(1): 100–108.

2018. 'Social Constructivism and International Ethics.' In Steele, Brent J., and Heinze, Eric A. (eds). *Routledge Handbook on Ethics in International Relations*, 116–130. London: Routledge.

Havercroft, Jonathan, and Duvall, Robert 2017. 'Challenges of an Agonistic Constructivism for International Relations: Comments on Antje Wiener's Theory of Contestation.' *Polity* 49(1): 156–164.

Haverland, Markus, and Yanow, Dvora 2012. 'A Hitchhiker's Guide to the Public Administration Research Universe: Surviving Conversations on Methodologies and Methods.' *Public Administration Review* 72(3): 401–408.

Head, Naomi 2020. 'A "Pedagogy of Discomfort"? Experiential Learning and Conflict Analysis in Israel-Palestine.' *International Studies Perspectives* 21(7): 78–96.

Helfer, Laurence R. 2003. 'Human Rights and Intellectual Property: Conflict or Coexistence?' *Minnesota Intellectual Property Review* 5(1): 47–61.

Heller, Kevin Jon 2022. 'Options for Prosecuting Russian Aggression Against Ukraine: A Critical Analysis.' *Journal of Genocide Research*, published online 6 July.

Heller, Regina, Kahl, Martin, and Pisoiu, Daniela 2012. 'The "Dark" Side of Normative Argumentation: The Case of Counterterrorism Policy.' *Global Constitutionalism – Human Rights, Democracy and the Rule of Law* 1(2): 278–312.

Hendrix, Cullen S., and Wong, Wendy H. 2013. 'When Is the Pen Truly Mighty? Regime Type and the Efficacy of Naming and Shaming in Curbing Human Rights Abuses.' *British Journal of Political Science* 43(3): 651–672.

Henning, C. Randall 2017. *Tangled Governance: International Regime Complexity, the Troika, and the Euro Crisis*. Oxford: Oxford University Press.

Henning, C. Randall 2019. 'Regime Complexity and the Organisations of Crisis and Development Finance.' *Development and Change* 50(1): 24–45.

Hernandez, Gleider 2017. 'The Responsibility of the International Legal Academic: Situating the Grammarian within the "Invisible College".' In D'Aspremont, J., Gazzini, T., Nollkaemper, A., and Werner, W. (eds). *International Law as a Profession*, 160–188. Cambridge: Cambridge University Press.

Hertogh, Mark, and Kirkham, Richard 2018. 'The Ombudsman and Administrative Justice: From Promise to Performance.' In Hertogh, M., and Kirkham, R. (eds). *Research Handbook on the Ombudsman*, 1–15. Cheltenham: Edward Elgar Publishing.

Hevener, Natalie K. 1983. *International Law and the Status of Women*. Nashville: Westview Publishing.

Hilde, Thomas C. 2012. 'Uncertainty and the Epistemic Dimension of Democratic Deliberation in Climate Change Adaptation.' *Democratization* 19(5): 889–911.

Hill, Christopher 2003. *The Changing Politics of Foreign Policy*. Basingstoke: Palgrave Macmillan.

Hill, Felicity, Aboitiz, Mikele, and Poehlman-Doumbouya, Sara 2003. 'Nongovernmental Organizations' Role in the Buildup and Implementation of Security Council Resolution 1325.' *Signs: Journal of Women in Culture and Society* 28(4): 1255–1269.

Hochschild, Arlie R. 1983. *The Managed Heart. Commercialization of Human Feeling*. Berkeley: University of California Press.

2004. 'What's in a Word? Torture.' *New York Times*, 23 May. www.nytimes.com/2004/05/23/opinion/what-s-in-a-word-torture.html.

Hofferberth, Matthias, and Weber, Christian 2015. 'Lost in Translation: A Critique of Constructivist Norm Research.' *Journal of International Relations and Development* 18(1): 75–103.

Hoffmann, Matthew J. 2009. 'Is Constructivist Ethics an Oxymoron?' *International Studies Review* 11(2): 231–252.

Hofius, Maren 2016. 'Community at the Border or the Boundaries of Community? The Case of EU Field Diplomats.' *Review of International Studies* 42(5): 939–967.

2020. 'Towards a "Theory of the Gap": Addressing the Relationship between Practice and Theory.' *Global Constitutionalism* 9(1): 169–182.

Hofius, Maren, Wilkens, Jan, Hansen-Magnusson, Hannes, and Gholiagha, Sassan 2014. 'Den Schleier lichten? Kritische Normenforschung, Freiheit und Gleichberechtigung im Kontext des "Arabischen Frühlings".' *Zeitschrift für Internationale Beziehungen* 21(2): 85–105.

Holmes, Marcus, and Wheeler, Nicholas J. 2020. 'Social Bonding in Diplomacy.' *International Theory* 12(1): 133–161.

Holtermann, Jakob v. H., and Madsen, Mikael R. 2015. 'European New Legal Realism and International Law: How to Male International Law Intelligible.' *Leiden Journal of International Law* 28(2): 211–230.

Holthaus, Leonie, and Steffek, Jens. 2020. 'Ideologies of International Organisation: Exploring the Trading Zones between Theory and Practice.' In Martill, B., and Schindler, S. (eds). *Theory as Ideology in International Relations: The Politics of Knowledge*, 187–208. Abingdon: Routledge.

Holzscheiter, Anna, Gholiagha, Sassan, and Liese, Andrea 2022. 'Advocacy Coalition Constellations and Norm Collisions: Insights from International Drug Control, Human Trafficking, and Child Labour.' *Global Society* 36(1): 25–48.

Hookway, Christopher 2013. '"The Principle of Peirce" and the Origins of Pragmatism.' In Malachowski, A. (ed). *The Cambridge Companion to Pragmatism*, 17–35. Cambridge: Cambridge University Press.

Hoover, Joseph 2012. 'Reconstructing Responsibility and Moral Agency in World Politics.' *International Theory* 4(2): 233–268.

Hopf, Ted 1998. 'The Promise of Constructivism in International Relations Theory.' *International Security* 23(1): 171–200.

Htun, Mala, and Weldon, Laurel S. 2012. 'The Civic Origins of Progressive Policy Change: Combating Violence against Women in Global Perspective, 1975–2005.' *American Political Science Review* 106(3): 548–569.

Hughes, Melanie M., Krook, Mona L., and Paxton, Pamela 2015. 'Transnational Women's Activism and the Global Diffusion of Gender Quotas.' *International Studies Quarterly* 59(2): 357–372.

Huijstee, M., Genovese, K., Daniel, C., and Singh, S. 2016. *Glass Half Full: The State of Accountability in Development Finance.* Report by 11 NGOs. 19 December. www.somo.nl/glass-half-full-2/.

Human Rights Council. 2015. 'The Role of Prevention in the Promotion and Prevention of Human Rights.' Report of the Office of the United Nations High Commissioner for Human Rights, 16 July. A/HRC/30/20.

Human Rights Watch. 2001. 'Torture Not an Option.' *Human Rights Watch Issue Backgrounder*, 19 November.

2008. 'Burma: China Should Push to Get Aid In.' In *Human Rights Watch News*, 10 May. www.hrw.org/news/2008/05/09/burma-china-should-push-get-aid.

2017. 'The Costs of International Advocacy: China's Interference in United Nations Human Rights Mechanisms.' Report, 5 September.

2020. 'Human Rights Dimensions of COVID-19 Response.' 19 March. www.hrw.org/news/2020/03/19/human-rights-dimensions-covid-19-response.

Hunt, Charles T. 2016. 'Emerging Powers and the Responsibility to Protect: Non-Linear Norm Dynamics in Complex International Society.' *Cambridge Review of International Affairs* 29(2): 761–781. https://doi.org/10.1080/09557571.2016.1166478.

Hunt, Charles T, and Orchard, Phil 2020. 'Consolidation and Contestation of the Responsibility to Protect.' In Hunt, C. T., and Orchard, P. (eds). *Constructing the Responsibility to Protect*, 1–27. London: Routledge.

Hunt, Paul 2017. 'Configuring the UN Human Rights system in the "Era of Implementation": Mainland and Archipelago.' *Human Rights Quarterly*. 39(3): 489–538.

Hunter, D. 2008. 'Civil Society Networks and the Development of Environmental Standards at International Financial Institutions.' *Chicago Journal of International Law* 8(2): 437–477.

Hurd, Ian 1999. 'Legitimacy and Authority in International Politics.' *International Organization* 53(2): 379–408.

Hurrell, Andrew 2002. 'Norms and Ethics in International Relations.' In Carlesnaes, W., Risse, T., Simmons, B. (eds). *Handbook of International Relations*, 57–84. London: SAGE.

Hutchison, Emma 2010. 'Trauma and the Politics of Emotions: Constituting Identity, Security and Community after the Bali Bombing.' *International Relations* 24: 65–86.

2016. *Affective Communities in World Politics. Collective Emotions after Trauma.* Cambridge: Cambridge University Press.

Hyde, Susan D. 2011. 'Catch Us if You Can: Election Monitoring and International Norm Diffusion.' *American Journal of Political Science* 55(2): 356–369.

ICAO. 2021. 'ICAO Council Condemns Belarus over 2021 Ryanair Flight Bomb Threat and Diversion.' 19 July. www.icao.int/Newsroom/Pages/ICAO-Council-strongly-condemns-Belarus-over-2021-Ryanair-flight-bomb-threat-and-diversion.aspx.

ICC. 2022. 'Statement of ICC Prosecutor, Karim A.A. Khan QC, on the Situation in Ukraine: "I have decided to proceed with opening an investigation".' 28 February. www.icc-cpi.int/news/statement-icc-prosecutor-karim-aa-khan-qc-situation-ukraine-i-have-decided-proceed-opening.

ICCPR. 1966. 'International Convention on Civial and Polical Rights.' www.ohchr.org/en/instruments-mechanisms/instruments/international-covenant-civil-and-political-rights (173 ratifications as of 7 October 2022). https://indicators.ohchr.org.

ICERD. 1965. 'International Convention on the Elimination of All Forms of Racial Discrimination (182 ratifications as of 7 October 2022).' https://indicators.ohchr.org/"\t"_blank.

ICESCR. 1966. 'International Covenant on Economic, Social and Cultural Rights (171 ratifications as of 7 October 2022).' https://indicators.ohchr.org.

ICRW 2019. *Toward a Feminist Foreign Policy in the United States*. Discussion Draft, October. Washington, DC: International Centre for Research on Women.

Ikenberry, John G., and Kupchan, Charles A., 1990. 'Socialization and Hegemonic Power.' *International Organization*, 44(3): 283–315.

ILC Study Group. 2006. 'Fragmentation of International Law: Difficulties arising from the Diversification and Expansion of International Law; Conclusions of the Work of the Study Group (A/CN.4/L.702).' 18 July.

Ilgit, Asli, and Prakash, Deepa 2019. 'Making Human Rights Emotional: A Research Agenda to Recover Shame in "Naming and Shaming."' *Political Psychology* 40(6): 1297–1313.

Immerwahr, Daniel 2019. *How to Hide an Empire: A History of the Greater United States*. New York: Farrar Straus and Giroux.

Inayatullah, Naeem, and Blaney, David 2004. *International Relations and the Problem of Difference*. London: Routledge.

Independent International Commission on Kosovo. 2000. *The Kosovo Report: Conflict, International Response, Lessons Learned: A Report from the Independent International Commission on Kosovo*. Oxford: Oxford University Press.

Inspection Panel. 2009. *Accountability at the World Bank: The Inspection Panel at 15 Years*. Washington, DC: The Inspection Panel, World Bank.

International Coalition for the Responsibility to Protect. 2020. www.responsibilitytoprotect.org/.

International Commission of Jurists. 2022. *Options for the Establishment of a Standing Independent Investigative Mechanism (SIIM)*. Geneva: International Commission of Jurists.

International Committee of the Red Cross. 2007. *Report on the Treatment of Fourteen "High Value Detainees" in CIA Custody*. Regional Delegation for United States and Canada. 14 February, Geneva.

International Court of Justice (ICJ). 2022. 'Press Release: Ukraine Institutes Proceedings against the Russian Federation and Requests the Court to Indicate Provisional Measures. No. 2022/4.' 27 February.

International Finance Corporation. 2012a. 'IFC Sustainability Framework: Policy and Performance Standards on Environmental and Social Sustainability, Access to Information Policy, Washington, DC, World Bank Group.' www.ifc.org/wps/wcm/connect/topics_ext_content/ifc_external_corporate_site/sustainability-at-ifc/policies-standards/ifcsustainabilityframework_2012.

International Finance Corporation. 2012b. *The International Bill of Human Rights and IFC Sustainability Framework*. Washington, DC: World Bank Group. www.ifc.org/wps/wcm/connect/topics_ext_content/ifc_external_corporate_site/sustainability-at-ifc/publications/ibhr_ifc_sustainability_framework.

Isachenkov, Vladimir 2014. 'Putin Signs Treaty to Add Crimea to Map of Russia.' *AP NEWS*, 18 March. https://apnews.com/article/ed0ea4d1515e41659494a156ed80c12e0.

IWDA. 2021. *Introducing the Australian Feminist Foreign Policy Coalition*. https://iwda.org.au/australian-feminist-foreign-policy-coalition/.

Jacob, Cecilia 2018. 'From Norm Contestation to Norm Implementation: Recursivity and the Responsibility to Protect.' *Global Governance* 24(3): 391–409.

2020. 'R2P as an Atrocity Prevention Framework: Concepts and Institutionalization at the Global Level.' In Jacob, C., and Mennecke, M. (eds). *Implementing the Responsibility to Protect: A Future Agenda*, 16–33. Abingdon: Routledge.

2021a. 'Regulatory Contestation: Steering toward Consistency in International Norm Implementation.' *International Studies Review* 23(4): 1349–1369. Online Advance, 1–21.

2021b. 'Institutionalising Prevention at the UN: International Organisation Reform as a Site of Norm Contestation.' *Global Governance* 27(2): 179–201.

2021c. 'The Status of Human Protection in International Law and Institutions: The United Nations Prevention and Protection Architecture.' *The Australian Year Book of International Law Online* 8(1): 110–133.

Jakobi, Anja P., and Loges, Bastian 2021. 'Urbanising Norms? Cities as Local Amplifiers in Global Norm Dynamics on HIV/AIDS Policies.' *Journal of International Relations and Development* 25: 54–78.

Jam v. IFC. 2019. The United States Court of Appeals for the District of Columbia Circuit No. 17–1011.

Jansson, Maria, and Eduards, Maud 2016. 'The Politics of Gender in the UN Security Council Resolutions on Women, Peace and Security.' *International Feminist Journal of Politics* 18(4): 590–604.

Jeff Wise. 2021. 'Why Belarus Grounding of Ryanair Flight Broke International Law.' *New York Magazine Intelligencer*, 24 May. https://nymag.com/intelligencer/2021/05/belarus-grounding-of-ryanair-flight-broke-international-law.html.

Jepperson, Ronald L., Wendt, Alexander, and Katzenstein, Peter 1996. 'Norms, Identity and Culture in National Security.' In Katzenstein, P. (ed). *The Culture of National Security: Norms and Identity in World Politics*, 33–75. New York: Columbia University Press.

Jervis, Robert 1997. 'System Effects.' In Jervis, R. (ed). *System Effects: Complexity in Political and Social Life*, 29–91. Princeton: Princeton University Press.

Jetschke, Anja, and Liese, Andrea 2013. 'The Power of Human Rights a Decade After.' In Risse, T., Ropp, S. C., and Sikkink, K. (eds). *The Persistent Power of Human Rights: From Commitment to Compliance*, 43–60. Cambridge: Cambridge University Press.

Joachim, Jutta M. 2008. *Agenda Setting, the UN, and NGOs: Gender Violence and Reproductive Rights*. Washington, DC: Georgetown University Press.

Joachim, Jutta M., and Schneiker, Andrea 2012. 'Changing Discourses, Changing Practices? Gender Mainstreaming and Security.' *Comparative European Politics* 10(5): 528–563.

Johansson-Nogués, Elisabeth, Vlaskamp, Martijn C., and Barbé, Esther (eds). 2020. *European Union Contested: Foreign Policy in a New Global Context*. Berlin and Heidelberg: Springer.

Johnson, Lyndon B. 1968. 'Special Message to the Senate Transmitting the Protocol Relating to the Status of Refugees.' *The American Presidency Project*. www.presidency.ucsb.edu/node/237750.

Johnson, Melissa, Davies, Sara E., True, Jacqui, and Morales-Riveros, Yolanda 2023. '"Patriarchal Reset" in the Asia Pacific during COVID-19: The Impacts on Women's Security and Rights.' *Pacific Review* 36(3): 603–630.

Johnston, Alastair Iain 2001. 'Treating International Institutions as Social Environments.' *International Studies Quarterly* 45(4), 487–515.

Johnstone, Ian 2011. *The Power of Deliberation: International Law, Politics and Organizations*. New York: Oxford University Press.

Jose, Betcy 2017. 'Not Completely the New Normal: How Human Rights Watch Tried to Suppress the Targeted Killing Norm.' *Contemporary Security Policy* 38(2): 237–259.

Joseph, Sara 2011. *Blame it on the WTO?: A Human Rights Critique*. Oxford: Oxford University Press.

Jurkovich, Michele 2020. 'What Isn't a Norm? Redefining the Conceptual Boundaries of "Norms" in the Human Rights Literature.' *International Studies Review* 22(3): 693–711.

Kammerhofer, Jörg 2005. 'Structural Uncertainty through Neo-Kelsenian Consistency: Conflicts of Norms in International Law.' *Papers of the European Society of International Law* 1–25.

Kardam, Nüket 2004. 'The Emerging Global Gender Equality Regime from Neoliberal and Constructivist Perspectives in International Relations.' *International Feminist Journal of Politics* 6(1): 85–109.

Karlsrud, John 2019. 'For the Greater Good?: "Good States" Turning UN Peacekeeping towards Counterterrorism.' *International Journal. Canada's Journal of Global Policy Anaylsis* 74(1): 65–83.

Karmanau, Yuras, and Baetz, Juergen 2014. 'Crimea to Vote to Split from Ukraine, Join Russia.' *AP NEWS*, 7 March. www.yahoo.com/entertainment/news/crimea-vote-split-ukraine-join-russia-233303911.html?guccounter=1.

Katsumata, Hiro 2009. 'ASEAN and Human Rights: Resisting Western Pressure or Emulating the West?' *Pacific Review* 5: 619–637.

Katzenstein, Peter 1996. 'Introduction: Alternative Perspectives on National Security.' In Katzesntein, P. (ed). *The Culture of National Security: Norms and Identity in World Politics*, 1–32. New York: Columbia University Press.

Kauffman, Craig M. 2017. *Grassroots Global Governance: Local Watershed Management Experiments and the Evolution of Sustainable Development*. New York: Oxford University Press.

Kauppi, Niilo, and Madsen, Mikael R. 2014. 'Fields of Global Governance: How Transnational Power Elites Can Make Global Governance Intelligible.' *International Political Sociology* 8(3): 324–330.

Kavalski, Emilian 2007. 'The Fifth Debate and the Emergence of Complex International Relations Theory: Notes on the Application of Complexity Theory to the Study of International Life.' *Cambridge Review of International Affairs* 20(36): 435–454. https://doi.org/10.1080/09557570701574154.

Keating, Vincent C. 2014. 'Contesting the International Illegitimacy of Torture: The Bush Administration's Failure to Legitimate Its Preferences within International Society.' *The British Journal of Politics and International Relations*, 16(1): 1–27.

Keck, Margaret E., and Sikkink, Kathryn. 1998. *Activists beyond Borders: Advocacy Networks in International Politics*. Ithaca: Cornell University Press.

Kellerman, Miles 2019. 'The Proliferation of the Multilateral Development Banks.' *Review of International Organization* 14: 107–145.

Kelley, Judith G. 2008. 'Assessing the Complex Evolution of Norms: The Rise of International Election Monitoring.' *International Organization* 62(2): 221–255.

Kelley, Judith G., and Simmons, Beth A. 2015. 'Politics by Number: Indicators as Social Pressure in International Relations.' *American Journal of Political Science* 59(1): 55–70.

Kennedy, David 2016. *A World of Struggle: How Power, Law, and Expertise Shape Global Political Economy*. Princeton: Princeton University Press.

Kennedy, Edward M. 1981. 'Refugee Act of 1980.' *International Migration Review* 15(1–2): 141–156.

Khundee, Supalak 2007. 'Thai Role Gets UK Backing Britain Tells Nitya, It Understands Kingdom's Unique Circumstances.' *The Nation*, 30 September.

Kim, Hun J., and Sharman, Jason C. 2014. 'Accounts and Accountability: Corruption, Human Rights and Individual Accountability Norms.' *International Organization* 68(2): 417–448.

Kim, Rakhyun E. 2020. 'Is Global Governance Fragmented, Polycentric, or Complex? The State of the Art of the Network Approach.' *International Studies Review* 22(4): 903–931. https://doi.org/10.1093/isr/viz052.

King, Desmond 2000. *Making Americans: Immigration, Race, and the Origins of the Diverse Democracy*. Cambridge, MA: Harvard University Press.

Kingsbury, Benedict 2010. 'The International Legal Order. International Law and Justice.' Working Paper 20003/1, History and Theory of International Law Series. Institute for International Law and Justice, New York University.

Kingsbury, Benedict, Krisch, Nico, and Stewart, Richard B. 2005. 'Emergence of Global Administrative Law.' *Law and Contemporary Problems* 68(15): 15–62.

Kirby, Paul, and Shepherd, Laura J. 2016. 'The Futures Past of the Women, Peace and Security Agenda.' *International Affairs* 92(2): 373–392.

2020. 'Women, Peace, and Security: Mapping the (Re) Production of a Policy Ecosystem.' *Journal of Global Security Studies* 6(3): 1–25.

Kirgis, Frederic L. 1987. 'Custom on a Sliding Scale.' *American Journal of International Law* 81(1): 146–151.

Kistler, Deborah, Thöni, Christian, and Welzel, Christian 2017. 'Survey Response and Observed Behavior: Emancipative and Secular Values Predict Prosocial Behaviors.' *Journal of Cross-Cultural Psychology* 48(4): 461–489.

Klaaren, Jonathan 2000. 'Post-Apartheid Citizenship in South Africa.' In Aleinikoff, A. T., and Klusmeyer, D. (eds). *From Migrants to Citizens: Membership in a Changing World*, 221–252. Washington, DC: Carnegie Endowment for International Peace.

Klabbers, Jan, Peters, Anne, and Ulfstein, Geir 2011. *The Constitutionalization of International Law*. Oxford: Oxford University Press.

Kleinlein, Thomas 2023. 'Matters of Interpretation: How to Conceptualize and Evaluate Change of Norms and Values in the International Legal Order.' In Krieger, H., and Liese, A. (eds). *Tracing Value Change in the International Legal Order: Perspectives from Legal and Political Science*, 64–81. Oxford: Oxford University Press.

Klotz, Audie 1995a. *Norms in International Relations: The Struggle against Apartheid*. Ithaca: Cornell University Press.

1995b. 'Norms Reconstituting Interests: Global Racial Equality and U.S. Sanctions against South Africa.' *International Organization* 49(3): 451–478.

2013. *Migration and National Identity in South Africa, 1860–2010*. Cambridge: Cambridge University Press.

2017. 'Racial Inequality.' In Dunne, T., and Reus-Smit, C. (eds). *Globalization of International Society*, 362–379. Oxford: Oxford University Press.

2018. 'The Power of Prejudice: The Race Gap in Constructivist International Relations Scholarship.' In Bertucci, M., Hayes, J., and James, P. (eds). *Constructivism and Its Critics*, 87–102. Ann Arbor: University of Michigan Press.

Klotz, Audie, and Boehme, Franziska 2022. *A Genealogy of Apartheid in International Law*. Paper presented at the International Studies Association Annual Meeting, Nashville.

Kornprobst, Markus, and Senn, Martin 2016. 'Introduction: Background Ideas in International Relations.' *The British Journal of Politics and International Relations* 18(2): 273–281.

Koschut, Simon 2014. 'Emotional (Security) Communities: The Significance of Emotion Norms in Inter-Allied Conflict Management.' *Review of International Studies* 40: 533–558.

2018. 'The Power of (Emotion) Words. On the Importance of Emotions for Discourse Analysis in IR.' *Journal of International Relations and Development* 21(3): 495–522.

Koskenniemi, Martti 2007. 'The Fate of Public International Law: Between Technique and Politics.' *Modern Law Review* 70(1): 1–30.

Kowert, Paul A. 2012. 'Completing the Ideational Triangle: Identity, Choice and Obligation in International Relations.' In: Shannon, V. P., and Kowert, P. A. (eds). *Psychology and Constructivism in International Relations: An Ideational Alliance*, 30–53. Ann Arbor: University of Michigan Press.

Krain, Matthew 2012. '"J'accuse"! Does Naming and Shaming Perpetrators Reduce the Severity of Genocides or Politicides?' *International Studies Quarterly* 56(3): 574–589.

Kramer, Paul A. 2006. *The Blood of Government: Race, Empire, the United States, and the Philippines*. Chapel Hill: University of North Carolina Press.

Krampf, Arie 2013. 'The Life Cycles of Competing Policy Norms. Localizing European and Developmental Central Banking Ideas.' KFG The Transformative Power of Europe, Working Paper No. 49 (Berlin).

Krasner, Stephen D. 1999. *Sovereignty: Organized Hypocrisy*. Princeton: Princeton University Press.

Kratochwil, Friedrich 1986. 'Of Systems, Boundaries, and Territoriality: An Inquiry into the Formation of the State System.' *World Politics* 39(1): 27–52. https://doi.org/10.2307/2010297.

1991. *Rules, Norms and Decisions: On the Conditions of Practical and Legal Reasoning in International Relations and Domestic Affairs*. Cambridge: Cambridge University Press.

1993. 'The Embarrassment of Changes: Neo-Realism as the Science of Realpolitik without Politics.' *Review of International Studies* 19(1): 63–80.

Kratochwil, Friedrich, and Ruggie, John G. 1986. International Organization: A State of the Art on an Art of the State.' *International Organization* 40(4): 753–775.

Krebs, Ronald R., and Jackson, Patrick T. 2007. 'Twisting Tongues and Twisting Arms: The Power of Political Rhetoric.' *European Journal of International Relations* 13(1): 35–66.

Kreft, Anne-Kathrin 2017. 'The Gender Mainstreaming Gap: Security Council Resolution 1325 and UN Peacekeeping Mandates." *International Peacekeeping* 24(1): 132–158.

Kreuder-Sonnen, Christian 2019. 'China vs the WTO: A Behavioural Norm Conflict in the SARS Crisis.' *International Affairs* 95(3): 535–552. https://doi.org/10.1093/ia/iiz022.

Kreuder-Sonnen, Christian, and Zürn, Michael 2020. 'After Fragmentation: Norm Collisions, Interface Conflicts, and Conflict Management.' *Global Constitutionalism* 9(2): 241–267. https://doi.org/10.1017/S2045381719000315.

Krieger, Heike, and Liese, Andrea 2019. 'A Metamorphosis of International Law? – Value Changes in the International Legal Order from the Perspectives of Legal and Political Science.' *KFG Working Paper Series No. 27.* Berlin Potsdam Research Group 'The International Rule of Law – Rise or Decline?' *Deutsche Nationalbibliothek.* https://d-nb.info/1217813039/34.

Krisch, Nico 2005. 'International Law in Times of Hegemony: Unequal Power and the Shaping of the International Legal Order.' *European Journal of International Law* 16(3): 369–408.

2014. 'The Decay of Consent: International Law in an Age of Global Public Goods.' *American Journal of International Law* 198(1): 1–40.

Krisch, Nico, and Kingsbury, Benedict 2006. 'Introduction: Global Governance and Global Administrative Law in the International Legal Order.' *European Journal of International Law.* 17(1), 1–13.

Krisch, Nico, Corradini, Francesco, and Reimers, Lucy L. 2020. 'Order at the Margins: The Legal Construction of Interface Conflicts over Time.' *Global Constitutionalism* 9(2): 343–363. https://doi.org/10.1017/S2045381719000327.

Krook, Mona L. 2011. 'Gendering Comparative Politics: Achievements and Challenges.' *Politics & Gender* 7(1): 99–105.

Krook, Mona L., and True, Jacqui 2012. 'Rethinking the Life Cycles of International Norms: The United Nations and the Global Promotion of Gender Equality.' *European Journal of International Relations*, 18(1): 103–127.

Kumar, Shashank P., and Rose, Cecily 2014. 'A Study of Lawyers Appearing before the International Court of Justice, 1999–2012.' *European Journal of International Law* 25(3): 893–917.

Kurowska, Xymena 2019. *The Politics of Cyber Norms: Beyond Norm Construction towards Strategic Narrative Contestation.* Brussels and Paris: EU Cyber Direct/EU Institute for Security Studies.

Laden, Anthony S., and Owen, David (eds). 2007. *Multiculturalism and Political Theory.* Cambridge: Cambridge University Press.

Lake, David A., Martin, Lisa L., and Risse, Thomas 2021. 'Challenges to the Liberal Order: Reflections on International Organization.' *International Organization* 75(2): 225–257.

Lake, David A., and Wiener, Antje 2023. 'Understanding Deep Contestation.' In Wiener, A., Lake, D. A., and Risse, T. (eds). *Deep Contestation of International Orders*. Oxford: Oxford University Press (in preparation).

Lake, Marilyn, and Reynolds, Henry 2008. *Drawing the Global Colour Line. White Men's Countries and the International Challenge of Racial Equality*. Cambridge: Cambridge University Press.

Lantis, Jeff S. 2016. 'Agentic Constructivism and the Proliferation Security Initiative: Modeling Norm Change.' *Cooperation and Conflict* 51(3): 384–400.

Lantis, Jeff S. and Wunderlich, Carmen 2018. 'Resiliency Dynamics of Norm Clusters: Norm Contestation and International Cooperation.' *Review of International Studies* 44(3): 570–593.

2022. 'Reevaluating Constructivist Norm Theory: A Three-Dimensional Norms Research Program.' *International Studies Review* online first.

Lau, Estelle T. 2006. *Paper Families: Identity, Immigration Administration, and Chinese Exclusion*. Durham: Duke University Press.

Laughland, Oliver, Urquhart, Conal, and Yuhas, Alan 2014. 'Crimea Referendum: Early Results Indicate 'Landslide' for Secession – As It Happened.' *The Guardian*, 16 March. www.theguardian.com/world/2014/mar/16/crimea-referendum-polls-open-live.

Lave, Jean, and Wenger, Etienne 1991. *Situated Learning: Legitimate Peripheral Participation*. Cambridge: Cambridge University Press.

Lavelle, K. 2011. *Legislating International Organisation: The US Congress, the IMF and the World Bank*. Oxford: Oxford University Press.

Leander, Anna 2008. 'Thinking Tools.' In Klotz, A., and Prakash, D. (eds). *Qualitative Methods in International Relations: A Pluralist Guide*, 11–27. New York: Palgrave.

Lebovic, James H., and Voeten, Erik 2006. 'The Politics of Shame. The Condemnation of Country Human Rights Practices in the UNCHR.' *International Studies Quarterly* 50(4): 861–888.

Lebow, Richard N., and Risse-Kappen, Thomas 1995. (eds). *International Relations Theory and the End of the Cold War*. New York: Columbia University Press.

Lechner, Silviya, and Frost, Mervyn. 2018. *Practice Theory and International Relations*. Cambridge: Cambridge University Press.

Legro, Jeffrey W. 1997. 'Which Norms Matter? Revisiting the 'Failure' of Internationalism.' *International Organization* 51(1): 31–63.

2020. 'The Transformation of Policy Ideas.' *American Journal of Political Science* 44(3): 419–432.

Lenton, Timothy M., Rockström, Johan, Gaffney, Owen, Rahmstorf, Stefan, Richardson, Katherine, Steffen, Will, and Schellnhuber, Hans J. 2019. 'Climate Tipping Points – Too Risky to Bet Against.' *Nature* 575: 592–595.

Lenz, Tobias, and Viola, Lora A. 2017. 'Legitimacy and Institutional Change in International Organizations: A Cognitive Approach.' *Review of International Studies* 43(5): 939–961.

Lesch, Max, and Zimmermann, Lisbeth. 2023. 'There's Life in the Old Dog Yet: Assessing the Strength of the International Torture Prohibition.' In Krieger, H., and Liese, A. (eds). *Tracing Value Change in the International Legal Order: Perspectives from Legal and Political Science*, 100–117. Oxford: Oxford University Press.

Lesser, Jeff 2013. *Immigration, Ethnicity, and National Identity in Brazil, 1808 to the Present.* Cambridge: Cambridge University Press.

Lewis, K. 2012. 'Citizen-Driven Accountability for Sustainable Development: Giving Affected People a Voice 20 Years On.' A Paper by the Independent Accountability Mechanisms Network. Accessed: 7 July 2016. http://siteresources.worldbank.org/EXTINSPECTIONPANEL/Resources/Rio20_IAMs_Contribution.pdf.

Liebowitz, Debra J., and Zwingel, Susanne 2014. 'Gender Equality Oversimplified: Using CEDAW to Counter the Measurement Obsession.' *International Studies Review* 16: 362–382.

Liese, Andrea 2009. 'Exceptional Necessity: How Liberal Democracies Contest the Prohibition of Torture and Ill-treatment When Countering Terrorism.' *Journal of International Law and International Relations* 5(1): 17–47.

Lindroos, Anja 2005. 'Addressing Norm Conflicts in a Fragmented Legal System: The Doctrine of Lex Specialis.' *The Nordic Journal of International Law* 74: 27–66.

Liste, Philip 2020. 'The Workings of Power in Transnational Law.' *TLI Think! Paper* 24/2020. https://papers.ssrn.com/sol3/papers.cfm?abstract_id=3756985.

Liu, Hin-Y., and Kinsey, Christopher 2018. 'Challenging the Strength of the Antimercenary Norm.' *Journal of Global Security Studies* 3(1): 93–110.

Locher, Birgit, and Prügl, Elisabeth 2001. 'Feminism and Constructivism: Worlds Apart or Sharing the Middle Ground?' *International Studies Quarterly* 45(1): 111–129.

Lu, Sidney X. 2019. *The Making of Japanese Settler Colonialism: Malthusianism and Trans-Pacific Migration, 1868–1961.* Cambridge: Cambridge University Press.

Lukas, Karin, Linder, Barbara, Kutrzeba, Astrid, and Sprenger, Claudia 2016. *Corporate Accountability: The Role and Impact of Non-Judicial Grievance.* Cheltenham, Edward Elgar Publishing.

Lynch, Cecilia 1999. *Beyond Appeasement: Interpreting Interwar Peace Movements in World Politics*. Ithaca: Cornell University Press.

Lyons, Gene M. 1989. 'In Search of Racial Equality: The Elimination of Racial Discrimination.' In Taylor, P., and Groom, A. J. R. (eds). *Global Issues in the United Nations' Framework*, 75–115. New York: St. Martin's.

Maass, Richard W. 2020. *The Picky Eagle: How Democracy and Xenophobia Limited U.S. Territorial Expansion*. Ithaca: Cornell University Press.

Macdonald, Kate, and Miller-Dawkins, May 2015. 'Accountability in Public International Development Finance.' *Global Policy* 6(4): 429–434.

Madokoro, Daisuke 2015. 'How the United Nations Secretary-General Promotes International Norms: Persuasion, Collective Legitimisation, and the Responsibility to Protect.' *Global Responsibility to Protect* 7(1): 31–55. https://doi.org/10.1163/1875984X-00701003.

Madsen, Mikael R. 2010. *La Genèse de l'Europe Des Droits de l'homme: Enjeux Juridiques et Stratégies d'Etat (France, Grande-Bretagne et Pays Scandinaves, 1945–1970)*. Strasbourg: Presses Universitaires de Strasbourg.

2011. 'Reflexivity and the Construction of the International Object: The Case of Human Rights.' *International Political Sociology* 5(3): 259–275.

2014. 'The International Judiciary as Transnational Power Elite.' *International Political Sociology* 8(3): 332–334.

2018. 'Who Rules the World: The Educational Capital of the International Judiciary.' *UC Irvine Journal of International, Transnational, and Comparative Law* 3: 97.

2021. 'The Narrowing of the European Court of Human Rights: Legal Diplomacy, Situational Self-Restraint and the Transformation of the Court.' *The European Convention on Human Rights Law Review* 2(2): 180–208.

Madsen, Mikael R., Cebulak, Pola, and Wiebusch, Micha 2018. 'Backlash against International Courts: Explaining the Forms and Patterns of Resistance to International Courts.' *International Journal of Law in Context* 14(2): 197–220.

Maliniak, Daniel, Peterson, Susan, Powers, Ryan, and Tierney, Michael J. 2017. 'TRIP 2017 Faculty Survey.' In *Teaching, Research, and International Policy Project*. Williamsburg, VA: Global Research Institute. https://trip.wm.edu/.

March, James G., and Olsen, Johan P. 1989. *Rediscovering Institutions*. New York: Free Press.

1998. 'The Institutional Dynamics of International Political Orders.' *International Organization* 52 (4): 943–969.

2004. 'The Logic of Appropriateness.' *ARENA Centre for European Studies Working Paper 04/09*. Oslo: University of Oslo.

Mares, Radu 2019, 'Securing Human Rights through Risk-Management Methods: Breakthrough or Misalignment?' *Leiden Journal of International Law* 32: 517–535.

Margulis, Matias E. 2013. 'The Regime Complex for Food Security. Implications for the Global Hunger Challenge.' *Global Governance* 19(1): 53–67.

Marshall, Catherine E., Ogden, Charles K., and Florence, Mary S. 1987. *Militarism versus Feminism: Writings on Women and War*. London: Virago Press.

Martin, Lisa 2013. 'Against Compliance.' In Dunoff, J. L., and Pollack, M. A. (eds). *Interdisciplinary Perspectives on International Law and International Relations: The State of the Art*, 591–610. Cambridge: Cambridge University Press.

Martin De Almagro, María 2018. 'Lost Boomerangs, the Rebound Effect and Transnational Advocacy Networks: A Discursive Approach to Norm Diffusion.' *Review of International Studies* 44(4): 672–693.

Martin-Mazé, Médéric 2017. 'Returning Struggles to the Practice Turn: How Were Bourdieu and Boltanski Lost in (Some) Translations and What to Do about It?' *International Political Sociology* 11(2): 203–220.

Mason, Michael 2005. *The New Accountability: Environmental Responsibility Across Borders*. London: Earthscan.

Matejova, Miriam, Parker, Stefan, and Dauvergne, Peter 2018. 'The Politics of Repressing Environmentalists as Agents of Foreign Influence.' *Australian Journal of International Affairs* 72(2): 145–162.

Mattern, Janice Bially and Zarazol, Ayşe 2016. 'Hierarchy in World Politics.' *International Organization* 70(3): 623–654.

Mattli, Walter, and Diez, Thomas 2014. *International Arbitration and Global Governance*. Oxford: Oxford University Press.

Max Fisher. 2013. 'Evo Morales's Controversial Flight over Europe, Minute by Heavily Disputed Minute.' *The Washington Post*, 3 July. www.washingtonpost.com/news/worldviews/wp/2013/07/03/evo-morales-controversial-flight-over-europe-minute-by-heavily-disputed-minute/.

May, Christopher, and Winchester, Adam (eds). 2018. *Handbook on the Rule of Law*. London: Edward Elgar Publishing. https://doi.org/10.4337/9781786432445.

Mayblin, Lucy, and Turner, Joe 2021. *Migration Studies and Colonialism*. Cambridge and Malden: Polity.

MBT Website. 2021. *AP Mine Ban Convention: Japan*. www.apminebanconvention.org/states-parties-to-the-convention/japan/.

McAdam, Jane 2020. 'Protecting People Displaced by the Impacts of Climate Change: The UN Human Rights Committee and the Principle of Non-Refoulement.' *American Journal of International Law* 114(4): 708–725.

McAfee, Noëlle 2004a. 'Public Knowledge.' *Philosophy and Social Criticism* 30(2): 139–157.

2004b. 'Three Models of Democratic Deliberation.' *The Journal of Speculative Philosophy* 18(1): 44–59.

McCarthy, Helen, Sharp, Ingrid, Beers, Laura, Sluga, Glenda, Donert, Celia, and Pankhurst, Helen 2015. 'Women, Peace and Transnational Activism: A Century On.' *History & Policy*, 30 March. www.historyandpolicy.org/dialogues/discussions/women-peace-and-transnational-activism-a-century-on.

McCarthy, Tom 2016. 'Donald Trump: I'd bring back "a hell of a lot worse than water boarding".' *The Guardian*, 7 February. www.theguardian.com/us-news/2016/feb/06/donald-trump-waterboarding-republican-debate-torture.

McCourt, David M. 2016. 'Practice Theory and Relationalism as the New Constructivism.' *International Studies Quarterly* 60(3): 475–485. www.jstor.org/stable/44510089.

2022. *The New Constructivism in International Relations Theory*: Bristol: Bristol University Press.

McIntyre, O., and Nanwani, S. (eds). 2020. *The Practices of the Independent Accountability Mechanisms: Towards Good Governance in Development Finance*. Leiden and Boston: Brill Njihoff.

McKay, Catriona L. 2012. 'Protecting the Silent Victim from Irregular Actors: Improving Non-State Compliance with the International Law of Environmental Protection in Armed Conflict.' In *ANU College of Law Research Paper* No. 12–18, ANU College of Law Honours Thesis 2011, https://ssrn.com/abstract=2082599.

McKeown, Adam 2011. *Melancholy Order: Asian Migration and the Globalization of Borders*. New York: Columbia University Press.

McKeown, Ryder 2009. 'Norm Regress: US Revisionism and the Slow Death of the Torture Norm.' *International Relations* 23(1): 5–25. https://doi.org/10.1177/0047117808100607.

Melucci, Alberto 1989. *Nomads of the Present: Social Movements and Individual Needs in Contemporary Society*. Philadelphia: Temple University Press.

Mende, Janne 2022. 'Norm Convergence and Collision in Regime Overlaps. Business and Human Rights in the UN and the EU.' *Globalizations* 19(5): 725–740.

Menkel-Meadow, Carrie 2019. 'Uses and Abuses of Socio-Legal Studies.' In Creutzfeld, N., Mason, M., and McConacchie, K. (eds). *Routledge Handbook of Socio-Legal Theory and Methods*, 35–57. Oxon: Routledge.

Mercer, Jonathan 1996. 'Approaching Emotion.' Paper Presented at the Annual Convention of the International Studies Association, San Diego, CA.

2005. 'Rationality and Psychology in International Politics.' *International Organization* 59(1): 77–106.

Meron, Theodor 2000. 'The Humanization of Humanitarian Law.' *American Journal of International Law* 94(2): 239–278.

2018. 'Closing the Accountability Gap: Concrete Steps toward Ending Impunity for Atrocity Crimes.' *The American Society of International Law*. 112(3): 433–451.

Merry, Sally E. 2006. 'Transnational Human Rights and Local Activism: Mapping the Middle.' *American Anthropologist* 108(1): 38–51. https://doi .org/10.1007/978-94-007-4710-4_10.

Michaels, Ralf, and Pauwelyn, Joost 2012. 'Conflict of Norms or Conflict of Laws?: Different Techniques in the Fragmentation of Public International Law.' *Duke Journal of Comparative & International Law* 22(3): 349–376.

Milanović, Marko 2009. 'A Norm Conflict Perspective on the Relationship between International Humanitarian Law and Human Rights Law.' *Journal of Conflict and Security Law* 14(3): 459–483.

2010. 'Norm Conflicts, International Humanitarian Law and Human Rights Law.' In Ben-Naftali, O. (ed). *Human Rights and International Humanitarian Law*, 1–36. Oxford: Oxford University Press.

Miller, John H., and Page, Scott E. 2007. *Complex Adaptive Systems: An Introduction to Computational Models of Social Life*. Princeton: Princeton University Press.

Mills, Kurt, and Karp, David J. (eds). 2015. *Human Rights Protection in Global Politics: Responsibilities of States and Non-State Actors*. Basingstoke: Palgrave Macmillan.

Minha, Donna 2020. 'The Possibility of Prosecuting Corporations for Climate Crimes before the International Criminal Court: All Roads Lead to the Rome Statute?' *Michigan Journal of International Law* 41(3): 491–540.

Ministry of Foreign Affairs of the People's Republic of China. 2021. 'Foreign Ministry Spokesperson Zhao Lijian's Regular Press Conference on May 25, 2021.' www.fmprc.gov.cn/mfa_eng/xwfw_665399/s2510_665401/ t1878445.shtml.

Mintrom, Michael, and True, Jacqui 2022. 'COVID-19 as a Policy Window: Policy Entrepreneurs and the Prevention of Violence Against Women.' *Policy and Society* 41(1): 143–154.

Misak, Cheryl 2000. *Truth, Morality and Politics: Pragmatism and Deliberation*. London: Routledge.

2004. 'Making Disagreement Matter: Pragmatism and Deliberative Democracy.' *The Journal of Speculative Philosophy* 18(1): 9–22.

Mitchell, Ronald B. 2002–19. 'International Environmental Agreements Database Project (Version 2018.1).' http://iea.uoregon.edu/.

Moghadam, Valentine M. 2005. *Globalizing Women: Transnational Feminist Networks*. Baltimore: Johns Hopkins University Press.

Moses, Dirk A., Duranti, Marco, and Burke, Roland, (eds). 2020. *Decolonization, Self-Determination, and the Rise of Global Human Rights Politics*. Cambridge: Cambridge University Press.

Müller, Harald 2001. 'Arguing, Bargaining, and All That: Communicative Action, Rationalist Theory and the Logic of Appropriateness in International Relations.' *European Journal of International Relations* 10(3): 395–435.

Müller, Jan-Werner 2015. 'Should the EU Protect Democracy and the Rule of Law inside Member States?' *European Law Journal* 21(2): 141–160.

Murcott, Melanie, and Webster, Emily 2020. 'Litigation and Regulatory Governance in the Age of the Anthropocene: The Case of Fracking in the Karoo.' *Transnational Legal Theory* 11(1–2): 144–164.

Murdie, Amanda M., and Davis, David R. 2012. 'Shaming and Blaming: Using Events Data to Assess the Impact of Human Rights INGOs: Shaming and Blaming.' *International Studies Quarterly* 56(1): 1–16.

Musa, Naim 2012. 'Malaysia in ASEAN: Foreign Policy on Non-Traditional Security Issues.' www.academia.edu/4219715/Malaysia_foreign_policy_after_mahathir_era.

Mwanza, Rosemary 2018. 'Enhancing Accountability for Environmental Damage under International Law: Ecocide as a Legal Fulfilment of Ecological Integrity.' *Melbourne Journal of International Law* 19(2): 586–613.

Nadelmann, Ethan A. 1990. 'Global Prohibition Regimes: The Evolution of Norms in International Society.' *International Organization* 44(4): 479–526.

Naude Fourie, A. 2012. 'The World Bank Inspection Panel's Normative Potential: A Critical Assessment and a Restatement.' *Netherlands International Law Review* LIX: 199–234.

NATO. 1999. 'NATO's Role in Relation to the Conflict in Kosovo.' www.nato.int/kosovo/history.html.

New York Times. 1915. 'Peace Talk Causes Suffrage Schism.' 25 April. www.nytimes.com/1915/04/25/archives/peace-talk-causes-suffrage-schism-mrs-pankhurst-opposes-sending.html.

2004. 'Transcript from Bush Speech on American Strategy in Iraq.' 24 May 2004. www.nytimes.com/2004/05/24/politics/transcript-from-bush-speech-on-american-strategy-in-iraq.html.

Niemann, Holger, and Schillinger, Henrik 2017. 'Contestation "All The Way Down"? The Grammar of Contestation in Norm Research.' *Review of International Studies* 43(1): 29–49.

Noor, Elina, and Qistina, T. N. 2017. 'Great Power Rivalries, Domestic Politics and Malaysian Foreign Policy.' *Asian Security* 13(3): 200–219.

Nuñez-Mietz, Fernando G., and García Iommi, Lucrecia 2017. 'Can Transnational Norm Advocacy Undermine Internalization? Explaining Immunization Against LGBT Rights in Uganda.' *International Studies Quarterly* 61(1): 196–209.

Nussbaum, Martha C. 2001. *Upheavals of Thought: The Intelligence of Emotions*. Cambridge: Cambridge University Press.

Odello, Marco E., and Burke, Róisín 2016. 'Between Immunity and Impunity: Peacekeeping and Sexual Abuses and Violence.' *The International Journal of Human Rights* 20(6): 839–853.

OECD. 2017. *OECD Due Diligence Guidance for Meaningful Stakeholder Engagement in the Extractive Sector*. Paris: OECD Publishing.

Ognibene, Lara, and Kariuki, Angela 2019. 'Standards in the Procedural Rights of Multilateral Environmental Agreements.' In Turner, S., Shelton, D., Razzaque, J., McIntyre, O., and May, J. (eds). *Environmental Rights: The Development of Standards*, 174–194. Cambridge: Cambridge University Press.

Oh, Arissa H. 2019. 'Japanese War Brides and the Normalization of Family Unification after World War II.' In Marinari, M., Hsu, M., and García, M. C. (eds). *A Nation of Immigrants Reconsidered: US Society in an Age of Restriction, 1924–1965*, 231–254. Champaign, IL: University of Illinois Press.

Olivius, Elisabeth, Hedstrom, Jenny, and Zin Mar, Phyo 2021. 'Feminist Peace or State Co-optation? The Women, Peace and Security Agenda in Myanmar.' *European Journal of Politics and Gender* 5(1): 25–43.

Ollivier, Maurice (ed). 1954. *The Colonial and Imperial Conferences from 1887 to 1937*. Ottawa: Queen's Printer.

O'Mahoney, Joseph 2014. 'Rule Tensions and the Dynamics of Institutional Change: From "to the Victor go the Spoils" to the Stimson Doctrine.' *European Journal of International Relations* 20(3): 834–857.

Onuf, Nicholas 1989. *World of Our Making: Rules and Rule in Social Theory and International Relations*. Columbia: University of South Carolina Press.

1994. 'The Constitution of International Society.' *European Journal of International Law* 5(1): 1–19. https://doi.org/10.1093/oxfordjournals.ejil.a035857.

Orbach, Barak 2012. 'What is Regulation?' *Yale Journal on Regulation Online* 30(1): 1–10.

Orchard, Phil 2014. *A Right to Flee: Refugees, States, and the Construction of International Society*. Cambridge: Cambridge University Press.

2018. *Protecting the Internally Displaced: Rhetoric and Reality*. London: Routledge.

Orchard, Phil, and Wiener, Antje 2024. 'Introduction.' In Orchard, P., and Wiener, A. (eds). *Contesting the World: Norm Research in Theory and Practice*, 1–25. Cambridge: Cambridge University Press.

Organisation for Economic Cooperation and Development (OECD). 2018. *Multilateral Development Finance: Towards a New Pact on Multilateralism to Achieve the 2030 Agenda Together*. Geneva: OECD. www.oecd.org/dac/financing-sustainable-development/development-finance-topics/Multilateral-Development-Finance-Highlights-2018.pdf.

Orsini, Amandine, Le Prestre, Philippe, Haas, Peter M., Brosig, Malte, Pattberg, Philipp, Widerberg, Oscar, Gomez-Mera, Laura, et al. 2020. 'Forum: Complex Systems and International Governance.' *International Studies Review* 22(4): 1008–1038. https://doi.org/10.1093/isr/viz005.

Ottawa Convention. 1997. 'Convention on the Prohibition of the Use, Stockpiling, Production and Transfer of Anti-Personnel Mines and on their Destruction.' https://geneva-s3.unoda.org/static-unoda-site/pages/templates/anti-personnel-landmines-convention/APLC%2BEnglish.pdf.

Owen, David, and Tully, James 2007. 'Redistribution and Recognition: Two Approaches.' In Laden, A. S., and Owen, D. (eds). *Multiculturalism and Political Theory*, 265–292. Cambridge: Cambridge University Press.

Oxfam. 2020. 'Small Group of Rich Nations Have Bought Up More Than Half the Future Supply of Leading COVID-19 Vaccine Contenders.' *Oxfam Press Releases*, 17 September. www.oxfam.org/en/press-releases/small-group-rich-nations-have-bought-more-half-future-supply-leading-covid-19.

Oxford Institute for Ethics, Law and Armed Conflict. n.d. 'Anchoring Accountability for Mass Atrocities: A Project to Research and Advise on the Permanent Support Needed to Fulfil International Investigative mandates.' www.elac.ox.ac.uk/research/anchoring-accountability-for-mass-atrocities/.

Paffenholz, Thania, Ross, Nick, Dixon, Steven, Shluchter, Anna-Lena, and True, Jacqui 2016. *Making Women Count – Not Just Counting Women*. New York: Inclusive Peace and Transition Initiative and UN Women.

Pahuja, Sundhya 2011. *Decolonising International Law: Development, Economic Growth and the Politics of Universality*. Cambridge: Cambridge University Press.

Panebianco, Stefania 2016. 'The Mediterranean Migration Crisis: Border Control versus Humanitarian Approaches.' *Global Affairs* 2(4): 441–445.

Panke, Diana, and Petersohn, Ulrich 2012. 'Why International Norms Disappear Sometimes.' *European Journal of International Relations* 18(4): 719–742.

2016. 'Norm Challenges and Norm Death: The Inexplicable?' *Cooperation and Conflict* 51: 3–19.

2017. 'President Donald J. Trump: An Agent of Norm Death?' *International Journal* 72(4): 572–579. https://doi.org/10.1177/0020702017740159.

Pantzerhielm, Laura, Holzscheiter, Anna, and Bahr, Thurid 2022. 'Governing Effectively in a Complex World? How Metagovernance Norms and Changing Repertoires of Knowledge Shape International Organization Discourses on Institutional Order in Global Health.' *Cambridge Review of International Affairs* 35(4): 592–617. https://doi.org/10.1080/09557571.2019.1678112.

Papanicolopulu, Irini 2016. 'The Duty to Rescue at Sea, in Peacetime and in War: A General Overview.' *International Review of the Red Cross* 98(2): 491–514.

Pappas, Gregory F. 2012. 'What Would John Dewey Say about Deliberative Democracy and Democratic Experimentalism?' *Contemporary Pragmatism* 9(2): 57–74.

Paris, Roland 2020. 'The Right to Dominate: How Old Ideas about Sovereignty Pose New Challenges for World Order.' *International Organization* 74(3): 453–489. https://doi.org/10.1017/S0020818320000077.

Park, Susan 2010. *The World Bank Group and Environmentalists: Changing International Organisation Identities*. London: Manchester University Press.

2017. 'Accountability as Justice for the Multilateral Development Banks? Borrower Opposition and Bank Avoidance to US Power and Influence.' *Review of International Political Economy* 24(5): 776–801.

2020. *Environmental Recourse at the Multilateral Development Banks*. Cambridge: Cambridge University Press.

2022. *The Good Hegemon: United States Power, Accountability as Justice, and the Multilateral Development Banks*. Oxford: Oxford University Press.

Park, Susan, and Vetterlein, Antje 2010. *Owning Development: Creating Policy Norms in the IMF and the World Bank*. Cambridge: Cambridge University Press.

Parker, Christine, and Braithwaite, John 2005. 'Regulation.' In Tushnet, M., and Cane, P. (eds). *The Oxford Handbook of Legal Studies*, 119–145. Oxford: Oxford University Press.

Parker, Christine, Scott, Colin, Lacey, Nicola, and Braithwaite, John 2004. 'Introduction.' In Parker, C., Scott, C., Lacey, N., and Braithwaite, J. (eds). *Regulating Law*, 1–12. Oxford: Oxford University Press.

Parnini, Syeda N. 2013. 'The Crisis of the Rohingya as a Muslim Minority in Myanmar and Bilateral Relations with Bangladesh.' *Journal of Muslim Minority Affairs* 33(2): 281–297.

Passoni, C., Rosenbaum, A., and Vermunt, E. 2016. *Empowering the Inspection Panel: The Impact of the World Bank's Safeguards Review*. Report, New York University School of Law. www.iilj.org/publications/empowering-the-inspection-panel/.

Paul, Kathleen 1997. *Whitewashing Britain: Race and Citizenship in the Postwar Era*. Ithaca: Cornell University Press.

Paul, T. V., Larson, Deborah W., and Wohlforth, William C. (eds). 2014. *Status in World Politics*. New York: Cambridge University Press.

Pauwelyn, Jost 2003. *Conflict of Norms in Public International Law. How WTO Law Relates to other Rules of International Law*. Cambridge: Cambridge University Press.

Paxton, Pamela, Hughes, Melanie M., and Green, Jennifer L. 2006. 'The International Women's Movement and Women's Political Representation, 1893–2003.' *American Sociological Review* 71(6): 893–920.

Payne, Rodger A. 2001. 'Persuasion, Frames and Norm Construction.' *European Journal of International Relations* 7(1): 37–61.

Peel, Jacqueline 2010. *Science and Risk Regulation in International Law*. Cambridge: Cambridge University Press.

Peel, Jacqueline, and Lin, Jolene 2019. 'Transnational Climate Litigation: The Contribution of the Global South.' *American Journal of International Law* 113(4): 679–726.

Peel, Jacqueline, and Osofsky, Hari M. 2020. 'Climate Change Litigation.' *Annual Review of Law and Social Science* 16: 21–38.

Peirce, Charles S. 1877. 'The Fixation of Belief.' *Popular Science Monthly* 12: 1–15. www.peirce.org/writings/p107.html.

1878. 'How to Make Our Ideas Clear.' *Popular Science Monthly*, January, 286–302. https://courses.media.mit.edu/2004spring/mas966/Peirce%201878%20Make%20Ideas%20Clear.pdf.

Peltner, Anne 2017. 'Competing Norms and Foreign Policy Change: Humanitarian Intervention and British Foreign Policy.' *International Politics* 54(6): 745–759.

Percy, Sarah 2007. *Mercenaries: The History of a Norm in International Relations*. Oxford: Oxford University Press.

2019. 'What Makes a Norm Robust: The Norm Against Female Combat.' *Journal of Global Security Studies* 4(1): 123–138.

Percy, Sarah, and Sandholtz, Wayne 2022. 'Why Norms Rarely Die.' *European Journal of International Relations*, September, Online First. https://doi.org/10.1177/13540661221126018.

Petrova, Margarita H. 2019. 'Naming and Praising in Humanitarian Norm Development.' *World Politics* 71(3): 586–630. https://doi.org/10.1017/s004388711800031X.

Pienaar, Sara 1987. *South Africa and International Relations between the Two World Wars*. Johannesburg: Witwatersrand University Press.

Polanyi, Karl 1957. *The Great Transformation*. New York: Rinehart.

Ponthieu, Aurélie 2016. 'Bounties not Bodies: Smugglers Profit from Sea Rescues Though No Clear Alternative Available.' *MSF Analysis*. https://msf-analysis.org/bounties-not-bodies-smugglers-profit-sea-rescues-though-no-clear-alternative-available/.

Posner, Richard A. 2003. *Law, Pragmatism and Democracy*. Cambridge, MA: Harvard University Press.

Power, Samantha 2016. 'Remarks at a UN Security Council Emergency Briefing on Syria.' 13 December. https://usun.state.gov/remarks/7607.

Pramendorfer, Elisabeth 2020. 'The Role of the Human Rights Council in Implementing the Responsibility to Protect.' *Global Responsibility to Protect* 12(3): 239–245.

Prantl, Jochen, and Nakano, Ryoko 2011. 'Global Norm Diffusion in East Asia: How China and Japan Implement the Responsibility to Protect.' *International Relations* 25(2): 204–223. https://doi.org/10.1177/0047117811404450.

Pratt, Simon F. 2018. 'Norm Transformation and the Institutionalization of Targeted Killing in the US.' *European Journal of International Relations* 25(3): 1–25. https://doi.org/10.1177/1354066118812178.

2020. 'From Norms to Normative Configurations: A Pragmatist and Relational Approach to Theorizing Normativity in IR.' *International Theory* 12(1): 59–82.

President of Russia. 2014. *Address by President of the Russian Federation*. http://en.kremlin.ru/events/president/news/20603.

Price, Richard M. 1997. *The Chemical Weapons Taboo*. Ithaca: Cornell University Press.

1998. 'Reversing the Gun Sights: Transnational Civil Society Targets Land Mines.' *International Organization* 52(3): 613–644.

2006. 'Detecting Ideas and Their Effects.' In Goodin, R. E., and Tilly, C. (eds). *The Oxford Handbook of Contextual Political Analysis*, 252–265. Oxford: Oxford University Press.

(ed). 2008. *Moral Limit and Possibility in World Politics*. New York: Cambridge University Press.

Price, Richard M., and Reus-Smit, Christian 1998. 'Dangerous Liaisons?: Critical International Theory and Constructivism.' *European Journal of International Relations* 4(3): 259–294.

Price, Richard M., and Sikkink, Kathryn 2017. 'From Micro to Neuro: Implications of Neuroscience and Moral Psychology for Research on International Norms.' *Memo for ISA Workshop 'Taking Stock of the Past to Shape the Future of Norm Studies.'* Baltimore, 21 February.

2021. *International Norms, Moral Psychology, and Neuroscience.* Cambridge: Cambridge University Press.
Price, Richard M., and Tannenwald, Nina 1996. 'Norms and Deterrence: The Nuclear and Chemical Weapons Taboos.' In Katzenstein, P. (ed). *The Culture of National Security: Norms and Identity in World Politics*, 114–152. New York: Columbia University Press.
Priest, Dana, and Gellman, Barton 2002. 'US Decries Abuse but Defends Interrogations.' *The Washington Post*, 26 December.
ProAsyl. 2013. 'Pushed Back: Systematische Menschenrechtsverletzungen an den griechisch- türkischen See- und Landgrenzen.' www.proasyl.de/wp-content/uploads/2013/11/Summary_Faelle_Deutsch_Pushed_Back.pdf.
Putnam, Hilary 2004. *Ethics without Ontology.* Cambridge, MA: Harvard University Press, 2004.
Quirk, Joel 2011. *The Anti-Slavery Project: From the Slave Trade to Human Trafficking.* Philadelphia: University of Pennsylvania Press.
Quirk, Joel, and Vigneswaran, Darshan 2015. 'Mobility Makes States.' In Vigneswaran, D., and Quirk, J. (eds). *Mobility Makes States: Migration and Power in Africa*, 1–34. Philadelphia: University of Pennsylvania Press.
Rajkovic, Nikolas, Aalberts, Tanja, and Gammeltoft-Hansen, Thomas 2016. 'Introduction: Legality, Interdisciplinarity, and the Study of Practices.' In Rajkovic, N., Aalberts, T., and Gammeltoft-Hansen, T. (eds). *The Power of Legality: Practices of International Law and Their Politics*, 1–25. New York: Cambridge University Press.
Ralph, Jason 2013. *America's War on Terror: The State of the American Exception from Bush to Obama.* Oxford: Oxford University Press.
2018. 'What Should Be Done? Pragmatic Constructivist Ethics and the Responsibility to Protect.' *International Organization* 72(1): 173–203.
2023. *On Global Learning. Pragmatic Constructivism, International Practice and the Challenge of Global Governance.* Cambridge: Cambridge University Press.
Ramirez, Bruno 2001. *Crossing the 49th Parallel: Migration from Canada to the United States, 1900–1930.* Ithaca: Cornell University Press.
Ramos, Jennifer M. 2013. *Changing Norms through Actions: The Evolution of Sovereignty.* New York: Oxford University Press.
Rapp, Stephen J. 2016. 'Bridging the Hague-Geneva Divide.' *Intersections.* Autumn/Winter: 11–13.
Ratti, Giovanni B. 2015. 'Negation in Legislation.' In Araszkiewicz, M., and Pleszka, K. (eds). *Logic in the Theory and Practice of Lawmaking*, 137–157. Cham: Springer.
Raustiala, Kal 2000. 'Compliance & Effectiveness in International Regulatory Cooperation.' *Case Western Reserve Journal of International Law* 32(3): 387–440.
Raustiala, Kal, and Victor, David G. 2004, 'The Regime Complex for Plant Genetic Resources.' *International Organization* 58(2): 277–309.
Razzaque, J. 2019 'A Stock-Taking of FPIC Standards in International Environmental Law.' In Turner, S., Shelton, D., Razzaque, J., McIntyre, O., and May, J. (eds). *Environmental Rights: The Development of Standards*, 195–221. Cambridge: Cambridge University Press.

Rees, Jonas H., Allpress, Jesse A., and Brown, Rupert 2013. 'Nie Wieder: Group-Based Emotions for In-Group Wrongdoing Affect Attitudes toward Unrelated Minorities: Never Again.' *Political Psychology* 34(3): 387–407.

Reike, Ruben, Sharma, Serena K., and Welsh, Jennifer M. 2015. 'Conceptualizing the Responsibility to Prevent.' In Sharma, S. K., and Welsh, J. M. (eds). *The Responsibility to Prevent: Overcoming the Challenges of Atrocity Prevention*, 21–37. Oxford: Oxford University Press.

Reiling, Carrie 2017. 'Pragmatic Scepticism in Implementing the Women, Peace and Security Agenda.' *Global Affairs* 3(4–5): 469–481.

Reiners, Nina 2022. *Transnational Lawmaking Coalitions for Human Rights*. Cambridge: Cambridge University Press.

Reinold, Theresa, 2023. 'The Prohibition on the Use of Force and its Justifications: Plus ca Change?' In Krieger, H., and Liese, A. (eds). *Tracing Value Change in the International Legal Order: Perspectives from Legal and Political Science*, 136–152. Oxford: Oxford University Press.

Reuters. 2021. 'Belarus Points to Hamas Bomb Threat in Plane Diversion, Hamas Rejects Claim.' 25 May. www.reuters.com/world/europe/belarus-points-hamas-bomb-threat-plane-diversion-hamas-rejects-claim-2021-05-24/.

2023. 'Norway Proposes 40% Gender Quota for Large and Mid-size Unlisted Firms.' 19 June. www.reuters.com/markets/europe/norwayproposes-40-gender-quota-large-mid-size-unlisted-firms-2023-06-19/.

Reus-Smit, Christian 2001. 'Human Rights and the Social Construction of Sovereignty.' *Review of International Studies* 27(4): 519–538.

2011. 'Struggles for Individual Rights and the Expansion of the International System.' *International Organization* 65(2): 207–242.

Rhoads, Emily Paddon 2016. *Taking Sides in Peacekeeping: Impartiality and the Future of the United Nations*. Oxford: Oxford University Press.

Rhoads, Emily Paddon, and Welsh, Jennifer 2019. 'Close Cousins in Protection: The Evolution of Two Norms.' *International Affairs* 95(3): 597–617.

Rice, Condoleezza 2008. 'U.S. Recognizes Kosovo as Independent State.' https://2001-2009.state.gov/secretary/rm/2008/02/100973.htm.

Rich, Bruce 1994. *Mortgaging the Earth: The World Bank, Environmental Impoverishment and the Crisis of Development*. Boston: Beacon Press.

Rich, Frank 2007. 'The "Good Germans" Among Us.' *Der Spiegel*, 15 October. www.spiegel.de/international/frank-rich-the-good-germans-among-us-a-511459.html.

Riis Andersen, Louise 2018. 'The HIPPO in the Room: The Pragmatic Push-Back from the UN Peace Bureaucracy against the Militarization of UN Peacekeeping.' *International Affairs* 94(2): 343–361.

Risse, Thomas 2000. '"Let's Argue!": Communicative Action in World Politics.' *International Organization* 51(1): 1–39.

Risse, Thomas, and Sikkink, Kathryn 1999. 'The Socialization of International Human Rights into Domestic Practices: Introduction.' In Risse, T., Ropp, Stephen C., and Sikkink, K. (eds). *The Power of Human Rights: International Norms and Domestic Change*, 1–38. Cambridge: Cambridge University Press.

Risse, Thomas, Ropp, Stephen C., and Sikkink, Kathryn (eds). 1999. *The Power of Human Rights. International Norms and Domestic Change*. Cambridge: Cambridge University Press.

2013. *The Persistent Power of Human Rights: From Commitment to Compliance.* Cambridge: Cambridge University Press.

Rivas, Althea-Marai, and Safi, Mariam 2022. 'Women and the Afghan Peace and Reintegration Process.' *International Affairs* 98(1): 85–104.

Roberts, Anthea 2017. *Is International Law International?* Oxford: Oxford University Press.

Rogers, Melvin L. 2009. 'Dewey, Pluralism, and Democracy: A Response to Robert Talisse.' *Transactions of the Charles S. Peirce Society* 45(1): 75–79.

Roht-Arriaza, Naomi 2006. *The Pinochet Effect: Transitional Justice in the Age of Human Rights*. Philadelphia: University of Pennsylvania Press.

Roosevelt, Eleanor 1948. 'On the Adoption of the Universal Declaration of Human Rights.' Speech Delivered 9 December, Paris, France. www.americanrhetoric.com/speeches/eleanorrooseveltdeclarationhumanrights.htm.

Rosenne, Shabtai, (ed). 1975. *League of Nations Conference for the Codification of International Law (1930)*. Dobbs Ferry: Oceana Publications.

Rosenthal, Uriel, Charles, Michael T., and T'Hart, Paul 1989. *Coping with Crises. The Management of Disasters, Riots and Terrorism.* Springfield: Charles C Thomas Publishers.

Rosert, Elvira 2019. 'Norm Emergence as Agenda Diffusion: Failure and Success in the Regulation of Cluster Munitions.' *European Journal of International Relations* 25(4): 1–29. https://doi.org/10.1177/1354066119842644.

Ross, Andrew A. G. 2006. 'Coming in from the Cold: Constructivism and Emotions.' *European Journal of International Relations* 12(2): 197–222.

2014. *Mixed Emotions: Beyond Fear and Hatred in International Conflict.* Chicago: University of Chicago Press.

Ross, Alf 2019. *On Law and Justice*, Holtermann, Jakob v. H. (ed.), Bindreiter, U. (trans.). Oxford: Oxford University Press.

Rousseau, Elise 2018. 'Power, Mechanisms, and Denunciations: Understanding Compliance with Human Rights in International Relations.' *Political Studies Review* 16(4): 318–330.

Ruggie, John G. 1982. 'International Regimes, Transactions, and Change: Embedded Liberalism in the Postwar Economic Order.' *International Organization* 36(2): 379–415. https://doi.org/10.1017/S0020818300018993.

1983. 'Human Rights and the Future International Community.' *Daedalus* 112(4): 93–110.

1993. 'Territoriality and Beyond: Problematizing Modernity in International Relations.' *International Organization* 47(1): 139–174.

2004. 'Reconstituting the Global Public Domain – Issues, Actors, and Practices.' *European Journal of International Relations* 10(4): 499–531.

Ruhl, Christian, Hollis, Duncan, Hoffman, Wyatt, and Maurer, Tim 2020. 'Cyberspace and Geopolitics: Assessing Global Cybersecurity Norm Processes at a Crossroads.' *Carnegie Endowment for International Peace.* https://carnegieendowment.org/2020/02/26/cyberspace-and-geopolitics-assessing-global-cybersecurity-norm-processes-at-crossroads-pub-81110.

Rüland, Anchalee 2018. 'Norms in Conflict: An Analysis of State Responses to Norm Conflict in Southeast Asia.' Ph.D. dissertation. Florence: European University Institute.

2022. *Norms in Conflict: Southeast Asia's Response to Human Rights Violations in Myanmar.* Lexington: The University Press of Kentucky.

Rüland, Anchalee, and Welsh, Jennifer M. 2024. 'Understanding and Resolving Norm Conflict.' In Orchard, P., and Wiener, A. (eds). *Contesting the World. Norm Research in Theory and Practice*, 43–63. Cambridge: Cambridge University Press.

Safety4Sea. 2019. 'Migrant Rescue Vessel Denied Access to EU Ports.' https://safety4sea.com/migrant-rescue-vessel-denied-access-to-eu-ports/.

Salter, Mark 2003. *Rights of Passage: The Passport in International Relations*. Boulder: Lynne Rienner Publishers.

Saltnes, Johanne D. 2019. 'Resistance to EU Integration? Norm Collision in the Coordination of Development Aid.' *Journal of European Integration* 41(4): 525–541.

Sanders, Rebecca 2011. '(Im)plausible Legality: The Rationalisation of Human Rights Abuses in the American "Global War on Terror".' *International Journal of Human Rights* 15(4): 605–626.

Sandholtz, Wayne 2007. *Prohibiting Plunder: How Norms Change*. Oxford: Oxford University Press.

2008. 'Dynamics of International Norm Change: Rules against Wartime Plunder.' *European Journal of International Relations* 14(1): 101–131.

2009. 'Explaining International Norm Change.' In Sandtholz, W., and Stiles, K. (eds). *International Norms and Cycles of Change*, 1–18. Oxford: Oxford University Press.

2016. 'The Multiple Paths to Norm Replacement.' Paper presented to the International Studies Association meeting, Atlanta, Georgia.

2017a. 'Domestic Law and Human Rights Treaty Commitments: The Convention against Torture.' *Journal of Human Rights* 16(1): 25–43.

2017b. 'International Norm Change.' In *Oxford Research Encyclopedia of Politics*. Oxford: Oxford University Press. https://oxfordre.com/politics/view/10.1093/acrefore/9780190228637.001.0001/acrefore-9780190228637-e-588.

2019. 'Norm Contestation, Robustness, and Replacement.' *Journal of Global Security Studies* 4(1): 139–146.

Sandholtz, Wayne, and Stiles, Kendall 2009. *International Norms and Cycles of Change*. Oxford and New York: Oxford University Press.

Sarfaty, Galit A. 2009. 'Why Culture Matters in International Institutions: The Marginality of Human Rights at the World Bank.' *American Journal of International Law* 103: 647–683.

2012. *Values in Translation: Human Rights and the Culture of the World Bank*. Stanford: Stanford University Press.

Sawer, Marian, and Grey, Sandra L. (eds). 2009. *Women's Movements: Flourishing or in Abeyance?* New York: Routledge.

Sawer, Marian, Banaszak, Lee A., Kantola, Johanna, and True, Jacqui 2023. *Handbook of Feminist Governance*. London: Edward Elgar Publishers.

Sawyer, Keith R. 2005. *Social Emergence: Societies as Complex Systems*. Cambridge: Cambridge University Press.

Schachter, Oscar 1977. 'The Invisible College of International Lawyers.' *Northwestern University Law Review* 72(2): 217–226.

Schenkkan, Nate, and Linzer, Isabel 2021. 'Out of Sight, Not Out of Reach: The Global Scale and Scope of Transnational Repression.' *Freedom House Report*. Washington, DC: Freedom House.

Schimmelfennig, Frank 2001. 'The Community Trap: Liberal Norms, Rhetorical Action, and the Eastern Enlargement of the European Union.' *International Organization* 55(1): 47–80.

Schmidt, Averell, and Sikkink, Kathryn 2019. 'Breaking the Ban? The Heterogeneous Impact of US Contestation of the Torture Norm.' *Journal of Global Security Studies* 4(1): 105–122. https://doi.org/10.1093/jogss/ogy036.

Schmidt, Dennis R. 2021. 'Complexity in International Society: Theorising Fragmentation and Linkages in Primary and Secondary Institutions.' *Complexity, Governance & Networks* 6(1): 94. https://doi.org/10.20377/cgn-105.

Schmidt, Sebastian 2014. 'Foreign Military Presence and the Changing Practice of Sovereignty: A Pragmatist Explanation of Norm Change.' *American Political Science Review* 108(4): 817–829. https://doi.org/10.1017/S0003055414000434.

Schneiker, Andrea 2020. 'Norm Sabotage: Conceptual Reflection on a Phenomenon That Challenges Well-Established Norms.' *International Studies Perspectives* 22(1): 1–18. https://doi.org/10.1093/isp/ekaa003.

Schrijver, Nico 2010. *Development with Destruction: The UN and Global Resource Management.* Bloomington: Indiana University Press.

Schrover, Marlou, and Moloney, Deirdre M. 2013. *Gender, Migration and Categorization: Mapping Distinctions between Migrants in Western Countries, 1945–2010.* Amsterdam: University of Amsterdam Press.

Scott, Shirley 2017. *International Law in World Politics: An Introduction.* 3rd edn. Boulder: Lynne Riener Publishers.

Searle, John R. 1995. *The Construction of Social Reality.* New York: Simon & Schuster.

Seidman, Gay W. 2000. 'Adjusting the Lens: What Do Globalizations, Transnationalism, and the Anti-Apartheid Movement Mean for Social Movement Theory?' In Guidry, J., Kennedy, M., and Mayer, Z. (eds). *Globalizations and Social Movements: Culture, Power, and the Transnational Public Sphere*, 339–357. Ann Arbor: University of Michigan Press.

Sending, Ole J. 2016. 'Agency, Order, and Heteronomy.' *European Review of International Studies* 3(3): 63–75.

Setzer, Joana, and Vanhala, Lisa C. 2019. 'Climate Change Litigation: A Review of Research on Courts and Litigants in Climate Governance.' *Wiley Interdisciplinary Reviews on Climate Change* 10(3): 1–19.

Shaffer, Gregory C., and Ginsburg, Tom 2012. 'The Empirical Turn in International Legal Scholarship.' *American Journal of International Law* 106(1): 1–46.

Shaffer, Gregoy C., and Pollack, Mark A. 2013. 'Hard and Soft Law.' In Dunoff, J. L., and Pollack, M. A. (eds). *Interdisciplinary Perspectives on International Law and International Relations: The State of the Art*, 197–222. Cambridge: Cambridge University Press.

Shalin, Dmitri N. 1992. 'Critical Theory and the Pragmatist Challenge.' *American Journal of Sociology* 98(2): 237–279.

Shiffman, Jeremy 2014. 'Knowledge, Moral Claims and the Exercise of Power in Global Health.' *International Journal of Health Policy and Management* 3(6): 297–299.

Sieber, Ulrich 2010. 'Legal Order in a Global World – The Development of a Fragmented System of National, International, and Private Norms.' In Max Planck Institute for Peace and the Rule of Law (ed). *Max Planck Yearbook of United Nations Law 14*, 1–49. London: Brill.

Sienknecht, Mitja 2021a. 'Rebel with a Cause – Rebel Responsibility in Intrastate Conflict Situations.' In Hansen-Magnusson, H., and Vetterlein, A. (eds). *The Routledge Handbook on Responsibility in International Relations*, 1–22. London: Routledge.

2021b. 'The PKK's Zig-Zag in Its Global Quest for Recognition.' In Geis, A., Clément, M., and Pfeiffer, H. (eds). *Armed Non-State Actors and the Politics of Recognition*, 109–129. Manchester: Manchester University Press.

Sienknecht, Mitja, and Vetterlein, Antje 2022. *Conceptualizing Responsibility(-gaps) in World Politics*. Manuscript under review, on file with the authors.

Sikkink, Kathryn 1993. 'Human Rights, Principled Issue-Networks, and Sovereignty in Latin America.' *International Organization* 47(3): 411–441.

2011. *The Justice Cascade: How Human Rights Prosecutions are Changing World Politics*. New York: W.W. Norton.

2013. 'The United States and Torture.' In Risse, T., Ropp, S. C., and Sikkink, Kathryn. (eds). *The Power of Human Rights: International Norms and Domestic Change*, 145–163. Cambridge: Cambridge University Press.

Sikkink, Kathryn, and Kim, Hun J. 2013. 'The Justice Cascade: The Origins and Effectiveness of Prosecutions of Human Rights Violations.' *Annual Review of Law and Social Science* 9(1): 269–285. https://doi.org/10.1146/annurev-lawsocsci-102612-133956.

Simmons, Beth A. 2009. *Mobilizing for Human Rights: International Law in Domestic Politics*. Cambridge: Cambridge University Press.

Simmons, Beth A., and Jo, Hyeran 2019. 'Measuring Norms and Normative Contestation: The Case of International Criminal Law.' *Journal of Global Security Studies* 4(1): 18–36. https://doi.org/10.1093/jogss/ogy043.

Skogly, Sigrun I. 2001. *The Human Rights Obligations of the World Bank and the International Monetary Fund*. London: Cavendish Publishing.

Sluga, Glenda 2013. *Internationalism in the Age of Nationalism*. Philadelphia: University of Pennsylvania Press.

Sluga, Glenda, and James, Carolyn (eds). 2015. *Women, Diplomacy and International Politics Since 1500*. Oxon: Routledge.

Smith, Karen E. 2010. *Genocide and the Europeans*. New York: Cambridge University Press.

Somer, Jonathan 2015. 'Non-State Armed Groups Continue to Cause Environmental Damage in Conflicts, yet States are Reluctant to Meaningfully Address their Conduct for Fear of Granting them Legitimacy.' *CEOBS Blog*, 4 December. https://ceobs.org/environmental-protection-and-non-state-armed-groups-setting-a-place-at-the-table-for-the-elephant-in-the-room/.

Sondermann, Elena, Ulbert, Cornelia, and Finkenbusch, Peter 2018. 'Introduction: Moral Agency and the Politics of Responsibility.' In Ulbert, C., Finkenbusch, P., Sondermann, E., and Debiel, T. (eds). *Moral Agency and the Politics of Responsibility*, 1–18. London: Routledge.

Stappert, Nora 2018. 'A New Influence of Legal Scholars? The Use of Academic Writings at International Criminal Courts and Tribunals.' *Leiden Journal of International Law* 31(4): 963–980.

2020. 'Practice Theory and Change in International Law: Theorizing the Development of Legal Meaning through the Interpretive Practices of International Criminal Courts.' *International Theory* 12(1): 33–58.

Staunton, Eglantine, and Ralph, Jason 2020. 'The Responsibility to Protect Norm Cluster and the Challenge of Atrocity Prevention: An Analysis of the European Union's Strategy in Myanmar.' *European Journal of International Relations* 26: 660–686.

Steinbrook, Robert 2020. 'A US Election Victory for Science and Public Health.' *British Medical Journal* 10 November: 371.

Stevenson, Hayley 2013. *Institutionalizing Unsustainability: The Paradox of Global Climate Change*. Berkeley: University of California Press.

Stimmer, Anette 2019a. 'Beyond Internalization: Alternate Endings of the Norm Life Cycle.' *International Studies Quarterly* 63(2): 270–280.

Forthcoming. 'Norm Contestation and Change in International Politics.' Cambridge: Cambridge University Press.

2024. 'The Interaction of Law and Politics in Norm Interpretation.' In Orchard, P., and Wiener, A. (eds). *Contesting the World: Norm Research in Theory and Practice*, 164–181. Cambridge: Cambridge University Press.

Stimmer, Anette, and Wisken, Lea 2019. 'The Dynamics of Dissent: When Actions are Louder than Words.' *International Affairs* 95(3): 515–533.

Stone, Deane, and Moloney, Kim (eds). 2019. *The Oxford Handbook of Global Policy and Transnational Administration*. Oxford: Oxford University Press.

Stone, Laurel 2015. 'Quantitative Analysis of Women's Participation in Peace Processes.' In O'Reilly, M., Ó Suilleabhan, A., and Paffenholz, T. (eds). *Reimagining Peacemaking: Women's Roles in Peace Processes*, 34, Annex II. Washington, DC: Institute for International Peace.

Strand, Vibeke B. 2019. 'Interpreting the ECHR in Its Normative Environment: Interaction between the ECHR, the UN Convention on the Elimination of All Forms of Discrimination against Women and the UN Convention on the Rights of the Child.' *The International Journal of Human Rights* 24(7): 979–992. https://doi.org/10.1080/13642987.2019.1574423.

Strezhnev, Anton, Kelley, Judith G., and Simmons, Beth A. 2021. 'Testing for Negative Spillovers: Is Promoting Human Rights Really Part of the "Problem"?' *International Organization* 75(1): 71–102.

Study Group of the International Law Commission. 2006. 'Fragmentation of International Law: Difficulties Arising from the Diversification and Expansion of International Law.' *Report of the Study Group of the International Law Commission*, finalised by Koskenniumi, M. 13 April, Geneva. https://legal.un.org/ilc/documentation/english/a_cn4_l702.pdf.

Subotic, Jelena 2017. 'Constructivism as Professional Practice in the US Academy.' *PS: Political Science & Politics* 50(1): 84–88.

Subotic, Jelena, and Zarakol, Ayşe 2013. 'Cultural Intimacy in International Relations.' *European Journal of International Relations* 19(4): 915–938.

Suchman, Mark C. 1995. 'Managing Legitimacy: Strategic and Institutional Approaches.' *Academy of Management Review* 20(3): 571–610.

Sullivan, Michael, and Solove, Daniel J. 2013. 'Radical Pragmatism.' In Malachowski, A. (ed). *The Cambridge Companion to Pragmatism*, 324–344. Cambridge: Cambridge University Press.

Susskind, Yifat, and Duarte, Diana 2019. 'Networked Advocacy.' In Davies, S. E., and True, J. (eds). *The Oxford Handbook of Women, Peace, and Security*, 792–802. New York: Oxford University Press.

Suzuki, Shogi 2009. *Civilization and Empire. China and Japan's Encounter with European International Society*. London: Routledge.

Taguba, Antonio M. 2004. 'Article 15-6 Investigation of the 800th Military Police Brigade.' *Federation of American Scientists* (FAS). https://fas.org/irp/agency/dod/taguba.pdf.

Talisse, Robert 2007. *A Pragmatist Philosophy of Democracy*. New York: Routledge.

Tallberg, Jonas and Zürn, Michael 2019. 'The Legitimacy and Legitimation of International Organizations: Introduction and Framework.' *The Review of International Organizations* 14(4): 581–606.

Tannenwald, Nina 1999. 'The Nuclear Taboo: The United States and the Normative Basis of Nuclear Non-use.' *International Organization* 53(3): 433–468.

2005. 'Stigmatizing the Bomb: Origins of the Nuclear Taboo.' *International Security* 29(4): 5–49.

Tarrow, Sidney G. 2005. *The New Transnational Activism*. Cambridge: Cambridge University Press.

TASS. 'Russia Supports ICAO's Investigation into Incident with Ryanair Flight.' 28 May. https://tass.com/politics/1295055.

Taylor, Sarah 2019. 'Advocacy and the Women, Peace and Security Agenda.' In Davies, S. E., and True, J. (eds). *The Oxford Handbook of Women, Peace, and Security*. New York: Oxford University Press.

Teitel, Ruti G. 2000. *Transitional Justice*. Oxford: Oxford University Press.

2011. *Humanity's Law*. Oxford: Oxford University Press.

Terman, Rochelle 2020. 'The Positive Side of Negative Identity: Stigma and Deviance in Backlash Movements.' *The British Journal of Politics and International Relations* 22(4): 619–630.

Terman, Rochelle, and Voeten, Erik 2018. 'The Relational Politics of Shame: Evidence from the Universal Periodic Review.' *The Review of International Organizations* 13(1): 1–23.

The Atlantic. 2007. 'Verschärfte Vernehmung.' 29 May. www.theatlantic.com/daily-dish/archive/2007/05/-versch-auml-rfte-vernehmung/228158/.

The Moscow Times. 2021. 'Lukashenko Defends "Legal" Plane Diversion to Belarus, Kremlin Backs Him.' 26 May. www.themoscowtimes.com/2021/05/26/lukashenko-defends-legal-plane-diversion-to-belarus-kremlin-backs-him-a74013.

The New York Times. 2020. 'City of Paris Fined Nearly $110,000 for Appointing Too Many Women.' 16 December. www.nytimes.com/2020/12/16/world/europe/paris-too-many-women-fine.html.

The White House. 2021. 'Statement by President Joe Biden on Diversion of Ryanair Flight and Arrest of Journalist in Belarus.' 24 May.

www.whitehouse.gov/briefing-room/statements-releases/2021/05/24/statement-by-president-joe-biden-on-diversion-of-ryanair-flight-and-arrest-of-journalist-in-belarus/.

Thoits, Peggy A. 2004. 'Emotion Norms, Emotion Work, and Social Order.' In Manstead, A. S. R., Frijda, N., and Fischer, A. (eds). *Feelings and Emotions. The Amsterdam Symposium*, 359–378. Cambridge: Cambridge University Press.

Thomas, Daniel C. 2001. *The Helsinki Effect: International Norms, Human Rights, and the Demise of Communism*. Princeton: Princeton University Press.

Thompson, B. 2017. 'Determining Criteria to Evaluate Outcomes of Businesses' Provision of Remedy: Applying a Human Rights-Based Approach.' *Business and Human Rights Journal* 2: 55–85.

Thörn, Håkan 2006. *Anti-Apartheid and the Emergence of a Global Civil Society*. Basingstoke: Palgrave Macmillan.

Tickner, Ann J., and True, Jacqui 2018. 'A Century of International Relations Feminism: From World War I Women's Peace Pragmatism to the Women, Peace and Security Agenda.' *International Studies Quarterly* 62(2): 221–233.

2002. *Stories, Identities and Political Change*. Lanham: Rowman and Littlefield.

Tomz, Michael 2007. *Reputation and International Cooperation*. Princeton: Princeton University Press.

Tooze, Adam 2023. 'This is Why "Polycrisis" is a Useful Way of Looking at the World Right Now.' Interview with Radio Davos, 15 February. Transcript published in World Economic Forum 2023. *Global Health*, 7 March. www.weforum.org/agenda/2023/03/polycrisis-adam-tooze-historian-explains/.

Torpey, John 1998. 'Coming and Going: On the State Monopolization of the Legitimate "Means of Movement".' *Sociological Theory* 16(3): 239–259.

True, Jacqui 2016. 'Explaining the Global Diffusion of the Women, Peace and Security Agenda.' *International Political Science Review* 37(3): 307–323.

2017. 'Ending Violence against Women in Asia: International Norm Diffusion and Global Opportunity Structures for Policy Change.' *UNRISD Working Paper*.

2020. 'Explaining the Global Diffusion of the Women, Peace and Security Agenda.' *International Political Science Review* 37(3): 307–323.

True, Jacqui, and Mintrom, Michael 2001. 'Transnational Networks and Policy Diffusion.' *International Studies Quarterly* 45(1): 27–57.

True, Jacqui, and Wiener, Antje 2019. 'Everyone Wants (a) Peace: The Dynamics of Rhetoric and Practice on "Women, Peace and Security".' *International Affairs* 95(3): 553–574.

True-Frost, Cora C. 2022. 'Listening to Dissonance at the Intersections of International Human Rights Law.' *Michigan Journal of International Law* 43(2): 361–421.

Tryggestad, Torunn L. 2009. 'Trick or Treat? The UN and Implementation of Security Council Resolution 1325 on Women, Peace and Security.' *Global Governance* 15(4): 539–557.

Tsebelis, George 2002. *Veto Players: How Political Institutions Work*. Princeton: Princeton University Press.

Tully, James 2002. 'The Unfreedom of the Moderns in Comparison to Their Ideals of Constitutional Democracy.' *The Modern Law Review* 65(2): 204–228.

Turner, Catherine 2019. '"Soft Ways of Doing Hard Things": Women Mediators and the Question of Gender in Mediation.' *Peacebuilding* 8(4): 383–401.

Turner, Stephen J., Shelton, Dinah L., Razzaque, Jona, McIntyre, Owen, and May, James R. (eds). 2019. *Environmental Rights: The Development of Standards*. Cambridge: Cambridge University Press.

Udall, L. 1997. *The World Bank Inspection Panel: A Three Year Review.* Washington, DC: Bank Information Center.

UN General Assembly. 1966. *International Covenant on Civil and Political Rights.* New York: United Nations.

1979. *Convention on the Elimination of All Forms of Discrimination against Women.* New York: United Nations. www.ohchr.org/sites/default/files/Documents/ProfessionalInterest/cedaw.pdf.

2006. *Human Rights Council: Resolution, adopted by the General Assembly.* A/RES/60/251. 3 April. Geneva: United Nations.

UN Women. 2015. *Preventing Conflict, Transforming Justice, Securing the Peace: A Global Study on the Implementation of United Nations Security Council Resolution 1325.* New York: UN Women.

2018. *Women's Meaningful Participation in Negotiating Peace and the Implementation of Peace Agreements: Report of the Expert Group Meeting.* New York: UN Women.

2021. *Beyond COVID-19: A Feminist Plan for Sustainability and Social Justice.* New York: UN Women.

UNHCR. 2015. 'Rescue at Sea: A Guide to Principles and Practices as Applied to Refugees and Migrants.' *UNHCR Brochures.* www.unhcr.org/publications/brochures/450037d34/rescue-sea-guide-principles-practice-applied-migrants-refugees.html.

UNHCR and IOM. 2019. 'UNHCR and IOM joint statement: International approach to refugees and migrants in Libya must change.' Geneva. www.unhcr.org/news/press/2019/7/5d2765d04/unhcr-iom-joint-statement-international-approach-refugees-migrants-libya.html.

Unifeed. 2021. 'UN/Russia Belarus Protasevich.' 28 May. www.unmultimedia.org/tv/unifeed/asset/2623/2623451/.

United Nations. 1946–7. *Yearbook of the United Nations.* New York: United Nations. www.un.org/en/yearbook.

1948. Universal Declaration of Human Rights, General Assembly Resolution 217A.

2000. *Protocol to Prevent, Suppress and Punish Trafficking in Persons, Especially Women and Children, Supplementing the United Nations Convention against Transnational Organized Crime.* New York: United Nations.

2005. 'Outcome Document of the 2005 World Summit.' 24 October. https://undocs.org/A/RES/60/1.

2012. 'Report of the Secretary-General's Internal Review Panel on United Nations Action in Sri Lanka.' https://digitallibrary.un.org/record/737299?ln=en.

2013. 'Human Rights due Diligence Policy on United Nations Support to Non-United Nations Security Forces.' A/67/775 – S/2013/110. 5 March. Geneva.

2014. 'Fulfilling Our Collective Responsibility: International Assistance and the Responsibility to Protect.' Report of the Secretary-General to the General Assembly, Sixty-eighth Session. A/68/947. 11 July. New York.

2015a. 'Human Rights Up Front: An Overview.' https://interagencystandingcommittee.org/system/files/overview_of_human_rights_up_front_july_2015.pdf.

2015b. 'Report of the Special Rapporteur on Extreme Poverty and Human Rights.' United Nations General Assembly 70th Session. A/70/274. www.un.org/en/ga/search/view_doc.asp?symbol=A/70/274.

2018. 'Report of the Special Rapporteur on the issue of human rights obligations relating to the enjoyment of a safe, clean, healthy, and sustainable environment.' United Nations General Assembly 73rd Session. A/73/188. https://undocs.org/A/73/188.

2022. 'Belarus Improperly Diverted Passenger Flight, Endangered Lives, International Civil Aviation Organization Senior Official Tells Security Council.' SC/15088. 31 October. https://press.un.org/en/2022/sc15088.doc.htm.

United Nations High Commissioner for Refugees (UNHCR). 2002. 'Background Note on the Protection of Asylum-Seekers and Refugees Rescued at Sea.' UNHCR.

United Nations Human Rights Council. 2015. 'The Role of Prevention in the Promotion and Prevention of Human Rights.' Report of the Office of the United Nations High Commissioner for Human Rights. A/HRC/30/20. 16 July. Geneva.

2019. 'Promotion of Truth, Justice, Reparation and Guarantees of Non-Recurrence: Report of the Special Rapporteur on the Promotion of Truth, Justice, Reparation and Guarantees of Non-Recurrence.' A/HRC/42/45. 11 July. Geneva.

2020. 'Overview of Consultations on the Contribution of the Human Rights Council to the Prevention of Human Rights Violations.' Report of the Rapporteurs. A/HRC/43/37. 14 January. Geneva.

United Nations Mandate of the Special Rapporteur on extrajudicial, summary or arbitrary executions, 'Letter to the Islamic Republic of Iran.' AL IRN 28/2020. 24 December 2020, 3.

United Nations Secretary General. 2013. 'The Universal, Indivisible, Interrelated, Interdependent and Mutually Reinforcing Nature of All Human Rights and Fundamental Freedoms.' Report of the Secretary-General. United Nations General Assembly. A/68/224. 23 July. New York.

2015. 'Report on Conflict-Related Sexual Violence.' S/2015/361. 2 June.

2016. 'Report on Conflict-Related Sexual Violence.' S/2016/361, 22 June.

2017. 'Report of the Secretary-General: Implementing the Responsibility to Protect: Accountability for Prevention.' A/71/1016 –S/2017/556. 10 August. New York. www.un.org/en/genocideprevention/documents/2017%20SG%20report%20on%20RtoP%20Advanced%20copy.pdf.

2019. 'Resolution 2493 (2019).' S/Res/2493. 29 October.

2020a. *Policy Brief: The Impact of COVID-19 on Women*. New York: United Nations.

2020b. 'Gender-based violence and Covid-19. Video Message by the Secretary General.' 4 May. www.un.org/sg/en/content/sg/statement/2020-04-05/secretary-generals-video-message-gender-based-violence-and-covid-19-scrolldown-for-french.

Universal Rights Group. 2017. 'How to Operationalize the Council's "Prevention" Mandate: The Effective Implementation of Paragraph 5F of GA Res. 60/251.' Permanent Mission of Norway to the United Nations, Universal Rights Group, and the Mission permanente de la Suisse auprés de l'Office des Nations Unies et des autres organisations internationals à Geneve. www.universal-rights.org/wp-content/uploads/2017/09/Glion_final_report.pdf.

United States Mission to the United Nations. 2022. 'Remarks at a UN Security Council Briefing on the ICAO Report on Belarus' Diversion of Ryanair Flight 4978.' 31 October. https://usun.usmission.gov/remarks-at-a-un-security-council-briefing-on-the-icao-report-on-belarus-diversion-of-ryanair-flight-4978/.

UNSC S/PV.7125. 2014. 'United Nations Security Council.' 7125th meeting. https://documents-dds-ny.un.org/doc/UNDOC/PRO/N14/250/46/PDF/N1425046.pdf?OpenElement.

UNSC S/PV.7134. 2014. 'United Nations Security Council.' 7134th meeting. https://documents-dds-ny.un.org/doc/UNDOC/PRO/N14/263/70/PDF/N1426370.pdf?OpenElement.

Urpelainen, Johannes 2010. 'Regulation under Eeconomic Globalization.' *International Studies Quarterly* 54(4): 1099–1121.

US Department of Justice. 2004. 'Memorandum for James B. Comey, Deputy Attorney General, Re: Legal Standards Applicable Under 18 USC. 2340-2340A.' Washington, DC: US Department of Justice.

US Department of State. 2016. 'Ambassador Power's Remarks at a UN Security Council Briefing on Syria.' 26 September. www.youtube.com/watch?v=SJjvUkuQ_4I.

2021. 'Holding the Lukashenka Regime and Its Enablers to Account.' 21 June. www.state.gov/holding-the-lukashenka-regime-and-its-enablers-to-account/.

Van Kersbergen, Kees, and Verbeek, Bertjan 2007. 'The Politics of International Norms: Subsidiarity and the Imperfect Competence Regime of the European Union.' *European Journal of International Relations* 13(2): 217–238.

Vandeveer, Stacy D., and Dabelko, Geoffrey D. 2001. 'It's Capacity, Stupid: International Assistance and National Implementation.' *Global Environmental Politics* 1(2): 18–29.

Vauchez, Antoine 2010. 'The Transnational Politics of Judicialization. Van Gend En Loos and the Making of EU Polity.' *European Law Journal* 16 (1): 1–28.

2014. 'Communities of International Litigators.' In Romano, C. P. R., Alter, K. J., and Shany, Y. (eds). *The Oxford Handbook of International Adjudication*, 655–668. Oxford: Oxford University Press.

Venzke, Ingo 2012. *How Interpretation Makes International Law: On Semantic Change and Normative Twists*. Oxford: Oxford University Press.

Vetterlein, Antje 2018. 'Responsibility Is More Than Accountability: The Conditions of Moral Agency of Corporate Social Responsibility.' *Contemporary Politics* 24(5): 545–567.

Vetterlein, Antje, and Hansen-Magnusson, Hannes 2020. 'The Rise of Responsibility in World Politics.' In Hansen-Mangnusson, H., and Vetterlein, A. (eds). *The Rise of Responsibility in World Politics*, 3–32. Cambridge: Cambridge University Press.

Vezina, Renee 2012. 'Combating Impunity in Haiti: Why the ICC Should Prosecute Sexual Abuse by UN Peacekeepers.' *Ave Maria International Law Journal* 1(2): 431–460.

Vincent, Raymond J. 1984. 'Racial Equality.' In Bull, H., and Watson, A. (eds). *The Expansion of International Society*, 239–254. Oxford: Clarendon Press.

Vitalis, Robert 2000. 'The Graceful and Generous Liberal Gesture: Making Racism Invisible in American International Relations.' *Millennium* 29(2): 331–356.

2015. *White World Order, Black Power Politics: The Birth of American International Relations*. Ithaca: Cornell University Press.

2017. 'UN Peace Operations and Conflicting Legitimacies.' *Journal of Intervention and Statebuilding* 11(3): 286–305.

Von Eschen, Penny M. 1997. *Race against Empire: Black Americans and Anti-Colonialism, 1937–1957*. Ithaca: Cornell.

Von Glahn, Gerhard, and Taulbee, James L. 2017. *Law Among Nations: An Introduction to Public International Law*. 11th ed. London: Routledge.

Vucetic, Srdjan 2011. 'Genealogy as a Research Tool in International Relations.' *European Journal of International Relations* 37(3): 1295–1312.

Wade, Robert H. 1997. 'Greening the Bank: The Struggle over the Environment 1970–1995.' In Kapur, D., Lewis, J., and Webb, R. C. (eds). *The World Bank: Its First Half Century*, 611–734. Washington, DC: Brookings Institute.

Walker, Neil 2008. 'Beyond Boundary Disputes and Basic Grids: Mapping the Global Disorder of Normative Orders.' *International Journal of Constitutional Law* 6(3–4): 373–396.

2014. *Intimations of Global Law*. Cambridge: Cambridge University Press.

Walker, Shaun 2020. 'Rule of Law Fears Remain in Poland despite EU Compromise.' *The Guardian (London)*. December 2020. www.theguardian.com/world/2020/dec/11/eu-fears-hungary-poland-compromise-not-end-of-story.

Waltz, Waldo E. 1937. *The Nationality of Married Women: A Study of Domestic Policies and International Legislation*. Champaign: University of Illinois Press.

Ward, Jon 2008. 'White House Says Waterboarding not Torture.' *The Washington Post*, 7 February.

Watt, Nicholas, and Wintour, Patrick 2015. 'How Immigration Came to Haunt Labour: The Inside Story.' *The Guardian*, 24 March.

Weaver, Catherine 2007. 'The World's Bank and the Bank's World.' *Global Governance* 13(4): 493–512.

Weber, Max 1977. *Critique of Stammler*, Oakes, G. (trans.). New York: Free Press.

Weldes, Jutta 1996. 'Constructing National Interests.' *European Journal of International Relations* 2(2): 275–318.

Wellens, Karel 2002. *Remedies against International Organisations*. Cambridge: Cambridge University Press.

Welsh, Jennifer M. 2013. 'Norm Contestation and the Responsibility to Protect.' *Global Responsibility to Protect* 5(4): 365–396.

2018. 'Humanitarian Actors and International Political Theory.' In Brown, C., and Eckersley, R. (eds). *The Oxford Handbook of International Political Theory*, 316–329. Oxford: Oxford University Press.

2019. 'The Individualization of War: Defining a Research Programme.' *Annals of the Fondazione Luigi Einaudi* 53(1): 9–28.

Wendt, Alexander E. 1987. 'The Agent-Structure Problem in International Relations Theory.' *International Organization* 41(3): 335–370.

1992. 'Anarchy is What States Make of It: The Social Construction of Power Politics.' *International Organization* 46(2): 391–425.

1999. *Social Theory of International Politics*. Cambridge: Cambridge University Press.

Wenger, Etienne 1998. *Communities of Practice: Learning, Meaning and Identity*. Cambridge: Cambridge University Press.

Wenham, Clare, Smith, Julia, Davies, Sara E., Feng, Huiyun, Grépin, Karen A., Harman, Sophie, Herten-Crabb, Asha, and Morgan, Rosemary 2020. 'Women are Most Affected by Pandemics – Lessons from Past Outbreaks.' *Nature*, 8 July. www.nature.com/articles/d41586-020-02006-z.

Westerman, Pauline C. 2013. 'Pyramids and the Value of Generality.' *Regulation and Governance* 7(1): 80–94.

Whalen, Jeni 2013. *How Peace Operations Work: Power, Legitimacy and Effectiveness*. Oxford: Oxford University Press.

2017. 'Dealing with Disgrace: Addressing Sexual Exploitation and Abuse in UN Peacekeeping.' In *Providing for Peacekeeping 15*. Brisbane: International Peace Institute.

Widmaier, Wesley W., and Glanville, Luke 2015. 'The Benefits of Norm Ambiguity: Constructing the Responsibility to Protect across Rwanda, Iraq and Libya.' *Contemporary Politics* 21(4): 367–383.

Wiebelhaus-Brahm, Eric 2016. 'Use, Abuse, and Disuse of Transitional Justice Norms in the Wake of the Arab Spring.' In Aman, M. A., and Aman, M. J. (eds). *The Middle East: New Order or Disorder?*, 413–439. Washington, DC: Policy Studies Organization/Westphalia Press.

Wiener, Antje 2004. 'Contested Compliance: Interventions on the Normative Structure of World Politics.' *European Journal of International Relations* 10(2): 189–234.

2007. 'The Dual Quality of Norms: and Governance beyond the State: Sociological and Normative Approaches to Interaction.' *Critical Review of International Social and Political Philosophy* 10(1): 47–69.

2008. *The Invisible Constitution of Politics: Contested Norms and International Encounters*. Cambridge: Cambridge University Press.

2009. 'Enacting Meaning-in-Use: Qualitative Research on Norms and International Relations.' *Review of International Studies* 35(1): 175–193.

2014. *A Theory of Contestation*. Berlin and Heidelberg: Springer.

2017a. 'Agency of the Governed in Global International Relations: Access to Norm Validation.' *Third World Thematics: A TWQ Journal* 2(5): 709–725.

2017b. 'A Theory of Contestation – A Concise Summary of Its Argument and Concepts.' *Polity* 49(1): 109–125.

2018. *Contestation and Constitution of Norms in Global International Relations*. Cambridge: Cambridge University Press.

2020. 'Norm(ative) Change in International Relations: A Conceptual Framework.' *KFG Working Paper Series No. 44*. Berlin Potsdam Research Group 'The International Rule of Law – Rise or Decline?' https://papers.ssrn.com/sol3/papers.cfm?abstract=3638205.

2022. 'Societal Multiplicity for International Relations: Engaging Societal Interaction in Building Global Governance from Below.' *Cooperation and Conflict* 57(3): 348–366.

Wiener, Antje, and Puetter, Uwe 2009. 'The Quality of Norms is What Actors Make of It: Critical Constructivist Research on Norms.' *Journal of International Law and International Relations* 5(1): 1–16.

Wiener, Antje, Börzel, Tanja A., and Risse, Thomas (eds). 2019. *European Integration Theory*. Oxford: Oxford University Press.

Wilkens, Jan, and Datchoua-Tirvaudey, Alvine R. C. 2022. 'Researching Climate Justice: A Decolonial Approach to Global Climate Governance.' *International Affairs* 98(1): 125–143. https://doi.org/10.1093/ia/iiab209.

Willetts, Peter 1982. 'Pressure Groups as Transnational Actors.' In Willetts, P. (ed). *Pressure Groups in the Global System: The Transnational Relations of Issue-Oriented Non-Governmental Organizations*, 1–27. New York: St. Martin's Press.

Williams, Owain D., and Rushton, Simon 2011. 'Private Actors and Global Health Governance.' In Williams, O. D., and Rushton, S. (eds). *Partnerships and Foundations in Global Health Governance*, 1–25. Basingstoke: Macmillan.

Wills, Siobhán 2013. 'Continuing Impunity of Peacekeepers: The Need for a Convention.' *Journal of International Humanitarian Legal Studies* 4: 47–80.

WILPF. 2016. 'Move the Money from War to Peace.' www.wilpf.org/move-the-money/.

2017. *Obstacles to Women's Meaningful Participation in Peace Efforts in Ukraine*. Geneva: Women's International League for Peace and Freedom.

2018. *Towards a Feminist Security Council: A Guidance Note for Security Council Members*. Geneva: Women's International League for Peace and Freedom.

Winston, Carla 2018. 'Norm Structure, Diffusion, and Evolution: A Conceptual Approach.' *European Journal of International Relations* 24(3): 638–661.

2020. 'Truth Commissions as Tactical Concessions: The Curious Case of Idi Amin.' *The International Journal of Human Rights* 25(3): 1–23.

Wiuff Moe, Louise, and Stepputat, Finn 2018. 'Introduction: Peacebuilding in an Era of Pragmatism.' *International Affairs* 94(2): 293–299.

Wolff, Jonas and Zimmermann, Lisbeth 2016. 'Between Banyans and Battle Scenes: Liberal Norms, Contestation, and the Limits of Critique.' *Review of International Studies* 42(3): 513–534.

Wong, Wendy H., Levi, Ron, and Deutsch, Julia 2017. 'The Ford Foundation: Building and Domesticating the Field of Human Rights.' In Seabrooke, L., and Hendriksen, L. F. (eds). *Professional Networks in Transnational Governance*, 82–100. Cambridge: Cambridge University Press.

Woo, Byungwon, and Murdie, Amanda 2017. 'International Organizations and Naming and Shaming: Does the International Monetary Fund Care about the Human Rights Reputation of Its Client?' *Political Studies* 65(4): 767–785.

Woods, N., and Lombardi, D. 2006. 'Uneven Patterns of Governance: How Developing Countries are Represented in the IMF.' *Review of International Political Economy* 13(3): 480–515.

Wright, C. 2007. 'From "Safeguards" to "Sustainability": The Evolution of Environmental Discourse Inside the International Finance Corporation.' In Stone, Diane and Wright, Christopher (eds). *The World Bank and Governance: A Decade of Reform and Reaction*, 67–87. London and New York: Routledge.

World Bank. 1993. *Environmental Assessment Sourcebook Updates, Number 1–5, Report 21923*. Washington, DC: World Bank.

2017. *Environmental and Social Framework*. Washington, DC: World Bank Group.

WTO. 2021a. 'Dispute Settlement Activity – Some Figures.' www.wto.org/english/tratop_e/dispu_e/dispustats_e.htm.

2021b. 'DS170: Canada – Term of Patent Protection.' www.wto.org/english/tratop_e/dispu_e/cases_e/ds170_e.htm.

Wunderlich, Carmen 2013. 'Theoretical Approaches in Norm Dynamics.' In Müller, H., and Wunderlich, C. (eds). *Norm Dynamics in Multilateral Arms Control: Interests, Conflicts, and Justice*, 20–47. Athens, GA: University of Georgia Press.

2020. *Rogue States as Norm Entrepreneurs: Black Sheep or Sheep in Wolves' Clothing?* Cham: Springer.

Young, Oran R. 1980. 'International Regimes: Problems of Concept Formation.' *World Politics* 32(3): 331–356.

Zagelmeyer, S., Bianchi, L., and Shemberg, A. 2018. 'Non-State Based Non-Judicial Grievance Mechanisms (NSBGM): An Exploratory Analysis.' A report prepared for the Office of the UN High Commissioner for Human Rights, University of Manchester. www.ohchr.org/Documents/Issues/Business/ARP/ManchesterStudy.pdf.

Zarakol, Ayşe 2011. *After Defeat. How the East Learned to Live with the West.* Cambridge: Cambridge University Press.

Zaum, Dominik 2013. 'International Organizations, Legitimacy, and Legitimation.' In Zaum, D. (ed). *Legitimating International Organizations*, 3–25. Oxford: Oxford University Press.

ZEIT. 2020. 'Paris muss Bußgeld wegen zu vieler Frauen in Führungspositionen zahlen.' *DIE ZEIT*, 15 December. www.zeit.de/politik/ausland/2020-12/paris-frauenquote-geldbusse-diskriminierung-fuehrungspositionen-anne-hidalgo.

Zimmerli, Walter C., and Aßländer, Michael S. 1996. 'Wirtschaftsethik.' In Nida-Rümelin, J. (ed). *Angewandte Ethik: Die Bereichsethiken und ihre theoretische Fundierung*, 290–345. Stuttgart: Alfred Kröner Verlag.

Zimmermann, Lisbeth 2016. 'Same Same or Different? Norm Diffusion between Resistance, Compliance, and Localization in Post-conflict States.' *International Studies Perspectives* 17(1): 98–115.

2017. *Global Norms with a Local Face: Rule-of-Law Promotion and Norm Translation*. Cambridge: Cambridge University Press.

Zimmermann, Lisbeth, Deitelhoff, Nicole, and Lesch, Maximilian 2018. 'Unlocking the Agency of the Governed: Contestation and Norm Dynamics.' *TWQ Journal* 2(5): 691–708.

Zvobgo, Kelebogile, and Loken, Meredith 2020. 'Why Race Matters in International Relations.' *Foreign Policy*, 19 June. https://foreignpolicy.com/2020/06/19/why-race-matters-international-relations-ir/.

Zwingel, Susanne 2012. 'How do Norms Travel? Theorizing International Women's Rights in Transnational Perspective.' *International Studies Quarterly* 56(1): 115–129.

2013. 'Translating International Women's Rights Norms: CEDAW in Context.' In Caglar, G., Prügl, E., and Zwingel, S. (eds). *Feminist Strategies in International Governance*, 111–126. New York: Routledge.

2015. *Translating International Women's Rights: The CEDAW Convention in Context*. London: Palgrave.

Index

Footnotes are indicated by n. after the page number, figures by fig. and tables by tab.

www.ingramcontent.com/pod-product-compliance
Lightning Source LLC
Chambersburg PA
CBHW070003170525
26858CB00005B/386

* 9 7 8 1 0 0 9 4 7 9 1 7 2 *